T0212734

Lecture Notes in Computer Science　　8872

Commenced Publication in 1973
Founding and Former Series Editors:
Gerhard Goos, Juris Hartmanis, and Jan van Leeuwen

More information about this series at http://www.springer.com/series/7410

Joaquin Garcia-Alfaro · Jordi Herrera-Joancomartí
Emil Lupu · Joachim Posegga
Alessandro Aldini · Fabio Martinelli
Neeraj Suri (Eds.)

Data Privacy Management, Autonomous Spontaneous Security, and Security Assurance

9th International Workshop, DPM 2014
7th International Workshop, SETOP 2014
and 3rd International Workshop, QASA 2014
Wroclaw, Poland, September 10–11, 2014
Revised Selected Papers

 Springer

Editors

Joaquin Garcia-Alfaro
Télécom SudParis
Evry
France

Jordi Herrera-Joancomartí
Universitat Autònoma de Barcelona
Bellaterra
Spain

Emil Lupu
Imperial College London
London
UK

Joachim Posegga
Universität Passau
Passau
Germany

Alessandro Aldini
University of Urbino
Urbino
Italy

Fabio Martinelli
Pisa Research Area
National Research Council - CNR
Pisa
Italy

Neeraj Suri
Technische Universität Darmstadt
Darmstadt
Germany

ISSN 0302-9743   ISSN 1611-3349   (electronic)
Lecture Notes in Computer Science
ISBN 978-3-319-17015-2   ISBN 978-3-319-17016-9   (eBook)
DOI 10.1007/978-3-319-17016-9

Library of Congress Control Number: 2015935044

LNCS Sublibrary: SL4 – Security and Cryptology

Printed on acid-free paper

Springer International Publishing AG Switzerland is part of Springer Science+Business Media
(www.springer.com)

Foreword from the DPM 2014 Program Chairs

This volume contains the proceedings of the 9th Data Privacy Management International Workshop (DPM 2014), held in Wrocław, Poland, on September 10, 2014, in conjunction with the 19th annual European research event in Computer Security (ESORICS 2014) symposium. The DPM series started in 2005 when the first workshop took place in Tokyo (Japan). Since then, the event has been held every year in different venues: Atalanta - USA (2006), Istanbul - Turkey (2007), Saint Malo -France- (2008), Athens - Greece (2009), Leuven - Belgium (2010), Pisa - Italy (2011), and Egham - UK (2012).

The aim of DPM is to promote and stimulate the international collaboration and research exchange on areas related to the management of privacy-sensitive information. This is a very critical and important issue for organizations and end users. It poses several challenging problems, such as translation of high-level business goals into system-level privacy policies, administration of sensitive identifiers, data integration and privacy engineering, among others.

In this workshop edition, 30 submissions were received and each of them was evaluated on the basis of significance, novelty, and technical quality. The Program Committee, formed by 40 members, performed an excellent task and with the help of additional 14 referees all submissions went through a careful anonymous review process (three or more reviews per submission). In the end, six full papers, accompanied by four short papers and one position paper were presented at the event. The final program also included a keynote talk by Jordi Herrera-Joancomartí.

We would like to thank everyone who helped in organizing the event, including all the members of the Organizing Committee of both ESORICS and DPM 2014. In particular, we would like to highlight and acknowledge all the efforts from the team of Mirosław Kutyłowski, for all their help and support. Our gratitude goes also to Pierangela Samarati, Steering Committee Chair of the ESORICS Symposium, for all her arrangements to make possible the satellite events. Our special thanks to the General Chair of DPM 2014, Jordi Castellà-Roca, as well as the Steering Committee member Guillermo Navarro-Arribas, for their unconditional help since the beginning of this event. Last but, by no means the least, we thank all the DPM 2014 Program Committee members, additional reviewers, all the authors who submitted papers, and all the workshop attendees.

Finally, we want to acknowledge the support received from the sponsors of the workshop: Institut Mines-Télécom, CNRS Samovar UMR 5157, Télécom SudParis, UNESCO Chair in Data Privacy, Internet Interdisciplinary Institute (IN3) from the Universitat Oberta de Catalunya; and projects CONSOLIDER INGENIO 2010 CSD2007-0004 ARES and TIN2011-27076-C03-02 CO-PRIVACY from the Spanish MICINN.

January 2015

Joaquin Garcia-Alfaro
Jordi Herrera-Joancomartí

Foreword from the SETOP 2014 Program Chairs

Autonomous and Spontaneous Security focuses on the dynamics of system behavior in response to threats, their detection, characterization, diagnosis, and mitigation in particular through architectural and behavioral reconfiguration. Such approaches are needed in Embedded Systems, Pervasive Computing, and Cloud environments, which bridge the physical, social, and computing worlds and challenge traditional security provisions from different perspectives. Systems must be agile and continue to operate in the presence of compromise, introspective, and self-protecting rather than just hardened, resilient to more complex threats, yet more vulnerable as they are physically accessible, widely heterogeneous, and need to integrate long-term legacy components.

Ensuring their resilience and protecting such systems at scale require novel solutions across a broad spectrum of computational and resource environments, which integrate techniques from different areas including security, network management, machine learning, knowledge representation, control theory, stochastic analysis, and software engineering among others.

As in previous years, SETOP 2014 was held in conjunction with ESORICS 2014. This year, we were hosted in the historic city of Wrocław, Poland and we combined presentations from SETOP 2014 and QASA 2014 in a unique program – the topics of the two workshops being closely related. In addition to the workshop presentations this year's program also included a keynote address by Professor Elisa Bertino on *Assessing Data Trustworthiness - Concepts and Research Challenges.*

We are grateful to our hosts and to the ESORICS Steering and Organizing Committees for hosting SETOP, to the members of the Program Committee and external reviewers. This year's workshop would certainly not have happened without the persistence, dedication, and effort of its General Chair Frédéric Cuppens to whom we are indebted.

Autonomous and Spontaneous Security is a challenging topic and we are grateful to the authors who submitted papers, the presenters, and attendees.

January 2015   Emil Lupu
                                                                                         Joachim Posegga

Foreword from the QASA 2014 Program Chairs

This post-proceedings volume contains the revised versions of papers presented at QASA 2014: 3rd International Workshop in Quantitative Aspects in Security Assurance, held on September 11, 2014 in Wrocław, as an affiliated event of ESORICS 2014.

The QASA workshop series responds to the increasing demand for techniques to deal with quantitative aspects of security assurance at several levels of the development life cycle of systems and services, from requirements elicitation to run-time operation and maintenance. The aim of QASA is to bring together researchers and practitioners interested in these research topics with a particular emphasis on the techniques for service-oriented architectures. The scope of the workshop is intended to be broad, including aspects as dependability, privacy, risk, and trust.

QASA 2014 received 15 submissions, each reviewed by at least 3 Program Committee members. The committee decided to accept 7 papers (after two rounds of evaluations) for the post-proceedings. The program also included two invited talks, given by Elisa Bertino on assessing data trustworthiness and Audun Jøsang on defining assurance levels for user and server authentication.

The presentations and the discussions during the workshop have shown that the area of quantitative security, in its many facets, is an active and interesting field of research.

We would like to thank the invited speakers, the authors of submitted papers, the members of the Program Committee, the external referees, and the sponsors, which are the EU projects SESAMO and SPECS and the IFIP WG 11.14 (NESSoS) on Secure Engineering. We are also grateful for the use of the EasyChair platform, which offered an effective and clear way of managing the entire review process as well as the post-proceedings production. Finally, we are also grateful to the Institute of Mathematics and Computer Science of the Wrocław University of Technology for providing the venue for QASA 2014.

January 2015

Alessandro Aldini
Fabio Martinelli
Neeraj Suri

9th International Workshop on Data Privacy Management — DPM 2014

General Chair

Jordi Castellà-Roca   Universitat Rovira i Virgili, Spain

Program Committee Chairs

Joaquin Garcia-Alfaro   Télécom SudParis, France
Jordi Herrera-Joancomartí   Universitat Autònoma de Barcelona, Spain

Publicity Chair

Guillermo Navarro-Arribas   Universitat Autònoma de Barcelona, Spain

Program Committee

Rainer Böhme	University of Münster, Germany
Ana Cavalli	Télécom SudParis, France
Frédéric Cuppens	Télécom Bretagne, France
Nora Cuppens-Boulahia	Télécom Bretagne, France
Josep Domingo-Ferrer	Universitat Rovira i Virgili, Spain
Nicola Dragoni	Technical University of Denmark, Denmark
Christian Duncan	Quinnipiac University, USA
David Evans	University of Derby, UK
Sara Foresti	Università degli Studi di Milano, Italy
Sebastien Gambs	University of Rennes 1, France
Flavio D. Garcia	Radboud University Nijmegen, The Netherlands
Paolo Gasti	New York Institute of Technology, USA
Stefanos Gritzalis	University of the Aegean, Greece
Marit Hansen	Unabhängiges Landeszentrum für Datenschutz, Germany
Artur Hecker	Télécom ParisTech, France
Sokratis Katsikas	University of Piraeus, Greece
Evangelos Kranakis	Carleton University, Canada
Pascal Lafourcade	IUT Clermont-Ferrand, France
Maryline Laurent	Télécom SudParis, France
Georgios Lioudakis	National Technical University of Athens, Greece
Giovanni Livraga	Università degli Studi di Milano, Italy
Javier Lopez	University of Málaga, Spain

Sotirios Maniatis   Hellenic Authority for Communications Privacy, Greece
Refik Molva   Eurécom, France
Guillermo Navarro-Arribas   Universitat Autònoma de Barcelona, Spain
Melek Önen   Eurécom, France
Cristina Perez-Sola   Universitat Autònoma de Barcelona, Spain
Silvio Ranise   Fondazione Bruno Kessler, Italy
Yves Roudier   Eurécom, France
Mark Ryan   University of Birmingham, UK
Pierangela Samarati   Università degli Studi di Milano, Italy
David Sanchez   Universitat Rovira i Virgili, Spain
Claudio Soriente   ETH Zürich, Switzerland
Alessandro Sorniotti   SAP Research, France
Vicenç Torra   Artificial Intelligence Research Institute, Spain
Yasuyuki Tsukada   NTT Communication Science Laboratories, Japan
Alexandre Viejo   Universitat Rovira i Virgili, Spain
Jens Weber   University of Victoria, Canada
Lena Wiese   University of Göttingen, Germany
Nicola Zannone   Eindhoven University of Technology, The Netherlands

Steering Committee

Josep Domingo-Ferrer   Universitat Rovira i Virgili, Spain
Joaquin Garcia-Alfaro   Télécom SudParis, France
Guillermo Navarro-Arribas   Universitat Autònoma de Barcelona, Spain
Vicenç Torra   Artificial Intelligence Research Institute, Spain

Additional Reviewers

Khalifa Toumi   Panagiotis Rizomiliotis
Hari Siswantoro   Samuel Paul Kaluvuri
Maria Koukovini   Alberto Blanco-Justicia
Eugenia Papagiannakopoulou   Maximilian Hils
Jannik Dreier   Aouadi Mohamed
Sebastian Luhn   Luis Vinh-Hoa La
Riccardo Traverso   Alexandru Ionut Egner

7th International Workshop on Autonomous and Spontaneous Security — SETOP 2014

General Chair

Frédéric Cuppens   Télécom Bretagne, France

Program Committee Chairs

Emil Lupu   Imperial College London, UK
Joachim Posegga Universität Passau, Germany

Program Committee

Habtamu Abie   Norwegian Computing Centre, Norway
Ehab Al-Shaer   University of North Carolina at Charlotte, USA
Fabrizio Baiardi   University of Pisa, Italy
Lorenzo Cavallaro Royal Holloway, University of London, UK
Ana-Rosa Cavalli   Télécom SudParis, France
Mauro Conti   Università di Padova, Italy
Jorge Cuellar   Siemens AG, Germany
Frédéric Cuppens   Télécom Bretagne, France
Nora Cuppens   Télécom Bretagne, France
Gabi Dreo-Rodosek Bundeswehr University Munich, Germany
William Fitzgerald EMC Information Systems International, USA
Dieter Gollmann   University of Hamburg, Germany
Stefanos Gritzalis University of the Aegean, Greece
Mohamed Hamdi   Sup'Com, Tunisia
Thorsten Holz   Ruhr University Bochum, Germany
Trent Jaeger   Pennsylvania State University, USA
Christian D. Jensen Technical University of Denmark, Denmark
Martin Johns   SAP AG, Germany
Kwok-yan Lam   National University of Singapore, Singapore
Jean Leneutre   Télécom Paris Tech, France
Javier Lopez   University of Málaga, Spain
Fabio Martinelli   IIT-CNR, Italy
Yves Roudier   Eurécom, France
Daniele Sgandurra Imperial College London, UK
Radu State   University of Luxembourg, Luxembourg
Neeraj Suri   Technische Universität Darmstadt, Germany
Elias Tragos   ICS-FORTH, Greece
Shengzhi Zhang   Florida Institute of Technology, USA

Steering Committee

Ana-Rosa Cavalli	Télécom SudParis, France
Frédéric Cuppens	Télécom Bretagne, France
Nora Cuppens-Boulahia	Télécom Bretagne, France
Jean Leneutre	Télécom ParisTech, France
Yves Roudier	Eurécom, France

Additional Reviewers

Ilaria Matteucci
Francesco Santini

3rd International Workshop on Quantitative Aspects in Security Assurance — QASA 2014

Workshop Chairs

Alessandro Aldini   University of Urbino, Italy
Fabio Martinelli   IIT-CNR, Italy
Neeraj Suri   Technische Universität Darmstadt, Germany

Program Committee

Alessandro Aldini   University of Urbino, Italy
Lujo Bauer   Carnegie Mellon University, USA
Jorge Cuellar   Siemens AG, Germany
Frédéric Cuppens   Télécom Bretagne, France
Javier Lopez   University of Málaga, Spain
Jesus Luna Garcia   Technische Universität Darmstadt, Germany
Fabio Martinelli   IIT-CNR, Italy
Catherine Meadows   Naval Research Laboratory, USA
Charles Morisset   Newcastle University, UK
Flemming Nielson   Technical University of Denmark, Denmark
Andrei Sabelfeld   Chalmers University of Technology, Sweden
Pierangela Samarati   Università degli Studi di Milano, Italy
Reijo Savola   VTT Technical Research Centre of Finland,
                           Finland
Ketil Stoelen   SINTEF, Norway
Neeraj Suri   Technische Universität Darmstadt, Germany
Herbert Wiklicky   Imperial College London, UK

Additional Reviewers

Cristina Alcaraz   Ana Nieto
Luciano Bello   Aida Omerovic
Gencer Erdogan   Cristian Prisacariu
Carmen Fernandez   Daniel Schoepe
Sebastian Hunt

Contents

Keynote Talks

Research and Challenges on Bitcoin Anonymity   3
   Jordi Herrera-Joancomartí

Data Trustworthiness—Approaches and Research Challenges 17
   Elisa Bertino

Assurance Requirements for Mutual User and Service
Provider Authentication 26
   Audun Jøsang

Data Privacy Management

Group Discounts Compatible with Buyer Privacy 47
   Josep Domingo-Ferrer and Alberto Blanco-Justicia

The Crypto-Democracy and the Trustworthy (Position Paper) 58
   Sébastien Gambs, Samuel Ranellucci, and Alain Tapp

Configuration Behavior of Restrictive Default Privacy Settings
on Social Network Sites. 77
   Markus Tschersich

Towards Inherent Privacy Awareness in Workflows 95
   Maria N. Koukovini, Eugenia I. Papagiannakopoulou,
   Georgios V. Lioudakis, Nikolaos Dellas, Dimitra I. Kaklamani,
   and Iakovos S. Venieris

Index Optimization for L-Diversified Database-as-a-Service 114
   Jens Köhler and Hannes Hartenstein

Privacy-Preserving Loyalty Programs. 133
   Alberto Blanco-Justicia and Josep Domingo-Ferrer

Secure Improved Cloud-Based RFID Authentication Protocol 147
   Sarah Abughazalah, Konstantinos Markantonakis, and Keith Mayes

Autonomous and Spontaneous Security

Environment–Reactive Malware Behavior: Detection and Categorization 167
   Smita Naval, Vijay Laxmi, Manoj S. Gaur, Sachin Raja,
   Muttukrishnan Rajarajan, and Mauro Conti

Metric for Security Activities Assisted by Argumentative Logic   183
  Tarek Bouyahia, Muhammad Sabir Idrees, Nora Cuppens-Boulahia,
  Frédéric Cuppens, and Fabien Autrel

Quantitative Aspects in Security Assurance

Calculating Adversarial Risk from Attack Trees: Control Strength
and Probabilistic Attackers   201
  Wolter Pieters and Mohsen Davarynejad

Analysis of Social Engineering Threats with Attack Graphs   216
  Kristian Beckers, Leanid Krautsevich, and Artsiom Yautsiukhin

Introducing Probabilities in Controller Strategies   233
  Jerry den Hartog and Ilaria Matteucci

Automatically Calculating Quantitative Integrity Measures
for Imperative Programs.   250
  Tom Chothia, Chris Novakovic, and Rajiv Ranjan Singh

Risk-Aware Information Disclosure   266
  Alessandro Armando, Michele Bezzi, Nadia Metoui, and Antonino Sabetta

Probabilistic Modelling of Humans in Security Ceremonies   277
  Christian Johansen and Audun Jøsang

High-Level Simulation for Multiple Fault Injection Evaluation   293
  Maxime Puys, Lionel Rivière, Julien Bringer, and Thanh-ha Le

Short Papers

Towards an Image Encryption Scheme with Content-Based Image
Retrieval Properties   311
  Bernardo Ferreira, João Rodrigues, João Leitão, and Henrique Domingos

A-PPL: An Accountability Policy Language   319
  Monir Azraoui, Kaoutar Elkhiyaoui, Melek Önen, Karin Bernsmed,
  Anderson Santana De Oliveira, and Jakub Sendor

Privacy-Preserving Electronic Toll System with Dynamic Pricing
for Low Emission Zones   327
  Roger Jardí-Cedó, Jordi Castellà-Roca, and Alexandre Viejo

Association Rule Mining on Fragmented Database   335
  Amel Hamzaoui, Qutaibah Malluhi, Chris Clifton, and Ryan Riley

Author Index   343

Keynote Talks

Research and Challenges on Bitcoin Anonymity

Jordi Herrera-Joancomartí[(✉)]

Dept. d'Enginyeria de la Informació i les Comunicacions,
Universitat Autònoma de Barcelona, 08193 Bellaterra, Catalonia, Spain
jordi.herrera@uab.cat

Abstract. Bitcoin has emerged as the most successful crypto currency
since its appearance back in 2009. Besides its security robustness, two
main properties have probably been its key to success: anonymity and
decentralization. In this paper, we provide a comprehensive description
on the details that make such cryptocurrency an interesting research
topic in the privacy community. We perform an exhaustive review of the
bitcoin anonymity research papers that have been published so far and
we outline some research challenges on that topic.

1 Introduction

Bitcoin is an online virtual currency based on public key cryptography, proposed in 2008 in a paper [1] authored by someone behind the Satoshi Nakamoto
pseudonym. It became fully functional on January 2009 and its broad adoption,
facilitated by the availability of exchange markets allowing easy conversion with
tradicional currencies (EUR or USD), has brought it to be the most successful
virtual currency.

However, in contrast to other virtual payments systems appeared so far,
the seminal paper [1] describing the Bitcoin system was not published in the
scientific arena but as a forum post on the Internet[1]. Furthermore, the practical development of the ideas proposed in such paper took place on January
2009, when the same author created the first block of the Blockchain and implemented a fully functional bitcoin wallet which allows to operate with such new
cryptocurrency. For this reason, the deployment of bitcoin took off without so
much attention from the research community and the first research papers on the
topic did not appear until late 2011 in the arXiv repository and later published
conferences and journals [2,3].

During the 2014, there has been an explosion in the publication of bitcoin
research papers, and well established conferences included the topic of *cryptocur-
recies* as a "topic of interest". Furthermore, specific workshops were created, like
the 1st Workshop on Bitcoin Research, held jointly with the 18th International
Conference Financial Cryptography and Data Security. The research performed
so far related to bitcoin has been very broad, not only in the technical research
arena but also in other disciplines, like business and economy, law or sociology.

---

[1] http://web.archive.org/web/20090131115053/http://bitcoin.org/.
http://p2pfoundation.ning.com/forum/topics/bitcoin-open-source.

© Springer International Publishing Switzerland 2015
J. Garcia-Alfaro et al. (Eds.): DPM/SETOP/QASA 2014, LNCS 8872, pp. 3–16, 2015.
DOI: 10.1007/978-3-319-17016-9_1

In this paper, we provide a comprehensive description of the key issues of the bitcoin system in order to allow to new comers to understand the scientific review performed later on. Then, we provide an exhaustive review of the papers that dealt with anonymity issues. Throughout the paper we identify and discuss interesting research challenges.

2   The Bitcoin System

In this section, we point out the main ideas that allow to understand the basic functionality of the bitcoin virtual currency. Such background is needed to understand the meaning of the research performed so far. However, the complexity of bitcoins makes impossible to provide a fully description of the system in this review, so interested readers can refer to [4] for a detailed and more extended explanation on the bitcoin system.

Bitcoin is a cryptocurrency based on accounting entries. For that reason, it is not correct to look at bitcoins as digital tokens since bitcoins are represented as a balance in a bitcoin account. A **bitcoin account** is defined by an Elliptic Curve Cryptography key pair[2]. The bitcoin account is publicly identified by its **bitcoin address**, obtained from its public key using an unidirectional function. Using this public information users can send bitcoins to that address[3]. Then, the corresponding private key is needed to spend the bitcoins of the account. Regarding this definition, it is easy to understand that any user can create any number of bitcoin addresses (generating the key pair) either using any standard crypto-software or self purpose created programs, like bitcoin wallets. Notice that if the user creates such bitcoin accounts in a private manner then, a priori, nobody can link the identity of the user with the value of a bitcoin address.

2.1   Bitcoin Payments

Payments in the bitcoin system are performed through transactions between bitcoin accounts. A **bitcoin transaction** indicates a bitcoin movement from source addresses to destination addresses. Source addresses are referred as **input addresses** in a transaction and destination addresses are named **output addresses**. As it can be seen in Fig. 1, a single transaction can have one or multiple input addresses and one or multiple output addresses.

A transaction details the exact amount of bitcoins to be transfered from each input address. The same applies to the output addresses, indicating the total amount of bitcoins that would be transfered at each account. For consistency, the total amount of the input addresses (source of the money) must be greater or equal than the total amount of the output addresses (destination of

---

[2] Bitcoin uses ECDSA with the curve secp256k1 implying private keys of 256 bit length.

[3] Notice that public key, address or bitcoin account are referring to the same concept.

Inputs

Previous output (index)	Amount	From address	Type	ScriptSig
e631567f352f...:1	3.02887912	1CGVyAgAx9gg1va5pGNVJtF6gdKpPUVTSf	Address	304402201700305a3d79a[....]2b985b15daa0ab9c50cd61449ca037dc9f0
c284ec14325f...:0	3.04042789	1GY84QPLfM9d4KqTjTbbHsb9BX9FF1kYQx	Address	3045022100e724004f2d3[....]91d95b56ad29f817f3e3259daffbd72f2a98
0fbec1d29b8e....0	2.99934316	1CGVyAgAx9gg1va5pGNVJtF6gdKpPUVTSf	Address	304402200f6e9b4281cb0[....]2b985b15daa0ab9c50cd61449ca037dc9f0
232715b3c51a...:1	3.00515088	17ALqzZFPbSqXz9aQhzgK6ts9htZfV8Mwu	Address	304402207311495478c1d[....]8d4656bf7613d47dd4e6a5b062d9fb6a34

Outputs

Index	Amount	To address	Type	ScriptPubKey
0	0.51682435	1LUHXNTsHPUGVJJeefPdb2rpdxtWoHrcKv	Address	OP_DUP OP_HASH160 d5936a017660c48be2adaa9a77153eccfdb8b0b8 OP_EQUALVERIFY OP_CHECKSIG
1	11.5569767	1HzAb4E1kZH4pDKoxML4KXBLPPyUootw4s	Address	OP_DUP OP_HASH160 ba51b9aee7595c72a2cbc1d4e3e90e356f77804 OP_EQUALVERIFY OP_CHECKSIG

Fig. 1. Bitcoin transaction example: four input addresses and two output addresses (data from blockexplorer.com).

the money)[4]. Furthermore, the bitcoin protocol forces that input addresses must spend the exact amount of a previous received transaction[5] and for that reason, in a transaction, each input address can unambiguously indicate the index[6] of the transaction in which the bitcoins were received (the field *Previous output (index)* in Fig. 1).

Finally, the owner of the input addresses should perform a digital signature using his private keys, proving that he is the real owner of such accounts[7].

Before accepting a payment from a standard transaction, the receiver should:

- Validate that the bitcoins of the input addresses are not previously spent.
- Validate that the digital signature is correct.

The first validation prevents doublespending in the bitcoin system and to allow such validation the system needs a ledger where all previous transactions are annotated. Before accepting the payment, the receiver needs to be sure that there is no any other transaction already in the ledger that has an input address with the same *Previous output (Index)* of the input addresses of the transaction that has to be validated. For that reason, the integrity of the system is based on the fact that this ledger is not modifiable, although it should be possible to add new transactions. In the bitcoin system, this append-only ledger is called blockchain[8].

---

[4] Although apparently both amounts should be the same, we will discuss later on in which situation the input value could be greater than the output value.

[5] Notice that in Fig. 1, there is two input addresses that are exactly the same which indicates that bitcoins have arrived in this bitcoin account in two separate transactions.

[6] A transaction is identified in the bitcoin system by its hash value.

[7] Although this is the standard form of bitcoin verification for regular bitcoin transfer transactions, the verification of a transaction can be much more complex and is based on a bitcoin transaction script language, a stack-based execution language (more details can be found in Chap. 5 of [4]).

[8] Note that the non-modifiable property of the blockchain imply that bitcoin payments are non reversible.

The second validation can be performed with the information included in the transaction itself together with the information of the transaction identified in the *Previous output (Index)*. Finally, it is worth to mention that the enforcement of spending the total amount of a previous transaction makes very difficult to perform exact payments in the bitcoin system (transactions with exactly a single input address and a single output address), and then users should collect the "change" of the payment in one of his addresses, as it is shown in Fig. 2. The address that collects the change in a transaction is referred as a *shadow address* and it belongs to the same user that performs the payment.

Inputs

Previous output (index)	Amount	From address	Type	ScriptSig
073a12d29e11...:0	0.706	1NYB35emL1yQunpExWhRM6CHBAzbJVx9Sd	Address	304402205d2b1[....]0a9b96e22abb02da6e3a03c1aa8c

Outputs

Index	Amount	To address	Type	ScriptPubKey
0	0.4	13osnkmwyYaER5tBPp5f9zWjWhpHwNgD66	Address	OP_DUP OP_HASH160 1ecdc8400fe436056bc1b18f9927ee1a7ce46443 OP_EQUALVERIFY OP_CHECKSIG
1	0.3059	1ATkLdK5icinT2c5F2NWoJYs8QWs4y5NUg	Address	OP_DUP OP_HASH160 67c81fc63d214d19696f25d1fd1fe360dabdf371 OP_EQUALVERIFY OP_CHECKSIG<

Fig. 2. A Bitcoin transaction where the owner of the address 1NYB35emL1yQunpEx-WhRM6CHBAzbJVx9S performs a payment of 0.4 bitcoins to the address 13osnkmwy-YaER5tBPp5f9zWjWhpHwNgD66 and collects the change in the address 1ATkLdK-5icinT2c5F2NWoJYs8QWs4y5NUg, the shadow address of this transaction (data from blockexplorer.com).

2.2 The Blockchain and the Mining Process

The **blockchain** is a general append-only ledger containing all bitcoin transactions performed since the system started to operate, back in 2009. Such approach implies that the size of the blockchain is constantly increasing (21 GB by September 2014) and, for that reason, scalability is probably the biggest challenge that the system faces. The blockchain is freely replicated and stored in different nodes of the bitcoin network, making the bitcoin a completely distributed system.

Transactions are included in the blockchain at time intervals, rather than in a flow fashion, and such addition is performed by collecting all new transactions of the system, compiling them together in a data structure, called blocks, and including the block at the top of the blockchain. Every time that a block containing a specific transaction is included in the blockchain such transaction is said to be a **confirmed transaction** since it has been already included in the blockchain and can be checked for doublespending prevention.

Blocks are data structures that mainly contain a set of transactions that have been performed in the system (see Fig. 3). To achieve the append-only property, addition of a block in the blockchain is a hard problem, so adding blocks to the blockchain is time and work consuming. Furthermore, every block is indexed using its hash value and every new block contains the hash value of the previous one (see the field *Previous block* in Fig. 3). Such mechanism ensures that the modification of a block from the middle of the chain would imply to modify all remaining blocks of the chain from that point to the top in order to match all hash values.

Block 125552

Hash: 000000000000000001e8d6829a8a21adc5d38d0a473b144b6765798e61f98bd1d
Previous block: 00000000000008a3a41b85b8b29ad444def299fee21793cd8b9e567eab02cd81
Time: 2011-05-21 17:26:31
Difficulty: 244 112.487774
Transactions: 4
Total BTC: 84.52
Size: 1,496 kilobytes
Merkle root: 2b12fcf1b09288fcaff797d71e950e71ae42b91e8bdb2304758dfcffc2b620e3
Nonce: 2504433986

Transactions

Transaction	Fee	Size (kB)	From (amount)	To (amount)
51d37bdd87...	0	0.135	Generation: 50 + 0.01 total fees	15nNvBTUdMaiZ6d3GWCeXFu2MagXL3XM1q: 50.01
60c25dda8d...	0	0.259	1HuppjXz7dPrt2a67LqacDW5T4VanFrpqC: 29.5	1B8vkT58i8KUPVJvvyQfrbc8Wjwu3vEarQ: 0.5 1BQbxzgRSLEsmv1JNc8MG76wdUgMwbsaww: 29
01f314cdd8...	0.01	0.617	1NdzSE6sHubscXJrv7jJn2gd4fL9L3ai6E: 0.03 1Jjv9m5VrRUE7VoktCsj18KUSqkqchhbum: 0.02 1HsYJJPqTn34DEjMnTb3VfKckX7ZcWPibm: 4.82	175FNxcLc1YrTwwG6TcsywcsHYdVqyhbwC: 0.01 1MueNMRJmcqVQeqE7v4dqogpNbhyxqq8R6: 4.85
b519286a10...	0	0.404	12DCoCVvDCkQShZ5RTh9bysgCkmkRMNQbT: 0.14 13CJwnnXJPwkzY4Xnaoqf8dnyNBwrHG9fe: 0.01	1Mos7p8fqJKBcYNRG1TdT5hBRxdMP6YHPy: 0.15

Fig. 3. Example of a bitcoin block (data from blockexplorer.com).

Adding a block to the blockchain is known as the **mining process**, a process that is also distributed and that can be performed by any user of the bitcoin network using specific-purpose software (and hardware). The mining process uses a hashcash proof-of-work system, first proposed by Adam Back as an anti-spam mechanism. The proof-of-work consists in finding a hash of the new block with a value lower than a predefined target[9]. This process is performed by brute force varying the nonce value of the block and hashing the block until the desired value is obtained. Once the value has been found, the new block becomes the top block of the blockchain and all miners discard their work on that block and move to the next one, by collecting new transactions and taking the hash of the top block as the previous block hash.

---

[9] Notice that the value of the target determines the difficulty of the mining process. Bitcoin system adjusts the target value depending on the hash power of the miners in order to set the throughput of new blocks to 1 every 10 min (in mean).

Mining new blocks is a structural task in the bitcoin system since it helps to confirm the transactions of the system. For that reason, and also assuming that mining implies a hard work, miners have to be properly rewarded. In the bitcoin system, miners are rewarded with two mechanisms. The first one provides them with newly created bitcoins. Every new block includes a special transaction, called generation transaction, (see the first transaction in Fig. 3) in which it does not appear any input address and the output address is determined by the miner who creates the block, who obviously indicates one of its own addresses[10]. The second rewarding mechanism is the fees that each transaction pays to the miner. The fee for each transaction is calculated by computing the difference between the total input amount and the total output amount of the transaction (notice that in example block of Fig. 3 the first transaction does not provide any fee while the second one generates a 0.01 fee). All fees collected from transactions in a block are included in the generation transaction.

2.3 The Bitcoin Network

The bitcoin system needs to disseminate different kinds of information, essentially, transactions and blocks. Since both data are generated in a distributed way, the system transmits such information over the Internet through a distributed peer to peer (P2P) network. Such distributed network is created by bitcoin users in a dynamic way, and nodes of the bitcoin P2P network [5] are computers running the software of the bitcoin network node. This software is included by default into bitcoin's full-client wallets, but it is not usually incorporated in light wallet versions, such as those running in mobile devices. It is important to stress such distinction in case to perform network analysis, because when discovering nodes in the P2P bitcoin network, depending on the scanning techniques, not all bitcoin users are identified, but only those running a full-client and those running a special purpose bitcoin P2P node. Furthermore, online bitcoin accounts, provided by major bitcoin Internet sites, can also be considered as a light weight bitcoin clients, so they do not represent a full bitcoin P2P node neither.

3   Bitcoin Anonymity

Anonymity is probably one of the properties that has been key for the success of the currency deployment. Anonymity in the bitcoin network is based on the fact that users can create any number of anonymous bitcoin addresses that will be used in their bitcoin transactions. This basic approach is a good starting point, but the underlaying non-anonymous Internet infrastructure, together with the availability of all bitcoin transactions in the blockchain, has proven to be an anonymity threat. In order to review the papers published on bitcoin anonymity, we group them in three different categories: those papers that exploit mainly

---

[10] The amount of a generation transaction is not constant and it is determined by the bitcoin system. Such value, started in 50 bitcoins, is halved every four years, fixing asymptotically to 21 millions the total number of bitcoins that will be ever created.

data obtained from the blockchain to derive some information from users or more general properties like usage patterns; papers that use bitcoin network information to identify users; and papers that propose mixing techniques to protect users anonymity.

3.1 Blockchain Analysis

A direct approach to analyze the anonymity offered by the bitcoin system is to dig information out of the blockchain. Since the blockchain includes all transactions performed by the system, a simple analysis provides information from which bitcoin addresses the money comes and to which bitcoin addresses it goes. However, since users in the bitcoin system can create any number of addresses, the main goal is to cluster all addresses in the blockchain that belong to the same user. As we will see, authors apply different techniques to perform such clustering.

The first research article on Bitcoins was published by Reid and Harrigan [2], a first version of which appeared in arXiv in July 2011. From the blockchain information, authors construct the transaction network and the user network. The former represents the flow of bitcoins between transactions, where each vertex represents a transaction and each directed edge indicates whether or not there is an input/output address that links the transactions. The latter represents the flow of bitcoin users over the time. To construct the user network, authors cluster addresses of the same user assuming that all input addresses of a transaction belong to the same user. Then, external information on bitcoin addresses is obtained from different Internet resources (like twitter posts, forums, specialized bitcoin applications -like bitcoin faucet-) to help the clustering process and to identify the users behind such clusters. All such information allow them to perform egocentric analysis and visualization, context discovery, flow and temporal analyses and they conclude that it is possible to associate many bitcoin addresses with each other, and with external identifying information. Furthermore, with appropriate tools, the activity of known users can be observed in detail.

In [6], Androulaky et al. take another step into clustering addresses. Taking into account the same idea of [2], where all input addresses of the same transaction are clustered, they added another heuristic using the output addresses of a transaction. Assuming that most transactions have only two output addresses, in the case that one of the two has already appeared in the blockchain, the other one will be a shadow address and can be clustered with the input addresses. Furthermore, they also apply behavior-based clustering techniques, K-Means and Hierarchical Agglomerative Clustering, to enhance the cluster creation. In order to perform such analysis, the authors generate synthetic data from a specific purpose bitcoin simulator that they developed. Data from the simulation has also the advantage to provide a ground truth for evaluating their clustering measures. With this simulation environment and the proposed techniques, authors indicate that the profiles of 40 % of bitcoin users can be unveiled.

Ron and Shamir [7] perform an analysis of bitcoin user behavior from the blockchain data, rather than trying to deanonymize user information. They also use the assumption that multiple input addresses belong to the same user in order to characterize user behavior. They conclude that until May 13th 2012 most of the new created coins remain unexpended in the minted addresses and that there was a huge number of tiny transactions that move fractions of bitcoins. Furthermore, they carefully analyze the largest transactions of the network until that moment and provide a detailed graph structure of their movements.

Papers reviewed so far perform a passive analysis in the sense that information of the blockchain is processed without any previous intervention. In [8] in order to better understand the traceability of Bitcoin flows, Meiklejohn *et al.* perform an active analysis. By performing payments from owned bitcoin addresses to known services (like mining pools, on-line wallets, gambling services, exchange sites, ...) they can identify such services later on in the corresponding blockhain transactions. Furthermore, they also browse the Internet in order to obtain user identification of other addresses. Then, they used two heuristics for clustering: the first one is the all input addresses belong to the same user (already used in [2,6,7]) and the second one identifies the shadow address of a transaction by looking the one between all output addresses that appeared for the first time in the blockchain (a similar approach than in [6], but not limited to two output address transactions). With their analysis, authors conclude that for large bitcoin transactions, it is possible to trace their movements and the bitcoin network does not offer enough anonymity, for instance for money laundry. Such traceability is even more sharp in case the analyzer is (or has access) to a central service, like a mining pool, an eWallet provider or a bitcoin exchange site.

In [9] Ober *et al.* empirically study global properties of the bitcoin transaction graph and their time evolution since bitcoin creation until January 6th, 2013. They distinguish from all bitcoin addresses what they call *used addresses*, those that have been used to perform a payment (that is an address present as an input address in some transaction). They also define an *active entity* as the owner of such addresses and, similar to other authors, cluster in a single *active entity* different used addresses that appear together as input in a transaction. The size of an entity is then the number of addresses included in the cluster. Authors deal the anonymity in the bitcoin network through the measure of k-anonymity. They conclude that to estimate the level of k-anonymity provided by bitcoin system is necessary to estimate the number of active entities since, for instance dormant coins (those included in an address not active for a long time) reduce the anonymity set. Furthermore, they also indicate that to better estimate the k-anonymity at a certain point of time, active entities should be defined based on a window time around this period (hours, days, weeks, ...). Then, an active entity is the one that have performed a payment within this window time. With their analysis, they conclude that the best strategy, which maximizes the anonymity set, is to be as small as possible (the best case, only one address for each cluster) and be active for the shortest possible time (the best case, single use address). Their analysis provides interesting facts, like for instance, that speculation is good for anonymity since it raises the bitcoin price and, so, the total number of active entities which in turns increase the anonymity set.

Spagnuolo *et al.* [10] present BitIodine, a tool to analyze the blockchain information. BitIodine parsers the blockchain information and provides a frontend to obtain different information. From basic address account balance, received or sent import amount or total number of transactions to more sophisticate information like address clustering (using multi-input addresses and shadow addresses), addresses labeling based on public information on the web or path computation between addresses. As a use case of the proposed tool, authors provide an interesting analysis on payments to CryptoLocker ransomware. They found a high correlation between the dates that infections were reported and the dates of payments performed to bitcoin addresses provided by the ransomware for unlocking the files. This is the first analysis performed with public available information (not backed up with information graved from underground forums) in which it is possible to estimate the amount of money generated by a ransomware software.

In [11], Ron and Shamir present an in deep analysis of bitcoin transactions performed by Dread Pirate Roberts, the person who ran first Silk Road marketplace. Based on the blockchain information and a published account, authors made a detailed analysis which provides enough information to show the power of data mining techniques to analyze specific transactions in a public ledger system like bitcoin.

As we have seen, clustering addresses of the bitcoin system belonging to the same user is the key research topic in blockchain analysis. Although some proposals have been performed so far, the dynamism of the bitcoin system still offers room for further analysis. For instance, some hypothesis on the heuristics to cluster such addresses depend on the behavior of the wallets and how are they programed to perform and receive payments. Such behavior has been modified since the publication of some papers and new functionalities of the system have emerged. For those reasons, as we will see later on, some of those hypotheses may not hold at present time and new heuristics should be analyzed. Furthermore, most research works perform address clustering with the help of external data (like forums post, tweets, etc.), then to cluster addresses with only the information provided by the blochchain is still an open challenge.

3.2 Traffic Analysis

As we already mentioned, the anonymity degree of users in the bitcoin system is also bounded by the underlying technologies used. Transactions in the bitcoin system are transmitted through a P2P network, so, as it was first pointed out in [2], the TCP/IP information obtained from that network can be used to reduce the anonymity of the system. Although it is true that most wallets are able to work over anonymous networks (TOR[11] or I2P[12]) a high number of bitcoin users do not use such services, and then, there is still room for network analysis.

Koshy *et al.* [12] perform an anonymity study based on real-time transaction traffic collected during 5 month. For that purpose, authors develop CoinSeer,

---

[11] https://www.torproject.org/.
[12] https://geti2p.net/.

a bitcoin client designed exclusively for data collection. For more than 5 million transactions, they collected information on the IP address from where the Coin-Seer received such transaction and, in the general case, they assigned as the IP corresponding to the transaction the one that broadcast the transaction for the first time. In order to perform a pure network analysis, authors do not apply any address clustering process, so only single input transactions (almost four million) are taken into account in the analyzed data set. Then, to match an IP with a bitcoin address, they consider a vote on the link between IP_i and $address_j$ if a transaction first broadcasted form an IP_i contains the bitcoin $address_j$ as input address. Authors also perform a similar analysis for output addresses and model the problem as an evaluation of association rules, identifying the corresponding confidence scores and the support counts for the rule. After their analysis, authors conclude that it is difficult to map IP addresses with bitcoin addresses by performing traffic analysis if bitcoin peers act properly, since the bindings authors could obtain between IP addresses and bitcoin addresses mainly come from anomalous transactions patterns. Furthermore, authors also indicate that some network configuration, like mixing services or eWallets, might conduct to erroneous assumptions when linking IP and bitcoin addresses.

In contrast to blockchain analysis, traffic analysis has received less attention from the researches probably due to the fact that the blockchain is ready available for analysis and network data has to be gathered. In fact, bitcoin network analysis is a hard topic due to the dynamism and size of such P2P network. The anonymity analysis performed by Koshy *et al.* seems to show that no information can be derived with this technique, but it is difficult to completely discard such approach since in their work authors do not provide any estimation regarding which part of the bitcoin P2P network represent the 2,678 peers they were able to monitor, and for the period of the analysis, no data of the size of the network is available from other sources. So, with only one work performed, whether or not network analysis can reveal private information from bitcoin users still remains an open problem. Furthermore, network analysis can be performed to identify not only the owner of an address but also the identity of other actors in the bitcoin community.

3.3   Mixing

In order to enhance the anonymity properties of the bitcoin system, some authors propose the use of mix services, a procedure that shuffles the information in order to hinder the relation between then input and the output values.[13] The goal is to allow bitcoin users to send bitcoins from one address to a mix service and receive from the mix service the bitcoins to another address that could not be linked with the original one. This service can be run by a central authority which receives payments and pays back to different addresses. However, such authority should be a trusted party since, on one hand, it is able to link addresses and,

---

[13] The main application of the mix concept, proposed by D. Chaum in [13] is the TOR network.

on the other hand, regarding the non-reversibility of the bitcoin payments, the mixer can receive the payment without sending back the bitcoins.

A basic mix service can be implemented using a multiple-input and multiple-output transaction, as it is described in CoinJoin [14]. The idea is that multiple users can jointly create a transaction with multiple input addresses[14] and multiple output addresses. To be a valid transaction, the transaction should be signed by all users participating in the mixing. Notice that partially signed transaction should circulate between users that mix their coins, although a meeting point server can be used. In that case, users should use an anonymous channel (TOR/I2P) to protect them in front of network attacks performed by the meeting point server. Furthermore, blind signatures may enforce that the meeting server does not learn linkability information between input and output address transactions. One of the problems of this proposal is that one of the anonymous users of the mix service can perform a DoS attack. Since the final valid transactions should be signed by all users that include bitcoins in the transactions, each mixing transaction never becomes valid in case the attacker simply does not sign any transaction in which he takes part. Despite these drawbacks, CoinJoin has been implemented in SharedCoin[15] or DarkWallet[16].

Möser *et al.* [15] perform an active analysis using reverse-engineering to understand the mode of operation of three mixing services: Bitcoin Fog[17], BitLaundry[18] and SharedCoin[19]. They perform mix procedures for each mix service for small bitcoin values using as a destination addresses one or multiple new generated ones. Then, they visualize the transaction graph of the addresses involved in the mixing. They conclude that while in Bitcoin Fog and SharedCoin it is hard to relate input and output transactions, for the Bitcoin Fog, they found a clear structure that allow to understand how the service works and may help an attacker to detect the output transactions.

Barber *et al.* propose in [16] a Fair Exchange Protocol that can be used as a two-party mixing protocol. The protocol uses the scripting functionality that bitcoin transactions provide and a cut-and-choose protocol. The paper only provides the description of each protocol phase as an isolated two party protocol assuming that both users have already been meet.

In [17], Bonneau *et al.* present Mixcoin, a centralized mixing system that relies on accountability. Users of the system obtain, prior the mixing phase, a signed warranty that can be used to prove, in case of the event, that the mixer entity has misbehaved. Authors point out that such public verifiable proof of misbehavior would discourage malicious mixing. However, there is still the

---

[14] At that point, it is important to note that some bitcoin uses, like the one described by CoinJoin, break the assumption that multiple input addresses in a transaction implies the same owner for all those input addresses, assumption that is taken as an heuristic for clustering addresses by almost all the anonymity papers.

[15] https://sharedcoin.com/.

[16] https://www.darkwallet.is/.

[17] http://bitcoinfog.com/.

[18] http://app.bitlaundry.com/.

[19] https://sharedcoin.com/.

possibility that the mixer could deanonymize users using his stored information. This thread is solved by concatenating several mixer services, thus reducing the strategy of a malicious mixer to a collusion with the other mixers. However, the mixer concatenation is not straight forward, since the proposed mixing protocol does not allow the users to choose the number of bitcoins to mix, because the scheme fixes a predefined amount. For that reason, mixing fees (that can be seen as the difference between the incoming and the outcoming bitcoin values) are difficult to apply without affecting the anonymity of users. To solve that point, authors propose randomized mixing fees so the fee is not a fraction of the mixed value, but the entire value that the user wants to mix, and the fee can be charged, or not, by the mixer with some predefined probability. Using such approach, the input addresses of the mix has the same value than output addresses or, in case the fee has been applied, there is no output address. This approach allows sequential mixing, but imposes a restriction on the fixed amount to be mixed and the minimum number of coins that users can mix, in order to keep a reasonable fee for the service.

Finally, Bissias *et al.* propose in [18] a system called Xim, a two-party mixing protocol designed as a multi-round protocol to enhance its anonymity properties. In fact, the core proposal is an anonymous partnering system that allows to find anonymously partners. Then, the mixing is performed using the Fair Exchange protocol proposed in [16]. They perform a comparative analysis of Xim with other proposals (MixCoin, SharedCoin, DarkWallet, CoinShuffle) and analyze different attacks on Xim. Sybil attacks and DoS attacks are discouraged by means of a carefully designed fee system.

Mix services provide a mechanism to mix bitcoin from different users in order to increase bitcoin user's anonymity. Proposals have moved from centralized systems to distributed protocols in order to increase user's privacy protection. Research in this topic ranges from atomic protocols that do not take into account the entire practical scenario (like how users can be paired or grouped anonymously) to specific proposals on how mixing fees can be calculated. In this field, open challenges include side channels attacks (within the mixing service and at communication level) and the integration of multiple mix services that, in its extreme case, yields the interesting concept of continual mixing, already proposed in [17]. Finally, It is also worth to mention that some proposals that initially were focused on improving bitcoin anonymity, implied a deep modification of the bitcoin protocol and, due such impossibility, some of those proposals have evolved in the creation of different currency proposals, like Zerocoin [19].

4   Conclusions

Bitcoin is a payment system based on a decentralized architecture that provides a mechanism to obtain multiple anonymous credentials, bitcoin addresses, that can be used to perform and receive payments. However, research performed so far has proven that the way the system uses such addresses may unveil some information from their owners. Since all transactions performed by the system are freely available in the blockchain for analysis, it allows to cluster different addresses of the same user and characterize some uses. Furthermore, if one of the addresses of the cluster can be mapped to a real identity, then the payment history of the entire cluster may disclose relevant information of that user. Although interesting research has been performed in this topic, the dynamism of the bitcoin ecosystem that constantly modifies and enhances the bitcoin usage implies that some of the hypotheses assumed for those blockchain analysis may not completely hold and, for that reason, blockchain analysis still presents interesting open questions.

Apart form the blockchain analysis, anonymity of the bitcoin system can be analyzed by gathering information from the P2P network used for payment communication. Since the P2P network uses the TCP/IP protocol, traffic analysis may reveal private information from users. However, such analysis is much more difficult to perform than the blockchain analysis since the bitcoin P2P network is highly dynamic. Although very few papers have been presented regarding this topic and results are not apparently optimistic, we think that there is still interesting network analysis that can be performed over the bitcoin P2P network.

In order to mitigate the anonymity reduction of the bitcoin system that can be performed using the techniques described above, the use of mix services have been proposed. Bitcoin mixes are services that allow a user to anonymize his bitcoins by mixing them with bitcoins of other users. Different proposals have been presented in this field showing that it is possible to design a mix service with a considerable level of security for the user. However, it is important to indicate that research in bitcoin mix services has to be performed carefully since developing this kind of services can be considered, from an economical or legal point of view, money laundering.

Finally, it is worth mention that research in the bitcoin ecosystem can be performed in other topics than anonymity, like for instance cryptography, network security or P2P network to name a few. On the other hand, besides the research lines that can be performed directly on the study of the bitcoin system itself, other approaches perform research using the bitcoin system as a tool. Examples of such approach are the design of secure multiparty computation or coin toss protocols. Furthermore, some structural parts of the bitcoin system, like the blochchain approach as an append-only ledger, may open interesting challenges for future developments on secure decentralized systems.

Acknowledgments. This work was partially supported by the Spanish Ministerio de Ciencia y Tecnologia (MCYT) funds under grants TIN2010-15764 "N-KHRONOUS" and TIN2011-27076-C03 "CO-PRIVACY".

References

1. Nakamoto, S.: Bitcoin: a peer-to-peer electronic cash system (2008). https://bitcoin.org/bitcoin.pdf
2. Reid, F., Harrigan, M.: An analysis of anonymity in the bitcoin system. In: Altshuler, Y., Elovici, Y., Cremers, A.B., Aharony, N., Pentland, A. (eds.) Security and Privacy in Social Networks, pp. 197–273. Springer, New York (2013)

3. Babaioff, M., Dobzinski, S., Oren, S., Zohar, A.: On bitcoin and red balloons. In: Proceedings of the 13th Association for Computing Machinery (ACM) Conference on Electronic Commerce, EC 2012, pp. 56–73. ACM, New York (2012)
4. Antonopoulos, A.M.: Mastering Bitcoins. O'Reilly Media, Sebastopol (2014)
5. Donet Donet, J.A., Pérez-Solà, C., Herrera-Joancomartí, J.: The bitcoin P2P network. In: Böhme, R., Brenner, M., Moore, T., Smith, M. (eds.) FC 2014 Workshops. LNCS, vol. 8438, pp. 87–102. Springer, Heidelberg (2014)
6. Androulaki, E., Karame, G.O., Roeschlin, M., Scherer, T., Capkun, S.: Evaluating user privacy in bitcoin. In: Sadeghi, A.-R. (ed.) FC 2013. LNCS, vol. 7859, pp. 34–51. Springer, Heidelberg (2013)
7. Ron, D., Shamir, A.: Quantitative analysis of the full bitcoin transaction graph. In: Sadeghi, A.-R. (ed.) FC 2013. LNCS, vol. 7859, pp. 6–24. Springer, Heidelberg (2013)
8. Meiklejohn, S., Pomarole, M., Jordan, G., Levchenko, K., McCoy, D., Voelker, G.M., Savage, S.: A fistful of bitcoins: characterizing payments among men with no names. In: Proceedings of the 2013 Conference on Internet Measurement Conference, IMC 2013, pp. 127–140. ACM, New York (2013)
9. Ober, M., Katzenbeisser, S., Hamacher, K.: Structure and anonymity of the bitcoin transaction graph. Future Internet 5(2), 237–250 (2013)
10. Spagnuolo, M., Maggi, F., Zanero, S.: BitIodine: extracting intelligence from the bitcoin network. In: Christin, N., Safavi-Naini, R. (eds.) FC 2014. LNCS, vol. 8437, pp. 452–463. Springer, Heidelberg (2014)
11. Ron, D., Shamir, A.: How did dread pirate Roberts acquire and protect his bitcoin wealth? In: Böhme, R., Brenner, M., Moore, T., Smith, M. (eds.) FC 2014 Workshops. LNCS, vol. 8438, pp. 3–15. Springer, Heidelberg (2014)
12. Koshy, P., Koshy, D., McDaniel, P.: An analysis of anonymity in bitcoin using P2P network traffic. In: Christin, N., Safavi-Naini, R. (eds.) FC 2014. LNCS, vol. 8437, pp. 464–480. Springer, Heidelberg (2014)
13. Chaum, D.L.: Untraceable electronic mail, return addresses, and digital pseudonyms. Commun. ACM 24(2), 84–90 (1981)
14. Maxwell, G.: Coinjoin: Bitcoin privacy for the real world. post on bitcoin forum. https://bitcointalk.org/index.php?topic=279249
15. Moser, M., Bohme, R., Breuker, D.: An inquiry into money laundering tools in the bitcoin ecosystem. In: eCrime Researchers Summit (eCRS), pp. 1–14, September 2013
16. Barber, S., Boyen, X., Shi, E., Uzun, E.: Bitter to better — how to make bitcoin a better currency. In: Keromytis, A.D. (ed.) FC 2012. LNCS, vol. 7397, pp. 399–414. Springer, Heidelberg (2012)
17. Bonneau, J., Narayanan, A., Miller, A., Clark, J., Kroll, J.A., Felten, E.W.: Mixcoin: anonymity for bitcoin with accountable mixes. In: Christin, N., Safavi-Naini, R. (eds.) FC 2014. LNCS, vol. 8437, pp. 481–499. Springer, Heidelberg (2014)
18. Bissias, G., Ozisik, A.P., Levine, B.N., Liberatore, M.: Sybil-resistant mixing for bitcoin. In: Proceedings of the 13th ACM Workshop on Workshop on Privacy in the Electronic Society, WPES 2014. ACM, New York (2014)
19. Miers, I., Garman, C., Green, M., Rubin, A.: Zerocoin: Anonymous distributed e-cash from bitcoin. In: 2013 IEEE Symposium on Security and Privacy (SP), pp. 397–411, May 2013

Data Trustworthiness—Approaches
and Research Challenges

Elisa Bertino[✉]

Computer Science Department and Cyber Center, Purdue University,
West Lafayette, IN, USA
bertino@cs.purdue.edu

Abstract. With the increased need of data sharing among multiple organizations, such as government organizations, financial corporations, medical hospitals and academic institutions, it is critical to assess and assure data trustworthiness so that effective decisions can be made based on data. In this paper, we first discuss motivations and relevant techniques for data trustworthiness. We then present an architectural framework for a comprehensive system for trustworthiness assurance and discuss relevant recent work. We highlight open research issues and research directions throughout the paper.

Keywords: Big data · Integrity · Trust management · Security · Policies

1 Introduction

Technology advances and novel software systems, including sensing devices, cyber-physical systems, smart mobile devices, cloud systems, data analytics, and social networks, are making possible to capture, and to quickly process and analyze huge amounts of data from which to extract information critical for society-relevant application domains. Examples of such domains include cyber security, homeland protection, healthcare, energy, transportation, and education. For example, in the security application domain, relevant tasks that can benefit from big data include anomaly detection and user monitoring for protection from insider threat [1]. In homeland protection, by analyzing and integrating data collected on the Internet and Web one can identify connections and relationships among individuals that may in turn help in detecting potential terrorists. By collecting and mining data concerning user travels and disease outbreaks one can predict disease spreading across geographical areas. And those are just a few examples; there are certainly many other application domains where big data can play a major role.

However, in order for analysts and decision makers to produce accurate analysis, make effective decisions and predictions, and take actions data must be trustworthy. Indeed, today's demand for data trustworthiness is stronger than ever. As many organizations are increasing their reliance on data for daily operations and critical decision making, data trustworthiness is arguably one of the most critical issues.

© Springer International Publishing Switzerland 2015
J. Garcia-Alfaro et al. (Eds.): DPM/SETOP/QASA 2014, LNCS 8872, pp. 17–25, 2015.
DOI: 10.1007/978-3-319-17016-9_2

Assuring data trustworthiness is however a difficult problem which often depends on the semantics of the application domain. Solutions for improving data, like those found in data quality, may be very expensive and may require access to data sources which may have access restrictions, because of data sensitivity. Also even when one adopts methodologies to assure that data are of good quality, errors may still be introduced and low quality data be used. Therefore a critical requirement is the ability to assess the trustworthiness of data so to be able to discard untrustworthy data, execute recovery operations to correct data, and strengthen defense measures.

The many challenges of assuring data trustworthiness require articulated solutions combining different approaches and techniques. In this paper we discuss some of those approaches and solutions, and introduce and highlight relevant research challenges. We also describe a cyclic framework for assessing trustworthiness for sensor data streams [2] and extensions to this framework. Throughout the paper we identify and discuss relevant research challenges.

2   Relevant Approaches and Techniques

Currently there is no comprehensive approach to the problem of high assurance data trustworthiness. However, several relevant techniques have been proposed in different areas of the computer science field that can be used as building blocks.

Integrity Models. The Biba integrity model [3] has been the first model specifically designed to assure integrity in information systems. This model is based on a hierarchical lattice of integrity levels, and integrity is defined as a relative measure that is evaluated at the subsystem level. A subsystem is some sets of subjects and data objects. An information system is defined as composed of a number of subsystems. In the Biba model the main integrity threat is that of a subject attempting to improperly change the behavior of another subject by supplying false or incorrect data. Under the Biba model each subject and data object in the system is assigned an integrity level from the hierarchical lattice of integrity levels. An integrity level associated with a subject indicates how much one can trust the subject with respect to supplying trustworthy data. Each data object is also assigned an integrity level, indicating how much the data object can be trusted. Based on such trust levels, the main principle of the Biba model is to prevent a more trusted subject from receiving data supplied by a less trusted subject. This principle then dictates how data access control is enforced. A drawback of the Biba model is that it is not clear how to assign appropriate integrity levels to subjects and data objects and which are the criteria for determining them. An interesting possibility would be to investigate whether reputation techniques [4] could be used to address such issue.

The approach by Clark and Wilson [5] is based on a clear distinction between military security and commercial security. They argue that security policies related to integrity, rather than disclosure, are of the highest priority in commercial information systems and that separated mechanisms are required for the enforcement of these policies. The model by Clark and Wilson has two key notions: well-formed transactions and separation of duty. A well-formed transaction is structured so that a subject cannot manipulate data arbitrarily, but only in constrained ways that ensure internal consistency of data. Separation of duty requires separating all operations into several subparts and that each subpart be executed by a different subject.

Semantic Integrity. Many commercial DBMS support the specification of conditions, often referred to as *semantic integrity constraints*, which data must satisfy. Examples of such conditions in a demographic database would be that the age of each individual in the database is an integer ranging between 0 and 140, and that the age of an individual must be lower than the ages of his/her living ancestors. Such constraints are used mainly for *data correctness and consistency*. As such semantic integrity techniques are unable to deal with the more complex problem of data trustworthiness in that they are not able to determine whether some data correctly reflect the real world and are provided by some reliable and accurate data source.

Data Quality. Data quality is a major problem in a wide range of information systems, ranging from data warehousing and business intelligence to customer relationship management and supply chain management. Data quality has been investigated from different perspectives, depending also on the precise meaning assigned to the notion of data quality. Data are of high quality "if they are fit for their intended uses in operations, decision making and planning" [6]. Alternatively, the data are deemed of high quality if they correctly represent the real-world construct to which they refer. Several theoretical frameworks have been proposed for understanding data quality. One framework aims at integrating the product perspective (conformance to specifications) and the service perspective (meeting consumers' expectations) [7]. Another framework is based on semiotics to evaluate the quality of the form, meaning and use of the data [8]. One highly theoretical approach analyzes the ontological nature of information systems to define data quality rigorously [9]. In addition to these more theoretical investigation, a considerable amount of research has been devoted to investigating and describing various categories of desirable attributes (or dimensions) of data quality. These categories commonly include accuracy, correctness, currency, completeness and relevance. Nearly 200 such terms have been identified and there is little agreement on their nature (are these concepts, goals or criteria?), their definitions or measures. Tools have also been developed for analyzing and repairing poor quality data, through the use for example of *record linkage techniques* [10].

Even though data quality is a very relevant to the problem of assessing and assuring data trustworthiness, it is not clear whether data quality methodologies scale for big data. Also such methodologies have been mainly designed to deal with data errors "naturally" introduced by mistakes in the applications and/or as result of human errors. As such they are unable to deal with environments in which malicious parties may carry deliberate data deception attacks. In addition, many such methodologies are based on the idea of correcting the data by using the "original data"; however in applications such as sensor-based applications, the original data may have disappeared by the time one realizes that there are errors in the collected data. Addressing such an issue would require a real-time data quality assessment process and the ability to quickly perform data recovery and correction actions.

Reputation Techniques. Reputation systems represent a key technology for securing collaborative applications from misuse by dishonest entities. A reputation system computes reputation scores about the entities in a system, which helps single out those entities that are exhibiting less than desirable behavior. Examples of reputation systems may be found in several application domains; E-commerce websites such as eBay (ebay.com) and Amazon (amazon.com) use reputation systems to discourage fraudulent activities. The EigenTrust [4] reputation system enables peer-to-peer file sharing systems to filter out peers who provide inauthentic content. The web-based community of Advogato.org uses a reputation system [11] for spam filtering. Reputation techniques can be useful in assessing data sources as shown by recent research [12].

3   A Cyclic Framework for Data Trustworthiness

Basic Approach. A cyclic and provenance-aware trust computation framework was proposed by Lim et al. [2] for data streamed from sensor networks. The goal of such framework is to support a continuous process by which: (a) data continuously streamed from a network of sensors are assessed with respect to their trustworthiness; and (b) sensors are continuously assessed based on the data they provide. In essence the goal of the framework is to assign each data item and sensor a *trust score*, that is, a number ranging in the [0,1] interval. By using such score, a user or application can compare inconsistent data and thus decide which data to use and which ones to discard. Low trust scores assigned to sensors may also be early signs of compromised or malfunctioning sensors.

The proposed framework is based on the heuristic that the more trustworthy data a sensor reports, the higher the sensor's trust score is. Moreover, the trustworthiness of a data item depends on the trust scores of the sensors which passed it towards the server node. The sensors through which a data item has been passed in the sensor network represent the provenance of such data item. By taking into account such interdependency relationship (see Fig. 1) between the trustworthiness of data items and sensors, a cyclic trust assessment process is executed in which the trust scores evolve gradually.

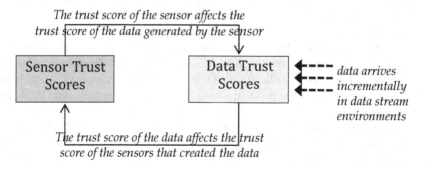

Fig. 1. Interdependency between the data and sensor trust scores

More specifically, in order to reflect the interdependency and continuous evolution properties in computing trust scores, the framework by Lim et al. maintains three different types of trust scores: *current*, *intermediate*, and *next trust scores*. We note that since new data items are continuously added to the stream, executing the cycle once whenever a new data item arrives is enough to reflect the interdependency and continuous evolution properties in the stream environment. The framework works as follows. Trust scores are initially computed based on the values and provenance of data items; we refer to these trust scores as *implicit trust scores*. To obtain these trust scores, two types of similarity functions are used: *value similarity* inferred from data values, and *provenance similarity* inferred from physical provenances. Value similarity is based on the principle that the more data items referring to the same real-world event have similar values, the higher the trust scores of these items are. As most sensor data referring to the same event follow the *normal distribution*, the approach for computing trust scores based on value similarity assumes a normal distribution. A data item that has a value far from the average value computed over all data item values observed during the same time window is thus assigned a lower trust score. Provenance similarity is based on the observation that different physical provenances of similar data values may increase the trustworthiness of data items. In other words, different physical provenances provide more independent data items. For more details on the approach and its experimental evaluation we refer the reader to [2].

A Collusion Attack. As the above framework essentially uses some simple statistical estimators based on value averages, collusions are possible by which several compromised sources collaborate in order to carry out a data deception attack [13]. Such an attack works as follow. Consider a sensor network consisting of 8 sensors all acquiring data about the same environment feature such as humidity. Suppose that a simple statistical test known as 3σ is used, by which values that are higher than three times the standard deviation with respect to the average are discarded. At round 1, all sensors are reliable, and the value accepted by the system (the average among all readings) is close to the actual value (small errors may occur due to device imperfections). At round 2, an adversary compromises three sensors, and alters the readings of these values such that the 3σ interval is skewed towards lower values. Since three distinct sensors report a lower value, the statistical test will conclude that the sensor reporting the highest value must be in error, since its value is outside the confidence interval. Therefore, its value is discarded, and the sensor is marked as less trustworthy for the next round. In the third round, the adversary shifts again its reported values, and manages to make the system to declare the sensor reporting the second highest value untrustworthy as well. This way, through careful selection of reported values, an attacker is able to circumvent the statistical test error detection technique. More importantly, the attacker manages to shift the accepted value far away from the actual value, thus succeeding in the data deception attack.

Protection Against Collusion Attacks. It is important to notice that conventional security approaches like encryption or digital signatures are ineffective against such an attack, as the attacker will alter the data before the data are encrypted and signed by the compromised sensor. Therefore different approaches must be devised.

A promising approach by Rezvani et al. [12, 14] is based on the observation that the above cyclic framework initially assigns the same trust score to all the sensors. Therefore, in order to improve the performance of the cyclic framework [2], Rezvani et al. combine two techniques:

1. *Robust variance estimation for the initial trust score of sensors.* The main idea is to include in the cyclic framework an initial stage in which an initial estimate of two noise parameters for each sensor is obtained; these parameters are bias and variance. Based on such estimate, in the next phase, an initial estimate of the data true values is provided using an estimator inspired by the Maximum Likelihood Estimation (MLE). In the third stage of the proposed framework, the initial estimate of the true values provided in the second stage is used to estimate the trustworthiness of each sensor based on the distance of sensor readings to such initial estimate.

2. *Characterization of the statistical distributions of errors.* It is important to notice that although using the previous technique makes the cyclic framework more robust than its original version which assigns equal trust scores to each sensor, experiments show that the attacker can still skew the results considerably. Thus, the previous technique is extended with a fourth stage based on a novel collusion detection mechanism for eliminating the contributions of the compromised sensors. Such detection mechanism is based on the observation that in a sophisticated collusion attack at least one of the compromised sensors will have highly non stochastic behavior; for example, in the attack scenario by Lim et al. [13], one of the compromised sensors is constrained to reporting values which must be very close to the skewed mean. On the other hand, the error of non-compromised sensors, even when it is large, comes from a large number of independent factors, and thus must roughly have a Gaussian distribution. Consequently, instead of looking just at the Root Mean Square (RMS) magnitude of errors of each sensor, one has to look at the statistical distribution of such errors, assessing the likelihood of whether they came from a normally distributed random variable. Sensors whose errors are highly unlikely to have come from a normally distributed random variable, possibly with a bias, are eliminated. Once the compromised sensors and their readings are eliminated, the noise parameters estimation and the MLE with known variances on the remaining readings are recomputed. Extensive experiments show that this approach is highly effective in detecting colluding attacks. We refer the reader to [12] for details of the approach and its experimental evaluation.

Open Research Issues. In the addition to the problem of collusion, there are many open research issues in the context of the cyclic framework approach which we discuss in what follows.

- *Similarity/dissimilarity of data.* Measuring data similarity is essential in the trust score computation. If we only handle numeric values, the similarity can be easily measured with the difference or Euclidean distance of the values. However, if the value is non-numeric (such as text data), we need to include modeling techniques able to take into account data semantics. For example, if data are names of places, we need to consider spatial relationships in the domain of interest. Possible approaches that can be used include semantic web techniques, like ontologies and description logics. Similarly, measuring provenance similarity is not easy especially when the provenance is complex. The edit distance which uses the minimum amount of distortion needed to transform one graph into another is the most popular similarity measure in graph theory. However, computing the edit distance for general graphs is known to be an NP-hard problem. Therefore, we need an approximate similarity measure method to efficiently compare graph-shape provenances.

- *Secure and efficient data provenance.* An important requirement for a data provenance trust model is that the provenance information be protected from tampering when flowing across the various parties. In particular, we should be able to determine the specific contribution of each party to the provenance information and the type of modification made (insert/delete/update). We may also have constraints on what the intermediate parties processing the data and providing provenance information can see about provenance information from previous parties along the data provisioning chain. An approach to address such problem is based on approaches for controlled and cooperative updates of XML documents in Byzantine and failure-prone distributed systems [15]. One could develop an XML language for encoding provenance information and use such techniques to secure provenance documents. Also it is critical that provenance be encoded efficiently especially for use in sensor networks. Recent approaches have been proposed based on data dictionary [16] and arithmetic coding techniques [17]. However, they need to be extended to support dynamic wireless networks.

- *Data validation through privacy-preserving record linkage.* In developing solutions for data quality, the use of record linkage techniques is critical. Such techniques allow a party to match, based on similarity functions, its own records with records by another party in order to validate the data. In our context such techniques could be used not only to match the resulting data but also to match the provenance information, which is often a graph structure. Also in our case, we need not only to determine the similarity for the data, but also the dissimilarity of the provenance information. In other words, if two data items are very much similar and their provenance information is very dissimilar, the data item will be assigned a high confidence level. In addition, confidentiality of provenance information is an important requirement because a party may have relevant data but have concerns or restrictions for the data use by another party. Thus application of record linkage technique to our context thus requires addressing the problem of privacy, the extension to graph-structured information, and the development of similarity/dissimilarity functions. Approaches have been proposed for privacy-preserving record linkage [18–20]. However those approaches have still many limitations, such as the lack of support for graph-structured information.

- *Correlation among data sources.* The relationships among the various data sources could be used to create more detailed models for assigning trust to each data source. For example, if we do not have good prior information about the trustworthiness of a particular data source, we may try to use distributed trust computation approaches such as EigenTrust [4] to compute a trust score for the data source based on the trust relationships among data sources. In addition, even if we observe that the same data is provided by two different sources, if these two sources have a very strong relationship, then it may not be realistic to assume that the data is provided by two independent sources. An approach to address such issue is to develop "source correlation" metrics based on the strength of the relationship among possible data sources. Finally, in some cases, we may need to know "how important is a data sources within our information propagation network" to reason about possible data conflicts. To address such issue one can apply various social network centrality measures such as degree, betweenness, closeness, and information centralities [21] to assign importance values to the various data sources.

4   Conclusions

In this paper we have discussed research directions concerning the problem of providing data that can be trusted by end-users and applications. This is an important problem for which multiple techniques need to be combined in order to achieve good solutions. In addition to approaches and ideas discussed in the paper, many other issues need to be addressed to achieve high-assurance data trustworthiness. In particular, data need to be protected from attacks carried through unsecure platforms, like the operating system, and unsecure applications, and from insider threats. Initial solutions to some of those data security threats are starting to emerge.

Acknowledgments. The work reported in this paper has been partially supported by the Purdue Cyber Center and the National Science Foundation under grant CNS-1111512.

References

1. Bertino, E.: Protection from Insider Threats. Morgan&Claypool, San Rafael (2012)
2. Lim, H.S., Moon, Y.-S., Bertino, E.: Provenance-based trustworthiness assessment in sensor networks. In: Proceedings of the 7th International Workshop on Data Management for Sensor Network (DMSN'10). Singapore (2010)
3. Biba, K.J.: Integrity Considerations for Secure Computer Systems. Technical Report TR-3153, Mitre (1977)
4. Kamvar, S.D., Schlosser, M.T., Garcia-Molina, H.: The eigentrust algorithm for reputation management in P2P networks. In: Twelfth International World Wide Web Conference, pp. 640–651. ACM (2003)
5. Clark, D.D., Wilson, D.R.: A comparison of commercial and military computer security policies. In: Proceedings of IEEE Symposium on Security and Privacy Symposium, Oakland (CA) (1987)
6. Juran, J.M.: Juran on Leadership for Quality—an Executive Handbook. Free Press, New York (1989)
7. Kahn, B., Strong, D., Wang, R.: Information Quality Benchmarks: Product and Service Performance. Communications of the ACM, vol. 45, pp. 184–192. ACM (2002)
8. Price, R., Shanks, G.: A semiotic information quality framework. In: IFIP International Conference on Decision Support Systems: Decision Support in an Uncertain and Complex World. Prato (Italy) (2004)

9. Wand, Y., Wang, R.Y.: Anchoring Data Quality Dimensions in Ontological Foundations. Communications of the ACM, vol. 39, pp. 86–95. ACM (1996)
10. Batini, C., Scannapieco, M.: Data Quality: Concepts, Methodologies and Techniques. Springer (2006)
11. Levien, R:. Attack resistant trust metrics. PhD thesis, University of California—Berkeley, CA, USA (2002)
12. Rezvani, M., Ignjatovic, A., Bertino, E., Jha, S.: Secure data aggregation for wireless sensor networks. IEEE transactions on dependable and secure computing. In press (2014)
13. Lim, H.S., Ghinita, G., Bertino, E., Kantarcioglu, M.: A game-theoretic approach for high-assurance of data trustworthiness in sensor networks. In Proceedings of IEEE 28th International Conference on Data Engineering (ICDE'12), Washington (DC) (2012)
14. Rezvani, M., Ignjatovic, A., Bertino, E., Jha, S.: A robust iterative filtering technique for wireless sensor networks in the presence of malicious attacks. poster abstract. In: Proceedings of ACM Sensys'13 Conference. Rome (Italy) (2013)
15. Mella, G., Ferrari, E., Bertino, E., Koglin, Y.: Controlled and cooperative updates of XML documents in byzantine and failure-prone distributed Systems. ACM Trans. Inf. Syst. Secur. **9**, 421–460 (2006)
16. Wang, C., Hussein, S.R., Bertino, E.: Dictionary based secure provenance compression for wireless sensor networks. IEEE transactions on parallel and distributed systems, in press (2014)
17. Hussein, S.R., Wang, C., Sultana, S., Bertino, E.: Secure data provenance compression using arithmetic coding in wireless sensor networks. In: Proceedings of 33rd IEEE International Performance Computing and Communications Conference (IPCCC 2014), Phoenix (AZ) in press (2014)
18. Scannapieco, M., Figotin, I., Bertino, E., Elmagarmid, A.: Privacy preserving schema and data matching. In: ACM SIGMOD International Conference on Management of Data, pp. 653–664 (2007)
19. Inan, A., Kantarcioglu, M., Bertino, E., Scannapieco, M.: A hybrid approach to private record linkage. In: 24th IEEE International Conference on Data Engineering, pp. 496–505 (2008)
20. Cao, J., Rao, F.-Y., Bertino, E., Kantarcioglu, M.: A hybrid private record linkage scheme: separating differentially private synopses from matching records. In: Proceedings of IEEE 31st International Conference on Data Engineering (ICDE'15), Seoul Korea in press (2015)
21. Jackson, M.O.: Social and Economics Networks. Princeton University Press, Princeton (2008)

Assurance Requirements for Mutual User and Service Provider Authentication

Audun Jøsang[✉]

University of Oslo, Oslo, Norway
josang@ifi.uio.no

Abstract. Several nations and organisations have published frameworks for assurance of user authentication in the context of eGovermnent. This reflects the importance that governments see in guaranteeing that only authorized users can access eGovernment services. However, in order to ensure trusted online interaction it is equally important to obtain assurance of authentication of service providers. Unilateral authentication is obviously insufficient for securing two-way interaction, so both user authentication assurance and service provider authentication assurance must be considered. Unfortunately there are currently no satisfactory frameworks for service provider authentication in the eGovernment context. This paper first describes and compares some of the current eAuthentication frameworks for user authentication. Then it proposes an eAuthentication framework for service provider authentication, and discusses how the two types of frameworks can be integrated and aligned.

1 Introduction

Entity authentication gives certainty about identities between interacting parties during online transactions. An entity is e.g. a person, organisation or a system. The entity's digital identity is a set of digitally encoded attributes that have been assigned to, or that characterise the entity. In order for an entity to be uniquely recognizable based on its digital identity it is normally required that one of the attributes is a unique name, typically called an identifier, within a specific name space. A username typically represents a person's digital identity within a local network or service domain. An Internet domain name typically represents an organisation's digital identity in the global domain of DNS (Domain Name System). These examples show that entities at each side of an online interaction typically source their identifiers from different name spaces, which has implications for how they mutually authenticate each other.

Entity authentication is a fundamental security component for trusted online interaction. Failed authentication, where an attacker is able to take on the identity of another entity, is a serious security threat that can have significant negative consequences. Authentication assurance expresses the certainty of correct

---

The work reported in this paper has been partially funded by eurostars project E!8324 OffPAD.

J. Garcia-Alfaro et al. (Eds.): DPM/SETOP/QASA 2014, LNCS 8872, pp. 26–44, 2015.
DOI: 10.1007/978-3-319-17016-9_3

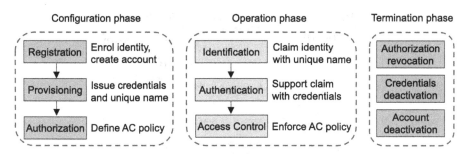

Fig. 1. Phases of Identity and Access Management

authentication in a network or domain. From a business perspective it is necessary to consider the cost of authentication which increases with the the level of assurance, so requiring high assurance must be based on a real business need. The basic principle is that higher risk associated with authentication failure must be mitigated by requiring higher authentication assurance.

The term IAM[1] (Identity and Access Management) denotes the security technologies that enable the intended authorized individuals to access the right resources at the right times for the right reasons. IAM can be described in terms of three separate phases where each phase contains a set of steps, as illustrated in Fig. 1.

The configuration phase covers the registration, provisioning and authorization steps. Authorization consists of specifying the entity's access permissions in the form of an AC (Access Control) Policy. Authorization must obviously be practiced, or delegated, by an authority in the organization, and results in the definition of AC rules in the system that controls access to resources. After initial completion of the configuration phase the entity is able to pass through the operation phase of IAM and can engage in trusted interactions. The configuration phase is revisited whenever necessary for updating identity, credential or authorization attributes. Although authentication can be seen as a single step in the operation phase, the correctness of authentication depends not only 1) on the correctness of the authentication step, but also 2) on the registration step, and 3) on the provisioning step during the configuration phase. Should any of these steps fail, then authentication will fail in general. Similarly, the correctness of access control requires that the correct identity has been authenticated, that an appropriate access policy has been defined in the authorization step, and that this policy is correctly enforced in the access control step. This paper focuses on the steps required for authentication, not on access control, so Fig. 1 is only meant to show how authentication and access control are complementary components of the IAM process. The termination phase is included in Fig. 1 for completeness, but is not directly relevant to the present study.

The terms *client* and *server* are typically used to denote the peer entities in a communication session. In reality, client and server systems are only agents for legal and/or cognitive entities such persons or organisations. The human user and the SP (Service Provider) organisation are both legal as well as cognitive

---

[1] http://www.gartner.com/it-glossary/identity-and-access-management-iam/.

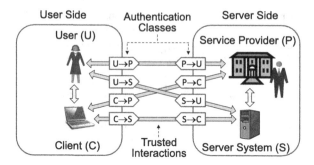

Fig. 2. General mutual entity authentication classes

entities. A person is assumed to be a cognitive entity because is possesses its own non-deterministic free will, in contrast to system entities that are considered to be deterministic without a free will. An organisation can also be considered to be cognitive in the sense that its actions are governed by persons who in turn are cognitive entities.

By taking into account the distinction between system entity (client or server) and legal/cognitive entity (person or organisation) there are (at least) two entities on each side of a communication session. Between the client side and the server side these entities can be connected with 4 separate bidirectional edges which represent different forms of entity authentication.

Figure 2 shows the 2×4 different classes of entity authentication resulting from the distinction between the human user and the client system on the user side, as well as between the SP organisation and the server system on the SP side. These 8 authentication classes are listed in Table 1.

Some of the entity authentication classes in Fig. 2 and Table 1 are relatively impractical, such as C→P and P→C, but the figure illustrates the generality of entity authentication when assuming that both the user side and SP side are non-atomic. U→P is e.g. practiced when authenticating customers over the

Table 1. Entity authentication classes

Authentication of user-side entities:
U→P: User authentication by the SP
U→S: User authentication by the server (commonly called *User authentication*)
C→P: Client authentication by the SP
C→S: Client authentication by the server
Authentication of SP-side entities:
P→U: SP authentication by the user
P→C: SP authentication by the client
S→U: Server authentication by the user (defined as *Cognitive server authentication*)
S→C: Server authentication by the client

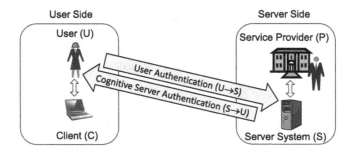

Fig. 3. Pragmatic end-to-end authentication

phone by asking questions about address, date of birth, customer number as well as by dialing credentials such as PIN codes directly on the phone.

For Internet and Web services applications the entity authentication classes U→S and S→U in Fig. 2 are the most important due to the requirement of end-to-end security in web service applications. In the typical case where a human user accesses an online service, semantic end-to-end communication takes place between the human user and the server system. It is therefore pragmatic to require mutual authentication between those two entities, as illustrated in Fig. 3.

Authentication type U→S, commonly known as *user authentication*, is a fundamental component of IAM on the Internet. User authentication is extensively studied in the literature, with a multitude of solutions in practical use, such as passwords, OTP (one-time password) devices, and biometrics.

Entity authentication type S→U in Figs. 2 and 3 has largely been ignored by researchers and industry. Authentication type S→U, which we call *cognitive server authentication*, focuses on how a human user can verify that a server belonging to the correct and intended SP is at the other end of an Internet connection. The lack of robust practical solutions for cognitive server authentication is a serious vulnerability which brings exposure to various types of attacks.

The TLS security protocol [9] combined with server certificates is commonly considered to provide server authentication. However, the TLS protocol alone can only provide server authentication type S→C in Fig. 2 because the authenticity of server certificates, and thereby of the server, are validated by the client system, not by the human user. In that sense, authentication based on TLS alone provides an inferior form of server authentication which we call syntactic server authentication. Additional elements as part of the user interface must be combined with TLS to enable cognitive server authentication type S→U, i.e. to enable the human user to authenticate the server system, and indirectly the SP, in a reliable way.

The concept of *authentication assurance* expresses the certainty of correct authentication. Several governments have articulated and published frameworks for user authentication assurance, with specific assurance levels defined as a function of factors such as identity registration assurance and authentication mechanism strength. Unfortunately, no similar frameworks have been articulated for server authentication.

This paper gives an overview of current eAuthentication frameworks for user authentication, and also proposes a framework for SP authentication, where each specific authentication assurance level is a function of a set of assurance factors. It is also proposes how frameworks for user and SP authentication can be integrated and aligned.

2   Frameworks for User Authentication

There exist several frameworks for user authentication in eGovernment contexts. They typically specify UAALs (User Authentication Assurance Levels) from UAAL-1 to UAAL-4, where the strongest authentication is UAAL-4. Some frameworks also define UAAL-0 for services where *"no assurance"* in real identity is required. The requirements for each UAAL is roughly harmonized across the various national or regional frameworks although there can be minor differences in terminology interpretation.

The risk level of a specific service reflects the potential negative impact in case of failed authentication. The required authentication assurance level shall balance that risk, meaning that if the risk of failed authentication is high, the required authentication assurance level must be correspondingly high too. The user authentication frameworks below specify authentication assurance levels according to this principle.

- **NIST SP800-63 (USA).** Title: *Electronic Authentication Guideline* [6]. This framework describes technical requirements for user authentication assurance levels that are specified in the E-Authentication Guidance for U.S. Federal Agencies [5].
- **FANR (Norway).** Title: *Framework for Authentication and Non-Repudiation in Electronic Communication with and within the Public Sector*[2] [27]. This is the official framework for user authentication in the the Norwegian Government sector. It is clearly inspired by the NIST framework above, but contains far less details.
- **STORK QAA (EU).** Title: *STORK (Secure Identity Across Borders Linked) QAA (Quality Authentication Assurance)* [16], where the assurance levels were adopted from the 2007 IDABC report: Identities for Authorities, Businesses and Citizens: Proposal for a multi-level authentication mechanism and a mapping of existing authentication mechanisms [12]. The STORK QAA has been adopted in the 2014 EU regulation eIDAS [10].
- **NeAF (Australia).** Title: *National e-Authentication Framework* [8], which is well structured and quite comprehensive when compared to previous frameworks. NeAF includes UAAL-0 aimed at anonymous access as well as pseudonymous user authentication.
- **e-Pramaan (India).** Title: *e-Pramaan: Framework for e-Authentication* [26]. This framework by the Indian Government represents an important companion for the Indian UID (Unique Identity) project and the biometric authentication

---

[2] Norwegian title: Rammeverk for autentisering og uavviselighet med og i offentlig sektor.

Table 2. Correspondence between assurance levels in user authentication frameworks

Authentication Framework	User Authentication Assurance Levels				
OMB / NIST **USA 2004 / 2011**	Little or no assurance (1)		Some (2)	High (3)	Very High (4)
FANR / FAD **Norway 2008**	Little or no assurance (1)		Low (2)	Moderate (3)	High (4)
STORK QAA **EU 2009**	No or minimal (1)		Low (2)	Substantial (3)	High (4)
NeAF **Australia 2009**	None (0)	Minimal (1)	Low (2)	Moderate (3)	High (4)
e-Pramaan **India 2012**	None (0)	Minimal (1)	Minor (2)	Significant (3)	Substantial (4)
IS 29115 **ISO/IEC 2013**	Low (Little or no) (1)		Medium (2)	High (3)	Very High (4)

program [4]. It includes UAAL-0 similarly to the earlier Australian NeAF. *Pramaan* is Hindi for *validation*.

– **ISO 29115.** Title: *Entity authentication assurance framework* [17]. This international standard from 2013 is to a large extent based on STORK QAA, but is also inspired by the other frameworks mentioned above.

The assurance level alignment of the above referenced authentication frameworks is illustrated in Table 2. It can be seen that there is a general consensus among the frameworks regarding the levels, although some of the frameworks use specific terms differently, so that e.g. level 4 can be described as giving 'High', 'Very High' or 'Substantial' assurance, depending on the particular framework. This might be a source of confusion, so that practitioners who need to map the authentication assurance levels of systems between e.g. USA and Australia, or between EU and India should be aware of the meaning behind the terms used in the respective frameworks.

The user authentication frameworks listed in Table 2 describe various factors that contribute to the robustness of the overall user authentication solution, as illustrated in Fig. 4 below, where the rectangles on the left-hand side represent assurance factors and the rectangle on the right-hand side represents the resulting assurance level which is dictated by the least level of all factors.

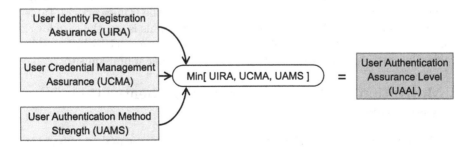

Fig. 4. Factors for user authentication assurance

Table 3. Corresponding terms for the authentication factors in ISO79115 and in this paper

ISO79115 terms		Terms used in this paper
Enrollment	=	User Identity Registration
Credential Management	=	User Credential Management
Entity Authentication	=	User Authentication Method

The terms used to describe each factor are generic for the purpose of this study. Other specific terms are often used in the frameworks listed in Table 2, but their interpretations are the same as those of the terms of Fig. 4. For example, the terms used in ISO 29115 and the corresponding terms in this study are listed in Table 3:

The three user authentication factors are briefly described below.

- **User Identity Registration Assurance (UIRA)** refers to the thoroughness of the process for enrolling new entities that are to be authenticated by the system. In case an entity is to be registered with identity attributes from other identity domains, such as name and postal address, then the registration strength will depend on the correctness of these attributes when they are imported.
- **User Credential Management Assurance (UCMA)** refers to the the estimated reliability and security of creation, distribution, usage and storage of the authentication credentials such as passwords, tokens and biometric profiles.
- **User Authentication Method Strength (UAMS)** refers to the intrinsic robustness of the specific solution used for authentication, such as password based, token based or biometrics based authentication, as well as any combination of these to form 2-factor solutions.

Figure 4 illustrates how the overall UAAL is a function of the three authentication assurance factors UIRA, UCMA and UAMS, according to the principle of the weakest link, meaning that the UAAL reflects the weakest the three factors. In practice, each UAAL dictates specific requirements for the UIRA, UCMA and UAMS factors, so that a specific UAAL is obtained only when all the requirements for that level are satisfied. For example, the UIRA requirements for UAAL 4 typically dictate that the user must present herself in person and produce official documents that get verified by the registrar. In contrast, there are typically no UIRA requirements for UAAL 1, so that a user can simply register any name during online registration. Some of the frameworks of Table 2 above do not include all three authentication factors. This is e.g. the case for the Norwegian FANR where user identity registration assurance (UIRA) is ignored because the correct registration of citizens is assumed as a prerequisite.

3   Motivation for Service Provider Authentication Assurance

TLS [9] provides cryptographically strong server authenticated in a technical sense. Unfortunately, typical implementations of TLS only offer syntactic server authentication by the client system, and not cognitive server authentication by the user. In order to provide meaningful server authentication a method that explicitly allows the user to authenticate the server system or the SP organisation is needed. The difference between server authentication by the client and server authentication by the user, which can be seen in Fig. 2, might seem subtle and insignificant, but is nevertheless absolutely crucial [19,21].

By analysing the security solution of TLS from a security usability perspective it can easily be seen that there are serious usability vulnerabilities that can easily be exploited by phishing attacks [19,20]. This is briefly explained below.

The standard implementation of TLS in web browsers provides various information elements to the user. Unfortunately this information is often insufficient to make an informed conclusion about the identity of the web server.

The closed padlock in the corner of a typical browser represents one element of security information indicating that the web traffic is encrypted with TLS, normally based on a server certificate. However, the lack of information about the identity and nature of the server is a security usability vulnerability.

Additional security information is contained in the server certificate that can be inspected e.g. by double-clicking on the padlock icon. The mental load of analysing the content of a server certificate is intolerable for most people, which represents another security usability vulnerability.

In case of Extended Validation (EV) Certificates the green address bar is also activated in all major browsers, addition to displaying the the padlock icon. The EV identity verification process requires the applicant organisation to prove exclusive rights to use a domain, confirm its legal, operational and physical existence, and to prove that the organisation has authorized the issuance of the Certificate. Paradoxically however, EV certificates do not eliminate confusion about the entity's identity. Figure 5 below shows the address bar of the UK bank NatWest in case (a) of its normal website (at the top), and (b) of its corresponding secure website equipped with an EV certificate (at the bottom).

The bottom of Fig. 5 shows the green address bar with EV certificate and domain name www.nwolb.com which is completely different from the domain name personal.natwest.com on the address bar of the normal website. This is

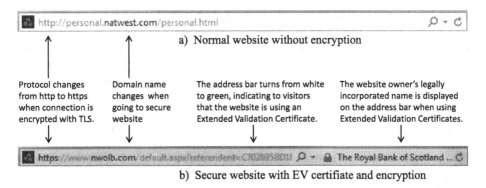

Fig. 5. Address bars of NatWest for normal website and for secure website with EV certificate

very misleading, and is unfortunately quite common because organisations often choose to operate secure websites with different servers and domain names than those of their normal websites. In addition, corporate names of organisations are often completely different from names used in public marketing, as can be seen on the address bar of the EV certificate which indicates the corporate name "The Royal Bank of Scotland" which is very different from "NatWest". To include a corporate name in the certificate and display it on the address bar therefore has minimal value for server authentication.

Criminal organisations can of course buy EV certificates by simply registering a cover business with physical presence. Names of such businesses can be chosen to be similar to those of legal organisations selected as targets of cyber attacks. In this way EV certificates for cover businesses can give web visitors who mistakenly access the criminal organisation's website a false sense of security. A criminal organisation targeting NatWest bank could e.g. buy the domain www.natwestbank.com and set up a business e.g. with corporate name "National Westbank Group". Paradoxically, a corresponding EV certificate would for most people appear more genuine than the real server certificate of the genuine NatWest bank.

From the user's perspective, the ordinary name and graphical logo represent the primary identity of the service provider. From the client browser's perspective only the server domain name represents identity because graphical logos and ordinary names can not be interpreted by TLS. The mismatch between the identifiers assumed by the user and by the client computer can be exploited by attackers to trick the user.

Another vulnerability is that distinct domain names can appear very similar, for example differing only by a single letter, or looking very similar, so that a false domain name may pass undetected. The following confusing domain names illustrate this.

www.bell-labs.com
www.bellabs.com
www.belllabs.com.

Confusion between similar domain names is easy to induce and can be very difficult to prevent. A realistic experiment was conducted during trial e-voting at municipal elections in Norway in 2011. In select municipalities citizens were invited to cast their votes online on the website `evalg.stat.no`. Two researchers set up a false e-voting website with the similar domain name `evalg-stat.no` and were able to trick several hundred people in their municipality to cast their votes through the false website [28]. This experiment demonstrated that despite cryptographically strong security, poor security usability made it simple for the researchers to obtain people's voting intentions, and to prevent people from actually voting, which is extremely serious. This experiment clearly shows the that the assurance of SP authentication is unsatisfactory.

One might think that domain name confusion can be avoided by combining the domain names with EV certificates, but this is not the case. The research laboratory "Bell Labs" has a server certificate for the domain name www.bell-labs.com

containing the corporate name "Alcatel-Lucent USA Inc" which for most people appears totally unrelated. This example shows that EV certificates do not assist users in understanding the identity of SP organisations. EV certificates can even be used to mislead while giving a false sense of security. Some organisations, such as financial institutions, feel pressured to buy EV certificates in order to make their online presence appear trustworthy, which in our opinion should be labeled trust extortion [21]. EV certificates are significantly more expensive that normal server certificates, so trust extortion is a necessary part of the business model for selling EV certificates.

The fundamental problem is that, although domain names are designed to be readable by humans, they provide poor usability for identifying organisations in the real world. Company names such as "NatWest" are suitable for dealing with organisations in the physical world, but not for global online identification and authentication. The consequence of this mismatch between names used in the online world and in the physical world is that users do not know which unique domain name to expect when accessing online services. Server authentication becomes meaningless when users do not know which domain name to expect.

Another problem with the current implementation of TLS is its dependence on the browser PKI that has a relatively large number of CAs (Certificate Authorities). This model creates many single points of total failure for Internet security. Several authors describe problems related to the browser PKI [13,22,30], where one major problem is that any CA can sign any certificate they want which amplifies the threat of false certificates appearing in the wild [23] and [24]. This problem is related to how the SSL PKI is built up, and not to the TLS protocol itself.

DNSSEC is a solution to ensure that the domain name given by the domain name system (DNS) is not modified to send a user to another place then originally intended by the owner of the domain name. DNSSEC builds on asymmetric cryptographic signing of DNS records in the name servers [3]. This is a strong hierarchical public key infrastructure, where the root-key is managed by The Internet Corporation For Assigned Names and Numbers (ICANN) [1]. ICANN also manage the root-servers for all top level domain names. DNSSEC (if checked by the user or its client) makes it hard for an attacker to make false DNS records and misleading a client system to a wrong server [2]. The recent RFC6698 [15] proposes the "DANE TLSA" protocol which uses DNSSEC as a basis for distributing certificates for TLS. This would allow the elimination of trust required in third party CAs, and would therefore provide a significantly stronger security assurance than that which currently can be provided by the browser PKIX [7], the PKI with X.509 certificates currently used with web browsers. With a proper implementation and widespread deployment of the DANE TLSA protocol it would be possible to phase out the problematic browser PKIX described below.

In summary, our analysis of current server authentication has exposed serious vulnerabilities that continue to be exploited by criminals to mount successful phishing attacks. A framework for server authentication assurance is needed to address these vulnerabilities.

4   Proposed Framework for Server Authentication

The existing authentication frameworks listed in Table 2 do not specifically focus on how users can make sure that an accessed online service actually is hosted by the correct and intended SP organisation. The Indian e-Pramaan framework describes a method based on "watermarks" [26], whereby the user selects an image and/or text during registration to a SP. When the user accesses the SP with their use name the next time, then the server of the SP shows the image and text (if it exists), which gives the user a way to confirm that this is the previously accessed SP before the user enters their password.

Research into the usability of such a system has shown that most users do not react if the "watermark" is replaced with a text describing that the service is undergoing an upgrade, and will enter their passwords anyway [29]. In addition it would be simple to imagine attacks where the image is extracted by some kind of proxy server, and delivered to the user by a malicious website.

US NIST SP800-63 describes similar examples of personalization measures to be implemented by the services. They also mention that there is no foolproof way to prevent the user (Claimant) from revealing any sensitive information to which he or she has access [6].

Because these documents focus on server side solutions, they are missing important points, which are the authentication of the server by the user. The frameworks propose applying simple methods for the user to authenticate the server and try to highlight some "best practices", at the same time pushing the technology for the user authentication to its limit. However, a specif framework for server authentication assurance would have to specify a more complete set of methods and principles for server authentication.

4.1   Identity Cognition and the Petname Model

The concept of identity cognition means that the relying party actively makes a judgment about the authenticated party's identity and decides whether characteristics of the entity comply with the relying party's explicit or implicit security policy. A basis for identity cognition is to understand the meaning of names, which can be challenging as explained in Sect. 3 above.

Three fundamental desirable properties of names described by Bryce 'Zooko' Wilcox-O'Hearn [33] are to be global[3], unique[4] and memorable[5]. To be memorable a name has to pass the so-called 'moving bus test' [25] which consists of testing whether an averagely alert person is able to correctly remember the name written on a moving bus for a definite amount of time, e.g. 10 min after the bus has passed. A name is unique if it is collision-free within the domain [31].

Wilcox-O'Hearn states with supporting evidence that no name space can be designed where names generally have all three desirable properties simultaneously. A visual analogy of this idea is created by placing the three properties

---

[3] Called *decentralized* in [33].

[4] Called *secure* in [33].

[5] Called *human-meaningful* in [33].

at the three corners of a triangle. In this triangle dubbed Zooko's Triangle, the three corners are never connected by a single line, only pairs of corners are connected. The edges joining the corners then illustrate the possible properties that a name space can have.

Wilcox-O'Hearn's idea was to design name spaces of global and unique names (pointers), and name spaces of memorable and unique names (petnames), and create mappings between the two types of name spaces. This is the *petname model* which consists of mapping a common name space of pointers to individual name spaces of petnames, which thereby combines all three desirable properties of names. A *petname system* is a system that implements the petname model.

The TrustBar [14] for the Firefox browser is a software solution that incorporates a petname system. The TrustBar solution consists of personalising every server certificate that the user wants to recognise by defining a personal petname for it [11]. The petname can e.g. consist of an image or a audible tune that the user can easily recognise. Unfortunately solutions like the TrustBar are not widely used.

A hardware-based implementation of the petname model is the experimental OffPAD device [32]. During the TLS handshake the petname system on the Off-PAD receives server certificates relayed via NFC communication from the client computer. In order to support cognitive server authentication, the server domain name (pointer) – received in a certificate – is mapped to a user-defined petname representing the service provider. The server certificate is also validated in the traditional way, which provides syntactic server authentication. Strengthened authentication assurance can be obtained by having server certificates signed under DNSSEC, which would give a very high Server Authentication Assurance Level according to the server authentication requirements described in Sect. 4.4 below.

4.2 Authentication Modalities

According to the X.800 standard, entity authentication is *"the corroboration that a peer entity in an association is the one claimed"* [18]. Here, 'association' means a connection, a session or a single instance of communication. We use the term 'interaction' as a general term for the same thing. So in case a victim user intends to connect to https:\\www.paypal.com, but is tricked into connecting to a phishing website called https:\\www.paypal.com, then the server certificate claims that the server identity is www.peypal.com which then is correctly authenticated according to X.800. However, something is clearly wrong here, and the failure to capture this obvious security breach indicates that the above definition of entity authentication is inadequate. What is needed is a richer modality of authentication.

We define three authentication modalities where *syntactic authentication* is the poorest, where *semantic authentication* is intermediately rich, and where *cognitive authentication* is the richest modality, as described next.

– **Syntactic entity authentication:** *The verification by the relying entity that the identity of the entity in an interaction is as claimed.*

This basic form of entity authentication is equivalent to peer-entity authentication as in X.800. Syntactic authentication alone does not provide any meaningful security and can e.g. not prevent phishing attacks since the relying party is indifferent to the identity of the authenticated entity.

- **Semantic entity authentication:** *The verification by the relying entity that the identity of the remote entity in an interaction is as claimed, and in addition the verification by the relying entity that the remote entity has semantic characteristics that are compliant with a specific security policy.*

  Semantic entity authentication can be enforced by an automated system e.g. with a white list of identities that have been authorized for interaction.

- **Cognitive entity authentication:** *The verification by the cognitive relying party that the identity of the remote entity in an interaction is as claimed, and in addition the verification by the relying entity that the remote entity has semantic characteristics that are compliant with a specific security policy, and in addition the appropriate presentation of semantic characteristics of the remote entity in a way that makes a cognitive relying party able to examine the true nature of the remote entity and to judge policy compliance.*

  Cognitive entity authentication requires the relying party to have cognitive reasoning power, such as in humans, animals or advanced AI systems. This authentication modality effectively prevents phishing attacks because users recognise the server identity and decides whether it is the intended one.

Technologies for service provider authentication are very different from those of user authentication, so mutual user and service provider authentication is highly asymmetrical. User authentication (class $[U \rightarrow S]$) typically takes place at the application layer e.g. with automated verification of passwords by the server system. On the other hand, service provider authentication (class $[S \rightarrow C]$) typically takes place at the transport layer e.g. with TLS authentication, where automated verification by the client system alone is insufficient so that human cognitive involvement might be required.

4.3   Factors for Server Authentication Assurance

It is important to involve the user when he or she registers to a new service, both to check if the place is correct and to show the user what to expect the next time. As most of the technical authentication processing is transparent, the users are easily deceived. It is therefore important to have solutions that allow users to understand the processes taking place during the authentication. As [29] pointed out, all 63 subjects who participated in an experiment entered user name and password even when TLS was not used, because they did not know the difference between the browser using TLS (as indicated by https) and not using TLS (as indicated by http).

Users have to understand how the security mechanisms work, not in detail, but have a general overview, and need to know and understand the required

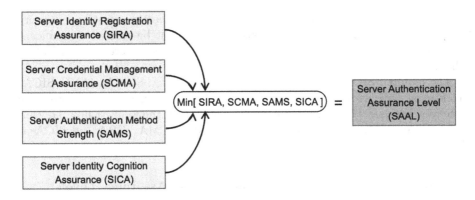

Fig. 6. Factors for server authentication assurance

security actions and security conclusions [19]. The higher the authentication risk level, the more this understanding is required.

The three assurance factors for user authentication assurance, as indicated in Fig. 4 does not cover the concept of identity cognition, because the authentication is executed by a system which simply applies syntactic identity recognition. However, for server authentication by humans it is necessary to introduce the assurance factor SICA (Server Identity Cognition Assurance). Identity cognition by the human user consists of paying attention to the presented server identity, understanding its nature, and making a decision whether it is the expected or desired identity for the specific communication session. Similarly to the case of user authentication frameworks, the assurance factors SAMS (Server Authentication Method Strength), SCMA (Server Credential Management Assurance) and SIRA (Server Identity Registration Assurance) are also used in case of server authentication frameworks as indicated in Fig. 6 where where the rectangles on the left-hand side represent assurance factors and the rectangle on the right-hand side represents the resulting server authentication assurance.

The purpose of introducing the additional SICA assurance factor in Fig. 6 is to explicitly require that the human user take a conscious choice after having recognised the specific server identity with its unique name. High SICA is not needed in case of low SAAL. It is acceptable to have a low SAAL when it would have little consequence that the user misunderstands the server identity and accesses the wrong server without knowing it. However, the SAAL must be higher when the consequence of accessing the wrong server is more severe. This also forces the SICA to be higher, which puts stronger requirements on the authentication methods and their usability, so that that human users can be certain that they access the intended server.

The security of a service extends beyond the server system and SP domain, and should include all users enrolled into it. This is difficult to achieve when serving millions of users. The responsibility to educate the users on how to use the services with adequate identity cognition assurance lies with the SP, as the SP can not expect all their users to have this knowledge prior to enrollment.

When planning a service there is always a trade-off between cost and security level, where ensuring SICA and educating users might be seen as a significant cost, but it may be worth the effort when the risk of wrong server authentication is high.

The required SAAL dictates the input factors (SIRA, SCMA, SAMS, SICA) which must have at least the same level as SAAL. Another way to express the same idea is to say that SAAL follows the principle of the weakest link, i.e. that SAAL is derived as the minimum level of SAMS, SCMA, SIRA and SICA as illustrated in Fig. 6.

4.4   Requirements for Server Authentication Assurance Levels

The present study is relatively high level, so a more thorough study is obviously necessary for specifying detailed requirements for the four factors of server authentication assurance levels illustrated in Fig. 6. The requirements we describe below are therefore intended as suggestions and input to the discussion around this topic. Server authentication assurance levels with their corresponding relative risk levels are briefly described first, followed by the requirements for each server authentication factor.

Server Authentication Assurance Levels (SAAL)

– **SAAL-1.** Minimal server authentication assurance is required when wrong server authentication would have minimal or no negative impact for services in this level, and attackers have little incentive to spoof the server, e.g. because the user does not provide sensitive information to the SP.
– **SAAL-2.** Low server authentication assurance is required when wrong server authentication would have some negative impact for services in this level, and attackers could have some incentive to spoof the server to mislead or steal user credentials or user information.
– **SAAL-3.** Moderate server authentication assurance is required when wrong server authentication would have significant negative impact, and attackers could have strong financial or political incentive to spoof the server to mislead or steal user credentials or user information.
– **SAAL-4.** High server authentication assurance is required when wrong server authentication would have severe negative impact for services in this level, and attackers could have strong financial or political incentive to spoof the server to mislead or steal user credentials or user information.

At this point in time there exist several different server authentication methods that can be used for the different assurance levels, some are not widely deployed although theoretical and implemented solutions exist. The list below is indicative for possible server authentication method strengths.

The management of server authentication credentials is quite different from that of user authentication credentials. The list below is indicative for possible server credentials management assurance.

Requirements for Server Credentials Management Assurance (SCMA)

1. **SCMA-1.** No specific requirements.
2. **SCMA-2.** Online installation on the client systems of PKI root public keys used for server certificate validation. Private server keys can be stored in server memory with adequate protection.
3. **SCMA-3.** Online installation on the client system of the the DNSSEC PKI root public key used for server certificate validation. Private DNSSEC server keys can be stored in server memory with adequate protection.
4. **SCMA-4.** The same requirements as for SCMA-3 above, but the PKI root public key must be installed manually on client systems, and private server keys must be installed, stored and processed in trusted hardware.

Requirements for Server Authentication Method Strength (SAMS)

1. **SAMS-1.** The server is identified by its domain name or IP address. Otherwise there are no specific requirements.
2. **SAMS-2.** It is sufficient to have a SSL/TLS connection with a valid SSL certificate. It must be possible to check if the certificate is valid, and to inspect the unique domain name of the SP.
3. **SAMS-3.** Server certificates based in DNSSEC is required in order to avoid the weakest link vulnerability of the browser PKI. DNSEC also ensures that results returned by DNS are authentic. Currently, DNSSEC is not widely implemented, and is not supported by all web browsers.
4. **SAMS-4.** The same requirements as for SAMS-3 above. In addition, a petname system is required to support identity cognition for the SP identity and name.

Incremental requirements for Server Identity Cognition Assurance (SICA)

- **SICA-1.** It is required that the unique name of the server can be inspected, e.g. on the browser address bar. This enables casual authentication.
- **SICA-2.** It is required that the server has a certificate validated by the browser, and that the domain name is displayed. This enables syntactic authentication.
- **SICA-3.** It is required that authentication policies for specific server identities are specified and enforced. This enables semantic authentication.
- **SICA-4.** It is required to use a petname system. In addition it is required that the user explicitly approves the petname in order to indicate satisfaction with the exact server identity in the communication. This enables cognitive authentication.

5   Concluding Remarks

It is important to observe that unequal assurance levels for user authentication and server authentication can be detrimental to the overall security of online service provision. For example, assume that a user is required to use strong user authentication when accessing an online service, while at the same time being unable to authenticate the service provider's identity. An obvious attack in this situation is to trick and direct the user to a false server, which would enable the attacker to collect user credentials which in turn could be used to masquerade as the user. It is therefore obvious that the assurance levels for user and server authentication need to be aligned in Internet mediated service access. Frameworks for user authentication and server authentication should therefore be considered in conjunction, and we encourage national governments with programs for online service provision to consider frameworks for both user authentication as well as server authentication, and to consider their relationship and inter-dependencies.

The lack of focus on service provider authentication by the user is currently a blind spot in the academic and industry information security communities. The intention of this paper is to create awareness for the need to have symmetry and balance in the assurance of mutual user and server authentication. With the recent publication of several mature frameworks for user authentication assurance, now is the time to establish frameworks for server authentication assurance.

References

1. Abley, J., Schlyter, J.: DNSSEC Trust Anchor Publication for the Root Zone (2010). http://data.iana.org/root-anchors/draft-icann-dnssec-trust-anchor.txt
2. Arends, R., Austein, R., Larson, M., Massey, D., Rose, S.: RFC 4033 - DNS Security Introduction and Requirements. IETF, March 2005. http://www.rfc-editor.org/
3. Ateniese, G., Mangard, S.: A new approach to DNS security (DNSSEC). In: Proceedings of the 8th ACM conference on Computer and Communications Security, CCS 2001, pp. 86–95. ACM, New York (2001)
4. Bhavan, Y., Marg, S.: Biometrics Design Standards For UID Applications. Unique Identification Authority of India, Planning Commission, New Delhi (2009)
5. Bolten, J.B.: E-Authentication Guidance for Federal Agencies - Memorandum to the Heads of All Departments and Agencies (OMB M-04-04). Technical report, Executive Office of Tthe President, Office of Management and Budget, Washington, D.C. 20503 (2004)
6. Burr, W.E. et al.: Electronic Authentication Guideline - NIST Special Publication 800–63 Rev. 1. Technical report, National Institute of Standards and Technology, December 2011
7. Cooper, D., Santesson, S., Farrell, S., Boeyen, S., Housley, R., Polk, W.: RFC 5280 - Internet X.509 Public Key Infrastructure Certificate and Certificate Revocation List (CRL) Profile. IETF, May 2008
8. National e-Authentication Framework (NeAF). Australian Government Information Management Office, Canberra (2009)
9. Dierks, T., Rescorla, E.: RFC 5246 - The Transport Layer Security (TLS) Protocol Version 1.2. IETF, August 2008. http://www.ietf.org/rfc/rfc5246.txt

10. EU. Regulation (EU) No 910/2014 of the European Parliament and of the Council of 23 July 2014 on electronic identification and trust services for electronic transactions in the internal market and repealing Directive 1999/93/EC (eIDAS Regulation). European Union (2014)
11. Ferdous, M.S., Jøsang, A., Singh, K., Borgaonkar, R.: Security Usability of Petname Systems. In: Jøsang, A., Maseng, T., Knapskog, S.J. (eds.) NordSec 2009. LNCS, vol. 5838, pp. 44–59. Springer, Heidelberg (2009)
12. Graux, H., Majava, J.: eID Interoperability for PEGS (Pan-European eGovernment services) - Proposal for a multi-level authentication mechanism and a mapping of existing authentication mechanisms. Technical report, EU IDABC (Interoperable Delivery of European eGovernment Services to public Administrations, Businesses and Citizens.) (2007)
13. Hayes, J.M.: The Problem with Multiple Roots in Web Browsers - Certificate Masquerading. In: 7th Workshop on Enabling Technologies, Infrastructure for Collaborative Enterprises (WETICE 1998). CAUSA Proceedings, pp. 306–313. IEEE Computer Society, Palo Alto, 17–19 June 1998
14. Herzberg, A., Gbara, A.: Protecting (even Naïve) Web Users from Spoofing and Phishing Attacks. Technical Report 2004/155, Cryptology ePrint Archive (2004)
15. Hoffman, P., Schlyter, J.: The DNS-Based Authentication of Named Entities (DANE) Transport Layer Security (TLS) Protocol: TLSA. IETF, August 2012. http://www.ietf.org/rfc/rfc6698.txt
16. Hulsebosch, B., Lenzini, G., Eertink, H.: Deliverable D2.3 - STORK Quality authenticator scheme. Technical report, STORK eID Consortium (2009)
17. ISO. ISO/IEC 29115:2013. Entity authentication assurance framework. ISO, Geneva, Switzerland (2013)
18. ITU. Recommendation X.800, Security Architecture for Open Systems Interconnection for CCITT Applications. International Telecommunications Union (formerly known as the International Telegraph and Telephone Consultantive Committee), Geneva (1991) (X.800 is a re-edition of IS7498-2)
19. Jøsang, A., AlFayyadh, B., Grandison, T., AlZomai, M., McNamara, J.: Security Usability Principles for Vulnerability Analysis and Risk Assessment. In: The Proceedings of the Annual Computer Security Applications Conference (ACSAC 2007), Miami Beach, December 2007
20. Jøsang, A., Møllerud, P.M., Cheung, E.: Web Security: The Emperors New Armour. In: The Proceedings of the European Conference on Information Systems (ECIS2001), Bled, Slovenia, June 2001
21. Jøsang, A.: Trust extortion on the internet. In: Meadows, C., Fernandez-Gago, C. (eds.) STM 2011. LNCS, vol. 7170, pp. 6–21. Springer, Heidelberg (2012)
22. Jøsang, A., Dar, K.S.: Server certificates based on DNSSEC. In: Proceedings of NordSec2011, Tallin, October 2011
23. Keizer, G.: Computerworld: DigiNotar dies from certificate hack caper (2011). http://www.computerworld.com/s/article/9220175/DigiNotar_dies_from_certificate_hack_caper
24. Microsoft. Microsoft Security Bulletin MS01-017 (March 22, 2001): Erroneous VeriSign-Issued Digital Certificates Pose Spoofing Hazard (2001). http://www.microsoft.com/technet/security/bulletin/MS01-017.asp
25. Miller, M.S.: Lambda for Humans: The PetName Markup Language. Resources library for E (2000). http://www.erights.org/elib/capability/pnml.html
26. Ministry of Communications and Information Technology. e-Pramaan: Framework for e-Authentication. Government of India, Delhi, Version 1.0, October 2012

27. Ministry of Government Administration Reform: Framework for Authentication and Non-Repudiation in Electronic Communication with and within the Public Sector (in Norwegian: Rammeverk for autentisering og uavviselighet i elektronisk kommunikasjon med og i offentlig sektor). Technical report, Norwegian Government (2008)

28. Kai, A.: Olsen and Hans Fredrik Nordhaug. Internet Elections: Unsafe in Any Home? Commun. ACM **55**(8), 36–38 (2012)

29. Schechter, S.E., Dhamija, R., Ozment, A., Fischer, I.: The emperor's new security indicators. In: IEEE Symposium on Security and Privacy, 2007. SP 2007, pp. 51–65, May 2007

30. Soghoian, C., Stamm, S.: Certified lies: detecting and defeating government interception attacks against SSL (Short Paper). In: Danezis, G. (ed.) FC 2011. LNCS, vol. 7035, pp. 250–259. Springer, Heidelberg (2012)

31. Stiegler, M.: Petname Systems. Technical Report HPL-2005-148, HP Laboratories Palo Alto, 15 August 2005

32. Varmedal, K.A., Klevjer, H., Hovlandsvåg, J., Jøsang, A., Vincent, J., Miralabé, L.: The OffPAD: requirements and usage. In: Lopez, J., Huang, X., Sandhu, R. (eds.) NSS 2013. LNCS, vol. 7873, pp. 80–93. Springer, Heidelberg (2013)

33. Bryce (Zooko) Wilcox-O'Hearn: Names: Decentralized, secure, human-meaningful: Choose two (2005). http://www.zooko.com/distnames.html

Data Privacy Management

Group Discounts Compatible with Buyer Privacy

Josep Domingo-Ferrer$^{(\boxtimes)}$ and Alberto Blanco-Justicia

Department of Computer Engineering and Mathematics, Universitat Rovira i Virgili,
Av. Països Catalans 26, 43007 Tarragona, Catalonia, Spain
{josep.domingo,alberto.blanco}@urv.cat

Abstract. We show how group discounts can be offered without forcing buyers to surrender their anonymity, as long as buyers can use their own computing devices (*e.g.* smartphone, tablet or computer) to perform a purchase. Specifically, we present a protocol for privacy-preserving group discounts. The protocol allows a group of buyers to prove how many they are without disclosing their identities. Coupled with an anonymous payment system, this makes group discounts compatible with buyer privacy (that is, buyer anonymity).

Keywords: Buyer privacy · Group discounts · Cryptographic protocols · Digital signatures

1 Introduction

Group discounts are offered by vendors to encourage consumers to use their services, to promote more efficient use of resources, to protect the environment, etc. Examples include group tickets for museums, stadiums or leisure parks, discounted highway tolls or parking fees for high-occupancy vehicles, etc. It is common for the vendor to require all group members to identify themselves, but in reality this is seldom strictly necessary.

We make the assumption that the important feature about the group is the *number of its members*, rather than their identities. A secondary feature that may often (not always) be relevant for a group discount is whether group members are physically together.

Anonymously proving the number of group members and their being together is trivial in a face-to-face setting with a human verifier, who can see that the required number of people are present. However, with an automatic verifier and/or in an on-line setting, this becomes far from obvious.

In this paper, we propose a method to prove the number of people in a group while preserving the anonymity of group members and without requiring specific dedicated hardware, except for a computing device with some wireless communication capabilities (*e.g.* NFC, Bluetooth or WiFi). Also, we explore the option to include payment in our proposed system, which is necessary for group discounts. We complete the description of our method with a possible

© Springer International Publishing Switzerland 2015
J. Garcia-Alfaro et al. (Eds.): DPM/SETOP/QASA 2014, LNCS 8872, pp. 47–57, 2015.
DOI: 10.1007/978-3-319-17016-9_4

anonymous payment mechanism, *scratch cards*. The method presented here is a generalization of a specific protocol for toll discounts in high-occupancy vehicles, whose patent we recently filed [5].

The rest of the paper is structured as follows. Section 2 describes the building blocks of our method, namely a digital signature scheme, a key management scheme, an anonymous payment scheme and wireless communication technologies; the latter technologies should be short-range in applications where one wants to check that the group members are physically together. Section 3 describes our actual group size accreditation method, including the required entities and protocols. The security and the privacy of our proposal are analyzed in Sect. 4. In Sect. 5, we give a complexity estimation of our approach and describe precomputation optimizations. Finally, Sect. 6 summarizes conclusions and future work ideas.

2   Building Blocks

Our group size accreditation method is based on an identity-based dynamic threshold $(IBDT)$ signature scheme, namely a particular case of the second protocol proposed in [6].

Threshold signature schemes are commonly based on (t, n)-threshold secret sharing schemes, such as the ones introduced in [1,10], and they require a minimum number t of participants to produce a valid signature. Dynamic threshold signature schemes differ from the previous ones in that the threshold t is not fixed during the setup phase, but is declared at the moment of signing. Our method takes advantage of this feature to find out how many users participated in the signature of a particular message, and consequently how many people form a group. If one wishes to prove that the signature is not only computed by at least t participants, but also that *these are together in the same place*, the above signature schemes need to be complemented with short-range communication technologies.

On the other hand, identity-based public key signature schemes, theorized by Shamir in [11] and with the first concrete protocol, based on the Weil pairing, developed by Boneh *et al.* in [3], allow public keys pk^U to be arbitrary strings of some length, which we call *identities*. These strings are associated with a user U and reflect some aspect of his identity, *e.g.* his email address. The corresponding secret key sk^U is then computed by a trusted entity, the certification authority (CA), taking as input the user's identity and, possibly, some secret information held only by the CA, and is sent to the user U through some secure channel. Identity-based public key signature schemes offer a great flexibility in key generation and management and our method takes advantage of this feature by proposing a key management scheme that allows preserving the anonymity of the participants.

Finally, in most group discounts, a fee must be paid after proving the number of group members, so an anonymous payment method is needed. Indeed, this method should not reveal additional information about the group members to the service provider.

2.1   IBDT Signature Scheme

We outline a general identity-based dynamic threshold signature scheme, namely the second protocol proposed in [6]. Our protocol will be a slight modification of this general case; we will point out differences when needed. A general *IBDT* signature scheme consists of the following five algorithms.

IBDT 1. *Setup is a randomized trusted setup algorithm that takes as input a security parameter λ, a universe of identities $\mathcal{ID}$ and an integer n which is a polynomial function of λ and upper-bounds the possible thresholds* (i.e. n is *the maximum number of users that can participate in a threshold signature). It outputs a set of public parameters* pms *and a master key pair* msk *and* mpk. *An execution of this algorithm is denoted as*

$$(\mathsf{pms}, \mathsf{mpk}, \mathsf{msk}) \leftarrow \mathsf{Setup}\,(\lambda, \mathcal{ID}, n).$$

IBDT 2. *Keygen is a key extraction algorithm that takes as input the public parameters* pms, *the master key pair* msk *and* mpk, *and an identity* $\mathbf{id} \in \mathcal{ID}$. *The output is a private key* $SK_{\mathbf{id}}$. *An execution of this algorithm is denoted as*

$$SK_{id} \leftarrow \mathsf{Keygen}\,(\mathsf{pms}, \mathsf{mpk}, \mathsf{msk}, \mathbf{id}).$$

IBDT 3. *Sign is a randomized signing algorithm that takes as input the public parameters* pms, *the master public key* mpk, *a user's secret key* $SK_{\mathbf{id}}$, *a message* Msg $\in \{0,1\}^*$ *and a threshold signing policy* $\Gamma = (t, S)$ *where* $S \subset \mathcal{ID}$ *and* $1 \le t \le |S| \le n$. *Note that, in our case, t will be strictly equal to $|S|$. Sign outputs a partial signature* $\sigma_{\mathbf{id}}$. *We denote an execution of this algorithm as*

$$\sigma_{\mathbf{id}} \leftarrow \mathsf{Sign}\,(\mathsf{pms}, \mathsf{mpk}, SK_{\mathbf{id}}, \mathsf{Msg}, \Gamma).$$

IBDT 4. *Comb is a deterministic signing algorithm which takes as input the public parameters* pms, *the master public key* mpk, *the secret key of the combiner user* $SK_{\mathbf{id}}$, *a message* Msg, *a threshold signing policy* $\Gamma = (t, S)$ *and a specific set S_t of t partial signatures. Comb outputs a global signature σ. We denote the action taken by the signing algorithm as*

$$\sigma \leftarrow \mathsf{Comb}\,(\mathsf{pms}, \mathsf{mpk}, SK_{\mathbf{id}}, \mathsf{Msg}, \Gamma, \{\sigma_{\mathbf{id}}\}_{\mathbf{id} \in S_t}).$$

IBDT 5. *Verify is a deterministic verification algorithm that takes as input the public parameters* pms, *a master public key* mpk, *a message* Msg, *a global signature σ and a threshold policy $\Gamma = (t, S)$. It outputs 1 if the signature is deemed valid and 0 otherwise. We denote an execution of this algorithm as*

$$b \leftarrow \mathsf{Verify}\,(\mathsf{pms}, \mathsf{mpk}, \mathsf{Msg}, \sigma, \Gamma).$$

For correctness, for any security parameter $\lambda \in \mathbb{N}$, any upper bound n on the group sizes, any universe $\mathcal{ID}$, any set of public parameters and master key pair $(\mathsf{pms}, \mathsf{mpk}, \mathsf{msk})$, and any threshold policy $\Gamma = (t, S)$ where $1 \leq t \leq |S|$, it is required that for

$$\sigma = \mathsf{Comb}\left(\mathsf{pms}, \mathsf{mpk}, SK_{\mathbf{id}}, \mathsf{Msg}, \Gamma, \{\sigma_{\mathbf{id}}\}_{\mathbf{id} \in S_t}\right),$$

$$\mathsf{Verify}\left(\mathsf{pms}, \mathsf{mpk}, \mathsf{Msg}, \sigma, \Gamma\right) = 1$$

whenever the values $\mathsf{pms}, \mathsf{mpk}, \mathsf{msk}$ have been obtained by properly executing the Setup algorithm, $|S_t| \geq t$, and for each $\mathbf{id} \in S_t$, $\sigma_{\mathbf{id}} \leftarrow \mathsf{Sign}(\mathsf{pms}, \mathsf{mpk}, SK_{\mathbf{id}}, \mathsf{Msg}, \Gamma)$ and $SK_{\mathbf{id}} \leftarrow \mathsf{Keygen}(\mathsf{pms}, \mathsf{mpk}, \mathsf{msk}, \mathbf{id})$.

2.2   Key Management

The anonymity provided by our accreditation method is a result of our key generation protocol and management solution. As we stated above, identity-based public key cryptosystems allow using arbitrary strings as public keys. In our protocol, every user U_i is given an ordered list of public keys that depend on some unique identifier of the user, such as his national identity card number, his phone number, the IMEI number of his phone or a combination of any of them. We will call this identifier $n_{U_i} = d_k^i d_{k-1}^i \ldots d_1^i$, where d_j^i is the j-th last digit of n_{U_i} and typically ranges from 0 to 9.

To generate the list of public keys from an identifier n_{U_i}, we choose a value $\ell < k$ and take the ℓ last digits of n_{U_i}. This results in a vector of public keys

$$\mathbf{PK}_{U_i} = \left\{\mathsf{pk}_1^{d_1^i}, \ldots, \mathsf{pk}_\ell^{d_\ell^i}\right\},$$

with every $\mathsf{pk}_j^{d_j^i}$ being an encoding of the digit and its position in n_{U_i}, for example:

$$\mathsf{pk}_j^{d_j^i} = j \,\|\, d_j^i,$$

where $\|$ is the concatenation operation. To illustrate this process, imagine $n_{U_i} = 12345678$ and $\ell = 4$. The resulting public key list would be

$$\mathbf{PK}_{U_i} = \{18, 27, 36, 45\}.$$

To prove the number of members in a group, the members will choose a common integer $j \in \{1, \ldots, \ell\}$ so that the j-th public key in their list, $i.e.$ $\mathsf{pk}_j^{d_j^i}$, is different for all of them. Then they will perform the required operations with these public keys and their corresponding private keys. Assuming that the values of the digits range from 0 to 9, this would provide anonymity to each of the users, since on average 10 % of people will share the same public key $\mathsf{pk}_j^{d_j^i}$ for some value of j.

Note that this approach limits the size of the groups that can be certified with our method to a maximum of 10. Moreover, intuition tells us that the closer the size of the group to this maximum size, the more difficult it becomes to find a value of j for which each user has a different public key. The probability that our protocol fails depends on the number of keys each user is given, ℓ, and the size of the group n; more specifically for $n \leq 10$:

$$F(\ell, n) = \left(1 - \frac{10(10 - 1)\ldots(10 - n + 1)}{10^n}\right)^{\ell},$$

that is very close to 1 for values of n close to 10.

The limit on the maximum value of n can be increased by assigning $d \geq 2$ digits of n_{U_i} to each of the ℓ public keys, instead of just one digit. By doing this, the maximum value for the size of the groups becomes 10^d, and the probability of failure, for values of $n \leq 10^d$, is

$$F(\ell, n, d) = \left(1 - \frac{10^d(10^d - 1)\ldots(10^d - n + 1)}{10^{dn}}\right)^{\ell}.$$

However, the price to be paid for choosing a larger d is a loss of anonymity, since, if more digits are associated to each public key, less users share the same public key. For example, for $d = 2$ a user would share each of his keys with only 1 % of the total number of users.

The service provider will choose ℓ and d depending on the maximum number of keys that a user can store, the maximum allowed group size and the anonymity level to be guaranteed.

2.3 Anonymous Payment Mechanisms

Group discounts are one of the applications of our method: after proving the group size, the group members must pay a fee that depends on that size. If proving the size has been done anonymously, it would be pointless to subsequently use a non-anonymous payment protocol (such as credit card, PayPal, etc.).

Hence, we need to use an anonymous payment mechanism along with our group size accreditation protocol. The simplest option for an anonymous payment method is to use cash if the application and the service provider allow it. Unfortunately, this will not always be the case, and other payment methods have to be taken into account. Electronic cash protocols such as [4] are good candidates for this role. Nowadays, Bitcoin [8] is a well-established electronic currency and, although it is not anonymous by design [9], it can be a good solution if accompanied by careful key management policies. Also, extensions of the original protocol as Zerocoin [7] provide anonymity by design.

For completeness, we propose in this work to use a much simpler approach, based on prepaid scratch cards that users can buy at stores using cash (for maximum anonymity). Each such card contains a code Pay.Code which the service provider will associate with a temporary account holding a fixed credit specified by the card denomination.

2.4 Communication Technologies

Our accreditation method requires communication among the members of a group and between the members and some type of verifying device. If we want to prove not only that a group has a certain number of members, but also that these are together, the interactions with the verifying device must rely on short-range communication technologies, like NFC, Bluetooth or WiFi.

During the accreditation protocol, the users' smartphones will be detected in some way by the verifying device and a communication channel will be established. The requirements and constraints of this process depend on the type of service and verifying devices, but nonetheless it is desirable that communication establishment be fast and not too cumbersome to the user.

We propose to use Bluetooth, and in particular *Bluetooth Low Energy* [2] to communicate with the verifying device. BLE solves some of the main limitations of traditional Bluetooth, *i.e.* reduces detection and bonding times, requires much less work by the user than NFC and has a shorter range than both Bluetooth and WiFi, which is desirable in a method like ours. Finally, BLE is implemented by most major smartphone manufacturers, at least in recent models, unlike NFC.

Regarding communication between the smartphones, any of the three mentioned technologies, or a combination of them (*e.g.* Bluetooth pairing through NFC messages) seems appropriate. The choice is up to the service provider.

3   Group Size Accreditation Method

A service that implements our accreditation method includes the following elements:

- A service provider (SP) that publishes a smartphone application App_U and distributes the necessary public parameters and keys of an *IBDT* signature scheme Π to users, after some registration process.
- A smartphone application App_U for each user U which:
  - allows computing signatures with Π on behalf of U;
  - allows computing ciphertexts with a public-key encryption scheme Π' selected by SP, under SP's public key pk^{SP};
  - can be run on master or slave mode, which affects how App_U participates in the accreditation protocol;
  - includes some certificate which allows checking the validity of pk^{SP};
  - implements some communication protocol, relying in short-range communication technologies, such as NFC or Bluetooth, to interact with the applications of the rest of the members of the group and with the verifying devices.
- Prepaid payment scratch cards available at stores. Each card includes a code Pay.Code that the SP associates to an account with a fixed credit specified by the card denomination.
- Verifying devices installed at suitable places in the provider's infrastructures which:
  - allow verifying signatures with Π;
  - hold the SP certificates as well as the keys needed to decrypt ciphertexts produced with Π' under pk^{SP};

- have short-range communication capabilities and implement some protocol to communicate with the users' devices.
- Some method to penalize or prevent the misuse of the system.

The complete accreditation protocol runs as follows:

Protocol 1. *System setup protocol.*

1. SP chooses the user identifier to be used as n_U and appropriate values for ℓ and d.
2. SP generates the parameters of the IBDT signature scheme Π as per Algorithm IBDT.Setup;
3. SP generates the parameters of the public-key encryption scheme Π'.

Protocol 2. *Registration protocol.*

1. A user U with identifier n_U authenticates himself to the service provider, face-to-face or by some other means. The user receives a PIN code pin_U.
2. The service provider associates to U a vector of public keys of Π, $\mathbf{PK_{id}}$ as described in Sect. 2.2.
3. The service provider computes the secret keys associated to $\mathbf{PK_{id}}$ as per Algorithm IBDT.Keygen:
$$\mathbf{SK_{id}} = \left(sk_1^{d_1^{\text{id}}}, \ldots, sk_\ell^{d_\ell^{\text{id}}} \right).$$
4. The user downloads the smartphone application App_U and, using the PIN code pin_U, completes the registration protocol and receives the system parameters and keys, as well as the public key pk^{SP}.

Protocol 3. *Credit purchase.*

1. A user buys a prepaid card for the system, e.g. a scratch card, from a store.
2. The card includes some code Pay.Code which has to be introduced in the smartphone application.

Protocol 4. *Group setup protocol.*

1. Some user U^*, among the group of users $U_1, \ldots, U_t$ who want to use the service, takes the leading role. This user will be responsible for most of the communication with the verifying device. U^* sets his smartphone application to run in master mode and the others set it to work in slave mode.
2. The users agree on a value $j \in \{1, 2, \ldots, \ell\}$ such that the value of the j-th public key in $\mathbf{PK_{id}}$ is different for every user.

Protocol 5. *Group size accreditation protocol.*

1. A verifying device detects the users' devices and sends them a unique time-stamped ticket T that may include a description of the service conditions and options.

2. *Each user U_i runs Algorithm* IBDT.Sign *to compute a partial signature with* Π *under his secret key* $\mathsf{sk}_j^{d_j^i}$ *on message*

$$\mathsf{Msg} = \left\langle \mathsf{T} \| \mathsf{pk}_j^{d_j^1} \| \dots \| \mathsf{pk}_j^{d_j^t} \right\rangle,$$

for the threshold predicate $\Gamma = (t, \{\mathsf{pk}_j^{d_j^1}, \dots, \mathsf{pk}_j^{d_j^t}\})$. *It sends the resulting partial signature* σ_i *to* U^*.

3. U^* *receives* $(\sigma_1, \dots, \sigma_t)$ *and runs Algorithm* IBDT.Comb *to combine these signatures and output a final signature* σ *on behalf of* $U_1, \dots, U_t$. U^* *sends to the verifying device*

$$\mathsf{Msg}' = \langle \mathsf{Msg}, \sigma \rangle.$$

4. *The verifying device checks the validity of the signature by running*

$$\mathsf{IBDT.Verify}(\mathsf{Msg}, \sigma, \mathsf{pk}_j^{d_j^1} \| \dots \| \mathsf{pk}_j^{d_j^t}, t).$$

Note that this signature will only be valid if all users $U_1, \dots, U_t$ *have collaborated in computing it, and thus it proves that the group of users is composed of at least t people. If the signature is not valid, the group will be penalized in an application-dependent way, e.g. with access denial, group discount denial, etc. Otherwise, the service provider grants access to the group of users and tells the group the amount* amount_t *they have to pay depending on the group size.*

Protocol 6. *Payment.*

1. *Each group member* U *in the (sub)set* P *of group members who want to collaborate in paying the bill sends to the verifying device via Bluetooth or WiFi his payment code encrypted under SP's public key:*

$$C_U = \mathsf{Enc}_{\mathsf{pk}^{SP}}(\mathsf{T} \| \mathsf{Pay.Code}_U),$$

where $\mathsf{Pay.Code}_U$ *is the code which user* U *obtained from a prepaid scratch card and where* Enc *is the public-key encryption algorithm of scheme* Π'.

2. *The verifying device decrypts the ciphertexts* $\{C_U : U \in P\}$ *to obtain the payment codes of the users in* P.

3. *The verifying device substracts the quantity* amount_t *divided by the cardinal of* P *to the accounts associated with the received payment codes.*

4   Security and Privacy Analysis

Security and privacy are offered by design in our proposal:

– The chosen IBDT scheme ensures unforgeability of signatures under chosen message attacks even when an attacker can choose arbitrarily the threshold signing policy. In this case, this means that, for any $t \geq 2$, no group of less than t buyers is able to deceive the service provider by producing a threshold signature with threshold t. Complete security proofs can be found in the original paper [6].

- No more than the pseudonyms and the number of participants of a group is revealed to the service provider during the execution of the protocol. Buyer anonymity is guaranteed by the key management scheme described in Sect. 2.2 *within the community of buyers sharing the same public key*. For example, if each public key is associated to a combination of d decimal digits, then on average this public key is shared by a community containing $10^{-d} \times 100\%$ of the total number of users.
- When payment is completely anonymous, whatever anonymity level achieved by key management is preserved after payment. For our given method, this is ensured when a given Pay.Code cannot be linked to a specific buyer. This can be achieved, for example, if the scratch card containing the Pay.Code is purchased using cash.

5 Performance Analysis

Our group size accreditation method is to be run by service providers, specialized verifying devices and the users' smartphones. Therefore, it is important that the computations of the underlying cryptographic protocol be as fast as possible, especially the algorithms that are executed by the smartphones, which have limited computational capabilities and rely on batteries.

In this section, we analyze the performance of the underlying *IBDT* signature scheme. This scheme is a pairing-based cryptographic protocol and as such, the required operations are performed in elliptic curve groups. We analyze its performance by counting the number of point multiplications, point exponentiations and pairings, which are the most costly operations.

Table 1 shows the number of these operations for each of the algorithms in the *IBDT* signature scheme. The number of operations is counted as a function of the maximum number of possible participants in a signature, n, and the size of the signing group t. As we stated previously, $t \leq n$.

Table 1. Operations required per algorithm

	Multiplications	Exponentiations	Pairings
Setup	0	$n + 4$	1
Keygen	$2n$	$4n$	0
Sign	$2n + 6$	$2n + 5$	0
Comb	$2n - t + 1$	$2n - t$	0
Verify	$n + 2$	$n + 1$	4

Note that the Sign and Comb algorithms, that are intended to be executed in the users' smartphones during the **group size accreditation protocol** (5), present what seems to be quite a high number of operations. This might be a problem if the devices in which these algorithms are to be executed do not have enough computational power. Moreover, these two algorithms should precisely be most efficient, since they are run most often, and possibly with time constraints. Therefore, it would be interesting if we could precompute some of their operations.

The Sign algorithm is a probabilistic protocol, that is, it has some random values in it that have to be refreshed each time it is executed. This limits the amount of operations in the algorithm that can be precomputed. On the other hand, most of the operations depend on static values, $e.g.$ keys and threshold policies Γ. Threshold policies contain the number of signers that will participate in a signature and their public keys. We assume that groups of users will be quite stable, $i.e.$ users will generally use services together with the same group members, or at least with a limited set of different groups. We can exploit this assumption by precomputing operations that only depend on static values and threshold policies.

The Comb algorithm obviously depends on the output of Sign, but it is a deterministic algorithm and some of its operations depend on static values and also on the threshold policies. Therefore, by the same assumption as before, we can precompute some of the operations.

These precomputations will divide the Sign and Comb algorithms in two phases each, one for precomputing values, which will be executed during the **group setup protocol** (4), and the other one performed during the **group size accreditation protocol** (5). The resulting number of operations in each of these phases is shown in Table 2.

Table 2. Precomputed and non-precomputed operations of the Sign and Comb algorithms (PC stands for precomputed)

	Multiplications	Exponentiations	Pairings
Sign PC	$2n + 2$	$2n + 1$	0
FastSign	2	4	0
Comb PC	$2n - 2t$	$2n - 2t$	0
FastComb	$3t + 1$	$3t$	0

6   Conclusions and Future Work

We have presented a privacy-preserving mechanism for group discounts. The method is built upon an $IBDT$ signature scheme, a concrete key generation and management solution, short-range communication technologies and anonymous payment mechanisms. Our complexity analysis and initial tests show that the method is usable in practice.

Future work will consist of implementing the protocol, testing it and developing a generic app for privacy-preserving group discounts that can be easily customized for specific applications.

Acknowledgments. Thanks go to Dr Carla Ràfols for advice on IBDT signatures. The following funding sources are acknowledged: Google (Faculty Research Award to the first author), Government of Catalonia (ICREA Acadèmia Prize to the first author and grant 2014 SGR 537), Spanish Government (project TIN2011-27076-C03-01 "CO-PRIVACY"), European Commission (FP7 projects "DwB" and "Inter-Trust") and Templeton World Charity Foundation (grant TWCF0095/AB60 "Co-Utility"). The authors are with the UNESCO Chair in Data Privacy. The views in this paper are the authors' own and do not necessarily reflect the views of Google, UNESCO or the Templeton World Charity Foundation.

References

1. Blakley, G.R.: Safeguarding cryptographic keys. In: Proceedings of the National Computer Conference, pp. 313–317. AFIPS Press, New York (1979)
2. Bluetooth SIG, Specification of the Bluetooth System (2013). https://www.bluetooth.org/en-us/specification/adopted-specifications
3. Boneh, D., Franklin, M.: Identity-based encryption from the Weil pairing. In: Kilian, J. (ed.) CRYPTO 2001. LNCS, vol. 2139, p. 213. Springer, Heidelberg (2001)
4. Chaum, D., Fiat, A., Naor, M.: Untraceable electronic cash. In: Goldwasser, S. (ed.) CRYPTO 1988. LNCS, vol. 403, pp. 319–327. Springer, Heidelberg (1990)
5. Domingo-Ferrer, J., Ràfols, C., Aragonès-Vilella, J.: Method and system for customized contactless toll collection in carpool lanes (in Spanish "Método y sistema de cobro sin contacto, por el uso de una vía, para vehículos de alta ocupación"), Spanish patent ref. no: P201200215. Date filed: February 28, 2012. Patent owner: Universitat Rovira i Virgili
6. Herranz, J., Laguillaumie, F., Libert, B., Ràfols, C.: Short attribute-based signatures for threshold predicates. In: Dunkelman, O. (ed.) CT-RSA 2012. LNCS, vol. 7178, pp. 51–67. Springer, Heidelberg (2012)
7. Miers, I., Garman, C., Green, M., Rubin, A.D.: Zerocoin: anonymous distributed e-cash from bitcoin. In: 2013 IEEE Symposium on Security and Privacy (SP), pp. 397–411. IEEE (2013)
8. Nakamoto, S.: Bitcoin: a peer-to-peer electronic cash system. Consulted, vol. 1 (2008). http://www.bitcoin.org/bitcoin.pdf
9. Reid, F., Harrigan, M.: An analysis of anonymity in the Bitcoin system. In: Altshuler, Y., Elovici, Y., Cremers, A.B., Aharony, N., Pentland, A. (eds.) Security and Privacy in Social Networks, pp. 197–223. Springer, New York (2013)
10. Shamir, A.: How to Share a Secret. Commun. ACM **22**, 612–613 (1979)
11. Shamir, A.: Identity-based cryptosystems and signature schemes. In: Blakely, G.R., Chaum, D. (eds.) CRYPTO 1984. LNCS, vol. 196, pp. 47–53. Springer, Heidelberg (1985)

The Crypto-Democracy and the Trustworthy (Position Paper)

Sébastien Gambs[1]([✉]), Samuel Ranellucci[2], and Alain Tapp[3]

[1] Université de Rennes 1 - INRIA/IRISA, Rennes, France
`sgambs@irisa.fr`
[2] Department of Computer Science, Aarhus University, Aarhus C, Denmark
`samuel@cs.au.dk`
[3] DIRO, Université de Montréal, Montréal, Canada
`tappa@iro.umontreal.ca`

Abstract. In the current architecture of the Internet, there is a strong asymmetry in terms of power between the entities that gather and process personal data (*e.g.*, major Internet companies, telecom operators, cloud providers, . . .) and the individuals from which this personal data is issued. In particular, individuals have no choice but to blindly trust that these entities will respect their privacy and protect their personal data. In this position paper, we address this issue by proposing an utopian crypto-democracy model based on existing scientific achievements from the field of cryptography. More precisely, our main objective is to show that cryptographic primitives, including in particular secure multiparty computation, offer a practical solution to protect privacy while minimizing the trust assumptions. In the crypto-democracy envisioned, individuals do not have to trust a single physical entity with their personal data but rather their data is distributed among several institutions. Together these institutions form a virtual entity called the Trustworthy that is responsible for the storage of this data but which can also compute on it (provided first that all the institutions agree on this). Finally, we also propose a realistic proof-of-concept of the Trustworthy, in which the roles of institutions are played by universities. This proof-of-concept would have an important impact in demonstrating the possibilities offered by the crypto-democracy paradigm.

Keywords: Privacy · Trust · Secure computation · Democracy

1 Introduction

The recent revelations from Snowden about the NSA's ability to eavesdrop on communications, as well as to track the digital traces left by Internet users, clearly demonstrates that we are currently moving towards an information age that is not so far from 1984. Since the original novel from Orwell, the concept of Big Brother has become a powerful meme. Indeed even if few people understand the subtleties of modern cryptography, the potential abuses resulting from the

© Springer International Publishing Switzerland 2015
J. Garcia-Alfaro et al. (Eds.): DPM/SETOP/QASA 2014, LNCS 8872, pp. 58–76, 2015.
DOI: 10.1007/978-3-319-17016-9_5

massive collection of personal data and the associated invasion of privacy is very present in people's mind. Thus, Big Brother is now synonymous of a dystopian future in literature, movies, arts and general culture.

The amount of information collected by Internet companies and third parties on individuals increases every day, both in quantity and in diversity. For instance, some actors have access to personal data such as social relationships, email content, income information, medical records, credit card and fidelity card usage, pictures taken through public and private cameras, personal files, navigation behavior, location, biometrics, data issued from quantified self, . . . , just to name a few. In addition, the ability to capture and record all aspects of life (both real and virtual) of users has increased dramatically recently due to new technological developments. For instance, Memoto[1] was originally a Kickstarter project whose objective was the development of a small camera worn by the user that would automatically generate a picture of its surroundings that would be associated with GPS position and the corresponding timestamp. Even more recently, the concept of Google glass has appeared to be very attractive to some users. However, its adoption will also certainly exacerbate the privacy concern of others.

On one hand, this massive collection of information raises many privacy issues since most data is personal and thus sensitive by nature. Already today, the accumulated amount of data collected is very significant but the possible abuses are still limited because its potential cannot be fully exploited, both for legal and technical reasons. For instance, the possibility of cross-referencing databases is often limited due to privacy laws regulating the gathering and processing of personal data. In addition, it is expected that the inference capabilities will increase dramatically as more and more data become available and gets concentrated in the hands of a few actors. Thus, we can reasonably believe that we do not have yet a full-fledged Big Brother because all this information is not accessible easily by one entity (except maybe the NSA).

On the other hand, the information captured could also be used in a number of useful and innovative manners. For instance, currently in Russia many cars are equipped with cameras in order to prevent corrupt policemen from charging a driver with a fictitious crime or to simplify insurance settlements. Thus, the record of this information can act as a safeguard against corruption. Coming from the quantified self movement, it has been suggested to rely on devices that regularly study your body while you shower to detect diseases and important changes such as pregnancy. Aggregate information also allows to pinpoint infections and cancers as well as their sources, such as poisoned wells.

With the advent of Big Data, machines will be able to perform fine-grained inferences that are not yet possible. While the basic statistical (actuarial) model is already at least as good (and often better) than experts at making predictions [BT02], machine learning has the potential for extracting even more useful information from large amount of data. This information can be used for good

---

[1] https://www.kickstarter.com/projects/martinkallstrom/
memoto-lifelogging-camera.

(*e.g.*, finding a link between some profiles and particular sicknesses) or for bad (*e.g.*, denying to someone the access to an health insurance because he is classified as a high risk profile). Ultimately, the machine might even become better at predicting the behavior of an individual than the person himself. For instance, a teenager has recently experienced the strange situation in which her father learned that she was pregnant due to a targeted advertisement that she received in her mailbox based on the profile constructed by the supermarket company out of her purchasing list[2].

One possibility for protecting privacy could be to work on anonymous or pseudonymous data. Unfortunately, anonymizing data in a sound and robust manner is a very difficult and sometimes even impossible task [Ohm10]. For instance, simply removing the personally identifiable information from the released data is usually insufficient to protect the privacy of a user. Indeed, it is possible that the combination of some attributes, which individually are innocuous, could act as a quasi-identifier and thus be used to de-anonymize the data. Thus, there is always the risk that an anonymous profile can be re-identified and linked to a real identity. In addition, if the data is composed of the queries or the mobility traces of a user, then this data is so rich that it can be used to build a very detailed profile of a user containing a lot of personal information. Even more, this profile (whether it is or not anonymous) can have a tangible impact of the life of the user. For instance, this profile might impact the price paid for a product or in an extreme case a service could be denied because of this profile, which is a form of discrimination.

Another possibility for an individual to protect his privacy would be to segregate himself from technology by not sharing information in any way. However, we believe that such an approach is both a step backward and impossible in practice as the digital traces of the actions of the user are collected often by systems that he is unaware of or he has limited or no control on. For instance, in most cities the users of a public transportation system constantly leave traces of their whereabouts through their transport pass. Thus, the main challenge is to be able to exploit the vast possibilities offered by the use of personal data in a secure and private manner.

In this position paper, we state our position regarding the utopian application of secure multiparty computation to democracy and propose a practical project on this theme. The outline of the paper is the following. First in Sect. 2, we discuss how trust is a central notion to any solution that stores and processes personal data. In particular, we highlight the trust assumptions that are usually made (implicitly or explicitly) by the current existing architectures. Then in Sect. 3, we introduce, what we coin as the "crypto-democracy utopia", in which cryptographic techniques are use to distributively implement a (virtual) trustworthy party that we coin as the Trustworthy. The role of the Trustworthy is to manage the processing and storing of personal data in a secure and private manner while minimizing the trust assumptions. Afterwords in Sect. 4, we review the

---

[2] http://www.nytimes.com/2012/02/19/magazine/shopping-habits.html?
pagewanted=1&_r=2&hp&.

state-of-the-art of cryptographic techniques such as secure multiparty computation and secret sharing that constitute the building blocks of our proposition for the Trustworthy before describing in Sect. 5 a proposition for a proof-of-concept downscale version of the Trustworhty. Finally, we conclude in Sect. 6.

2 Architecture of Trust

Trust is an essential and unavoidable concept strongly linked to security and privacy. However, it is also a notion that cannot be easily and universally defined. In this section, we discuss the notion of trust and we make explicit the trust assumptions done by existing architectures. This will enable us later to put in perspective the trust assumptions that we are making ourselves with our approach in the following sections.

Making Trust Explicit. In cryptography, trust is one of the fundamental element. At the same time it is often left aside and not defined explicitly. For instance, most of the fundamental results in cryptography assume that the main participants, Alice and Bob, are themselves cryptographers, that they each have access to a computer that is fully secure and under their control and that the software they execute on this computer is well known and understood by them. In addition, when involved in the protocol other assumptions that are sometimes made is that Alice and Bob perform no other task when participating to the protocol and that they do not run several sessions of the protocol in parallel. The adversary model has also to define precisely the capacities of the attacker, both in terms of the attacks that it can performed and the ressources he can used (*e.g.*, memory, computational power, eavesdropping capability, . . .) Thus, in practice in order for the protocol to be *really* secure, several trust assumptions have to be made.

In a different context, when using a smartphone a user has to trust that the hardware (*e.g.*, the SIM card) and software installed on his device are secure and will not leak private information about him without his consent. In addition, when the user downloads an application on the App Store, the user trusts that Apple has verified the behavior and the code of the application and that there is no risk in using it. In practice, these trust assumptions can be betrayed if the smartphone is infected by malware or if information leaks out of the device through a malicious application. On the Internet, when the user gives his data to a company or a cloud provider, in some sense he is doing an act of faith that this entity will respect his privacy. Similarly, when navigating on the web, for the user to believe that a website will forget the digital traces left by his interactions if it follows the *Do Not Track* Initiative is also a kind of wishful thinking.

Trust is also a central ingredient of public-key infrastructures in which certification authorities are responsible for certifying the identity of an entity or in its decentralized version of the Web of Trust (*i.e.*, through PGP-like solutions). Finally, even in quantum cryptography in which the security of the protocol is supposed to depend on the physical laws of quantum mechanics, ultimately one has to trust the hardware provided by the quantum cryptography company.

More Crypto Does Not Mean More Trust. Adding more cryptography to a particular service does not necessarily make it more trustworthy. For instance, a few years ago the debit card in Canada were equipped with a secure chip and a PIN in contrast with the credit cards themselves (at that time). Thus, one can say that the debit card was more trustworthy as it relies on more advanced cryptography and clearly provide more security, but was is really the case? In reality, several persons were facing serious issues after being stolen their PIN. Indeed, the reaction of the bank was that the system in place is secure and that the users are guilty of not having protected their PIN. Those unlucky customers were having the burden of proof, mainly because the security of the system was unquestioned. In contrast, the lack of security of the credit card was such that the bank would have almost no capacity to contradict a person claiming not to have made a purchase. Of course, the total cost of the fraud for credit cards was huge and the lack of security was clearly very costly for the credit card company, and thus indirectly for their clients. Still this example illustrates that stronger cryptography does not automatically improve trust. Another common example is the situation in which a user is forced due to the password policy to choose a very complex password and to change it very frequently. In this situation, it is often the case that the user will end up writing his very secret password on a post-it next to his screen or that he will never log out. This situation also exemplifies that adding more security features can sometimes lead to less security if it is not balanced with usability. In addition, the user also has to trust that the current implementation of cryptographic primitives is indeed doing what it is supposed to do.

One Should Not Have to Trust the Goodwill of Others. Another aspect of trust concerns the potential corruption of insiders. In particular, it is very dangerous to base security on trusting trust users as illustrated by the following anecdote. In this anecdote, one of the author was asked by one of his colleague why he is using a Gmail account instead of the email system provided by his department. In particular, his colleague insisted that he should not share all this private data, personal email and other sensitive information with companies such as Google. This means that the colleague was putting more trust on the technical support of the department than on Google itself. The response of the author to this criticism is very simple. On one hand, it is true that most of the staff from technical support in charge of the email accounts are very nice persons that it know the members of the department for a long time. Thus, it can be assumed that they do not to spy on the members of the department. On the other hand, one can easily imagine a scenario in which a conflict might arise between a person from the technical support and a professor, in which case the access to the email account might become problematic. In contrast, while Google also has incentives to spy on email (*e.g.*, for personalized services and targeted advertising), it has no interest in leaking this data while an angry member of the technical support might be tempted to do so. One typical trust assumption is that rational players have to be honest, which unfortunately does not protect against a fully malicious player.

To summarize, while cryptography is a prerequisite to build security, in all known systems there is also a question of trust. For instance, the user might have to trust software, laws, computers, networks, companies, humans or governments. Thus, the fundamental question is always: who are you ready to trust and to which extent. In particular, while trust assumptions *always* have to be made, one should aim for a solution in which these trust assumptions are minimal, realistic and consistent. In particular, we believe that the security and privacy guarantees provided by an architecture should not depend on the trust that one puts on a *single* entity. In the following sections, we will discuss how cryptography can reduce the semantic gap between the security provided in theory, the one achieved in practice and the one perceived by the end user.

3   The Crypto-Democracy Utopia

We believe that society is in need of an elegant solution to answer to the ever growing privacy concerns. This solution should provide strong privacy guarantees while still bringing the benefits of the knowledge that can be extracted from the collected data. While we recognize that the suggestion of an entity, collecting and managing all private and public information, evokes right away the dystopian Big Brother, in this section we will describe an utopian alternative based on sound science. In particular, we believe that techniques originating from secure multiparty computation can reconcile the antagonist needs of privacy and the ability to exploit personal data for the benefit of individuals and the greater good. While this utopian dream is already possible in theory with existing cryptographic techniques, realizing it in practice requires a significant increase in computation power and communication efficiency as well as algorithmic advances, not to mention a deep social revolution. However, both technology and cryptography are improving at a fast pace. For instance during the last 50 years, the processing capacity of computers has been multiplied by a factor close to a 1000 times per decade. Thus, what seems to be out of reach of current technology might become possible a near future. In addition, new breakthroughs in cryptography have been invented on a regularly basis. For instance, the concept of fully homomorphic encryption was only materialized in 2009 [Gen09] but its efficiency has been improved rapidly under thorough efforts of the cryptography community.

The Trustworthy. In this section, we propose a cryptographic approach to democracy, which is respectful of the privacy of citizens due to the way personal data is managed. In a nutshell, a set of carefully chosen independent institutions will implement a virtual entity, called the *Trustworthy*, in a distributed and secure manner using known cryptographic techniques. The Trustworthy would be responsible for managing the public and private information related to individuals. None of the institutions would have directly access to the private data. Instead a precise access structure would specify the level of collaboration necessary between these different institutions before it is possible to extract or use data from the Trustworthy. For instance, one possible access structure could be that a majority of the institutions have to be involved before the private information considered can be retrieved from the system, while another one could be that unanimity is required if the piece of data considered is really sensitive. In addition, to having the capacity to retrieve the data, the institutions would be able to compute over it (provided that the predefined number of institutions accept to collaborate), thus creating new knowledge. Note that the users are not involved in this computation as once a user has trusted the Trustworthy with his data, the Trustworthy can perform operations on it without further interaction with the user. Another objective of those institutions is to guarantee the correctness and appropriate behavior of the equipment, software and infrastructure under their control. This is especially important for the access points in which new fresh data can be entered in the trusted third, both to avoid the possibility of introducing fake data in the system and also to ensure that the data of a user does not leak at this entrance point.

Choice of Institution and Access Structure. The choice of institutions that will be part of the distributed implementation of the Trustworthy is a central aspect of the system and many scenarios are possible. However, in all cases, the choice of the institutions should be done in a way reaching a *quasi-consensus* in society. In practice, this does not mean that each citizen would have to trust all the institutions. On the contrary, if unanimity is required before data can be accessed then it is enough if each individual trusts that at least one of the elected institutions behaves in way that protect his privacy and civil rights. In addition, the structure chosen to reach this utopian goal is likely to be different from the ones that are currently used in most democratic countries. In particular, we believe that in order to avoid the transformation of the trusted third into Big Brother, each institution should not be under the control of the same entity (*e.g.*, the government). Instead these institutions should represent in a balanced way different categories of the population and groups of interests. Examples of institutions could be a political party, a college of professionals, a religious group, the supreme court, a data protection authority or a non-profit organization, just to cite a few. Of course, the set of institutions does not need to be fixed for eternity and new institutions with a clear mandate could be elected to participate to the realization of the crypto-democracy.

For a given set of institutions, there are many possible designs for the access structure. In a nutshell, an access structure is a set of rules specifying the type of collaboration and consensus required from institutions to retrieve or compute on data. An access structure stating that the collaboration of at least k amongst n institutions is needed is both generic and powerful as it encapsulates access policies such as majority, unanimity and quorum. Of course, not all type of data should require the same threshold but we believe that the previously stated ones cover most useful situations. In addition even if not all data should be treated equally, having too many different access structures could render the system unnecessarily complex.

Consistent, Simple and Self-Explanatory Trust Model. In the crypto-democracy paradigm, there is a strong correlation between the trust assumptions that are made in theory and how they should really be in practice. In particular, all institutions would certify that the entrance point in which data is fed into the system, including its hardware and software, is compliant with what is publicly expected to guarantee that there is no undue monitoring of the data. Furthermore, when the unanimity access structure is applied, it is clear from the user point of view that he only has to trust a single institution in being honest in order to trust the system, which is exactly in concordance with the theory. Another important aspect of trust is how robust is the system under the corruption of some institutions. Indeed, having a friend that works in an institution and is willing to provide private data is one thing, but having a corrupted friend in each institution is a conspiracy.

Hardware, Software and Infrastructure Requirements. In practice, each institution would need to own a super computer or a dedicated cluster and to have a team of cryptographers and security experts. In addition, each institution should scrutinize and monitor very carefully all the materials and the employees working under their supervision, with a special care to the entrance point for fresh data. While such requirements have a non-negligible cost, we believe that trust, privacy and security are sufficiently important concepts to deserve such an investment. For instance in Montreal, there is currently the project to build a new bridge that will cost around 5 billions US dollars. While the project is fundamental for the city, this bridge is only one among others connecting the island of Montreal to the rest of Quebec. In comparison, the large data center that Google constructs in Singapore costs 120 millions US dollars and thus 5 billions would pay for 40 of them.

4   State-of-the-Art in Secure Computation

In this section, we give a brief overview of the existing modern cryptographic techniques that could be used to implement the crypto-democracy. In theory at least, those techniques provide all the necessary ingredients to concretize the different aspects discussed in the previous sections. However to realize them in practice, the following issues have to be tackled: cost, speed, and scalability. After reviewing the state-of-the-art of the cryptographic primitives in this section and discussing the current existing implementations of such technologies, we describe in the next section a proposal for a downscale version of the Trustworthy that can be realistically implemented at a very reasonable cost.

4.1   Secure Multiparty Computation

Informally, *secure multiparty computation* [Gol09, CD14, CDN14] (which we simply call *secure computation* for the rest of this paper) is the field of cryptography studying how to securely and privately implement a distributed function that depends on the private inputs of many participants. Another way to phrase it is to say that the objective of secure computation is to emulate a trusted third party (*e.g.*, the Trustworthy) through a distributed protocol between participants without actually requiring that every participant trust everyone else. Security is generally defined with respect to a particular adversary model, which captures the actions that can be performed by dishonest participants. For instance, some participants might be *honest-but curious*, meaning that they follow the recipe of the protocol but collude together by exchanging their knowledge and information about the messages they have seen in order to break the privacy of the input of honest participants. In a stronger adversary model, participants can be *fully malicious* and cheat arbitrarily. In this setting, in addition of breaking the privacy of the input of honest participants, the objective of the adversary can be to attack the correctness of the protocol (*i.e.*, by influencing its output) or its robustness (*i.e.*, by making it abort). Thereafter, we will use the term "*trust model*" to encompass at the same time the adversary model considered as well as the trust assumptions that are made (both implicit and explicit).

More formally, we can define the general task of secure computation in the following manner.

Definition 1 (Secure computation). *With respect to a particular trust model T, a protocol securely computes a function f, if for any input $X = (x_1, ..., x_n)$ provided by n participants, as long as the trust assumptions of T are not betrayed, all participant only learn $f(X)$ and no additional information leaks from the protocol.*

This definition does not prevent the function itself from revealing sensitive information regarding the private input of specific participant (this issue is magnified if several functions are computed on this private data).This problem has been thoroughly studied in the literature and approaches such as the notion of differential privacy have been proposed to mitigate this issue [DMNS06, Dwo08].

4.2 Secret Sharing

Secret sharing [Sha79] is a cryptographic technique that can be used to distribute a secret between several participants in such a way that only a legitimate group of participants can reconstruct the secret. For instance, in a k-out-of-n secret sharing scheme, any set of k or more participants out of n can reconstruct the secret but less then k participants have absolutely no information on the secret. In this way, the code of a bank safe could be split in such way that it can be reconstructed only if two out of three vice presidents join their personal shares (*i.e.*, piece of the information). Most of the existing secret sharing schemes are information-theoretically secure, which means that an unauthorized group does not have in his hands the information to reconstruct the secret regardless of his computational power.

In this paper, we use secret sharing as a tool enabling users to distribute their secret across several institutions. In addition, secret sharing often forms the basis of secure computation protocols. More precisely, several protocols relies on an extension of secret sharing known as verifiable secret sharing. In standard secret sharing, if the shares are corrupted then the secret is lost and cannot be reconstructed. In contrast, Verifiable Secret sharing [CGMA85] allows the reconstruction of the secret as long as a restricted amount of shares remain uncorrupted. Thus, verifiable secret sharing ensures the validity of the data.

4.3   Secure Computation with an Honest Majority

The two fundamental results of secure computation have appeared the end of the eighties [GMW87, CCD88]. In a nutshell, these results consist in generic constructions showing that under the assumption that strictly more than two thirds of the participants are honest then *any* function can be computed securely. Thus, as long as strictly less than one third of the participants are malicious, regardless of their technological and computational power, they will not be able to learn information about the inputs of honest participants or force the protocol to output an incorrect result. Thereafter, we denote by n the total number of participants involved in the secure computation and t the number of malicious (*i.e.*, corrupted) participants. Most of these early protocols for secure computation relies on multiplication and addition over a large field rather than on bits and NAND gates but they can be applied to compute any generic boolean circuit. In particular, these protocols are not efficient because each multiplication (*i.e.*, AND gate) require interactions between all participants.

Although the original techniques for secure computation are now approximately 25 years old, the field is still very active. The generic construction for secure computation requiring a strict majority of honest participants was originally presented in [RBO89] but that construction require a secure broadcast channel. Since then, more efficient solutions have been designed. The construction of [BTH08] only requires linear communication complexity in the number of players for each multiplication gate but can only tolerate $t < n/3$ corrupt players. The construction of [BSFO12] requires approximately $O(n \log n)$ communication bits per multiplication gate and can tolerate any minority of malicious participants. With respect to the asynchronous setting, the construction proposed in [CHP13] is secure as long as $t < n/3$, and has a communication complexity proportional to the number of players multiplied by the number of multiplication gates of the circuit representing the function to be computed. The work of [CDI+13] can tolerate up to $n(1/2 - \epsilon)$ for any $\epsilon > 0$ (a smaller value epsilon increases the size of the constant) of malicious players and achieves a linear communication complexity in the number of players per multiplication gate. Finally, other theoretically interesting protocols include [DIK+08, DIK10].

4.4   Secure Computation Without Honest Majority

In some situations, the assumption that two thirds or a majority of the participants are honest may be too strong. For instance, a government might be unwilling to share information if there is a risk that the other parties might leak some information (thus breaching the privacy property). It might be also the case that the information is so sensitive and trust so limited that participants only trust that a particular party will protect their data. In particular, this means that even if up to $n-1$ participants are corrupted, the protocol is still secure. For this setting, it was shown in [Cle86] that certain distributed tasks are impossible without an honest majority. Thus it is impossible to achieve secure computation in full generality in this context without making either computational assumptions or physical assumptions such as the availability of trusted hardware.

A powerful and elegant solution is to base the construction of secure computation on a cryptographic primitive called *oblivious transfer* [Rab81, EGL85, Cré88]. In this asymmetric bipartite primitive, the sender sends two messages in the oblivious transfer and the receiver gets to choose one of these values. In addition, the sender is oblivious to the choice of the receiver (*i.e.*, he gets no information about this choice) and the receiver does not learn any information on the message he did not choose to learn. This primitive can be implemented using computational assumptions and is universal in the sense that the secure computation of any function can be implemented even if almost all participants are corrupted.

The protocol proposed in [NNOB12] is based on [CvdGT95] and provides secure computation solely from oblivious transfer. Both protocols first shares the inputs between two participants. Once this sharing has occurred the parties can perform operations such as AND, OR and XOR on distributed bits by relying on oblivious transfer. The latest construction only requires a constant number of bits of communication per gate. When extended to multiple participants, the complexity grows linearly in the number of players and the size of the circuit to be evaluated. Another construction of interest for secure computation is the IPS compiler named after its authors [IPS08] (an optimization was presented in [LOP11]). In these constructions, the participants imagine virtual players taking part in a protocol with honest majority evaluating the function in question. The participants will not just simulate these players but each player will verify by relying on oblivious transfer that a small minority of theses imagined players are acting honestly. As such, since making the protocol with honest majority fail would require that a participant corrupt a majority of virtual players, the honest participant will detect any effective cheating except with negligible probability. The communication complexity of [LOP11] is proportional to the size of circuits multiplied by the number of players.

Finally, more recent protocols [DPSZ12, DKL+13, KSS13, KS13, WNL+14] allow the evaluation of circuits with a complexity that is linear in the size of the circuit and the number of players, with the aid of pre-processing using somewhat homomorphic encryption. These protocols rely on the idea of multiplicative triples in the information-theoretic setting.

4.5 Applications

In principle, the range of applications of secure computation is extremely large but relatively few implementations exist. The first public implementation was realized by Ivan Damgård and his team [BCD+09]. This implementation was used in the context of an auction for the production rights of sugar beets.

More precisely in Denmark, farmers can buy and sell production rights and the secure computation was used to find the market equilibrium price and the amount bought and sold for that price. The implementation consists of an honest majority protocol with three institutions. The event involved roughly 1200 farmers and took roughly half an hour. Since, the protocol is repeated annually.

Secure computation can also used to perform general statistical data analysis. For instance, it was shown in [WH12], that by using fully homomorphic encryption, private linear regression on 4194304 elements can be completed in 256 minutes. Similarly, secure computation has also found applications in financial data analysis. In [BTW12], a solution was developed to analyze financial data in a private fashion for the ITL (Estonian Association of Information Technology and Telecommunications). This protocol is run roughly every six months. Another existing application of secure computation that was recently proposed is the detection of satellite collisions [KW13].

Secure computation can also protect the privacy of genetic and medical data [KBLV13, EN13]. In terms of performance in [KBLV13], the authors have compared the secure version of an algorithm against the standard algorithms and showed that the private algorithm was roughly 720 times slower. However, it is expected that further advances in secure computation will significantly reduce this factor. In addition, for some computations for which the privacy aspect is of paramount importance, this factor may not be so detrimental. Open source implementations of secure computation can be found in [MNPS04, BDNP08, EFLL12]

5   Proposal for a Scaled down Trustworthy

In order to demonstrate the practicality of the crypto-democracy, we propose in this section a preliminary implementation for a minimalistic Trustworthy. More precisely, we would like to use this significantly scaled down version of the Trustworthy as a proof-of concept to study the usefulness and feasibility of this type of initiative. In addition, another important contribution of such a project is to raise the awareness and interest of the security and privacy communities as well as the public at large. This implementation of the Trustworthy would use 5 independent universities as institutions. The main objectives of this implementation is to store in a secure and private manner the sensitive data belonging to users and to be able to conduct privacy-preserving data analysis for research in fields such as medicine and humanities. In particular, the Trustworthy can be used to provide meaningful non-trivial statistics on the data collected while ensuring that no single entity will be able to access this data in clear.

In this position paper, we only outline the main features of this implementation. However following the publication of paper, if we observe that the interest generated is sufficient, then we are planning to publish a technical report providing more details about the implementation.

5.1   Choice of Institutions

Relying on universities to play the role of institutions when implementing the Trustworthy seems to be a natural choice. Indeed, universities appear as a relevant choice because they are relatively independent and are trustworthy to the eye of the public. They also generally have the resources as well as expertise (in particular if they have a good security or cryptography research team) to guarantee the security and trust with respect to the software, hardware and network required by such an endeavor. Furthermore, we believe that it should not be difficult to find 5 universities spread around the world that would be sufficiently motivated to participate to this project.

Once the institutions have been selected, it will be essential to define a clear governance structure. For instance, no single university should be the sole master of the Trustworthy. Rather, we propose that the direction, decisions and computations that the trusted third will take should be decided by a simple majority structure in which each institution has exactly one vote. In addition, for specific data that have a higher degree of sensibility a stronger constraint such as unanimity across the institutions can be implemented. In this situation, no computation will be performed on the data unless all the institutions agree on this. In particular the Trustworthy cannot reveal information locked with an unanimity threshold with a majority vote but a majority vote would be enough to restrict the access to the data of a user or to discard it.

5.2   Functionalities Provided by the Trustworthy

In this section, we discuss in more details the data that will be secure by the Trustworthy and the functionalities that it will provide to users. For this first implementation, we believe that we should limit the functionalities offered to a few that will demonstrate the potential of the approach but can already be realized today with the current state of technology. However at the end of this section, we suggest other functionalities that are somewhat more advanced and could be added later.

- *Secure note.* Basically, this functionality simply corresponds to the possibility for the user to store, access and modify a text file in an online manner in the Trustworthy. This text file could be use to keep safe information such as password, passport number or credit card details. Typically, this file could be search by the user like a standard document and should not be too large.
- *Encrypted files.* The Trustworthy could be used to encrypt files chosen by the user and be responsible for protecting the secrecy of the key. For instance, the encrypted file could be stored on the hard drive of the user or on a cloud provider like Dropbox, Google drive or Microsoft drive. However, the key would be given to the Trustworthy, who would be responsible for decrypting the files if requested by the user.
- *Private email.* Offering the functionality of a private email service is a natural service that could be implemented through the Trustworthy. This functionality

would enable persons to exchange information in a truly private manner and by requesting that the email contains only text, this would not require a huge amount of storage.

– *Private survey.* This last functionality is the most complex but also the most This last functionalityinteresting feature of our proposal. Basically, the Trustworthy would be responsible for conducting surveys, for instance in the context of a research project in medicine or humanities. The respondent of a survey would login and fill it privately. Afterward, the data of his particular survey will never be reconstructed and seen by anyone in clear but rather statistics could be computed on the aggregate data of the different respondents to the survey and then made public. To ensure that the information of a particular user is sufficiently hidden into the global data, a condition on the minimal number of responses could be predefined before any analysis can be conducted on the data. In addition, ideally the list of statistics that will be computed should be known by all beforehand and the output should be sanitized to ensure privacy.

All the data stored on the Trustworthy should be secure according to some threshold, which might vary depending on the sensitivity of the data or the privacy expectations of users. For instance, in the case of the secure note, private email and encrypted files the user could decide by himself which threshold he want to use while for the survey this threshold should be fixed in advance and publicly known before the experiment starts (*i.e.*, before respondents begin to answer to the survey). In order to reconstruct the private data or to compute on it, *at least* the number of institutions required by the threshold have to cooperate together.

In practice, we envision that users will access to the Trustworthy in a transparent manner through their browser. Each user should have a unique identity and connect through a university of his choice using the corresponding software. This software should be open-source so that it can be inspected by anyone as well as being guaranteed and checked by the institutions. First when connecting, a mutual authentication protocol is run in which the user securely authenticates to the trusted third and vice-versa.

5.3   Implementing the Trustworthy

For the functionalities that only need to perform secret sharing then the Shamir scheme will be used. All symmetric encryption should be made using a standard encryption scheme with long keys (*e.g.*, AES with a 256 bits key). The keys used should be created uniformly at random in order to ensure a strong level of security.

– *Communication structure.* All the communications done between the user and the institutions are secured through the use of a public-key cryptosystem with a large key (possibly in conjunction with a protocol such as TLS) while the communications exchanged between the institutions are secure through the use of symmetric encryption. We also assume that the computer of the user is secure enough such that malware cannot intercept the information entered by the user in his web browser when connecting to the Trustworthy.

– *Identification and authentication.* All the interactions between the Trustworthy and a user will be done through his browser. Several standard authentication techniques such as the use of a passphrase or two-way authentication based on certificates could be used but of course their applicability and security have to be evaluated in more details with respect to the architecture developed in the project. While the security provided by the authentication mechanism used is of paramount importance for ensuring the privacy and integrity of the users' data entrusted to the Trustworthy, a full discussion of the different alternatives for authentication as well as their pros and cons is out of the scope of this paper. Note however that if the adversary is able to impersonate a specific user during authentication, this only jeopardize the privacy of the data of this user but not of the data of all users.

– *Secure note.* The corresponding text file should be compressed, encrypted and then saved on the hard drive of each institution. The key will be stored in the Trustworthy using a secret sharing scheme with a threshold defined by the user. The user can view and modify his file online and securely through a web application running on his browser.

– *Encrypted files.* Similarly to the previous functionality, the Trustworthy would only be responsible to store the key needed to decrypt the encrypted files. The user can choose whether he want to store these files on a disk under his control or on a server of his choice. The Trustworthy offers the possibility to perform an online encryption and decryption of these files.

– *Private email.* This functionality could be implemented by having the email sent a particular user stored in the Trustworthy using a secret sharing scheme such as that no institution would have a direct access to the content of these emails. In addition each email could itself be encrypted with the public key of the recipient. Only this recipient would be allowed to retrieve the corresponding shares once he has authenticated to the Trustworthy. As one of the assumptions is that the different institutions forming the Trustworthy are spread all around the world, the privacy of the emails would be ensured even if one of these institutions is requested to hand over the information it has (*e.g.*, similarly to what happen to Lavabit and Silent Circle).

– *Private survey.* The private survey functionality can be implemented by combining the techniques described in [BTH08] and [BCD+09]. The survey can be represented in binary format as well as an integer to speed-up calculations. In a nutshell, the integer would be stored using a redundant representation (base 2, integer and base 1 for small integer) to simplify the computations. Data consistency between the binary and the integer representation will be verified by the Trustworthy. Examples of possible operations on the survey data include AND and NOT (for the binary representation), the sum and multiplication (for integer representation) and the transfer from binary to integer (or vice-versa). It is also straightforward to compute if an encrypted value is smaller or larger than a particular threshold. The implementation that we propose is powerful enough to compute interesting non-trivial statistics.

For instance, we could easily compute the percentage of female participants whose age is between 32 and 40 years with both diabetes and the Coeliac disease. More precisely, this statistic requires the computation of 2 inequalities and 3 multiplications for each user in the survey. However, as the scalability increases with the number of users, this computation could be performed with only a constant number of messages sent.

The cost per institution will be quite low as most of the infrastructure is already provided by the university. With respect to the additional hardware needed, we believe that a 3000$ server under the responsibility of each institution should be sufficient to start the project. In particular, since the Trustworthy is mainly responsible of the storing of the encryption keys (at least for the secure notes and the encrypted files functionalities), the memory requirements are relatively small. By far, the main investment for the practical realization of this project will be the creation of the appropriate software although indirect but limited costs have also to be taken into account (*e.g.*, for the maintenance and possible upgrades). We believe that a two-year period for conducting this project is realistic.

Other *internal* functionalities need to be added to the Trustworthy. For instance, it should be possible to reshare information with a new threshold, which corresponds in practice to transforming the data encoded from one secret sharing to another. In case of a hardware malfunction, it should be possible to retrieve the corresponding data. Finally, it should also be possible to permanently remove data from the servers (and the backup) if a user request it, thus implementing a form of right to be forgotten. This functionality could be implemented for instance by erasing the corresponding shares at the level of each institution upon the user's request.

6   Conclusion

Our main objective in this paper was to show that the field of secure computation can help to the improvement of democracy. In particular, we have highlighted how using current technologies, we could implement the Trustworthy, which is a ideal trusted third party that could manage our personal data. The objective of the Trustworthy is to ensure a high degree of actual and perceived privacy while simplifying our lives. In order to show the feasibility of the approach, we have also propose a realistic project, achievable with limited financial resources that is interesting and powerful enough to generate interest and to enable researchers to experiment on this concept.

In the future, we would like to investigate also additional functionalities that could be added to the project once the basic functionalities described previously have been implemented. For instance, we hope that the system will be powerful and fast enough to perform more complex functions on the private survey data such as advanced data mining or machine learning algorithms.

Acknowledgments. Sébastien is supported by the Inria large scale project CAPPRIS (Collaborative Action on the Protection of Privacy Rights). Samuel is supported by the European Research Commission Starting Grant 279447, the Danish National Research Foundation and The National Science Foundation of China for the Sino-Danish Center for the Theory of Interactive Computation.

References

[BCD+09] Bogetoft, P., Christensen, D.L., Damgård, I., Geisler, M., Jakobsen, T., Krøigaard, M., Nielsen, J.D., Nielsen, J.B., Nielsen, K., Pagter, J., Schwartzbach, M., Toft, T.: Secure multiparty computation goes live. In: Dingledine, R., Golle, P. (eds.) FC 2009. LNCS, vol. 5628, pp. 325–343. Springer, Heidelberg (2009)

[BDNP08] Ben-David, A., Nisan, N., Pinkas, B.: Fairplaymp: a system for secure multi-party computation. In: Proceedings of the 15th ACM conference on Computer and Communications Security, pp. 257–266. ACM (2008)

[BSFO12] Ben-Sasson, E., Fehr, S., Ostrovsky, R.: Near-linear unconditionally-secure multiparty computation with a dishonest minority. In: Safavi-Naini, R., Canetti, R. (eds.) CRYPTO 2012. LNCS, vol. 7417, pp. 663–680. Springer, Heidelberg (2012)

[BT02] Bishop, M.A., Trout, J.D.: 50 years of successful predictive modeling should be enough: lessons for philosophy of science. Philos. Sci. **69**, 197–208 (2002)

[BTH08] Beerliová-Trubíniová, Z.: Perfectly-secure MPC with linear communication complexity. In: Canetti, R. (ed.) Theory of Cryptography. LNCS, vol. 4948, pp. 213–230. Springer, Heidelberg (2008)

[BTW12] Bogdanov, D., Talviste, R., Willemson, J.: Deploying secure multi-party computation for financial data analysis. In: Keromytis, A.D. (ed.) Financial Cryptography and Data Security. LNCCS, vol. 7397, pp. 57–64. Springer, Heidelberg (2012)

[CCD88] Chaum, D., Crépeau, C., Damgård, I.: Multiparty unconditionally secure protocols. In: Proceedings of the Twentieth Annual ACM Symposium on Theory of Computing, pp. 11–19. ACM (1988)

[CD14] Crépeau, C., Desrosiers, S.P.: Introduction to cryptographic protocols (2014, unplublished manuscript)

[CDI+13] Cohen, G., Damgård, I.B., Ishai, Y., Kölker, J., Miltersen, P.B., Raz, R., Rothblum, R.D.: Efficient multiparty protocols via log-depth threshold formulae. In: Canetti, R., Garay, J.A. (eds.) CRYPTO 2013, Part II. LNCS, vol. 8043, pp. 185–202. Springer, Heidelberg (2013)

[CDN14] Cramer, R., Damgård, I., Nielsen, J.B.: Secure Multiparty Computation and Secret Sharing - An Information Theoretic Approach (2014, unplublished manuscript)

[CGMA85] Chor, B., Goldwasser, S., Micali, S., Awerbuch, B.: Verifiable secret sharing and achieving simultaneity in the presence of faults. In: 26th Annual Symposium on Foundations of Computer Science, pp. 383–395. IEEE (1985)

[CHP13] Choudhury, A., Hirt, M., Patra, A.: Asynchronous multiparty computation with linear communication complexity. In: Afek, Y. (ed.) DISC 2013. LNCS, vol. 8205, pp. 388–402. Springer, Heidelberg (2013)

[Cle86] Cleve, R.: Limits on the security of coin flips when half the processors are faulty. In: Proceedings of the Eighteenth Annual ACM Symposium on Theory of Computing, pp. 364–369. ACM (1986)

[Cré88] Crépeau, C.: Equivalence between two flavours of oblivious transfers. In: Pomerance, C. (ed.) CRYPTO 1987. LNCS, vol. 293, pp. 350–354. Springer, Heidelberg (1988)

[CvdGT95] Crépeau, C., van de Graaf, J., Tapp, A.: Committed oblivious transfer and private multi-party computation. In: Coppersmith, D. (ed.) CRYPTO 1995. LNCS, vol. 963, pp. 110–123. Springer, Heidelberg (1995)

[DIK+08] Damgård, I., Ishai, Y., Krøigaard, M., Nielsen, J.B., Smith, A.: Scalable multiparty computation with nearly optimal work and resilience. In: Wagner, D. (ed.) CRYPTO 2008. LNCS, vol. 5157, pp. 241–261. Springer, Heidelberg (2008)

[DIK10] Damgård, I., Ishai, Y., Krøigaard, M.: Perfectly secure multiparty computation and the computational overhead of cryptography. In: Gilbert, H. (ed.) EUROCRYPT 2010. LNCS, vol. 6110, pp. 445–465. Springer, Heidelberg (2010)

[DKL+13] Damgård, I., Keller, M., Larraia, E., Pastro, V., Scholl, P., Smart, N.P.: Practical covertly secure MPC for dishonest majority – Or: breaking the SPDZ limits. In: Crampton, J., Jajodia, S., Mayes, K. (eds.) ESORICS 2013. LNCS, vol. 8134, pp. 1–18. Springer, Heidelberg (2013)

[DMNS06] Dwork, C., McSherry, F., Nissim, K., Smith, A.: Calibrating noise to sensitivity in private data analysis. In: Halevi, S., Rabin, T. (eds.) TCC 2006. LNCS, vol. 3876, pp. 265–284. Springer, Heidelberg (2006)

[DPSZ12] Damgård, I., Pastro, V., Smart, N., Zakarias, S.: Multiparty computation from somewhat homomorphic encryption. In: Safavi-Naini, R., Canetti, R. (eds.) CRYPTO 2012. LNCS, vol. 7417, pp. 643–662. Springer, Heidelberg (2012)

[Dwo08] Dwork, C.: Differential privacy: a survey of results. In: Agrawal, M., Du, D.-Z., Duan, Z., Li, A. (eds.) TAMC 2008. LNCS, vol. 4978, pp. 1–19. Springer, Heidelberg (2008)

[EFLL12] Ejgenberg, Y., Farbstein, M., Levy, M., Lindell, Y.: SCAPI: the secure computation application programming interface. IACR Cryptol. ePrint Arch. **2012**, 629 (2012)

[EGL85] Even, S., Goldreich, O., Lempel, A.: A randomized protocol for signing contracts. Commun. ACM **28**(6), 637–647 (1985)

[EN13] Erlich, Y., Narayanan, A.: Routes for breaching and protecting genetic privacy (2013). arXiv preprint arXiv:1310.3197

[Gen09] Gentry, C.: A fully homomorphic encryption scheme. Ph.D. thesis, Stanford University (2009)

[GMW87] Goldreich, O., Micali, S., Wigderson, A.: How to play any mental game or a completeness theorem for protocols with honest majority. In: Proceedings of the Nineteenth Annual ACM Symposium on Theory of Computing, pp. 218–229. ACM (1987)

[Gol09] Goldreich, O.: Foundations of Cryptography. Cambridge University Press, Cambridge (2009)

[IPS08] Ishai, Y., Prabhakaran, M., Sahai, A.: Founding cryptography on oblivious transfer – efficiently. In: Wagner, D. (ed.) CRYPTO 2008. LNCS, vol. 5157, pp. 572–591. Springer, Heidelberg (2008)

[KBLV13] Kamm, L., Bogdanov, D., Laur, S., Vilo, J.: A new way to protect privacy in large-scale genome-wide association studies. Bioinformatics **29**(7), 886–893 (2013)

[KS13] Keller, M., Scholl, P.: Efficient, oblivious data structures for MPC (2013). Cryptology ePrint Archive, Report 2014/137

[KSS13] Keller, M., Scholl, P., Smart, N.P.: An architecture for practical actively secure MPC with dishonest majority. In: Proceedings of the 2013 ACM SIGSAC Conference on Computer and Communications Security, pp. 549–560. ACM (2013)

[KW13] Kamm, L., Willemson, J.: Secure Floating-Point Arithmetic and Private Satellite Collision Analysis (2013)

[LOP11] Lindell, Y., Oxman, E., Pinkas, B.: The IPS compiler: optimizations, variants and concrete efficiency. In: Rogaway, P. (ed.) CRYPTO 2011. LNCS, vol. 6841, pp. 259–276. Springer, Heidelberg (2011)

[MNPS04] Malkhi, D., Nisan, N., Pinkas, B., Sella, Y.: Fairplay-secure two-party computation system. In: USENIX Security Symposium, pp. 287–302, San Diego, CA, USA (2004)

[NNOB12] Nielsen, J.B., Nordholt, P.S., Orlandi, C., Burra, S.S.: A new approach to practical active-secure two-party computation. In: Safavi-Naini, R., Canetti, R. (eds.) CRYPTO 2012. LNCS, vol. 7417, pp. 681–700. Springer, Heidelberg (2012)

[Ohm10] Ohm, P.: Broken promises of privacy: responding to the surprising failure of anonymization. UCLA Law Rev. **7**, 1701–1776 (2010)

[Rab81] Rabin, M.O.: How to exchange secrets with oblivious transfer (1981)

[RBO89] Rabin, T., Ben-Or, M.: Verifiable secret sharing and multiparty protocols with honest majority. In: Proceedings of the Twenty-First Annual ACM Symposium on Theory of Computing, pp. 73–85. ACM (1989)

[Sha79] Shamir, A.: How to share a secret. Commun. ACM **22**(11), 612–613 (1979)

[WH12] Wu, D., Haven, J.: Using Homomorphic Encryption for Large Scale Statistical Analysis (2012)

[WNL+14] Wang, X., Nayak, K., Liu, C., Shi, E., Stefanov, E., Huang, Y.: Oblivious Data Structures. Cryptology ePrint Archive, Report 2014/185 (2014)

Configuration Behavior of Restrictive Default Privacy Settings on Social Network Sites

Analyzing the Combined Effect of Default Settings and Interface Style

Markus Tschersich[(✉)]

Deutsche Telekom Chair of Mobile Business and Multilateral Security,
Goethe University Frankfurt, Theodor-W.-Adorno-Platz 4,
60323 Frankfurt am Main, Germany
`markus.tschersich@m-chair.de`

Abstract. Research about privacy in the context of social network sites has not addressed yet how users behave with restrictive default privacy settings. Literature about default settings and the sharing of personal information in social network sites lacks empirical insight into how restrictive default privacy settings influences the behavior of users. To gain empirical insight, a social network site privacy interface prototype was built to investigate the influence of default settings and interface style on the privacy configuration behavior of users. Results show configuration behavior differences between participants having restrictive or permissive privacy default settings. Further, interfaces with multiple pages of privacy settings induce participants to keep their default settings.

Keywords: Social Network Site · Privacy by Default · Privacy · Default setting · Interface

1 Introduction

Research in the area of privacy is a growing field in the information systems literature [1]. Current research about privacy in the context of social network sites (SNS) has not addressed yet how restrictive default privacy settings that do not share personal information without the explicit decision of the users, influences the behavior of users. Research strands about user behavior with software defaults and the sharing behavior of users are contradictory in the case of restrictive default privacy setting.

Literature in the field of default settings emphasizes that owing to several reasons like e.g. lack of awareness [1] and laziness [2,3], users tend to keep default settings. Consequently, when users of SNS behave similarly, more restrictive default privacy settings could lead to less shared personal information on SNS. On the other hand, users register to SNS in order to share personal information with others. This satisfies their needs to lower feelings of loneliness and to

© Springer International Publishing Switzerland 2015
J. Garcia-Alfaro et al. (Eds.): DPM/SETOP/QASA 2014, LNCS 8872, pp. 77–94, 2015.
DOI: 10.1007/978-3-319-17016-9_6

increase feelings of social capital [4]. On SNS with restrictive default privacy settings users cannot satisfy these needs without actively deviating from the default.

Users perform a privacy calculus by weighing between the benefits and costs of revealing personal information [5], before actually revealing personal information. Throughout this decision process and driven by their need to share personal information, users often underestimate possible risks owing to an "it wont happen to me" mentality [6]. By contrast, concepts like Privacy by Default (PbDef) [7] aim to prevent users from potential privacy threats. PbDef obliges platform providers to have the most restrictive privacy option as the preselected one for all settings that manage the revelation of personal information [8]. In online services that process personal information (like SNS), the most restrictive option is that no-one could access personal information besides the owner of the information itself. To grant other users access to personal information, everybody needs to decide explicitly what and with whom she/he wants to share.

Privacy professionals promote PbDef as a powerful concept to reduce the risk of privacy violation of the users that are also caused by the underestimation of risks by users [8,9]. Therefore, privacy professionals suggest the implementation of PbDef to all services that work with personal information. The European Commission shares the opinion of privacy professionals about the potentials of PbDef to protect the rights of citizens. Thus, as part of the European Union legislation process the European Commission and the European Parliament passed the draft law that makes PbDef binding for online service providers [10].

Providers of SNS expect PbDef to have a negative impact on the functionality of the platform and their business models [11]. The success of SNS, however, is determined by user participation, especially by sharing personal information [12]. Thus, concerns of providers are grounded in expecting less user participation owing to PbDef with its restrictive default privacy settings.

Findings of both research strands (status quo, users need) are contradictory in the case of restrictive default privacy settings and literature lacks empirical insight into how users really behave on SNS with restrictive default privacy settings and how different privacy settings influence the configuration behavior of their privacy. To provide first insights regarding this topic, our research analyzes how users differ in their configuration behavior of privacy settings by having different restrictive default privacy settings. To identify impacts by the interface we analyze the combined effect with different interface styles. This also enables a better assessment of concerns and chances of PbDef regulation in the case of SNS. To do so, we first describe the theoretical background of our research and our hypotheses in Sect. 2. Following that, in Sect. 3 we presente our methodology, including a description of our research prototype to execute the study. Section 4 presents the data collected during the study and the results of the tests. In Sect. 5 the results, implications and limitations are discussed followed by a conclusion in Sect. 6.

2   Theoretical Background

Various aspects in the field of privacy on SNS are covered in the literature [12–14]. SNS are defined to be about profiles and the connection between users [15]. Studies investigated how self-disclosure on SNS is influenced by gender [16] or culture [17] as well as what kind of personal information users disclose on their profiles on SNS [17]. Further, research investigates and describes the decision-making process performed by users before revealing personal information on SNS. The privacy calculus describes that users are performing a trade-off between the benefits and costs of their self-disclosure on SNS prior to the decision of whether to disclose personal information or not [1,6,18,19]. It is also found that trust plays an important role in this decision-making process, because it influences the perceived benefits and costs of the revelation [13].

Research also investigated why users share personal information within communities [5,20,21] and how they handle their privacy settings [22–24]. Users participate on SNS owing to several reasons. They desire identification within the community and have a need for self-verifying feedback from the community [25]. Therefore, it is important for them to present themselves within the community [26,27]. Further, communicating and sharing personal information on the SNS brings users plenty of social capital [28] and reduces feelings of loneliness [5,29].

Default settings have been investigated in numerous different domains and fields of application. Influences have been identified in the configuration of security settings of WiFi access points [30], in the purchase of seat reservations on railways [31], to the percentage of organ donors [32] and to response rates in web surveys [33]. The common theme is that users tend to accept default settings, so that defaults can also be seen as a de facto regulation [30]. Literature about opt-in and opt-out also confirms that users tend to keep preselected options [3]. Literature puts this behavior down to the status quo bias [4,34].

Several possible reasons for not changing the default settings and keeping the status quo exist: cognitive and physical laziness; perceiving default settings as correct; perceiving endorsement from the provider; or using defaults as a justification for choice [3,4,35–37]. In the case of privacy settings in SNS, literature shows that permissive default privacy options keep users off from configuring their privacy settings [23]. Having a plethora of reasons for not changing default settings, we expect that users with restrictive or permissive default settings will tend to keep close to their preselected default privacy settings. Therefore, we hypothesize:

H1: Users with restrictive or permissive default privacy settings differ in their configuration behavior of privacy settings on SNS.

When privacy settings are spread over multiple pages, users can have difficulties in getting an overview of their own privacy configurations. Further, a broader understanding of their own sharing behavior is limited [38,39]. Thus, overall complexity can be increased by more privacy settings and a finer granulation [39]. An increased complexity will reduce the transparency of the interface that will also lead users to keep their default settings [2]. Higher complexity of an interface can also require more technical skills to understand the interface [2]. Thus, the style of an interface can also affect the configuration behavior by users of their privacy settings. Therefore, we hypothesize:

H2: Users having a structured or unstructured interface differ in their configuration behavior of privacy settings on SNS.

The previously described findings about user behavior in the context of default settings and different interface styles also indicate a combined effect. Therefore, we hypothesize:

H3: Users having different restrictive default privacy settings and using a different interface differ in their configuration behavior of privacy settings on SNS.

3 Methodology

Hypotheses were checked in an experimental setting with an independent-measures study design. As our independent variables, we have two dimensions each with two conditions. The first dimension concerns the restrictiveness of the default settings. Each participant is assigned to either Privacy by Default with the preselected option that only the user herself can see her own personal information; or the opposite, that the whole SNS can see the personal information of the user. The second dimension concerns the interface. Each participant is assigned either to have all privacy settings in a list on one page or categorized in a menu with multiple pages. Based on the two dimensions with their conditions, four different groups have been built in the intersections of the conditions as displayed in Fig. 1.

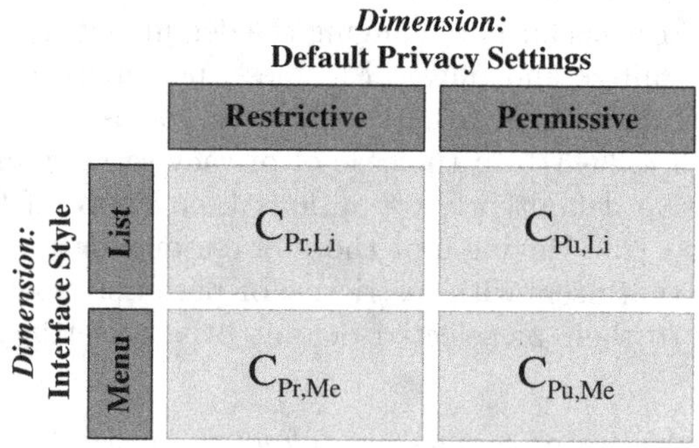

Fig. 1. Experimental groups

We analyzed the differences among the four groups for 14 different privacy settings of SNS. Relevant privacy settings were collected and clustered based on SNS that are popular in Germany: Facebook, Google+, LinkedIn, Xing, and StudiVZ. From the pool of privacy settings of these SNS, we selected for our analysis those settings that allow drawing conclusions regarding the personality of a user (e.g. personality, location, etc.). The selected settings were clustered with regard to their functionality. This results in three categories: Profile Information, Status Updates, and Media. The selected privacy settings and their grouping according to the identified categories are shown in Table 1.

Table 1. Analyzed privacy settings

Cat.	No.	Privacy settings
Profile information	1	Who can see the date of your birthday?
	2	Who can see your year of birth?
	3	Who can see whether you are interested in boys or girls?
	4	Who can see your relationship status?
Status updates	5	Who is allowed to see your status updates?
	6	Who will be informed about changes in your profile?
	7	Who is allowed to see updates about your location?
	8	Who is allowed to add information to your timeline?
	9	Who is allowed to see entries on your timeline added by others?
	10	Who is allowed to tag you in status updates?
	11	Who is allowed to tag you in photos?
Media	12	Who is allowed to see your photo albums?
	13	Who is allowed to see the location of your photos?
	14	Who is allowed to see your videos?

The dependent variable of the configuration behavior of participants is measured by the selected privacy option for each setting. Every participant can choose between options with different access rights for their personal information.

3.1 Participants

We focused on students with an active account on a social network. Overall 632 students participated in the study. An a priori power analysis with an expected effect size of $r = .50$ computed a required total sample size of at least 420 (105 per group) participants to get a power of .95 [40]. We met the requirements of the power analysis with our sample size of a total of 632 participants, as shown in Table 2.

Participants were motivated to participate in the study by prizes raffled among all participants that worked with the privacy interface prototype and filled out a subsequent questionnaire. Table 2 shows the distribution of the participants into the four experimental groups as well as their gender, age, and the period of time they have been using SNS. The proportion of male and female participants is comparable among all four groups. Likewise, the average ages as well as the time of SNS usage are similar within all four experimental groups.

Table 2. Sociodemographic data

	$C_{Pr,Me}$	$C_{Pr,Li}$	$C_{Pu,Me}$	$C_{Pu,Li}$	Total
Participants	115	198	126	193	632
Male	64	115	70	114	363
Female	46	73	53	77	249
No anser	5	10	3	2	20
Age					
Average Age	20.09	21.21	21.57	20.82	20.96
SD	5.33	5.97	6.65	4.61	5.63
SNS usage					
Average Years	4.78	4.91	4.81	4.70	4.81
SD	2.33	2.32	2.46	2.18	2.34

The frequency of using SNS for private purposes is comparable for all experimental groups as displayed in Fig. 2. About 70 % of the participants allocated to the interface style with privacy settings in the form of a list visit SNS several times a day. In the groups having a menu interface style the proportion of participants visiting SNS every day is over 60 %. The other participants, for the most part, visit SNS at least several times a week. Consequently, participants of our study have a high experience with SNS owing to the high frequency of their usage.

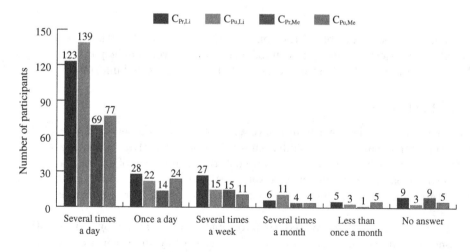

Fig. 2. Frequency of SNS usage

In addition, the distribution of the number of friends is also similar for all experimental groups, as shown in Fig. 3. Only a small portion of participants

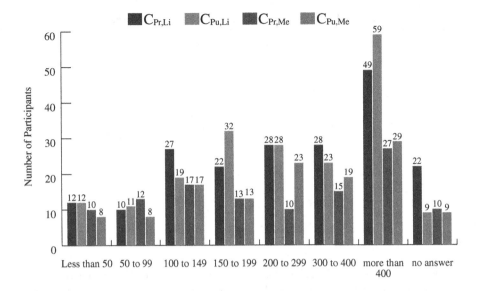

Fig. 3. Number of friends on SNS

per group have fewer than 100 friends on SNS. About 30 % of all experimental groups have more than 400 friends. The rest of the participants have from 100 to 400 friends.

3.2 Privacy Interface Prototype

A Privacy Interface Prototype was built to collect the needed data for the analysis. The developed prototype is built based on web-technologies that are platform-independent. After the development, the prototype was tested with all popular web browsers.

The prototype gives the opportunity to simulate the privacy configuration interfaces from SNS based on the two analyzed dimensions, but also to display instructions and questionnaires before and after the privacy interface. Furthermore, the prototype measures the duration that participants spend on each page. Participants can move between the pages through buttons at the bottom of each page.

The privacy configuration interface is composed of those privacy settings that are part of our analysis. To test the influence of the interface style, two different layouts of interfaces, as shown in Fig. 4 can be displayed by the prototype. In the first layout that simulates the interface style of (a) List, all analyzed privacy settings are laid out one below the other. In the second layout that simulates the interface style of (b) Menu, the analyzed privacy settings are spread over multiple pages grouped by the identified categories. The category Profile Information is displayed as the first page after starting the privacy interface prototype. With a menu on the left side participants can navigate between the pages of the categories to configure those privacy settings.

(a) List   **(b) Menu**

Fig. 4. Screenshots of the privacy interface prototype

Independently of the interface style, next to the description of each privacy setting a button exists to configure the privacy setting. A pull-down menu opens by clicking on this button and shows all available options as demonstrated in the example of restrictive default privacy settings in Fig. 5. In this menu each participant has the opportunity to choose between the following privacy options: (1) Everybody, (2) Friends of Friends, (3) Friends, (4) List (Subgroup of Friends), or (5) Only me. Initially, the default value based on the particular condition is shown on the button. Participants can change the privacy settings until they finalize the whole session of the privacy interface prototype and move to the next page with a questionnaire. When an option is changed, the button shows the latest selected option and this option is saved to the database of the prototype.

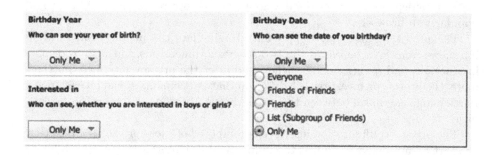

Fig. 5. Configuration of privacy settings

3.3 Procedure

Participants were asked to open the website with the privacy interface prototype in their web-browser. Initially, a page with instructions was shown describing the procedure of the study and instructing participants that the privacy interface requires them to configure privacy settings as they would do it on SNS with their personal information. Regarding the purpose of the study, participants were informed that we want to understand how they configure their privacy settings on SNS. They were not told that we are especially focusing on their configuration behavior with regard to different default privacy settings and interface styles.

On the next page, the interface of the privacy settings was displayed to the participants. In this step, the participants were randomly allocated to one of the four experimental groups based on both analyzed dimensions with each of the two conditions. For those experimental groups ($C_{Pr,Li}$, $C_{Pr,Me}$) that have the condition of restrictive default settings the option Only me was preselected to all privacy settings as proposed by PbDef. For the other experimental groups ($C_{Pu,Li}$, $C_{Pu,Me}$) we simulated the opposite - that all personal information is available on the SNS. The privacy settings of participants had been set to the option Everybody as the preselected option. Besides the default setting and based on the second analyzed dimension, participants had been allocated to one of the previously described interface styles.

All experimental groups were now asked to configure their privacy settings accordingly to their preferences, but were not forced to change any of the settings. Participants could quit the session of the privacy settings configuration by clicking on the button *Next* to move forward to the next page. Following that, they were asked some questions regarding their age, gender and usage behavior on SNS. Figure 6 summarizes the procedure of the study.

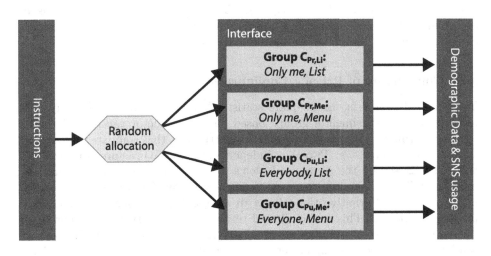

Fig. 6. Procedure of the study

4   Results

For each of the 14 analyzed privacy settings the participants had been able to choose from the previously described five options. It was required to code the

Table 3. Coding of privacy options

Code	Value
1	Everybody
2	Friends of Friends (FoF)
3	Friends
4	List (Subgroup of Friends)
5	Only me

privacy options to be able to run statistical analysis. We coded the options from 1 (Everybody) to 5 (Only me) as shown in Table 3.

In the following, descriptive statistics as well as the results of the statistical test are described in more detail.

4.1   Descriptive Statistics

For each of the analyzed privacy settings, we calculated the mean and the standard deviation based on the collected and coded data. This was done for all four experimental groups separately. Results for all groups are listed in Table 4. A separate comparison for each interface style shows that groups with restrictive default privacy settings ($C_{Pr,Li}$, $C_{Pr,Me}$) have a higher mean than groups with permissive settings ($C_{Pu,Li}$, $C_{Pu,Me}$). The difference between the means is even higher for the menu interface layout compared to the list layout. Standard deviations for each setting are comparable for all groups.

4.2   Comparison of Privacy Configuration Behavior

To test our hypothesis, an adequate statistical test is required to identify differences in our experimental groups based on two predictor variables: Default Privacy Setting and Interface Layout. Parametric tests that compare the ratio of systematic variance (e. g. Two-Way Independent ANOVA) require homoscedasticity [41]. Based on the results of Leven's test we found that this assumption was not fulfilled. Therefore, we used the Scheirer-Ray-Hare (SHR) test [42], a non-parametric alternative that allows to analyze the combined effect of two predictor variables. This ranking-based test is more conservative compared to the parametric Two-Way Independent ANOVA, but it allows investigation of the combined effect, even for the presence of heteroscedasticity. The SHR test gives results about the significance of the effect on the privacy configuration behavior of each analyzed dimension separately and of the combined effect. A p-value of $p < .05$ implies that H0 can be rejected under the 5-percent level. According to this a p-value of $p > .05$ implies that we have to reject the tested hypothesis.

As displayed in Table 5, results show the significant effect of the default setting on the configuration behavior for all 14 analyzed privacy settings. Therefore, we can see hypothesis H_1 as fulfilled. Further, results show that a significant effect

Table 4. Descriptive statistics

No.	$C_{Pr,Li}$		$C_{Pu,Li}$		$C_{Pu,Me}$		$C_{Pr,Me}$	
	$\bar{x}$	SD	$\bar{x}$	SD	$\bar{x}$	SD	$\bar{x}$	SD
1	3.05	1.06	2.73	1.11	2.61	1.19	3.17	1.06
2	3.53	1.29	2.93	1.34	2.94	1.44	3.49	1.31
3	3.58	1.44	2.67	1.47	2.87	1.57	3.32	1.58
4	3.48	1.23	2.89	1.31	2.82	1.19	3.30	1.16
5	2.99	0.74	2.73	0.78	1.65	0.98	4.11	1.00
6	3.70	1.04	3.20	1.09	1.90	1.39	4.50	0.88
7	3.93	1.06	3.40	1.26	1.98	1.51	4.61	0.78
8	3.52	0.97	2.87	0.98	1.67	1.01	4.15	1.00
9	3.49	1.08	2.80	1.02	1.63	0.98	4.17	1.03
10	3.35	0.95	2.89	0.89	1.73	1.09	4.26	0.97
11	3.47	0.98	2.92	0.98	1.77	1.15	4.30	0.92
12	3.19	0.82	2.86	0.83	1.69	1.00	4.23	0.97
13	3.78	1.07	3.17	1.15	1.72	1.11	4.44	0.92
14	3.55	1.07	3.03	0.99	1.74	1.10	4.26	1.06

Table 5. Results of Scheirer-Ray-Hare test

No.	Default setting		Interface style		Default*Interface	
	df	p-value	df	p-value	df	p-value
1	1	.000	1	.886	1	.596
2	1	.000	1	.880	1	.590
3	1	.000	1	.710	1	.092
4	1	.000	1	.128	1	.392
5	1	.000	1	.003	1	.000
6	1	.000	1	.648	1	.000
7	1	.000	1	.157	1	.000
8	1	.000	1	.661	1	.000
9	1	.000	1	.263	1	.000
10	1	.000	1	.119	1	.000
11	1	.000	1	.227	1	.000
12	1	.000	1	.034	1	.000
13	1	.000	1	.073	1	.000
14	1	.000	1	.412	1	.000

on the configuration behavior is measured only for privacy settings concerning the access to timeline updates and access to photo albums. We need to reject hypothesis H_2 for the 12 privacy settings with a p-value of $p > .05$.

For all analyzed privacy settings allocated to categories Status Updates and Media a significant combined effect of the Default Setting and the Interface style is measured. There is no significant combined effect on privacy settings in the category *Profile Information*. Thus, we need to reject hypothesis H_3 for the four privacy settings of category Profile Information, but results confirm the hypothesis H_3 for privacy settings in categories Status Updates and Media.

5   Discussion

The aim of this study was to understand how users' configuration behavior of default privacy settings is affected by the restrictiveness of default settings and the style of privacy interfaces. Results show a significantly different privacy configuration behavior between the participants of the groups having restrictive ($C_{Pr,Li}$, $C_{Pr,Me}$) or permissive ($C_{Pu,Li}$, $C_{Pu,Me}$) default privacy settings. Independent of interface styles, users tend to keep close to the preselected options or to keep default settings. This applies to all 14 analyzed privacy settings of our study. Thus, results are in line with research about users' behavior with default settings in other domains [2–4].

However, the dimension of the interface style does not have a significant effect on the configuration behavior of the participants for all settings. Besides the privacy settings for the access to status updates and photo albums, a significant difference between interface style list ($C_{Pr,Li}$, $C_{Pu,Li}$) and menu ($C_{Pr,Me}$, $C_{Pu,Me}$) is measured for none of the analyzed privacy settings. This is the result of similar behavior for the two experimental groups in each interface style that can clearly be seen in the radar chart (Fig. 7). The two experimental groups having the interface style of list (solid lines) are both close to the option Friend. Experimental groups having the interface style of menu (dotted lines) are in general both oriented to the preselected options of *Everybody* and *Only me*.

Results for the combined effect of both analyzed dimensions show a significant change in the configuration behavior of privacy settings in the categories *Status Updates* and *Media*. For these settings, the difference between experimental groups having restrictive or permissive default privacy settings is also influenced by the conditions of the interface style. As displayed in Fig. 7, at least for the categories *Status Updates* and *Media*, the difference between mean values having the interface style of list is smaller than the difference between mean values having the interface style with multiple pages. For the privacy settings of the category *Profile Information* the mean values of all four experimental groups are close to each other. That results in the non-significant result of the combined effect.

Based on the test results of the combined effect, it can be concluded that users having an interface with multiple pages tend to keep default settings for the analyzed privacy settings of the categories *Status Updates* and *Media*. Analysis of the

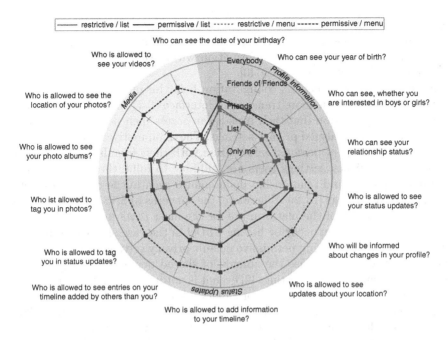

Fig. 7. Mean values of experimental groups per privacy setting

settings of category *Profile Information*, shows that participants are more willing to deviate from the default. We presume that this effect is less due to the settings themselves, but more due to the order of the categories. The category of *Profile Information* was the first page shown to the participants after starting the privacy interface prototype. Thus, participants were able to configure theses privacy settings directly. To adjust the privacy settings of the other categories they had to switch actively to another page, what was most probably not done by the majority of participants. This is in line with related research that less transparency is one reason for users to keep default settings [2]. Furthermore, higher granularity and placing settings on multiple pages can increase the complexity of the interface [39]. If users do not have enough technical skills to compensate for the higher complexity, it will also result in keeping their the default settings [2].

One can summarize, that also in the case of restrictive default privacy settings the status quo bias cannot be overcome by users' needs that require a deviation from the defaults. An interface style with multiple pages strengthens this effect on those pages that are not shown directly to the users.

5.1   Implications for Regulators and Platform Providers

Results of our study show that users behave differently whether they have restrictive or permissive default privacy settings. Concerns of platform providers seems to be confirmed that users will share less personal information in the case of PbDef. Users will share their personal information to a smaller number of addressees due to the more restrictive privacy settings. This will reduce the overall exchange of personal information within the network that could be critical for the success of the SNS [43].

Hence, the privacy settings configuration behavior of users also depends on the interface style. In the more transparent interface (list) the majority of participants favored the option that their friends can access their personal information for the majority of analyzed privacy settings. The main motivator for users to use SNS is the exchange of personal information with their friends [27]. In the case of transparent privacy settings users are still able to fulfill their need for social capital, enjoyment, and relationship-maintenance even in the case of restrictive default privacy settings [13, 29]. Therefore, the concerns of SNS providers regarding the functionality of the platform are for the most parts unfounded.

Hence, problems can occur by having PbDef in the case of a less transparent privacy interface. By having permissive default privacy setting a less transparent privacy interface can increase the amount of shared personal information compared to less shared default settings [2] even it is not in line with the expectations of users. In the case of PbDef SNS providers need to increase the transparency of the privacy interface to support users in fulfilling their needs in SNS. That also implies a deviation from restrictive default privacy settings.

Expectations of the EC on PbDef can be seen as fulfilled based on the results of the study. Users that are not deviating from their default setting e.g. owing to less transparent interfaces are still protected from an unintended revelation until they are able to adjust privacy settings according to their needs and requirements. Hence, business innovation or business models are also not blocked by PbDef regulation.

5.2 Limitations

The study is limited to several aspects. The analyzed sample is limited to students. Even though literature shows that younger persons use SNS more often than older ones [44] other generations are also of interest. Literature describes a relationship between age and the number of friends on SNS [45] and that younger users have more friends compared to older ones. Both findings depict a difference in usage behavior between generations. Therefore, the results of this study might not be applicable to other age groups of SNS users. Additionally, cultural aspects could also have a relevant effect on the configuration behavior of privacy settings. Especially, settings like sexual-orientation or relationship-status could be more sensitive in other cultures compared to the Western-Europe (German) culture [13].

Our study focused on SNS used in a private context. SNS with a private focus (e.g. Facebook) differ in their requirements and characteristics from business SNS (e.g. LinkedIn) or corporate SNS [46, 47]. Furthermore, personal information like sexual-orientation or relationship status are also not relevant in a professional context. Therefore, the configuration behavior of privacy settings can deviate.

The analyzed effect of the privacy configuration behavior of users is based on short-term decisions. In a real life scenario, users might be motivated to deviate from restrictive default settings at a later point in time, owing to the comments of their peers, the media or other external pressures. Thus, we cannot necessarily conclude the long-term behavior of users. Further, the behavior of the participants could be biased by the fact that due to the design of the study their personal information is never threatened. In a scenario where personal information are affected by their decision behavior is might be different.

Additionally, the prototype of our study was just composed out of the privacy interface. Usually, privacy interfaces of current SNS are hidden in the options or menus, besides other options. Therefore, aspects like awareness of privacy settings in general are not be covered by the results.

5.3   Future Research

As mentioned before, it is needed to identify the long-term effect of default privacy settings on the privacy configuration behavior of users on SNS. In addition, the effect of default privacy settings in interfaces with multiple pages needs further investigations. The order of analyzed categories in the interface needs to be randomized to find out whether the effect of keeping default settings is grounded in the order of categories or in the privacy settings themselves.

To counteract less shared personal information owing to restrictive default privacy settings in privacy interfaces with multiple pages, research is needed to build better interfaces. Requirements need to be identified and design guidelines need to be built to improve transparency in those privacy interfaces. Furthermore, open research fields include how experiences with SNS, the frequency of usage or the privacy sensitivity of users correlates with the configuration of privacy settings by having more restrictive default privacy settings.

6   Conclusion

With our study of 632 participants in an experimental setting, we gained empirical insight into the field of restrictive default privacy settings in the context of SNS. We built a better understanding of differences in privacy configuration behavior based on default settings or the interface style.

The findings of our study show that users' configuration behavior by users of privacy settings on SNS differs depending on the preselected option of privacy settings. Furthermore, the style of the privacy interface also partly influences the configuration behavior of privacy settings by users. Privacy interfaces with multiple pages keep users from changing their default settings, whereas interfaces that have all privacy settings in a list are more transparent and support users in deviating from the default option to adjust the privacy settings according to their needs.

Concluding, our study also demonstrate that in the case of restrictive default privacy settings users' needs that require the revelation of personal information also do not outweight the status quo bias. Having an interface style with less transparency strengthens this effect on those privacy settings that need further clicks to be accessible.

References

1. Smith, H.J., Dinev, T., Xu, H.: Information privacy research: an interdisciplinary review. MIS Q. **35**(4), 989–1016 (2011)
2. Shah, R.C., Kesan, J.P.: Policy through software defaults. In: Proceedings of the 2006 International Conference on Digital Government Research, pp. 265–272. Digital Government Society of North America (2006)
3. Bellman, S., Johnson, E.J., Lohse, G.L.: On site: to opt-in or opt-out?: it depends on the question. Commun. ACM **44**(2), 25–27 (2001)
4. Samuelson, W., Zeckhauser, R.: Status quo bias in decision making. J. Risk Uncertain. **1**(1), 7–59 (1988)
5. Burke, M., Marlow, C., Lento, T.: Social network activity and social well-being. In: Proceedings of the SIGCHI Conference on Human Factors in Computing Systems, pp. 1909–1912. ACM (2010)
6. Dinev, T., Hart, P.: An extended privacy calculus model for e-commerce transactions. Inf. Syst. Res. **17**(1), 61–80 (2006)
7. Cavoukian, A.: Privacy by design (leading edge). IEEE Technol. Soc. Mag. **31**(4), 18–19 (2012)
8. Cavoukian, A.: Privacy by design (2008). http://privacybydesign.ca/content/uploads/2009/08/7foundationalprinciples.pdf
9. Schaar, P.: Privacy by Default: Airbag für die Informationsgesellschaft (2009). https://www.bfdi.bund.de/bfdi_forum/showthread.php?t=3365
10. European Parliament. Report on the proposel for a regulation of the European Parliament and of the Council on the protection of individuals with regard to the processing of personal data and on the free movement of such data (General Data Protection Regulation) (2014). http://www.europarl.europa.eu/sides/getDoc.do?pubRef=-%2F%2FEP%2F%2FTEXT%2BREPORT%2BA7-2013-0402%2B0%2BDOC%2BXML%2BV0%2F%2FEN&language=EN#title1
11. Europe versus Facebook. Facebook's views on the proposed data protection regulation (2012). http://www.europe-v-facebook.org/FOI_Facebook_Lobbying.pdf
12. Brooks, L., Anene, V.: Information disclosure and generational differences in social network sites (2012)
13. Krasnova, H., Veltri, N.F.: Privacy calculus on social networking sites: explorative evidence from germany and USA. In: 2010 43rd Hawaii International Conference on System Sciences (HICSS), pp. 1–10. IEEE (2010)
14. Litt, E.: Understanding social network site users privacy tool use. Comput. Hum. Behav. **29**(4), 1649–1656 (2013)
15. Boyd, D.M., Ellison, N.B.: Social network sites: definition, history, and scholarship. J. Comput. Mediated Commun. **13**(1), 210–230 (2008)
16. Taraszow, T., Aristodemou, E., Shitta, G., Laouris, Y., Arsoy, A.: Disclosure of personal and contact information by young people in social networking sites: an analysis using facebook profiles as an example. Int. J. Media Cult. Polit. **6**(1), 81–101 (2010)
17. Nosko, A., Wood, E., Molema, S.: All about me: disclosure in online social networking profiles: the case of facebook. Comput. Hum. Behav. **26**(3), 406–418 (2010)

18. Chellappa, R.K., Sin, R.G.: Personalization versus privacy: an empirical examination of the online consumers dilemma. Inf. Technol. Manage. **6**(2–3), 181–202 (2005)
19. Culnan, M.J., Bies, R.J.: Consumer privacy: balancing economic and justice considerations. J. Soc. Issues **59**(2), 323–342 (2003)
20. Ellison, N., Steinfield, C., Lampe, C.: Spatially bounded online social networks and social capital. Int. Commun. Assoc. **36**, 1–37 (2006)
21. Lampe, C., Ellison, N.B., Steinfield, C.: Changes in use and perception of facebook. In: Proceedings of the 2008 ACM Conference on Computer Supported Cooperative Work, pp. 721–730. ACM (2008)
22. Bonneau, J., Preibusch, S.: The privacy jungle: on the market for data protection in social networks. In: Moore, T., Pym, D., Ioannidis, C. (eds.) Economics of Information Security and Privacy, pp. 121–167. Springer, Boston (2010)
23. Gross, R., Acquisti, A.: Information revelation and privacy in online social networks. In: Proceedings of the 2005 ACM Workshop on Privacy in the Electronic Society, pp. 71–80. ACM (2005)
24. Lewis, K., Kaufman, J., Christakis, N.: The taste for privacy: an analysis of college student privacy settings in an online social network. J. Comput. Mediated Commun. **14**(1), 79–100 (2008)
25. Forman, C., Ghose, A., Wiesenfeld, B.: Examining the relationship between reviews and sales: the role of reviewer identity disclosure in electronic markets. Inf. Syst. Res. **19**(3), 291–313 (2008)
26. Koroleva, K., Brecht, F., Goebel, L., Malinova, M.: Generation facebook-a cognitive calculus model of teenage user behavior on social network sites. In: Proceedings of AMCIS 2011 (2011)
27. Pempek, T.A., Yermolayeva, Y.A., Calvert, S.L.: College students' social networking experiences on facebook. J. Appl. Dev. Psychol. **30**(3), 227–238 (2009)
28. Granovetter, M.: The strength of weak ties: a network theory revisited. Sociol. Theory **1**(1), 201–233 (1983)
29. Burke, M., Marlow, C., Lento, T.: Feed me: motivating newcomer contribution in social network sites. In: Proceedings of the SIGCHI Conference on Human Factors in Computing Systems, pp. 945–954. ACM (2009)
30. Shah, R.C., Sandvig, C.: Software defaults as de facto regulation the case of the wireless internet. Inf. Commun. Soc. **11**(1), 25–46 (2008)
31. Goldstein, D.G., Johnson, E.J., Herrmann, A., Heitmann, M.: Nudge your customers toward better choices. Harvard Bus. Rev. **86**(12), 99–105 (2008)
32. Johnson, E.J., Goldstein, D.: Do defaults save lives? Sci. New York then Washington **302**, 1338–1339 (2003)
33. Jin, L.: Improving response rates in web surveys with default setting the effects of default on web survey participation and permission. Int. J. Mark. Res. **53**(1), 75–94 (2011)
34. Kahneman, D., Knetsch, J.L., Thaler, R.H.: Anomalies: the endowment effect, loss aversion, and status quo bias. J. Econ. Perspect. **5**, 193–206 (1991)
35. Dhar, R., Nowlis, S.M.: The effect of time pressure on consumer choice deferral. J. Consum. Res. **25**(4), 369–384 (1999)
36. Iyengar, S.S., Lepper, M.R.: When choice is demotivating: can one desire too much of a good thing? J. Pers. Soc. Psychol. **79**(6), 995 (2000)
37. Kesan, J.P., Shah, R.C.: Setting software defaults: perspectives from law, computer science and behavioral economics. Notre Dame L. Rev. **82**, 583 (2006)
38. Hargittai, E., ct al.: Facebook privacy settings: who cares? First Monday **15**(8) (2010). http://firstmonday.org/article/view/3086/2589

39. Stern, T., Kumar, N.: Improving privacy settings control in online social networks with a wheel interface. J. Assoc. Inf. Sci. Technol. **65**(3), 524–538 (2014)
40. Faul, F., Erdfelder, E., Lang, A.-G., Buchner, A.: G* power 3: a flexible statistical power analysis program for the social, behavioral, and biomedical sciences. Behav. Res. Meth. **39**(2), 175–191 (2007)
41. Field, A.: Discovering Statistics using IBM SPSS Statistics. Sage, London (2013)
42. Scheirer, C.J., Ray, W.S., Hare, N.: The analysis of ranked data derived from completely randomized factorial designs. Biometrics **32**, 429–434 (1976)
43. Krasnova, H., Hildebrand, T., Guenther, O., Kovrigin, A., Nowobilska, A.: Why participate in an online social network? an empirical analysis (2008)
44. Archambault, A., Grudin, J.: A longitudinal study of facebook, linkedin, and twitter use. In: Proceedings of the SIGCHI Conference on Human Factors in Computing Systems, pp. 2741–2750. ACM (2012)
45. Quinn, D., Chen, L., Mulvenna, M.: Does age make a difference in the behaviour of online social network users? In: 2011 International Conference on Internet of Things and 4th International Conference on Cyber, Physical and Social Computing (iThings/CPSCom), pp. 266–272. IEEE (2011)
46. Richter, A., Riemer, K.: Corporate social networking sites-modes of use and appropriation through co-evolution. In: ACIS 2009 Proceedings (2009)
47. DiMicco, J.M., Geyer, W., Millen, D.R., Dugan, C., Brownholtz, B.: People sense-making and relationship building on an enterprise social network site. In: 42nd Hawaii International Conference on System Sciences, HICSS 2009, pp. 1–10. IEEE (2009)

Towards Inherent Privacy Awareness in Workflows

Maria N. Koukovini[1]([✉]), Eugenia I. Papagiannakopoulou[1],
Georgios V. Lioudakis[1], Nikolaos Dellas[2], Dimitra I. Kaklamani[1],
and Iakovos S. Venieris[1]

[1] School of Electrical and Computer Engineering, National Technical University
of Athens, Heroon Polytechniou 9, 15773 Athens, Greece
`mariza@icbnet.ece.ntua.gr`
[2] SingularLogic S.A., Al. Panagouli and Siniosoglou, 14234 Nea Ionia, Greece

Abstract. This paper presents a holistic approach to the realisation
of *Privacy by Design* in workflow environments, ensuring that workflow models are rendered privacy-aware already at their specification
phase. In this direction, the proposed framework, considering the particular technical requirements stemming from data protection principles,
is centred around the following features: a novel, ontology-based approach to workflow modelling, which manages, unlike all other existing
technologies, to adequately capture privacy aspects pertaining to workflow execution; the appropriate codification of privacy requirements into
compliance rules and directives; an automated procedure for the verification of workflow models and their subsequent transformation, if needed,
so that they become inherently privacy-aware before being deployed for
execution.

Keywords: Privacy compliance · Workflow modelling · Verification ·
Ontologies

1 Introduction

In current distributed and dynamic environments, workflows [15] have emerged
as a prominent technology, fuelled also by the proliferation of Service Oriented
Architectures (SOA) and their loose-coupling nature. However, workflow systems are characterised by serious privacy implications, since they natively rely
to a large extent on access to and exchange of data. In fact, privacy pertains to
all three core workflow perspectives [12], as it is closely related to the tasks being
executed themselves (control perspective), the flow and processing of information (data perspective) and legitimate resource allocation (resource perspective).
Besides, workflows are often based on and foster collaboration within heterogeneous environments and among many stakeholders, something that significantly
complicates the direct and effective use of already existing solutions to privacy
protection. The key challenge arising in such context is that the various activities must no longer be considered only "in isolation" but also with respect to

© Springer International Publishing Switzerland 2015
J. Garcia-Alfaro et al. (Eds.): DPM/SETOP/QASA 2014, LNCS 8872, pp. 95–113, 2015.
DOI: 10.1007/978-3-319-17016-9_7

operational and data flows, resulting in a holistic view across the corresponding procedures; in other words, required mechanisms (e.g., access control) must be effectively enforced regarding not only individual actions but also large-scale interrelations thereof at the workflow level.

In light of these issues, an earlier paper, presented in DPM 2011, provided preliminary ideas on inherently privacy-aware workflows [16]. This paper revises and extends that work, by describing a concrete framework implemented towards fulfilling fundamental privacy requirements for workflow systems [14]; its contribution is highlighted in Sect. 1.2, after an overview of related work (Sect. 1.1).

1.1   Related Work

Workflow systems are typically split in two broad categories, *business* and *scientific*. The former constitute a well-established area, supported by various tools and languages, among the most mature of which are BPMN [27] and YAWL [2]. BPMN is the de facto modelling standard; it supports quite a few control patterns, explicitly models access to and flow of data and possesses basic resource capturing capabilities. Still, it does not allow for fine-grained data modelling, nor does it provide for sophisticated resource assignment schemes or complex resource allocation constraints, like Separation of Duties. YAWL supports most control flow patterns and is powerful in capturing resourcing requirements; nevertheless, it lacks constructs explicitly capturing data elements and dependencies. Finally, scientific workflows [21] do not even address the issue of assigning tasks to different resources, let alone associated authorisation considerations, due to the fact that, after their initiation, their execution proceeds mostly automatically. Moreover, even data modelling suffers from certain limitations, such as the lack of means for the detailed specification of the exchanged information itself.

From another viewpoint, a number of approaches have appeared in the literature aiming at ensuring that security and privacy are enforced during workflow execution. RBAC-WS-BPEL [6] specifies an extension to WS-BPEL, in order to implement role-based access control in workflows, while in [5] extensions to OrBAC [9] are introduced for handling access and flow control in both intra- and inter-organisational workflow environments. In these solutions, however, security policies are eventually enforced at run-time and not during workflow formation. The formal modelling of authorisation constraints as part of the workflow model specification is proposed in [31,32], while approaches like [30] go one step further by transforming, in a model-driven fashion, security goals modelled in the context of process models into concrete security implementations. Still, such work considers requirements specification to be under the control of the designer as *part of* the modelling procedure and not as an automated functionality performed *on* generated models, guided by a trusted knowledge base.

The latter can be achieved through either compliance-aware design or compliance checking mechanisms. In the former, requirements are automatically enforced in the design phase of new business processes [10,19]. Conversely, compliance checking takes place in a post-design step, thus separating the modelling phase of a process model from the checking phase. Respective approaches, like

[4,11,18], are mostly based on formal methods, in order to ascertain the fulfilment of diverse requirements, while another field of related work deals with measuring the compliance degree of a given process model [20]. The above, albeit important and influential, are rather general-purpose frameworks, hence not always able to support particular needs related to privacy. In this direction, some interesting works have recently appeared (e.g., [3,26,29]), emphasising on important facets of privacy awareness and propose solid solutions. Nevertheless, the workflow definition tools they are based on do not provide for adequate expressiveness regarding all privacy-related aspects, and, therefore, important factors are not considered in detail; finally, they do not address the issue of transforming workflow models towards privacy-compliant executable specifications.

1.2 Contribution and Structure of the Paper

In order to overcome the limitations of related work, in the context of EU FP7 DEMONS [1] a holistic solution for inherently privacy-aware workflow models has been developed. Inline with *Privacy by Design*, referring to the philosophy and approach of embedding privacy directly into the design and operating specifications of information technologies and systems [8], the proposed approach is characterised by the following features: the inclusion, at the workflow model level, of structures able to support the *in-design* specification of privacy policies, leading to targeted privacy configurations enforceable at run-time; the automatic verification of workflow models against privacy provisions; their automatic transformation in the case of detected violations.

Operationally, the general idea is the following. A workflow model, as specified by its designer, is subject to automatic verification and transformation in order to become privacy-aware. In this context, a number of models is leveraged (Fig. 1). The Workflow Model comprises an innovative ontological approach to workflow modelling, encompassing a variety of features for the incorporation of privacy aspects in workflow specifications. Its verification and transformation are based on access and usage control rules provided by a Policy Model; the latter comprises a sophisticated approach for privacy-aware access control, documented in [24,25]. Reasoning in the Policy Model results in the formation of Compliance Directives, used to regulate the verification and transformation procedure. All the above are grounded on a semantically rich Information Model, organised in two levels of representation, notably abstract and concrete. Its basic advantage is that it provides for fine-grained description of the underlying concepts and their relationships. Information, Policy, and Workflow Models, as well as the Compliance Directives, are all implemented as ontologies, providing for high expressiveness, formal and machine-interpretable semantics, semantic consistency and interoperability, and inference of knowledge.

The rest of the paper is outlined as follows. In Sect. 2 an overview of the Information Model is provided, while Sect. 3 describes the adopted approach for workflow modelling, focusing on its features fostering the incorporation of privacy aspects. A brief description of Compliance Directives follows in Sect. 4, whereas Sect. 5 describes the basic ideas of the verification and transformation

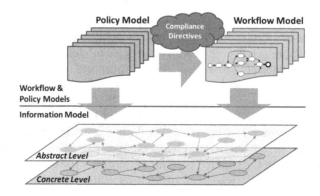

Fig. 1. Models and ontologies

procedure. Before concluding the paper, Sect. 6 provides an example, highlighting key aspects of the framework.

2   Information Model

The day-to-day operation of an organisation involves a variety of entities, like machines, users and data[1]. We consider two representation levels; the *concrete level* refers to well-specified entities, e.g., named humans, while the *abstract level* enables referring to entities by using abstractions, especially their semantic type and attributes.

At a concrete level, the set of *Users* (U) represents human entities, while this of *Organisations* (Org) describes internal divisions (e.g., departments) or external parties (e.g., sub-contractors). The various machinery comprise the *Machines* (M) set, providing hosting to *Operation Containers* (OpC) that offer *Operation Instances* (OpI). Operation Instances correspond to actual implementations of functionalities, while Operation Containers bundle collections of Operation Instances provided by the same functional unit[2]. Finally, information comprises the set of *Data* (D).

All above elements constitute instantiations of their semantic equivalents described at the abstract level. Users are assigned with *Roles* (R), Operation Instances provide implementations of *Operations* (Op), while data, organisations, machines and operation containers have *types*, reflecting the semantic class they fall under; thus, sets of *Data Types* (DT), *Organisation Types* $(OrgT)$, *Machine Types* (MT) and *Operation Container Types* $(OpCT)$ are defined. The semantic model also includes *Context Types* $(ConT)$, enabling the definition of contextual parameters, *Attributes* (Att), leveraged for describing properties and

---

[1] Naturally, the information model may vary; still, several concepts (e.g., roles, operations, data types, etc.) are pervasive and are the focus of the following.

[2] In Web Services terms, Operation Containers correspond to a service *interface*, whereas Operation Instances represent the associated *operations* [28].

characteristics of other elements, and *Purposes* (*Pu*) justifying instantiation of workflow models, as well as access requests.

Figure 2 provides an overview of the Information Model Ontology (IMO). As shown, all abstract concepts comprise classes, characterised by intra- and inter-class relations. The former define AND- and OR- hierarchies, enabling the inheritance of attributes and the specification of dependencies. Specifically, the `isA` and `isPartOf` object properties describe, respectively, the specialisation of a concept and the inclusion of an entity to another; the `DataTypes` class is in addition characterised by the `moreDetailedThan` property, reflecting a partial order of information according to its detail level. Inter-class relations describe associations between concepts of different semantic classes, such as the roles that may act for a purpose (`mayActForPurpose`), or the attributes characterising a concept (`hasAttribute`).

The individuals of the `Attributes` class are associated with an identifier (`AttributeNames`), a type, that can be a usual type (e.g., "Integer") or an entity from the IMO itself, and —optionally— a value, which can be an ontological element, or an arbitrary string, declared using the `hasValue` and `hasStringValue` properties, respectively. A valued attribute is considered *immutable*, as opposed to *mutable* attributes, the values of which are free to be determined during the specification of a workflow model or even at execution time. Finally, instances of the `DataIO` class map an operation with its inputs and outputs, indicating also the corresponding flow types, along with attributes further characterising each input/output relation, as well as the associated `States`; the latter refer to different states of information, such as "anonymised" vs. "identifiable" (cf. Sect. 3.2).

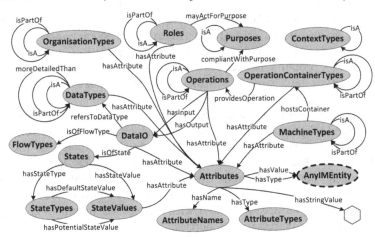

Fig. 2. Information Model Ontology (IMO).

3   Workflow Model

In general terms, a workflow describes a series of actions with well-defined sequential relations and information dependencies among them. A workflow under execution is referred to as a *workflow instance*, whereas its specification is provided by a *workflow model*.

The most fundamental artefacts of a workflow model are *tasks* and *flows*. The former represent actions to be executed within the workflow, each describing the *operation* performed by an *actor* on an *asset*. Flows express dependencies between tasks, are represented through directed edges and are of two types: *control* and *data*. A control flow dependency $t_A \xrightarrow{f_c} t_B$ between two tasks t_A and t_B means that t_B is executed only after the execution of t_A is completed; what the edge transfers is the thread of control, potentially accompanied by the necessary control parameters. On the contrary, a data flow dependency $t_A \xrightarrow{f_d} t_B$ assumes both tasks continuously under execution, with t_B, however, being dependant on the *stream* of data produced by t_A. Further, a workflow model is complemented by the operational *purposes* it is meant to serve, and the potential *initiators*, denoting entities authorised to initiate the workflow.

Definition 1. A *workflow model* is a tuple $\langle T, F_C, F_D, Init, WFPu \rangle$, such that: T is a finite set of tasks $\langle t_1, t_2, \ldots, t_n \rangle$; F_C and F_D are sets of directed edges, expressing the control flow and data flow relations among tasks; $Init$ is the set of human actors allowed to trigger the workflow execution; $WFPu \subseteq Pu$ denotes the purposes for which the workflow is intended to be executed.

The core part of the Workflow Model Ontology (WMO) is shown in Fig. 3. All concepts participating in a workflow specification are represented by instances of the corresponding classes, while OWL object properties model their relationships with each other and with IMO elements. Every workflow model is represented as an instance of the `WorkflowModels` class, comprising its reference semantic entry; this is associated to sets of `Initiators` and `WFPurposes` individuals, through the `initiatedBy` and `servesPurpose` properties. Class `Initiators` indicates, through property `refersToActor`, those `ActorEntities` (cf. Sect. 3.2) constituting initiators of workflows, while `refersToPurpose` maps members of the class `WFPurposes` to IMO's `Purposes`.

Tasks and edges are represented through the classes `TaskNodes` and `Edges`, respectively, while the latter is further subclassed by `DataEdges` and `ControlEdges`, denoting the two types of flows, F_D and F_C. In that respect, the `includesTask` and `includesEdge` properties map a `WorkflowModels` instance with the tasks and edges contained therein. Additionally, given that flows constitute directed edges, each has exactly one source and one destination task; therefore, instances of `Edges` are associated with `TaskNodes` instances through the `hasSource` and `hasDestination` properties.

3.1   Expressions, Logical Relations, Variables

In the direction of achieving rich expressiveness, two useful tools are *expressions* and *logical relations*. The latter allow specifying logical structures of concepts. For instance, a task may not be assigned to one type of actor; its definition may

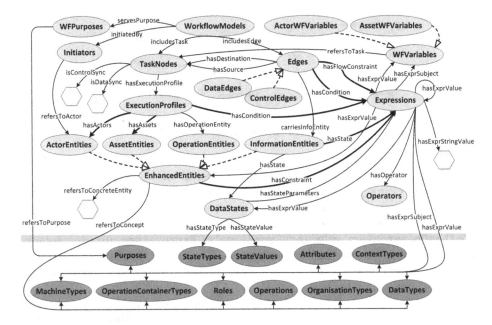

Fig. 3. The Workflow Model Ontology (WMO). Dark-shaded ovals denote IMO classes.

include a set of heterogeneous entities that must jointly undertake its execution (AND), a set of alternative actors, inclusive (OR) or exclusive (XOR), or combinations thereof.

Definition 2. Let $\mathcal{F}$ be the class of all functions on a set S, such that each $\phi_i(V) \in \mathcal{F}$ is a well-formed formula built up from the n-ary operators AND, OR and XOR, the unary operator NOT, and a set V of variables; a *logical relation* is a logical structure $\phi(S')$, such that $\phi \in \mathcal{F}$ and $S' \subseteq S$.

Thick lines in Fig. 3 imply the use of logical relations for structuring workflow elements; they are implemented by means of the `LogicalRelations` class (Fig. 4). Instances of its subclasses `ANDRelations`, `ORRelations`, `XORRelations` represent the AND, OR and XOR operators. Ontological instances participating in logical relations are referenced through the `posRelatedTo` and `negRelatedTo` properties, with the latter modelling the use of the NOT operator.

Expressions enable the definition of conditions (e.g., contextual) and constraints on concepts; they comprise ternary relations assigning a value to a subject through an operator, or logical structures of such triples.

Definition 3. An *atomic expression* is a tuple ⟨*exprSubject, operator, exprValue*⟩, such that: *exprSubject* is the reference concept; *operator* ∈ *Operators*, the latter being a set of operators, such as `equals`, `greaterThan`, `sameAs`, etc.; *exprValue* is the value assigned to the *exprSubject*. An *expression* is either an atomic expression or a logical relation thereof.

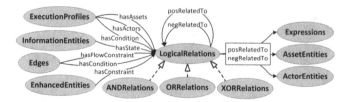

Fig. 4. Logical relations in the WMO.

Ontologically, expressions are modelled by means of the `Expressions` and `LogicalRelations` classes; instances of the former essentially model atomic expressions, whereas the latter provide for structuring composite expressions. Appropriate properties serve for indicating the subject (`hasExprSubject`), operator (`hasOperator`) and value (`hasExprValue`) of `Expressions`. An expression's subject and object can be instances of the WMO or IMO, or arbitrary, i.e., concepts not defined semantically; in such case, the `hasExprStringValue` property is used for assigning a String value.

Fostering the expression of powerful constraints, *workflow variables* provide reference "handles" serving as abstractions of the underlying objects, thus allowing to describe relative relations and dependencies. For instance, a constraint such as "the actor of task t_B should be the same as the one of t_A" can be defined, whatever the actors of t_A and t_B are.

Workflow variables are grouped under the WMO `WFVariables` class; notable individuals are `thisInstanceInitiator` and `thisInstancePurpose`, implying the initiator and purpose of a workflow instance, `thisTaskActor` and `this TaskAsset`, pointing at the actor and asset of the current task, and `this`, referring to the current entity. Further, its subclasses `ActorWFVariables` and `Asset-WFVariables` include variables referring to the actors and assets of all tasks in a workflow.

3.2   Workflow Entities

The core constituents of tasks are actors, operations and assets, while for flows, the exchanged information is essential for edges definition. A comprehensive approach for modelling these elements is adopted, centred around *enhanced entities*; the latter describe elements that their definition is either concrete, or abstract and constrained.

Definition 4. An *enhanced entity* is defined as ⟨*conConcept | abConcept, Constr*⟩, where: *conConcept* denotes a concrete element; *abConcept* denotes a concept expressed at the abstract level; *Constr* is an expression used to refer to concepts satisfying given conditions.

Despite the semantic and structural differences of actors, assets, operations and information, the corresponding entities share common features and therefore, to some extent, a uniform representation; thus, the associated WMO classes (Fig. 3) are all subclasses of `EnhancedEntities`. Each instance indicates the entity's semantic type and the constraints that describe said abstract entity, through the `refersToConcept` and `hasConstraint` properties, while if the entity is defined concretely, the `refersToConcreteEntity` property is used instead.

Information entities, used for flows specification, are further enriched with *states*, serving as indicators of the effect that the execution of preceding tasks has had on each information entity. A data state is characterised by a *type* and a *value*, incorporated in the information model as the sets ST and SV, being the instances of IMO classes `StateTypes` and `StateValues`. A state may also be described through some parameters.

Definition 5. A *data state* is defined as the tuple $\langle st, sv, params \rangle$, where: $st \in ST$ is its type, $sv \in SV$ is its value, and *params* is an expression describing state in more detail, by defining values for associated state attributes.

Ontologically, each data state comprises an instance of the `DataStates` WMO class; its type, value and parameters are indicated by the `hasStateType`, `has-StateValue` and `hasStateParameters` properties (Fig. 3), while the state itself is assigned to an `InformationEntity` by means of the `hasState` property. Nevertheless, when a certain state characterises parts of the referenced information entity and not the entity as a whole, `hasState` points to an appropriate expression. Therein, the *exprSubject* corresponds to the appropriate data type, the *exprValue* has the form prescribed by Definition 5, while the operator used is `inState`.

3.3 Workflow Tasks

A *task* corresponds to a unit of work in a workflow; assuming a workflow model WM, its tasks comprise the set T_{WM} and are ontologically defined as WMO `TaskNodes` class instances. A task's core element is its *operation*, i.e., the functionality it implements. A task is also characterised by a *synchronisation behaviour* [17].

Definition 6. A *task* $t_i \in T_{WM}$ is a tuple $\langle op, EP_i, dataSync_i, controlSync_i \rangle$, such that: $op \in Op$, EP_i is a set of execution profiles, and $dataSync_i, controlSync_i \in \{true, false\}$ determine the synchronisation behaviour of t_i.

Unlike other approaches where the definition of a task is "monolithic", this approach introduces the concept of *execution profiles*, enabling the specification of variations regarding the execution of a task. This concerns two aspects: differentiated execution based on some *conditions*, and capturing the dependencies between the task's actors, assets and operation constraints, that is, precisely defining their valid combinations. Therefore, each task $t_i \in T_{WM}$ is associated with a non-empty set EP_i of execution profiles:

Definition 7. An *execution profile* $ep_{i,j} \in EP_i$, associated to a task $t_i \in T_{WM}$, is a tuple $\langle \phi(Actors_{WM}), \phi(Assets_{WM}), oe, taskConditions \rangle$, such that:

$\phi(Actors_{WM})$ and $\phi(Assets_{WM})$ are logical relations on the sets of actor and asset entities, *oe* is an operation entity, and *taskConditions* is an expression defining conditions for the profile to be executed.

Task conditions describe real-time constraints external to the workflow specification (e.g., contextual factors), or spanning beyond task boundaries, that cannot be expressed on the basis of referenced entities' attributes alone.

Execution profiles are modelled through individuals of the ExecutionProfiles WMO class, appropriately linked to EnhancedEntities (sub-classes) instances. Task conditions are indicated through the hasCondition property, pointing at an Expressions or a LogicalRelations instance, while the hasExecutionProfile property associates a TaskNodes instance with its ExecutionProfiles.

Execution profiles provide a powerful mechanism for incorporating security policies in workflow models. Profiles reflect authorisation statements, describing conditional variants of an operation's execution, with actor(s), asset(s) and real-time parameters being interdependent. The important role of *entities* should not be neglected here, since they foster attribute-based constraints on actors, assets and the operation, while workflow variables and purpose consideration provide for SoD/BoD [7] enforcement and compliance with the purpose requirement.

Finally, the two synchronisation parameters, implemented by the isControl-Sync and isDataSync properties, indicate if a task being the *join* point of multiple incoming control or/and data flows synchronises these flows. *dataSync*, in particular, comprises a useful mechanism in controlling data linkability; its value determines whether the task processes separately each distinct input and directly passes the result to following tasks ("False"), or waits to receive input from all incoming edges before proceeding with the processing ("True").

3.4   Modelling Flows

Flow of control and data is represented through directed *edges* and as instances of the ControlEdges and DataEdges classes. Data and control edges share the same characteristics: each connects two tasks and denotes the flow direction, the information exchanged, the underlying conditions, and other flow properties; the distinction between them stems from the semantics of the connected operations regarding the manner they receive and consume information.

Definition 8. In a workflow model *WM*, an *edge* $e_i \in F_C \cup F_D$, with $F_C \cap F_D = \emptyset$, is defined as a tuple $\langle t_s, t_d, ie^k, flowCond_i, flowConstr_i \rangle$, where: t_s, $t_d \in T_{WM}$ are the source and destination tasks; ie^k is a set of k information entities; $flowCond_i$ and $flowConstr_i$ are expressions describing the conditions and constraints of e_i. An edge e_i is either a *control edge* ($e_i \in F_C$) or a *data edge* ($e_i \in F_D$).

Flow conditions and constraints are both defined as expressions. The former are analogous to task conditions and should hold in order for the transition among two tasks implied by the edge to be performed, supporting, when needed, conditional branching of control or data flow. The latter are conceptually close to the "implementation" attribute of the Send and Receive types of Tasks defined in BPMN [27]; they do not describe elements of the workflow model, but rather low-level properties describing their interaction. Conditions and constraints are ontologically implemented as `Expressions` or logical relations thereof, connected with edges through the `hasCondition` and `hasFlowConstraint` properties. Moreover, `carriesInfoEntity` connects edges with `InformationEntities` denoting exchanged information.

4   Compliance Directives

The verification of a workflow with respect to privacy compliance is performed based on its ontological representation (cf. Sect. 3) and on a set of *Compliance Directives*, that indicate the terms under which the workflow is acceptable. Directives are generated through reasoning over the Policy Model; its main elements are access control *rules*, used for defining *permissions*, *prohibitions* and *obligations* over *actions*, i.e., structures that, similar to execution profiles, indicate an operation performed by an actor on an asset.

Definition 9. An *access control rule* is a structure:

$$\left.\begin{array}{l} Permission \\ Prohibition \\ Obligation \end{array}\right\} (pu, act, preAct, cont, postAct)$$

where *act* is the action that the rule applies to; $pu \in Pu$ is the purpose for which *act* is permitted/prohibited/obliged to be executed; $cont \in \mathcal{P}(ConT)$ is a structure of contextual parameters; *preAct* is a structure of actions that should have preceded; *postAct* refers to the action(s) that must be executed following the rule enforcement.

The Policy Model provides an intelligent foundation for rule-based knowledge extraction, providing a manifold of advances compared to similar works. Its detailed description is out of scope of this paper; the reader is referred to [24,25].

Directives creation takes place on the basis of the pairs of all interacting tasks contained in the initial workflow, along with their corresponding interactions (i.e., connecting edges) themselves, what is being referred to as the *Bilateral Associations* (BA) of the workflow. That is, BAs refer to the initial (unverified) form of the workflow, as opposed to rules, that are defined within the Policy Model, are independent from any workflow and are used in order to extract Compliance Directives, considering the particular BAs of the workflow. The reason for choosing this pair-wise fragmentation for the initial processing at the level of Directives generation is that a BA essentially constitutes the elementary unit of flow. Thus, the instructions received are richer in semantics, since it is not only the tasks that matter, but also their interrelations. The main types of Directives considered are:

Bilateral Validity Directive (BVD): A directive of this type refers to one BA, indicating, for a given purpose and initiator among the specified ones, one valid actor–operation–asset combination for each task and a valid specification of the relationship connecting the two tasks; the latter may refer to the edge as has been defined by the designer, a different edge specification, or even one or more tasks that must be inserted in between the two tasks, so that the control or data flow between them is consistent. All other types of directives presented below refer, in most cases, to a specific BVD, reflecting the fact that requirements and prohibitions may depend on the existence and the different valid specifications of the tasks originally appearing in the workflow.

Input Requirement Directive (IRD): A task, though being "in principle" accepted, needs to receive some additional input, not included in the BA under consideration. The directive specifies the required input, (optionally) its source, and the task within a valid BA that needs to receive it.

Output Requirement Directive (ORD): A task specified within a valid BA must provide (some of) its output to a certain task (or structure thereof). An ORD defines the task in a valid BA that must communicate the data, the data themselves and the task structure that must receive them.

Task Presence Directive (TPD): A task structure must execute, complementing reference BA tasks. If applicable, a TPD also indicates the relative position or data association with respect to the BA task the required one(s) must be found in; for example, a task may require that another has preceded at some point in the workflow.

Task Forbiddance Directive (TFD): A task must not be executed in the context of a workflow, either at any point or within certain parts of the flow. Each of these directives refers to a task defined by a BVD, specifying the task structure with which the task under consideration is not allowed to coexist, along with their relative position, if applicable.

Flow Forbiddance Directive (FFD): A task is not allowed to have read access to two or more types of information during a single execution instance. Given a valid BA, such a directive prescribes a forbidden additional incoming flow, by specifying the data it is not allowed to receive but also, potentially, a particular task that they must not come from.

All types of directives may optionally be associated with a contextual condition under which the indicated specification, requirement or forbiddance must apply. Furthermore, a precondition or a postcondition may be defined, denoting the fact that said directive is enforceable if a task, or structure thereof, precede, respectively follow. Directives may additionally be characterised by a *compliance profile*, providing for the definition of variations and guiding their proper enforcement. For instance, in a hypothetical TPD, the compliance profile may define that the required task must have been executed *immediately before* the reference task, and, in particular, in a *blocking* sense, meaning that it must have completed before considered BA executes.

5 Workflow Verification

The compliance verification and consequent transformation of a workflow model are performed following the provisions prescribed by the Compliance Directives (Sect. 4); the procedure is outlined in Algorithm 1.

Algorithm 1. VerifyWorkflowModel

Input: WM
Output: WM_V
1: $PIP \leftarrow$ CreatePurposeInitiatorPairs
2: $IS \leftarrow$ GenerateInstanceSubgraphs(WM)
3: $BA \leftarrow \emptyset$
4: **for each** is **in** IS **do**
5:     BA.add(ExtractInitialBA(is))
6: **end for**
7: $D \leftarrow$ VerifyInitialBA(BA, PIP)
8: $VPIP \leftarrow$ GetValidPIP(PIP, D)
9: $VIS \leftarrow \emptyset$
10: **for each** is **in** IS **do**
11:     $C_{is} \leftarrow$ GenerateCases(is, $VPIP$, D_{VB})
12:     $VC_{is} \leftarrow \emptyset$
13:     **for each** c **in** C_{is} **do**
14:         $D_c \leftarrow$ ExtractCaseDirectives(c, D)
15:         $[FN, DN, IPrN, IPoN, ExN, StN] \leftarrow$ GetNorms(D_c)
16:         $T \leftarrow$ TopologicalSort(c)
17:         $\overline{T} \leftarrow$ InverseTopologicalSort(T)
18:         $vc \leftarrow$ ApplyNorms(c, $[FN, DN, IPrN, IPoN, ExN, StN]$, T, $\overline{T}$)
19:         **if** $vc \neq \emptyset$ **then**
20:             VC_{is}.add(vc)
21:         **end if**
22:     **end for**
23:     $vis \leftarrow$ MergeCases(VC_{is})
24:     **if** $vis \neq \emptyset$ **then**
25:         VIS.add(vis)
26:     **end if**
27: **end for**
28: **if** $VIS \neq \emptyset$ **then**
29:     $WM_V \leftarrow$ MergeInstanceSubgraphs(VIS)
30: **else**
31:     $WM_V \leftarrow \emptyset$
32: **end if**
33: **return** WM_V

As said, the directives are generated on the basis of Bilateral Associations (BA). In order for the latter to be extracted, first the workflow model is decomposed to *instance subgraphs* (*IS*); these correspond to the different variants the workflow may take, based on the values assigned to all constraints associated with its flow.

Definition 10. Given a workflow model *WM*, the set of *Instance Subgraphs IS* consists of all different unique execution variants of *WM*. Each subgraph *is* $\subseteq$ *IS* is a tuple $\langle T^{is}, F_C^{is}, F_D^{is} \rangle$, such that: $T^{is} \subseteq T$ is a subset of *WM* tasks; F_C^{is} and F_D^{is} are sets of edges, expressing the control and data flow relations among tasks of T^{is}, so that for any vector of values over the conditions related to all edges $e_i \in F_C^{is} \cup F_D^{is}$, including the constraints on their information entities, *is* will either be executed as a whole, or it will not be executed.

That is, when the execution of a task implies conditional branching of the consequent flows based on edge constraints, the mutually exclusive constraint spaces of outgoing edges are separately considered, resulting in an execution tree; its leaves represent the space of instance subgraphs. The concept of instance subgraphs has been often used in workflow science, since it makes easier to handle by breaking up the workflow into manageable components (e.g., [22]).

Based on *IS*, the Bilateral Associations (*BA*) are created (3–6), and thereupon verified using the Policy Model, resulting in the set *D* of Directives (7). The cartesian combination of purposes and initiators (*PIP*) is then reduced to those pairs appearing, according to *D*, to be valid (*VPIP*), whereas *D* drives the verification of each $is \in IS$ (10–27).

The first step in the verification of an instance subgraph *is* concerns the extraction of the different *cases* (C_{is}), derived from the Bilateral Validity Directives (BVD) associated with *is*. Each case *c* reflects an execution variant of *is*, where each task can be executed in a unique manner and all edges between tasks are the ones prescribed by the corresponding BVDs. To make this more clear, for every BA $\langle t_i, e_k, t_{i+1} \rangle$, each derived BVD comprises a structure $\langle t_i^*, e_k^*, t_{i+1}^* \rangle$, where t_i^* and t_{i+1}^* incorporate exactly one execution profile each, and e_k^* is the edge appropriately adapted. It is important to stress that e_k^* may include additional tasks mediating t_i^* and t_{i+1}^*; this is often the case, e.g., with tasks performing data anonymisation or encryption. Eventually, each case *c* is a projection of *is*, according to a valid combination of $\langle t_i^*, e_k^*, t_{i+1}^* \rangle$ structures, derived from the BVDs.

The generation of cases C_{is} is followed by their verification and appropriate transformation (13–22), considering also the rest of Directives. In this context, the behavioural *norm* of each task *t* in a case *c* is extracted by the directives D_c pertaining to the case. Essentially, norms comprise groups of compliance patterns that span across all Directives types and can be verified together for *t*.

Forbiddance Norms (*FN*) reflect requirements implied by TFD and FFD. Provisions described by *Direct Norms* (*DN*) concern tasks that should be present in the workflow directly connected with *t* via an edge, either incoming or outgoing. On the other hand, *Indirect Pre-* (*IPrN*) and *Indirect Post- Norms* (*IPoN*) indicate tasks that should precede, respectively follow, the execution of *t*, with relative position other than direct connection, whereas an *Existence Norm* (*ExN*) implies the need for a task to exist in the workflow at any position. *State Norms*

(StN), derived from BVD, reflect requirements related to data state (cf. Sect. 3.2). Finally, norms can be *conditional* or *definite*, depending on whether the corresponding Directives are associated with pre- and/or post-conditions, or not.

All tasks comprising the case are verified against the associated norms. Therefore, tasks are topologically sorted [13], providing for both forward and backward traversal, and the application of the norms for the progressive transformation of the case c takes place, resulting in its verified version vc (or in failure). The procedure begins and finishes with the application of forbiddance provisions; the reason is that, on the one hand, the case may be rejected at the very beginning due to some conflict implied by FN, while, on the other hand, checking against forbiddances is deemed necessary following any transformations that may have happened due to the application of the other types of norms.

The latter takes place in three phases; first, the definite provisions are applied, followed by the conditional ones. In each phase, direct norms precede indirect pre- and post- norms; the reason why indirect norms are not applied together, as is the case with direct, is that post- norms require traversing the tasks of the case in a backward manner. Third, norms related with data state are applied, in order to perform the corresponding verification and transformation after all other norms have been applied and, consequently, all task additions and flow modifications they imply have already been enforced.

After this loop has been executed over all cases C_{is}, the cases VC_{is} found to be valid are being merged (23), providing the verified instance subgraph vis; merging concerns the aggregation of the tasks representing the same activity in the different cases, and the unification of the corresponding edges. Similarly, when verification of all instance subgraphs is complete, the verified ones (VIS) are merged providing the final verified workflow model WM_V (29). In other words, similarly to the decomposition of the initial workflow model to instance subgraphs and cases, the final WM_V is assembled from its elementary parts, i.e., its cases and verified instance subgraphs, into a unified specification. Intuitively, in order for the workflow verification to be successful, there should be at least one verified case vc resulting from the procedure.

The basic scheme summarised in Algorithm 1 has some variants concerning mostly the repetitive execution of certain parts, in order for a case, a subgraph, or the model as a whole, to be verified again; this is in order to capture potential privacy flaws that the modification may have introduced. For instance, two new tasks, introduced during verification, may conflict with each other, which cannot be captured by the initial directives. Hence, repetition of some procedures is necessary, until the workflow "converges" to a definitive structure. This is part of ongoing optimisation work, which, along with the detailed description of the sub-algorithms used in Algorithm 1, is beyond this paper scope.

6   Example

Figure 5 provides a simple example inspired by the healthcare domain, on the basis of a workflow originally consisting of only one BA. Following the verification procedure in Sect. 5, the workflow specified by the designer (Fig. 5a)

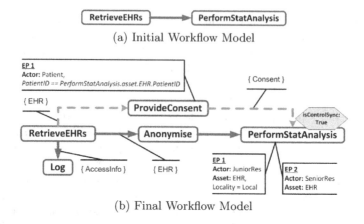

(a) Initial Workflow Model

(b) Final Workflow Model

Fig. 5. Workflow verification example

is transformed to its privacy-compliant equivalent (Fig. 5b), with the following modifications:

- The task `PerformStatAnalysis` is linked to two execution profiles, denoting the fact that individuals holding the role `JuniorRes` are authorised to perform it only on EHRs in which the field `Locality` has the value "Local", while the role `SeniorRes` is not subject to any constraints. This is due to the two BVDs derived for the BA in question, that provide two different valid specifications for the task `PerformStatAnalysis` and the same valid specification for the task `RetrieveEHRs`, for the purpose of `MedicalResearch` and the initiator `Researcher`, leading to the formation of two different cases for the unique instance subgraph.
- The task `Anonymise` is inserted between the two tasks, as also prescribed by both BVDs, for preventing read access to selected fields of processed EHRs.
- The task `Log` is inserted for accountability purposes, receiving as input the `AccessInfo` produced by `RetrieveEHRs`; this is required by an ORD linked to both BVDs and is enforced during Direct Norms application for the task `RetrieveEHRs`.
- The task `ProvideConsent` is inserted, to ensure that the corresponding patients (data subjects) have given their consent for processing their medical records. This is the result of the enforcement of an IRD, again linked to both BVDs, during Direct Norms application for the task `PerformStatAnalysis`. The compliance profile of the particular directive has the value "path-binding", indicating that the required task must receive its input (EHR) from a task along the data path providing analogous information to `PerformStatAnalysis`, i.e., `RetrieveEHRs`. Further, the task `PerformStatAnalysis` is annotated with `isControlSync` to be "True", so that it cannot execute without the reception of consent. Finally, the prescribed specification for `ProvideConsent` requires that its actor must be the patient, the EHR of whom is being processed by the task `PerformStatAnalysis`, implying a form of BoD.

7   Conclusions

This paper has presented an innovative framework towards *by design* privacy-aware workflow models. Inherent compliance is primarily based on two mechanisms: a comprehensive workflow modelling approach able to capture the privacy aspects *in* the workflow specification, and a procedure for the automatic privacy-aware verification and transformation of workflows, resulting in compliant specifications.

As regards the modelling approach, the cornerstone here is the concept of *execution profiles*. First, each comprises by itself an authorisation statement concerning the execution of an operation by some actor(s) on some asset(s), provided that certain conditions hold. Second, they define conditional variants of the task, thus introducing flexibility of authorisations based on the real-time parameters. And third, the elements comprising a profile are defined in great detail following the expressiveness provided by the *entities* primitive, also supported by various features, as are data states, workflow variables, and the explicit consideration of *purpose*. This way, it couples ideas stemming from a wide spectrum of security areas, including SoD/BoD [7], contextual security policies [9], as well as attribute-based [33] and privacy-aware [23] access control.

Going a step further, the proposed framework enables the automatic verification of workflow models, as far as their compliance with privacy principles is concerned, along with their subsequent transformation. This way, it provides for their enhancement with privacy-related features already at design-time, thus enabling inherent privacy awareness.

Finally, it is to be noted that the solution has been successfully leveraged in the context of EU FP7 DEMONS [1] for introducing privacy awareness in a number of real-world scenarios, in the demanding area of network monitoring.

Acknowledgment. This research was supported by the European Commission, in the frame of the FP7 DEMONS project.

References

1. FP7 ICT DEMONS (DEcentralized, cooperative, and privacy-preserving MONitoring for trustworthinesS). http://www.fp7-demons.eu/
2. van der Aalst, W.M.P., ter Hofstede, A.H.M.: YAWL: yet another workflow language. Inf. Syst. **30**(4), 245–275 (2005)
3. Alhaqbani, B., Adams, M., Fidge, C.J., ter Hofstede, A.H.M.: Privacy-aware workflow management. In: Glykas, M. (ed.) Business Process Management. SCI, vol. 444, pp. 111–128. Springer, Heidelberg (2013)
4. Awad, A., Weidlich, M., Weske, M.: Visually specifying compliance rules and explaining their violations for business processes. J. Visual Lang. Comput. **22**, 30–55 (2011)
5. Ayed, S., Cuppens-Boulahia, N., Cuppens, F.: Deploying security policy in intra and inter workflow management systems. In: International Conference on Availability, Reliability and Security (ARES) (2009)

6. Bertino, E., Crampton, J., Paci, F.: Access control and authorization constraints for WS-BPEL. In: International Conference on Web Services (2006)
7. Botha, R.A., Eloff, J.H.P.: Separation of duties for access control enforcement in workflow environments. IBM Syst. J. **40**(3), 666–682 (2001)
8. Cavoukian, A.: Privacy by design: origins, meaning, and prospects for assuring privacy and trust in the information era. In: Yee, G. (ed.) Privacy Protection Measures and Technologies in Business Organizations: Aspects and Standards. IGI Global, Hershey (2012)
9. Cuppens, F., Cuppens-Boulahia, N.: Modeling contextual security policies. Int. J. Inf. Secur. **7**(4), 285–305 (2008)
10. Goedertier, S., Vanthienen, J.: Designing compliant business processes with obligations and permissions. In: Eder, J., Dustdar, S. (eds.) BPM Workshops 2006. LNCS, vol. 4103, pp. 5–14. Springer, Heidelberg (2006)
11. Governatori, G., Hoffmann, J., Sadiq, S., Weber, I.: Detecting regulatory compliance for business process models through semantic annotations. In: Ardagna, D., Mecella, M., Yang, J. (eds.) Business Process Management Workshops. LNBIP, vol. 17, pp. 5–17. Springer, Heidelberg (2009)
12. Jablonski, S., Bussler, C.: Workflow Management: Modeling, Concepts, Architecture and Implementation. International Thomson Computer Press, London (1996)
13. Kahn, A.B.: Topological sorting of large networks. Commun. ACM **5**(11), 558–562 (1962)
14. Koukovini, M.N., Papagiannakopoulou, E.I., Lioudakis, G.V., Dellas, N., Kaklamani, D.I., Venieris, I.S.: Privacy compliance requirements in workflow environments. In: Cruz-Cunha, M.M. (ed.) Handbook of Research on Digital Crime, Cyberspace Security, and Information Assurance. IGI Global, Hershey (2014)
15. Koukovini, M.N., Papagiannakopoulou, E.I., Lioudakis, G.V., Dellas, N., Kaklamani, D.I., Venieris, I.S.: Workflow modeling technologies. In: Khosrow-Pour, M. (ed.) Encyclopedia of Information Science and Technology, pp. 5348–5356. IGI Global, Hershey (2015)
16. Koukovini, M.N., Papagiannakopoulou, E.I., Lioudakis, G.V., Kaklamani, D.I., Venieris, I.S.: A workflow checking approach for inherent privacy awareness in network monitoring. In: Garcia-Alfaro, J., Navarro-Arribas, G., Cuppens-Boulahia, N., de Capitani di Vimercati, S. (eds.) DPM 2011 and SETOP 2011. LNCS, vol. 7122, pp. 295–302. Springer, Heidelberg (2012)
17. Koukovini, M.N., Papagiannakopoulou, E.I., Lioudakis, G.V., Dellas, N.L., Kaklamani, D.I., Venieris, I.S.: An ontology-based approach towards comprehensive workflow modelling. IET Softw. **8**(2), 73–85 (2014)
18. Leyla, N., Mashiyat, A.S., Wang, H., MacCaull, W.: Towards workflow verification. In: Proceedings of the 2010 Conference of the Center for Advanced Studies on Collaborative Research, CASCON 2010 (2010)
19. Lu, R., Sadiq, S.K., Governatori, G.: Compliance aware business process design. In: ter Hofstede, A.H.M., Benatallah, B., Paik, H.-Y. (eds.) BPM 2007 Workshops. LNCS, vol. 4928, pp. 120–131. Springer, Heidelberg (2008)
20. Lu, R., Sadiq, S., Governatori, G.: Measurement of compliance distance in business processes. Inf. Syst. Manag. **25**, 344–355 (2008)
21. Ludäscher, B., Altintas, I., Bowers, S., Cummings, J., Critchlow, T., Deelman, E., De Roure, D., Freire, J., Goble, C., Jones, M., Klasky, S., McPhillips, T., Podhorszki, N., Silva, C., Taylor, I., Vouk, M.: Scientific process automation and workflow management. In: Shoshani, A., Rotem, D. (eds.) Scientific Data Management, Chap. 13. Computational Science Series. Chapman & Hall, London (2009)

22. Meda, H.S., Sen, A.K., Bagchi, A.: On detecting data flow errors in workflows. J. Data Inf. Qual. **2**(1), 4:1–4:31 (2010)
23. Papagiannakopoulou, E.I., Koukovini, M.N., Lioudakis, G.V., Dellas, N., Kaklamani, D.I., Venieris, I.S.: Privacy-aware access control. In: Khosrow-Pour, M. (ed.) Encyclopedia of Information Science and Technology, pp. 4403–4411. IGI Global, Hershey (2015)
24. Papagiannakopoulou, E.I., et al.: Leveraging ontologies upon a holistic privacy-aware access control model. In: Danger, J.-L., Debbabi, M., Marion, J.-Y., Garcia-Alfaro, J., Heywood, N.Z. (eds.) FPS 2013. LNCS, vol. 8352, pp. 209–226. Springer, Heidelberg (2014)
25. Papagiannakopoulou, E.I., Koukovini, M.N., Lioudakis, G.V., Garcia-Alfaro, J., Kaklamani, D.I., Venieris, I.S., Cuppens, F., Cuppens-Boulahia, N.: A privacy-aware access control model for distributed network monitoring. Comput. Electr. Eng. **39**(7), 2263–2281 (2013)
26. Short, S., Kaluvuri, S.P.: A data-centric approach for privacy-aware business process enablement. In: van Sinderen, M., Johnson, P. (eds.) IWEI 2011. LNBIP, vol. 76, pp. 191–203. Springer, Heidelberg (2011)
27. The Object Management Group (OMG): Business Process Modeling Notation (BPMN) Version 2.0, OMG Specification, January 2011
28. The World Wide Web Consortium (W3C): Web Services Description Language (WSDL) Version 2.0, W3C Standard, June 2007
29. Witt, S., Feja, S., Speck, A., Prietz, C.: Integrated privacy modeling and validation for business process models. In: Proceedings of the 2012 Joint EDBT/ICDT Workshops, EDBT-ICDT 2012. ACM (2012)
30. Wolter, C., Menzel, M., Schaad, A., Miseldine, P., Meinel, C.: Model-driven business process security requirement specification. J. Syst. Architect. **55**(4), 211–223 (2009)
31. Wolter, C., Schaad, A.: Modeling of task-based authorization constraints in BPMN. In: Alonso, G., Dadam, P., Rosemann, M. (eds.) BPM 2007. LNCS, vol. 4714, pp. 64–79. Springer, Heidelberg (2007)
32. Wolter, C., Schaad, A., Meinel, C.: Task-based entailment constraints for basic workflow patterns. In: Proceedings of the 13th Symposium on Access Control Models and Technologies, SACMAT 2008. ACM (2008)
33. Yuan, E., Tong, J.: Attributed based access control (ABAC) for web services. In: Proceedings of the IEEE International Conference on Web Services, ICWS 2005. IEEE Computer Society (2005)

Index Optimization for L-Diversified Database-as-a-Service

Jens Köhler$^{(\boxtimes)}$ and Hannes Hartenstein

Karlsruhe Institute of Technology (KIT), Steinbuch Centre for Computing (SCC)
and Institute of Telematics, Zirkel 2, 76131 Karlsruhe, Germany
{jens.koehler,hartenstein}@kit.edu

Abstract. Preserving the anonymity of individuals by technical means when outsourcing databases to semi-trusted providers gained importance in recent years. Anonymization approaches exist that fulfill anonymity notions like ℓ-diversity and can be used to outsource databases. However, indexes on anonymized data significantly differ from plaintext indexes both in terms of usage and possible performance gains. In most cases, it is not clear whether using an anonymized index is beneficial or not.

In this paper, we present Dividat, an approach that makes anonymized database outsourcing more practical and deployable by optimizing the indexing of ℓ-diversified data. We show that the efficiency of anonymized indexes differs from traditional indexes and performance gains of a factor of 5 are possible by optimizing indexing strategies. We propose strategies to determine which indexes should be created for a given query workload and used for a given query. To apply these strategies without actually creating each possible index, we propose and validate models that estimate the performance of anonymized index tables a-priori.

Keywords: Database-as-a-service · Anonymized indexes · ℓ-diversity · Performance optimization

1 Introduction

Outsourcing services and data to external providers has become increasingly attractive with the advent of cloud computing. However, while benefits in terms of scalability, elasticity and cost effectiveness are expected, data outsourcing also induces risks. One of the most important risks constitutes privacy loss of individuals [1]. The use of Database-as-a-Service (DaaS) offerings of external *storage providers* (SPs) often implies loosing control over the outsourced database, as even trustworthy SPs can be prone to third party attacks. To minimize the risk of data disclosure, data records can be encrypted by a trusted client before being outsourced. To retrieve records, the trusted client has to retrieve the encrypted records and decrypt them. As encrypted records are indistinguishable to the SP, indexes are necessary to efficiently retrieve encrypted records that match certain criteria. These indexes, however, can undermine the privacy of individuals again.

© Springer International Publishing Switzerland 2015
J. Garcia-Alfaro et al. (Eds.): DPM/SETOP/QASA 2014, LNCS 8872, pp. 114–132, 2015.
DOI: 10.1007/978-3-319-17016-9_8

One way to preserve the privacy of individuals in indexes is to anonymize the outsourced indexes. If an index contains two records *(John, Flu)* and *(John, None)*, John's privacy might be considered preserved as the illness of the individual named John cannot be determined with a probability higher than $\frac{1}{2}$. This anonymization concept where each value assignment that can be used to identify individuals has to map to at least ℓ assignments of sensitive values is referred to as ℓ-diversity [2]. As ℓ-diversified indexes contain plaintext rather than encrypted records, the SP can evaluate queries for records that match certain criteria.

Existing anonymization approaches for the DaaS setting [3–5] that generate an ℓ-diverse representation of a set of data typically do not address the creation of indexes on the anonymized data. The *efficiency of anonymized indexes* that contain anonymized plaintext records varies a lot depending on the query, the index content and the anonymity requirements, as we show in this paper. To determine which indexes should be created and used, approaches to assess the efficiency of anonymized index tables for specific queries are necessary.

In this paper, we propose Dividat (ℓ-**DIV**ers**I**fied **DAT**abases), an approach that makes use of ℓ-diversified indexes to make query execution more efficient. In particular, the contributions of this paper are the following:

- **A performance behavior inspection of ℓ-diversified indexes** to show that the efficiency of ℓ-diversified index tables heavily depends on the query, the content of the index and the anonymity requirements.
- **Indexing strategies** to determine which anonymized index tables should be created for a given workload and which index tables should be used.
- **Performance models** to estimate the performance of anonymized indexes a-priori without actually creating each possible index.

The paper is structured as follows: In Sect. 2 anonymization notions and concepts are introduced and related work is summarized. In Sect. 3 we investigate the influencing factors for the performance of anonymized index tables and show how optimized indexing strategies can be derived from performance models. We validate our models in Sect. 4 and discuss our approach in Sect. 5. Finally, the paper is concluded in Sect. 6.

2   Fundamentals and Related Work

2.1   Anonymity Notions and Techniques

In order to quantify the level of anonymity, several anonymity notions have been proposed [6]. Relevant in the context of this paper is the notion of ℓ-diversity [2]. The general concept of ℓ-diversity is applied for scenarios in which data is organized in a set of records that link identifiers to values of an attribute that is considered to be sensitive. The set of records is ℓ-diverse if for each identifier there are at least ℓ records with ℓ distinct sensitive values.

To deal with the fact that the set of identifying attributes might depend on the attacker (and his/her background knowledge), the formal definition of

Table 1. Anatomization example. QID: {Name, ZIP}, sensitive attributes: {ZIP, Illness}

Name	ZIP	Illness
John	12345	Flu
Eve	12349	Headache
Marc	12345	Asthma
Dan	23456	Cancer

(a) Plaintext

GID	Enc
1	Enc(John, 12345, Flu)
1	Enc(Eve, 12349, Headache)
2	Enc(Marc, 12345, Asthma)
2	Enc(Dan, 23456, Cancer)

(b) Encrypted data at SP

GID	Name	GID	ZIP	GID	Illness
1	John	1	12345	1	Flu
1	Eve	1	12349	1	Headache
2	Marc	2	12345	2	Asthma
2	Dan	2	23456	2	Cancer

(c) Anatomized data at SP (*anatomized view*)

ℓ-diversity builds on the notion of a quasi-identifier (QID). A QID is a set of attributes that can be used as if it were an identifier because of the attacker's background knowledge[1].

All records that have the same QID value form a so-called *QID-block*. The notion of ℓ-diversity requires that each QID-block has to be linked to at least ℓ different, well-represented sensitive attribute values. Thus, attackers that can link individuals to a QID value via background knowledge can determine an individual's correct sensitive attribute value only with a probability of $\frac{1}{\ell}$. Formally, ℓ-diversity is defined as follows [2]: A QID-block is ℓ-diverse if it contains at least ℓ well-represented values for the sensitive attribute S. A table is ℓ-diverse if every QID-block is ℓ-diverse.

To anonymize datasets to adhere to privacy notions like ℓ-diversity, a variety of approaches such as *anatomization* [4], *generalization* [8], *permutation* [9], *perturbation* [10,11] and *suppression* [8] exist. For the DaaS use-case where data is repeatedly updated and queried for records that satisfy specific conditions, the concept of anatomization is the prevalent anonymization method [3–5].

The focus of this paper is on *optimizing indexes* for anatomized data rather than on presenting yet another anonymization approach. Therefore, we build on existing approaches that ensure that the SP only has an *anatomized view* on the data [3–5]: All sensitive attributes that are not contained in the QID (*SensOnly* in the following) are stored in one table, each sensitive attribute that

---

[1] Formally a QID is defined as follows [7]: Given a population of entities U that are contained in the data and the set of total entities U', an entity-specific table $T(A_1, ..., A_n)$, $f_c : U \rightarrow T$ and $f_g : T \rightarrow U'$, where $U \subseteq U'$. A quasi-identifier of T, written QID, is a set of attributes $A_i, ..., A_j \subseteq \{A_1, ..., A_n\}$ where: $\exists p_i \in U$ such that $f_g(f_c(p_i)[QID]) = p_i$. Intuitively, f_c maps an entity p_i on its according record in table T. QID is a quasi-identifier if there exists a mapping f_g that can map the record $f_c(p_i)$ back to the original entity p_i based on the attributes contained in QID.

is contained in the QID (*QidSens*) is stored in a separate table and the remaining attributes (*QidOnly*) are stored in another table. Records are anonymized in batches of ℓ records. Each batch is assigned a group identifier (GID) to not lose the relations of the attribute values entirely. Based on the GID, each attribute that is contained in the QID maps to at least ℓ different values that are sensitive. Thus, the anatomized data representation can be considered ℓ-diverse.

Example: The relation shown in Table 1a can be anatomized as shown in Table 1c to guarantee 2-diversity with a QID {Name, ZIP} and sensitive attributes {ZIP, Illness}. For instance, the QID attribute combination "John, 12345" can be mapped on 2 different values for the sensitive attribute Illness. However, information is lost by anatomization: A query for the ZIP code of the records with the name "John" would return "12345" *and* "12349".

Approaches that provide anonymized DaaS remedy this loss of information by outsourcing encrypted versions of the records along with the anatomized data [4,5]. In the previous example, if the attribute values of GID 1 match a query, the encrypted records Enc(John, 12345, Flu) and Enc(Eve, 12349, Headache) can be retrieved from Table 1b and sent back to the trusted client of the query issuer. The trusted client then has to decrypt them and potentially discard false positive records that do not match the original query.

2.2 Related Approaches

The problem of confidential database outsourcing was addressed in the DaaS community by using encryption [12], confidentiality preserving indexing structures [13–15] and partitioning of attributes across multiple SPs [16–18]. While encrypting a database preserves data confidentiality and therefore the anonymity of individuals[2], indexing structures are needed for efficient query execution. Confidentiality preserving indexing structures can be used to query outsourced data efficiently, but can also induce information flows that allow attackers[3] with a certain background knowledge to reveal sensitive attributes [19].

Privacy preserving data publishing aims at preserving the privacy of individuals by anonymizing the data before publishing it. Traditional proposals for anonymized data publishing [6] focus on anonymizing and publishing a batch of data once. Recent approaches [20–23] also address the problem of publishing multiple versions of a dataset or even data streams, allowing to perform insert, delete and update operations on a published dataset.

Nergiz et al. [3,4] propose to leverage the findings of the data publishing community in DaaS scenarios. Their concept builds on anatomization of a data table into QID and sensitive attributes. By storing newly inserted records in an encrypted table that is completely transferred to and searched by a trusted client when evaluating queries, Nergiz et al. can guarantee that queries return newly inserted records. Vimercati et al. [5] propose to fragment databases and

---

[2] While this argument holds from a technical perspective, it is not always true from a legal perspective.

[3] This is especially true for attackers that are able to monitor the queries.

only loosely couple the fragments by assigning each attribute value a group and mapping the groups of different attributes on each other. Unlike Nergiz et al. [3,4] they support sensitive attributes that are contained in the QID. They showed that the anonymity properties of such anatomized databases are comparable to the ℓ-diversity notion. Dividat extends the approaches of Nergiz et al. and Vimercati et al. by examining in which cases it is beneficial for query execution performance to build pre-joined index tables based on the anatomized data.

Query optimization approaches for classical, non-anonymized databases [24–26] aim at finding an optimized query execution plan that minimizes the induced cost. Other approaches make use of *materialized views* to execute queries more efficiently that would otherwise require expensive joins and projections [27,28]. In classical query optimization the query has to be evaluated as efficiently as possible *and* return correct results. Correctness is not a necessary condition in our case as a trusted client post-processes the results. With Dividat the SP can partially evaluate a query and lets the trusted client evaluate the rest of a query if it is expected to be more efficient. Our approach also takes into account the ℓ-diversified data structure that originates from anatomization to a-priori determine which materialized views should be created before the data is even present. However, Dividat builds on classic approaches in the sense that it leverages the query optimization capabilities of the SP's database management system.

3   Performance-Optimized Indexes

Executing queries based on anatomized data as shown in Table 1c requires to join tables. Especially for big datasets, joining is considered expensive in terms of performance [29]. To avoid joins, materialized index tables that contain all attributes that are relevant to execute a query can be built by pre-joining the anatomized data. Such materialized index tables from anatomized data can increase query execution performance. However, as we will show in Sect. 3.1 a materialized index table that contains all relevant attributes for a query is not always the most efficient choice and choosing the optimal index table for a query can have a large performance benefit. In Sect. 3.2, we show how to develop an optimized indexing strategy. To decide which index tables should be *created* by the SP and which of the created index tables should be *used* to execute a given query, the overheads induced by different index tables need to be quantified without actually executing the query. We propose models that can be used to quantify these overheads in Sect. 3.3.

3.1   Possible Performance Savings

To investigate the potential performance benefits by optimizing the usage of anonymized indexes, we conducted empirical measurements. All measurements presented in this section are based on a PostgreSQL[4] database run on a machine

---

[4] http://www.postgresql.org/.

with 4 GB RAM and a 2.50 GHz QuadCore CPU. The data on which we executed queries contained 30.000 records with three attributes, for which values were chosen uniformly and independently at random: *gender* with two possible values, *synth1* and *synth2* with a varying value domain that depends on the measured scenario. The anonymity requirements were set to $QidOnly = \{gender\}$, $QidSens = \{synth1\}$ and $SensOnly = \{synth2\}$. We can show that optimizing the usage of index tables can improve performance even in very simple scenarios such as the investigated one.

Definition (Single Selection): A query performs a *single selection* on an attribute iff it selects only records that contain a *single* specific value for this attribute. *Example:* The query SELECT *...WHERE ZIP=12345 AND Phone=34622 AND Illness=None performs single selections on *ZIP*, *Phone* and *Illness*.   □

Definition (Multi Selection): A query performs a *multi selection* on an attribute iff it selects only records that contain one out of a set of values the attribute can take. *Example:* The query SELECT * ...WHERE ZIP=12345 AND Phone < 35638 AND (Illness=None OR Illness=Flu) performs multi selections on *Phone* and *Illness*.   □

First, we investigate the **dependency of query latency on the number of queried values.** We measured the execution time of random queries that contained single selections on *gender* and multi selections (based on $\leq$ and $\geq$ operators) selecting a varying number of values for both *synth1* and *synth2* based on different index tables. The results are shown in Fig. 1a. Executing the queries on a non-anonymized plaintext table provides the best results, but does not enforce the privacy requirements. Executing the queries based on an 3-diversified index table that contained *gender* and *synth1* (*gender-synth1* in Fig. 1a) performs best if less than 7 values are selected each for *synth1* and *synth2*. Otherwise, it is most efficient to evaluate the query on an index table that does not contain *synth1* and *synth2* but just *gender*. The measurements show that the optimal index table choice heavily depends on the query and performance differences of more than a factor of 5 exist between index tables (see gender vs. gender-synth1-synth2 for 16 selected values each for *synth1* and *synth2* in Fig. 1a).

Second, we investigate the **dependency of the query latency on the data's structure.** We measured the latency of random queries on varying datasets that differed in the number of values in the domain of the attributes *synth1* and *synth2*. The results are shown in Fig. 1b. With a bigger value domain for *synth1* / *synth2*, the latencies decrease as fewer records match the executed queries. The measurements show that the optimal index table choice for the executed query heavily depends on the value domain of *synth1* and *synth2*. For instance, executing the query based on the anonymized index table containing *gender*, *synth1* and *synth2* (*gender-synth1-synth2* in Fig. 1b) is the worst choice if *synth1*'s and *synth2*'s value domain includes 5 values each but is the best choice for value domains that contain 15 values each or more.

Third, we investigate the **dependency of the query latency on the diversity factor ℓ.** We measured the execution time of random queries that just

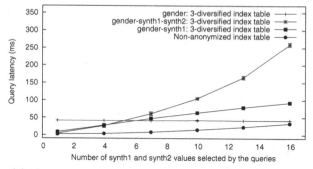

(a) Varying number of queried synth1 and synth2 values.

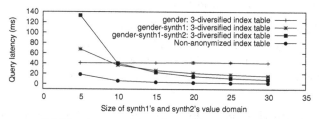

(b) Varying synth1 and synth2 value domains

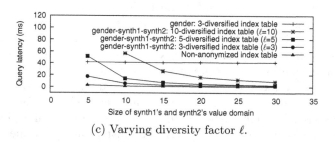

(c) Varying diversity factor ℓ.

Fig. 1. Performance differences between index tables with varying parameters.

contained a single selection on each attribute (e.g., ...WHERE gender=male AND synth1=1 AND synth2=2). The measured query latencies for a varying value domain of both *synth1* and *synth2* are shown in Fig. 1c. The measurements show that the optimal index table choice depends on *synth1*'s and *synth2*'s value domain *and* the anonymization factor ℓ. It is more efficient to use the anonymized index table *gender-synth1-synth2* than the *gender* index table if $\ell = 5$ and *synth1*'s as well as *synth2*'s value domain contains 10 values each. However, if $\ell = 10$, it is more efficient to execute the query based on the *gender* index table.

The measurements of the exemplary scenario presented in this section show that the usefulness of anonymized index tables to execute queries more efficiently heavily differs and an anonymized index table that contains all attributes for a given query is not necessarily the best choice. We will provide the rationale why this is the case in Sect. 3.3.

3.2   Index Optimization Strategies

The conducted measurements show that the efficiency of ℓ-diverse index tables heavily depends on (a) the data's structure, (b) the ℓ-diversity requirements and (c) the executed queries. Thus, to optimize the usage of indexes, information on these influencing factors is necessary. While the ℓ-diversity requirements are well specified and statistics can be kept by the SP to derive the data's structure, the queries executed in the future are in general not predictable. In this section, we propose strategies on how to adaptively determine which index tables should be used to *execute a specific query* and which index tables should be *created*.

Query Execution Strategy: As the optimal index table to execute a query depends on the query itself, for each query q that is executed an optimized decision has to be made on which existing index table I induces the lowest query latency. To make this decision, the expected query latency $l(I, q)$ needs to be estimated for each index table I and the index table with the minimum expected latency needs to be chosen. As this decision has to be made on-demand upon incoming queries, the latency estimation has to be performed efficiently and actually executing the query to determine the index tables' efficiency is not an option. A model that allows to a-priori assess the expected query latency $l(I, q)$ for each index table is needed. We propose such a model in Sect. 3.3.

Index Creation Strategy: The SP stores anonymized records in anatomized tables that allow to create index tables on-demand without interacting with the trusted client. The choice which set of index tables can be considered optimal and should be created does not necessarily depend only on the expected query workload $\mathcal{Q}$ but also on the storage overhead induced by the index tables. Both the storage overhead N_I of a single index table I and the query latency $l(I, q)$ that is induced when executing a query q on index table I can be estimated based on models we propose in Sect. 3.3. Based on these models, the query latency induced by a given set of index tables $\mathcal{I}$ for a given workload $\mathcal{Q}$ can be calculated as $\sum_{q \in \mathcal{Q}} \min_{I \in \mathcal{I}} l(I, q)$. Furthermore, the storage overhead of a set of index tables $\mathcal{I}$ can be calculated as $\sum_{I \in \mathcal{I}} N_I$. Both metrics can be considered by applying a weight w_l to the latency overhead and a weight w_s to the storage overhead according to the user's individual preferences:

$$o(\mathcal{I}, \mathcal{Q}) = w_l \cdot \frac{1}{|\mathcal{Q}|} \sum_{q \in \mathcal{Q}} \min_{I \in \mathcal{I}} l(I, q) + w_s \cdot \sum_{I \in \mathcal{I}} N_I \qquad (1)$$

To find a set of index tables $\mathcal{I}$ that minimizes the overhead $o(\mathcal{I}, \mathcal{Q})$, the query workload $\mathcal{Q}$ that will be executed needs to be known. We will propose two options to get hold of the workload in this section:

Option 1 - User interaction: One way to address the problem is to let the user specify the queries that need to be efficiently executable and for which index tables should be created. The user can state *precise queries* that should be executable as efficiently as possible (e.g., ...WHERE 2 < age < 11 AND name = john). However, in reality it is often not possible for the user to specify the *precise* queries that will be executed in the future. In this case, it suffices if the user can specify *abstract queries*, i.e., the expected average number of selected values for each attribute $|q_a|$ for each query (e.g., $|q_{age}| = 8, |q_{name}| = 1$).

We propose an efficient algorithm that runs in $O(|A_q|)$ (where A_q is the set of relevant attributes for query q) to determine the index table I that minimizes the overhead function o for a single query q in [30]. SPs can use the algorithm to determine the optimal index table for each user specified query and create the tables from the anatomized view.

Option 2 - Dynamic Self-Optimization: In some cases it might be hard for the user to specify beforehand the average number of selected values per attribute for a query or even to specify the kind of queries to be executed. Another way to address the problem is monitoring the query workload and adapting the indexing strategy to it. To characterize the workload, a sliding window of the last x queries can be taken as reference for future queries. Based on these queries, a set of index tables that minimizes the overhead function in Eq. 1 can be determined. To limit the storage overhead and to avoid excessive performance loss for inserting, updating and deleting records in all index tables, the number of index tables should be limited to a certain number. The resulting optimization problem can be solved by the SP in regular intervals to check whether the indexing strategy should be adapted. While solving this optimization problem is out of scope of this paper, we provide a formal description of the optimization problem in [30] and leave a deeper inspection of the problem for future work.

3.3   Performance Models

To evaluate Eq. 1, one needs to be able to determine the storage overhead N_I of an index table and the query latency $l(I, q)$ for executing a query based on an index table. In this section, we propose models that capture the trade-off between ℓ-diversity requirements and induced storage as well as query latency overheads. We propose a storage overhead model to a-priori quantify the storage overhead N_I a given index table induces and a query latency model that estimates the execution time $l(I, q)$ of a query q on a given index table I.

Storage Overhead Model (SO-model): By multiplying the number of index table records with the storage space needed to store a single record, the storage overhead induced by an index table I can be exactly calculated. For an index table I that contains the set of attributes A_I the number of records N_I that are contained in the index table can be calculated as:

$$N_I = \ell^{|QidSens \cap A_I| + \delta(|SensOnly \cap A_I|) + \delta(|QidOnly \cap A_I|)} \cdot N_M \qquad (2)$$

where $\delta(x) = \{ \begin{array}{l} 1 \text{ if } x > 0 \\ 0 \text{ else} \end{array}$ and N_M is the number of outsourced records.

Index table I can be built by joining all tables of the anatomized view on the GID that contain attributes included in A_I. For each sensitive attribute that is contained in the QID and the index table ($QidSens \cap A_I$), the attribute's

QidSens table in the anatomized view that contains ℓ records for each GID has to be joined. Each such table increases the number of entries in the result of the join by factor ℓ. Furthermore, if a sensitive attribute that is not part of the QID is contained in A_I, i.e., $SensOnly \cap A_I$ is not empty, the table containing the sensitive attributes has to be joined as well. As this table contains ℓ records for each GID, this increases the result of the join by factor ℓ.

Query Latency Model (QL-model): The query latency, i.e., the time needed to retrieve the matching records from an index table, depends on many factors like the used database system, the disk latency and the hardware configuration. We abstract from most of them by making the following assumption.

Assumption I: *The query latency $l(I, q)$ of executing query q on index table I linearly depends on the number of records $r(I, q)$ that are contained in the index table and match query q.*

$$l(I, q) = c \cdot r(I, q) + f \tag{3}$$

We show in Sect. 4.1 that Assumption I holds.

To apply the QL-model shown in Eq. 3, the parameters c, f and $r(I, q)$ have to be determined. We propose an analytical model that can be used to estimate the number of records $r(I, q)$ in an index table I that match query q later (see MR-model). Modeling c and f analytically like $r(I, q)$ is hard, as they depend on a variety of factors (e.g., indexing structures, disk latency, caching effects, database implementation, etc.). To determine the parameters for an existing index table I, execution times $(e_1, e_2, \ldots, e_n)$ of multiple queries $q_1, q_2, \ldots, q_n$ that return a different number of records $(r(I, q_1) \neq r(I, q_2))$ can be measured. Simple linear regression can then be used to determine parameters c and f that provide the best fit for the following system of equations: $e_i = c \cdot r(I, q_i) + f, i = 1 \ldots n$.

The resulting parameterized model can be used to determine a query execution strategy for incoming queries. To determine an index creation strategy, the parameters cannot be determined for each potential index table in most cases as this would imply to actually build each index table.

Assumption II: *The parameters c and f are independent from the data's structure, i.e., they only depend on the size of the index table N_I.*

Based on Assumption II, to approximate the parameters for non-existing index tables, c and f can be determined for each possible index table size N_I by building an according index table and measuring the query latency. The value domain of N_I is small, as N_I directly depends on the number of index table attributes in $SensOnly$, $QidOnly$ and $QidSens$ (see Eq. 2). The calculated c, f parameter values can be reused for all index tables with N_I entries without having to build each of them. In Sect. 4.1 we show that Assumption II holds.

Matching Records Model (MR-model): The query latency to evaluate a query q on an index table I depends on the number of records $r(I, q)$ contained in the index table that match the query. In the following we will provide analytical models that can be used by the QL-model to a-priori estimate the number of returned records $r(I,q)$ of a query q that is evaluated based on a given index table I. For simplicity, we initially make the following assumption.

Assumption III: *The attributes' values are independently distributed. We discuss in which cases this assumption can be neglected in Sect. 4.2.*

For simplicity and without loss of generality we presume that queries have a specific form that every query can be mapped on: For each contained attribute, the query filter contains conditions that are concatenated with OR operators. Conditions on distinct attributes are concatenated with AND operators.

Multi Selection Model: Given a set of data with N_M records where all attribute values are uniformly and independently distributed and a required diversity of ℓ. The expected number of matching records for a query q that is evaluated on an index table I can be calculated as:

$$r(I,q) = \prod_{a \in A_I} \frac{|q_a|}{|V_a|} \cdot N_I \tag{4}$$

where V_a is the set of possible values for attribute a, i.e., $|V_a|$ denotes the cardinality of attribute a that is contained in statistics maintained by the SP. The variable q_a denotes the set of values the query selects for attribute a. *Selectivity* is the percentage of records that contain specific attribute values. As attribute a is uniformly distributed, the average selectivity of a amounts to $\frac{|q_a|}{|V_a|}$. Furthermore, as the attribute values are assumed to be independently distributed, the combined selectivity of multiple attributes concatenated with AND clauses can be calculated multiplying the selectivity of single attributes. Multiplying this "combined selectivity" with the number of records in the anonymized index table results in the estimated number of records that are selected by a query.

The assumption of uniformly distributed attribute values does not hold for real use-cases. For non-uniformly distributed attribute values the model in Eq. 4 produces inaccurate predictions. To account for non-uniformly distributed attribute values, the frequency of attribute values can be maintained in statistics kept by the SP. In the following we will denote the occurrence probability of value v for attribute a as $p_a(v)$.

Non-uniformly Multi Selection Model: Based on the occurrence probabilities, the expected number of matching records for a query q that is evaluated on an index table I can be calculated as follows:

$$r(I,q) = \prod_{a \in A_I} \sum_{v \in q_a} p_a(v) \cdot N_I \tag{5}$$

The selectivity of a multi selection amounts to $\sum_{v \in q_a} p_a(v)$ as it suffices for a record to contain any attribute value that is selected in the multi selection. This corresponds to the OR clauses that concatenate conditions on the same attribute.

4   Evaluation

The SO-model (Eq. 2) has been analytically derived and accurately calculates the number of records that are contained in an index table that was built from

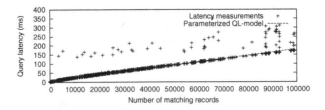

Fig. 2. Linear dependency: Number of matching records vs. query latency

an anatomized view. We validate the QL-model in Sect. 4.1 and investigate the applicability of the MR-model for non-uniform and interdependent attribute value distributions in Sect. 4.2.

4.1 QL-model Validation

We measured the latencies of queries that were executed on a variety of index tables and checked whether the execution times are consistent with our models. The measurements were conducted in the same setup that we described in Sect. 3.1. As exploring the entire parameter space of possible index tables that might occur is not feasible, we generated scenarios according to the 2^k-factorial design method [31], i.e., we fixed two choices for each parameter and investigated every possible parameter choice combination. We chose between 3 and 5 for the ℓ-parameter and between one or two sensitive attributes that are also contained in the QID or no sensitive attributes at all. Regarding data structure, we chose between uniformly and irregularly distributed attribute values and fixed the size of *synth1*/*synth2*'s value domain to either 20 or 2000. For each configuration, we measured the latencies of 6000 queries that select either 1,4,7,10,13 or 16 values.

Validating Assumption I: *The query latency linearly depends on the number of matching records.*

The measured query latency subject to the number of records that matched the query of one configuration is shown in Fig. 2. Except for some outliers (∼60 outliers vs. 6000 measurements), the query latency measurements linearly depend on the number of matching records for the investigated configuration and parameterizing the QL-model as described in Sect. 3.3 results in a good fit (cf. the dotted line in Fig. 2). Measurements of the other configurations confirmed this finding (see [30]).

Validating Assumption II: *The parameters c, f of the QL-model for a given index table can be reused for other index tables that contain other data, but the same number of records N_I.*

Based on our measurements, we parameterized the QL-model for each index table we created from our 2^k-factorial design (see Table 2). The parameters indicate that the data's structure, i.e., the number of attribute values and their distribution, is not a significant influencing factor for the parameters c and f. Thus, the parameters can be determined once for an index table and can then

Table 2. Comparing the measured values for each given anonymity parameter choice underlines the independence of the c, f parameters from the data structure for each investigated 2^k-factorial design configuration.

Anonymity parameter choices (affecting N_I)	Data structure		c	f
	Val. domain size	Uniform data dist.		
$\ell=3$, $|SensOnly|=0$, $|QidSens|=0$	20	Yes	0.00159	1.81
		No	0.00161	1.73
	2000	Yes	0.00164	1.80
		No	0.00163	1.64
$\ell=3$, $|SensOnly|=1$, $|QidSens|=0$	20	Yes	0.00138	2.26
		No	0.00137	2.03
	2000	Yes	0.00138	2.94
		No	0.00139	1.99
$\ell=3$, $|SensOnly|=1$, $|QidSens|=1$	20	Yes	0.00172	5.49
		No	0.00172	5.22
	2000	Yes	0.00178	5.69
		No	0.00173	5.45
$\ell=5$, $|SensOnly|=0$, $|QidSens|=0$	20	Yes	0.00159	1.81
		No	0.00161	1.73
	2000	Yes	0.00164	1.80
		No	0.00163	1.64
$\ell=5$, $|SensOnly|=1$, $|QidSens|=0$	20	Yes	0.00147	1.92
		No	0.00143	2.36
	2000	Yes	0.00143	2.71
		No	0.00142	2.85
$\ell=5$, $|SensOnly|=1$, $|QidSens|=1$	20	Yes	0.00192	12.58
		No	0.00192	12.43
	2000	Yes	0.00190	13.01
		No	0.00192	12.47

be reused for other index tables that contain different data but have the same anonymity requirements and therefore contain the same number of records N_I without actually building them.

To confirm the **validity of the general QL-model** in combination with the MR-model, we measured the deviation of the measured real latency from the latency that our parameterized models predicted. We performed these measurements for each configuration of the 2^k-factorial design. The aggregated results are shown in Fig. 3. The x-axis represents the absolute deviation of the QL-model from the real latencies in milliseconds. On the y-axis, the number of queries

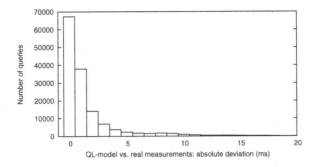

Fig. 3. Aggregated deviations: QL-model predictions vs. real measurements (histogram)

with the according deviation from the models are shown. The measurements show that, the predictions of the QL-model very closely matches the actual query latency. Combined with our results that query latency linearly depends on the number of matching records this finding also strongly indicates that our matching records model is sound.

4.2 Applicability of the MR-model

We based the analytical models to predict the number of records matching a query in an index table on **Assumption III** of independent attribute value distributions. In this section we show in which cases Assumption III is really necessary to correctly apply the models to derive a *query execution strategy* and an *index creation strategy*.

When deriving a **query execution strategy** for a given query q, the query q is exactly known and Eq. 5 can be applied. The validation of the QL-model presented in Sect. 4.1 included uniformly as well as irregularly distributed attribute values and showed that the QL-models can accurately predict the query latency in both cases. As query latency linearly depends on the number of matching records (cf. Sect. 4.1) this strongly indicates that our MR-model is sound for independently distributed attribute values. If the attribute value distributions depend on each other, using the proposed models leads to an overhead prediction error that depends on the strength of the attribute dependency. Even in the field of query optimization the assumption of independent attributes is often made and errors are accepted [25, 26]. Thus, this issue remains a challenging problem for future work for query optimization in general.

When determining an **index creation strategy**, the models are applied on query workloads instead of single queries. In this setting, we can prove that our models are sound even if the attribute value distributions depend on each other under certain assumptions. Intuitively this can be explained by the fact that the prediction errors of our models even out. An overview of the assumptions that need to be made to apply the MR-models is shown in Table 3 depending on the attribute value distribution and the available information that can be provided.

Table 3. Correctness of the models for index table creation vs. input information and data characteristics

Attr. value distribution	Available information		
	Precise queries	Abstract queries	Past workload
Uniform/Independent	✓	✓	✓
	Equation 4	Equation 4	Equation 4
Irregular/Independent	✓	If a_1 holds	✓
	Equation 5	Equation 4	Equation 5
Uniform/Dependent	if a_2 holds	if a_2 holds	if a_2 holds
	Equation 4	Equation 4	Equation 4
Irregular/Dependent	if a_2 holds	if a_2 holds	if a_2 holds
	Equation 4	Equation 4	Equation 4

Assumption a_1: selected values uniformly distributed.
Assumption a_2: selected value combinations uniformly dist.

If the attribute values are uniformly and independently distributed, Eq. 4 can be used to correctly determine the average number of matching records for a set of queries. In this case, is does not matter whether the user specified the expected queries in a *precise* or *abstract* way (cf. Sect. 3.3) or whether the SP adapts the strategy dynamically based on the *past workload*.

If the attributes are irregularly but independently distributed, Eq. 5 can be applied to correctly determine the average number of matching records if the user specified precise expected queries or the SP adapts the index strategy based on the past workload. If the user only specified abstract queries, Eq. 4 still can be correctly applied if the selected values by future queries are uniformly distributed (cf. Theorem 1). In case a user can only specify abstract queries, she is very likely not able to specify how the values selected by the future queries are distributed and possibly has to assume that they are uniformly distributed.

Theorem 1. *Let's assume that the assumption of uniformly distributed attribute values does not hold for a set of data. Equation 4 can be used to accurately calculate the expected number of matching records if the values selected by the queries are uniformly distributed.*

Proof: See [30] for the proof.

Furthermore, if it can be assumed that value combinations selected by future queries are uniformly distributed, it can also be shown that Eq. 4 can be used to correctly calculate the expected number of matching records even if the attributes are *not* independently distributed (cf. Theorem 2). In this case Eq. 4 is applicable to minimize the performance overhead for index tables that contain interdependently distributed attribute values.

Theorem 2. *Let's assume that the assumption of uniformly and/or independently distributed attribute values does not hold for a set of data. Equation 4 can be used to accurately calculate the expected number of matching records if the value combinations selected by queries are uniformly distributed.*

Proof: See [30] for the proof.

5   Discussion, Limitations, Future Work

Functionality of Dividat: We addressed selections of records based on equality and inequality conditions as query constructs in this paper. However, the proposed concepts and models can be applied to most other SQL conditions. For instance, LIKE operators constitute *multi selection* in our terminology. The parameters c and f of the QL-model (cf. Sect. 3.3) have to be determined for each type of multi selection as they might differ depending on indexing approaches that are utilized by the underlying database system used by the SP.

We considered query latency as one of the main optimization goals in this paper. While this is true for many use cases, applications exist that update the outsourced data at a high frequency. For these applications the performance of INSERT, UPDATE and DELETE operations should be included in the optimization process. Our QL-model can be applied to those operations analogously to SELECT operations. The optimization problem (cf. Eq. 1) to determine which index tables should be created for a query workload can be easily extended to also consider the overhead for these additional operations.

Overheads Induced by Dividat: Our models require statistical data that needs to be maintained and queried to optimize the execution strategy for each query. These processes induce a performance overhead on their own. The problem of processing statistical information in traditional query optimization closely resembles the problem at hand and can be applied in this context as well [24–26].

The choice which index tables should be created has to be made a-priori based on the predicted future data structure and the query behavior. These predictions are not necessarily accurate. Dividat allows the SP to build index tables without help from the trusted client. Thus, once the predicted state differs too much from reality, a new prediction can be made and the indexing strategy can be adapted without inducing any overhead for the trusted client.

The Dividat approach aims to minimize the overhead induced at the SP to evaluate incoming queries based on existing index tables. It considers both latency overhead and storage demand of the index tables. In our future work we plan to extend the models to consider additional factors such as the network transmission overhead and the crypto overhead for the trusted client that is induced by transmitted false-positive records that do not match the query. This will enable the SP to develop indexing strategies to optimize the overall query execution performance from a user's perspective.

6   Conclusion

In this paper we proposed Dividat, an approach to outsource databases while preserving the ℓ-diversity-based anonymity of individuals. Compared to previous approaches, Dividat enhances query execution performance by optimizing the use of anonymized index tables. Measurements showed that the query latency of naively built anonymized index tables can differ up to a factor of 5 from the optimal reachable latency. We proposed optimization strategies for index creation and query execution based on models that a-priori estimate the efficiency of ℓ-diversified index tables. The models were shown to accurately predict the efficiency of index tables. The proposed models can be used for index optimization but can also be seen as a starting point for an in-depth analysis to quantify the costs of database ℓ-diversification. While our measurements already gave an impression of the performance cost induced by ℓ-diversification of outsourced databases, a more generic analysis of the question "What is the cost that comes with database ℓ-diversification?" is a matter of future work.

References

1. De Capitani di Vimercati, S., Foresti, S., Samarati, P.: Managing and accessing data in the cloud: Privacy risks and approaches.: In Proceedings of the 7th International Conference on Risk and Security of Internet and Systems (CRiSIS), pp. 1–9 (2012)
2. Machanavajjhala, A., Kifer, D., Gehrke, J., Venkitasubramaniam, M.: L-diversity: Privacy beyond k-anonymity. ACM Trans. Knowl. Discov. Data (TKDD) **1**, 3 (2007)
3. Nergiz, A.E., Clifton, C.: Query processing in private data outsourcing using anonymization. In: Li, Y. (ed.) DBSec. LNCS, vol. 6818, pp. 138–153. Springer, Heidelberg (2011)
4. Nergiz, A.E., Clifton, C., Malluhi, Q.M.: Updating outsourced anatomized private databases. In: Proceedings of the International Conference on Extending Database Technology (EDBT), pp. 179–190 (2013)
5. De Capitani di Vimercati, S., Foresti, S., Jajodia, S., Livraga, G., Paraboschi, S., Samarati, P.: Extending loose associations to multiple fragments. In: Wang, L., Shafiq, B. (eds.) DBSec 2013. LNCS, vol. 7964, pp. 1–16. Springer, Heidelberg (2013)
6. Fung, B.C.M., Wang, K., Chen, R., Yu, P.S.: Privacy-preserving data publishing: A survey of recent developments. ACM Comput. Surv. (CSUR) **42**, 14:1–14:53 (2010)
7. Sweeney, L.: k-anonymity: a model for protecting privacy. Intl. J. Uncertainty Fuzziness Knowl. Based Syst. **10**(05), 557–570 (2002)
8. Bayardo, R., Agrawal, R.: Data privacy through optimal k-anonymization. In: Proceedings of the IEEE 21th International Conference on Data Engineering (ICDE), pp. 217–228 (2005)
9. Zhang, Q., Koudas, N., Srivastava, D., Yu, T.: Aggregate query answering on anonymized tables. In: Proceedings of the IEEE 23th International Conference on Data Engineering (ICDE), pp. 116–125 (2007)
10. Gedik, B., Liu, L.: Location privacy in mobile systems: A personalized anonymization model. In: Proceedings of the 25th IEEE International Conference on Distributed Computing Systems (ICDCS), pp. 620–629 (2005)
11. Kikuchi, H., Basu, A., Vaidya, J.: Perturbation based privacy preserving slope one predictors for collaborative filtering. In: Dimitrakos, T., Moona, R., Patel, D., McKnight, D.H. (eds.) IFIPTM 2012. IFIP AICT, vol. 374, pp. 17–35. Springer, Heidelberg (2012)

12. Popa, R.A., Redfield, C., Zeldovich, N., Balakrishnan, H.: Cryptdb: Protecting confidentiality with encrypted query processing. In: Proceedings of the 23rd ACM Symposium on Operating Systems Principles (SOSP), pp. 85–100 (2011)
13. Hacigumus, H., Iyer, B., Li, C., Mehrotra, S.: Executing SQL over encrypted data in the database-service-provider model. In: Proceedings of SIGMOD (2002)
14. Damiani, E., De Capitani di Vimercati, S., Jajodia, S., Paraboschi, S., Samarati, P.: Balancing confidentiality and efficiency in untrusted relational DBMSs. In: Proceedings of CCS (2003)
15. De Capitani di Vimercati, S., Foresti, S., Jajodia, S., Paraboschi, S., Samarati, P.: On information leakage by indexes over data fragments. In: Proceedings of the 1st International Workshop on Privacy-Preserving Data Publication and Analysis (PrivDB) (2013)
16. Ciriani, V., De Capitani di Vimercati, S., Foresti, S., Jajodia, S., Paraboschi, S., Samarati, P.: Combining fragmentation and encryption to protect privacy in data storage. ACM Trans. Inf. Sys. Secur. (TISSEC) **13**, 22:1–22:33 (2010)
17. Aggarwal, G., Bawa, M., Ganesan, P., Garcia-Molina, H., Kenthapadi, K., Motwani, R., Srivastava, U., Thomas, D., Xu, Y.: Two can keep a secret: A distributed architecture for secure database services. In: Proceedings of CIDR (2005)
18. Jünemann, K., Köhler, J., Hartenstein, H.: Data outsourcing simplified: Generating data connectors from confidentiality and access policies. In: Proceedings of the Workshop on Data-intensive Process Management in Large-Scale Sensor Systems (CCGrid-DPMSS) (2012)
19. Ceselli, A., Damiani, E., De Capitani di Vimercati, S., Jajodia, S., Paraboschi, S., Samarati, P.: Modeling and assessing inference exposure in encrypted databases. ACM Trans. Inform. Sys. Secur. (TISSEC) **8**, 119–152 (2005)
20. He, Y., Barman, S., Naughton, J.: Preventing equivalence attacks in updated, anonymized data. In: Proceedings of the IEEE 27th International Conference on Data Engineering (ICDE), pp. 529–540 (2011)
21. Fung, B.C.M., Wang, K., Fu, A.W.-C., Pei, J.: Anonymity for continuous data publishing. In: Proceedings of the International Conference on Extending Database Technology (EDBT), pp. 264–275 (2008)
22. Xiao, X., Tao, Y.: M-invariance: towards privacy preserving re-publication of dynamic datasets. In: Proceedings of the ACM International Conference on Management of Data (SIGMOD), pp. 689–700 (2007)
23. Zhou, B., Han, Y., Pei, J., Jiang, B., Tao, Y., Jia, Y.: Continuous privacy preserving publishing of data streams. In: Proceedings of the International Conference on Extending Database Technology (EDBT), pp. 648–659 (2009)
24. Ioannidis, Y.E.: Query optimization. ACM Comput. Surv. (CSUR) **28**(1), 121–123 (1996)
25. Chaudhuri, S.: An overview of query optimization in relational systems. In: Proceedings of the 17th ACM Symposium on Principles of Database Systems (PODS), pp. 34–43 (1998)
26. Haas, P.J., Ilyas, I.F., Lohman, G.M., Markl, V.: Discovering and exploiting statistical properties for query optimization in relational databases: a survey. Stat. Anal. Data Min. **1**(4), 223–250 (2009)
27. Goldstein, J., Larson, P.-A.: Optimizing queries using materialized views: a practical, scalable solution. In: Proceedings of the ACM International Conference on Management of Data (SIGMOD), pp. 331-342 (2001)
28. Chaudhuri, S., Krishnamurthy, R., Potamianos, S., Shim, K.: Optimizing queries with materialized views. In: Proceedings of the 11th International conference on Data Engineering, pp. 190–200 (1995)

29. Hellerstein, J.M., Stonebraker, M.: Predicate migration: Optimizing querieswith expensive predicates. In: Proceedings of the 1993 ACM International Conference on Managementof Data (SIGMOD), pp. 267–276 (1993)
30. http://dsn.tm.kit.edu/english/dividat.php
31. Jain, R.: The Art of Computer System Performance Analysis: Techniques for Experimental Design, Measurement, Simulation and Modeling. John Wiley, New York (1991)

Privacy-Preserving Loyalty Programs

Alberto Blanco-Justicia and Josep Domingo-Ferrer[⊠]

Department of Computer Engineering and Mathematics, Universitat Rovira i Virgili,
Av. Països Catalans 26, 43007 Tarragona, Catalonia, Spain
{alberto.blanco,josep.domingo}@urv.cat

Abstract. Loyalty programs are promoted by vendors to incentivize loyalty in buyers. Although such programs have become widespread, they have been criticized by business experts and consumer associations: loyalty results in profiling and hence in loss of privacy of consumers. We propose a protocol for privacy-preserving loyalty programs that allows vendors and consumers to enjoy the benefits of loyalty (returning customers and discounts, respectively), while allowing consumers to stay anonymous and empowering them to decide how much of their profile they reveal to the vendor. The vendor must offer additional reward if he wants to learn more details on the consumer's profile. Our protocol is based on partially blind signatures and generalization techniques, and provides anonymity to consumers and their purchases, while still allowing negotiated consumer profiling.

Keywords: Loyalty programs · Customer privacy · Anonymization · Blind signatures · E-cash

1 Introduction

Loyalty programs are marketing efforts implemented by vendors, especially retailers, that are aimed at establishing a lasting relationship with consumers. In a loyalty program, the vendor pursues two main goals: (i) to encourage the consumer to make more purchases in the future (returning customer); (ii) to allow the vendor to profile the consumer in view of conducting market research and segmentation (profiled customer). In order to lure consumers into a loyalty program, the vendor offers them rewards, typically loyalty points that consumers can later exchange for discounts, gifts or other benefits offered by the vendor. Normally, enrollment to loyalty programs involves some kind of registration procedure, in which customers fill out a form with their personal information and are granted a loyalty card, be it a physical card (magnetic stripe or smartcard) or a smartphone application.

Market analysis and client segmentation are carried out by building profiles of individual customers based on their personal information, which customers supply to the vendor during enrollment to the loyalty program, and their purchase records, collected every time customers present their loyalty cards. The profiles thus assembled are used in marketing actions, such as market studies and targeted advertising.

© Springer International Publishing Switzerland 2015
J. Garcia-Alfaro et al. (Eds.): DPM/SETOP/QASA 2014, LNCS 8872, pp. 133–146, 2015.
DOI: 10.1007/978-3-319-17016-9_9

Although loyalty programs have become widespread, they are experiencing a loss of active participants and they have been criticized by business experts and consumer associations. Criticism is mainly due to privacy issues, because it is not always clear whether the benefits vendors offer in their loyalty programs are worth the loss of consumer privacy caused by profiling [6,8,14,16].

Loyalty programs can offer clear advantages to both vendors and consumers, like returning customers and special discounts, respectively. However, privacy concerns regarding buyer profiling affect more and more the acceptance of such programs, as the public awareness on the dangers of personal information disclosure is increasing.

1.1   Contribution and Plan of This Paper

In this work we propose a protocol for privacy-preserving loyalty programs that allows vendors and consumers to enjoy the benefits of loyalty, while preserving the anonymity of consumers and empowering them to decide how accurately they reveal their profile to the vendor. In order to encourage customers not just to return but also to disclose more of their profile, the vendor must offer additional rewards to consumers. Thus, vendors *pay* consumers for their private information. On the other hand, consumers become aware of how much their personal data are worth to vendors, and they can decide to what extent they are ready to reveal such data in exchange for what benefits.

To empower consumers as described above, we provide them with a mechanism that allows them to profile themselves, generalize their profiles and submit these generalized profiles to the vendor in an anonymous way. There are some technical challenges to be overcome:

- The proposed mechanism should prevent vendors from linking the generalized profiles to the identity of buyers, to particular transactions or to particular loyalty points submitted for redemption.
- To prevent straightforward profiling by the vendor, payment should be anonymous. In online stores, to completely achieve anonymity, the buyers should use some kind of anonymous payment system, such as Bitcoin [12], Zerocoin [11], some other form of electronic cash [5], or simply scratch cards with prepaid credit anonymously bought, say, at a newsstand. In physical stores, it would be enough to pay with cash.
- Consumers should not be able to leverage their anonymity to reveal forged profiles to the vendor, which would earn them rewards without actually revealing anything on their real purchase pattern.

Our proposed mechanism, thus, needs to take care of the two main aspects of loyalty programs. First, it has to provide a way to obtain and submit loyalty points in an anonymous and unlinkable way; that is, a customer should be able to submit a particular loyalty point to a vendor, but the vendor should not be able to link that particular loyalty point to the transaction in which it was issued. Second, our mechanism must allow customers to build their own generalized profiles from their purchase history, but it must prevent customers to forge false profiles and vendors to link the generalized profiles to particular customers. We will show later that these two aspects can be tackled in a similar way.

The paper is organized as follows. Sect. 2 describes a traditional loyalty program and presents the requirements and security properties our new protocol should satisfy. In Sect. 3 we introduce a cryptographic protocol based on partially blind signatures that is the basis of our proposed solution. Sect. 4 discusses a generalization strategy that our protocol will follow. In Sect. 5 we present our privacy-preserving loyalty program protocol. In Sect. 6 we analyze the performance of the system in terms of computation and communication complexity. Finally, Sect. 7 summarizes our conclusions and plans for future work.

2   Loyalty Programs

Our method aims to offer all the functionalities of loyalty programs; that is, to allow vendors to reward returning customers with loyalty points and profile returning customers based on their purchase histories. The novelty is that our scheme empowers customers with the ability to decide how accurately they disclose their purchase histories to vendors.

A simple and perhaps the most widespread approach to implement a loyalty program is to have a centralized server, owned and operated by some vendor $\mathcal{V}$, that stores the information on the program participants. This information includes all the personal data the participants gave to the vendor when they enrolled to the program, their balance of loyalty points, and their history of purchases. Each customer is given a loyalty card which contains the identifier of her record in the server's database. Each time a customer buys at a store and presents her loyalty card, her record in the server is updated, by adding to it the items she bought and modifying her balance of loyalty points if needed. In this way, all transactions by each customer can be linked to each other using the customer's identifier. Even if the customer provided false information when she enrolled to the loyalty program, all of her transactions would be linked anyway. Hence, discovering the customer's identity in one individual transaction (*e.g.* through the credit or debit card used for payment) would allow linking her entire profile to her real identity.

If control over profiling and purchase histories is to be left to customers, a centralized approach does not seem a good solution. Moreover, we should also ensure that individual transactions cannot be linked to each other unless desired by the customer. To do so, we will let each customer manage locally and anonymously her own balance of loyalty points and history of purchases.

2.1   A Privacy-Preserving Alternative

Our proposed mechanism follows the decentralized approach. To allow local management of loyalty points and purchase receipts by the customer, we treat points and receipts as anonymous electronic cash that is issued by vendors and which can only be redeemed at the vendor who issued it. Moreover, the concrete implementation of the loyalty program should discourage customers from transferring loyalty points and purchase receipts among them. Purchase histories will be built by the vendor from the individual purchase receipts of all products purchased by each customer *that the customer allows the vendor to link together*; furthermore, the customer can decide how generalized/coarsened are the product descriptions in the purchase receipts she allows the vendor to link to one another.

Our proposed loyalty program protocol suite consists of the following procedures:

- SETUP. Algorithm run by some designated entity, which, on input a security parameter, outputs the parameters of the system. These parameters can be common to several vendors.
- VENDORSETUP. Protocol run by a vendor V in which the specific loyalty program is set up. Also, V obtains the public parameters of the system and a key pair.
- ENROLL. Protocol run by some customer C whereby C is given access to the loyalty program and the means to participate in it, typically a loyalty card or a smartphone application.
- USE. Interactive protocol run between some V and C, in which C inputs the name of a product she wants to buy and obtains a purchase receipt which proves that C has purchased the product from V.
- SUBMIT. Interactive protocol run between some V and C, in which C submits a list of possibly generalized purchase receipts to V, in order to get loyalty points.
- ISSUE. Interactive protocol run between some V and C, in which C obtains a certain amount of loyalty points.
- REDEEM. Interactive protocol run between some V and C, in which C submits a certain amount of loyalty points to V to obtain some benefits.

2.2 Desirable Properties

We can state the following requirements for loyalty points and purchase receipts:

- **Correctness.** Loyalty points issued by a V to a C following the ISSUE protocol are accepted by the same V running the REDEEM protocol. Similarly, purchase receipts given by V to some C during the USE protocol will be accepted by the same V in the SUBMIT protocol, even if they have been generalized.
- **Unforgeability.** It should be impossible to any malicious customer or any coalition of malicious customers and vendors to forge new loyalty points or receipts issued by a vendor V, regardless of how many original loyalty points or receipts they own from V.
- **Anonymity.** Loyalty points and purchase receipts should be granted in an anonymous way. A vendor should be unable to learn anything about a customer redeeming points or submitting receipts, other than the customer legitimately owns them. This should hold even if the vendor colludes with other vendors or customers.

- **Controlled linkability.** A customer $\mathcal{C}$ should be able to decide whether a submitted purchase receipt can be linked to other purchase receipts submitted by $\mathcal{C}$ to the same vendor $\mathcal{V}$.

3 Anonymous Tokens with Controlled Linkability

As stated in the previous section, loyalty points and purchase receipts have requirements in line with those of anonymous electronic cash and anonymous electronic credentials. These well-known technologies use blind signatures and/or zero-knowledge proofs of knowledge [2,3,5,13]. We will treat points and receipts using a construction that we call anonymous tokens with controlled linkability. These tokens will be realized by using partially blind signatures with some additional features.

3.1 Partially Blind Signatures

Blind signature protocols are interactive protocols between a requester and a signer, in which the signer produces a digital signature of a message submitted by the requester, but does not learn anything about the message content. This primitive was introduced by Chaum in [4] and has since been used in a vast array of privacy related protocols, such as e-cash, electronic voting and anonymous credential systems. An inherent drawback of blind signature protocols is that the signer cannot enforce a certain format on the message. Traditionally, this problem has been solved using *cut-and-choose* techniques, in which the requester of a signature generates and blinds a number n of messages, the signer asks the requester to unblind all messages but a randomly chosen one, checks whether all unblinded messages conform to the required format and, if yes, signs the only message that remains blinded. Using *cut-and-choose* techniques solves the problem (the probability that the requester succeeds in getting a non-conformant message signed is upper-bounded by $1/n$), but it does so at the cost of high computation and communication overheads.

Partially blind signatures were introduced by Abe in [1] as an alternative to *cut-and-choose* protocols. In a partially blind signature protocol, the requester and the signer agree on a public information that is to be included in the signed message, the signer can be sure that such information is really included, and the requester can be sure that the signed message remains blinded to the signer.

We use a partially blind signature scheme from bilinear pairings presented in [17]. This scheme satisfies the requirements of completeness, partial blindness and unforgeability against one-more forgery under chosen message attacks, and thus it is considered secure. Security proofs can be found in the original paper. Additionally, this scheme produces short signatures, it is computationally efficient and allows aggregate verification of signed messages bearing the same agreed public information.

3.2 Controlled Linkability of Tokens

The use of partially blind signatures will ensure that a submitted token cannot be linked to an issued token, nor to the customer to whom it was issued. However, if vendors are to be allowed to build customer profiles from anonymous purchase receipts, there must be a mechanism whereby, if allowed by the customer, the vendor can verify that several submitted purchase receipt tokens really correspond to the same (anonymous) customer, even if receipts have been generalized by the customer prior to submission. Note that if all (ungeneralized) purchase receipts from the same customer could be linked, customer anonymity would be problematic in spite of partially blind signatures: a very long and detailed profile is likely to be unique and goes a long way towards leaking the customer's identity.

Thus, we propose a mechanism that allows customers to decide which purchase receipt tokens can be linked together, by employing an additional identifier as part of the secret message in the partially blind signature. This identifier is chosen by the customer for each receipt token at the moment of token issuance. If a customer picks a fresh random number for each issued purchase receipt, then none of this customer's receipts will be linkable to each other; however, if the customer uses the same identifier for a group of purchase receipt tokens at the time of token issuance, then all of the tokens in this group can be verifiably linked together by the vendor after they are submitted.

3.3 Description

Anonymous tokens with controlled linkability are operated in four phases:

- In the *setup* phase, a certification agency generates the public parameters of the partially blind signature scheme.
- In the *key generation* phase, users (*i.e.* vendors and customers) get their key pairs from the certification agency.
- In the *issuance* phase, a token corresponding to some loyalty points or to a purchase receipt is generated by a customer, it is signed in a partially blind way by a vendor and it is returned to the customer.
- Finally, in the *verification* phase, a customer submits previously generated tokens to a vendor, who in turn verifies that each token was correctly signed. If tokens correspond to purchase receipts, the vendor may verify whether the submitted tokens are linked with each other and/or with previously submitted tokens.

Setup. This algorithm is executed once by a certification authority to set up the system parameters. It takes as input a security parameter λ. The algorithm chooses bilinear groups $(\mathbb{G}_1, \mathbb{G}_T)$ of order $q > 2^\lambda$, an efficiently computable bilinear map $e : \mathbb{G}_1 \times \mathbb{G}_1 \to \mathbb{G}_T$, a generator $g \in \mathbb{G}_1$ and collision-resistant hash functions $H : \{0,1\}^* \to \mathbb{Z}_q^*$ and $H_0 : \{0,1\}^* \to \mathbb{G}_1$. The public parameters are $\mathsf{pms} = \{\mathbb{G}_1, \mathbb{G}_T, e, q, \lambda, g, H, H_0\}$.

Key Generation. A vendor gets a secret key $sk_{\mathcal{V}} = x \in_R \mathbb{Z}_q^*$ and a public key $pk_{\mathcal{V}} = g^x$, and publishes his public key.

Token Issuance. A customer wants to obtain from a vendor a token with an agreed public information c (this information may specify a number of loyalty points or a purchase receipt for a certain product). This is an interactive protocol which produces a partially blind signature on public information c, and a secret message containing a unique identifier α of the token and a (possibly) unique identifier y. The protocol is depicted in Fig. 1 and described next:

1. The customer chooses a value for y, either from a list of previously used values or by generating a new one uniformly at random from $\mathbb{Z}_q^*$.
2. The customer and the vendor agree on a public string $c \in \{0,1\}^*$.
3. The customer chooses random $\alpha, r \in_R \mathbb{Z}_q^*$ and builds the message $m = (\alpha, y)$. Then, the customer blinds the message by computing $u = H_0(c\|m)^r$ and sends u to the vendor.
4. The vendor signs the blinded message by computing $v = u^{(H(c)+sk_{\mathcal{V}})^{-1}}$ and sends it back to the customer.
5. The customer unblinds the signature by computing $\sigma = v^{r^{-1}}$. The resulting tuple $T = \langle c, m, \sigma \rangle$ is the token.

An execution of this protocol, between a vendor $\mathcal{V}$ and a customer $\mathcal{C}$, is denoted by $T = \langle c, m, \sigma \rangle = \mathsf{Issuance}(\mathcal{V}, \mathcal{C}, c, y)$.

Customer		**Vendor**
$y \in \mathbb{Z}_q^*$		$sk_{\mathcal{V}}$
	$\xleftarrow{\quad c \in \{0,1\}^* \quad}$	
$\alpha, r \in_R \mathbb{Z}_q^*$		
$m = (\alpha, y)$		
$u = H_0(c\|m)^r$	$\xrightarrow{\quad u \quad}$	
	$\xleftarrow{\quad v \quad}$	$v = u^{(H(c)+sk_{\mathcal{V}})^{-1}}$
$\sigma = v^{r^{-1}}$		
$T = \langle c, m, \sigma \rangle$		

Fig. 1. Token issuance protocol

Token Verification. The submission and verification of a token is an interactive protocol between a customer and a vendor. The customer submits the token $T = \langle c, m, \sigma \rangle$ and the vendor returns `accept` or `reject` as a result of the verification. Informally, the vendor checks that the signature on the token is valid and has been produced by himself; then, if the value y contained in the message matches the one of a previously submitted token, the tokens are grouped. The protocol is outlined in Fig. 2 and described next:

1. The customer sends $T = \langle c, m, \sigma \rangle$ to the vendor.
2. The customer parses the message m as (α, y).
3. The vendor verifies the signature by checking the equality

$$e(g^{H(c)} \cdot pk_{\mathcal{V}}, \sigma) \stackrel{?}{=} e(g, H_0(c||m)).$$

If the above equality holds, check whether the token has already been spent (verify whether a token with the same α has previously been submitted). If the verification was successful and the token has not been spent yet, mark it as spent and send an accept message to the customer. Otherwise, send a reject message to the customer.
4. Finally, the vendor checks whether the identifier value y is the same as the one in a previously spent token. If yes, link the new token with that previous one.

An execution of this protocol involving a customer $\mathcal{C}$, a vendor $\mathcal{V}$ and a token T is denoted as $\mathsf{accept/reject} = \mathsf{Verification}(\mathcal{V}, \mathcal{C}, T)$.

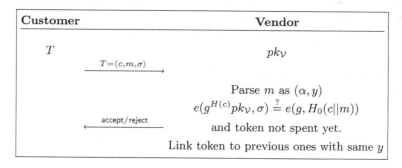

Fig. 2. Verification protocol

Aggregate Verification. This protocol allows the customer to aggregate signatures of messages bearing the same public information by just multiplying the resulting signatures. If there is a list of tokens $\{T_1, \ldots, T_n\}$, where $T_i = \langle c_i, m_i, \sigma_i \rangle$, and $c_i = c$ for $1 \leq i \leq n$, a customer can aggregate the partially blind signatures by computing $\sigma_{agg} = \prod_{i=1}^{n} \sigma_i$ and submitting $T_{agg} = \langle c, \{m_1, \cdots, m_n\}, \sigma_{agg} \rangle$. The vendor can then verify the validity of the aggregated token by checking the equality

$$e(g^{H(c)} \cdot pk, \sigma_{agg}) \stackrel{?}{=} e(g, \prod H_0(c||m_i)).$$

3.4   Security Analysis

The desirable security features that were described in Sect. 2.2 are satisfied by the above protocol suite, as argued below.

- **Correctness.** If the partially blind signature scheme is correctly computed, the verification equation will pass, because

$$e(g^{H(c)} \cdot pk, \sigma) = e(g^{H(c)+x}, \sigma)$$
$$= e(g^{H(c)+x}, v^{r^{-1}})$$
$$= e(g^{H(c)+x}, u^{(H(c)+x)^{-1} \cdot r^{-1}})$$
$$= e(g^{H(c)+x}, H_0(c||m)^{r \cdot r^{-1} \cdot (H(c)+x)^{-1}})$$
$$= e(g, H_0(c||m)^{r \cdot r^{-1} \cdot (H(c)+x) \cdot (H(c)+x)^{-1}})$$
$$= e(g, H_0(c||m)).$$

- **Unforgeability.** Unforgeability is provided by the partially blind signature scheme. The security proofs can be found in the original work in [17].
- **Anonymity.** No information on the user is obtained by a server during the protocol. Submitted tokens cannot be linked to issued tokens or to the identity of a requester or prover because of the *partial blindness* property of the signature scheme.
- **Controlled linkability.** When a token is issued, the identifying value y is only known to the customer who generated the token, due to the *partial blindness* of the signature. Hence, if two verified tokens contain the same identifying value y, there are two possibilities: (i) both tokens were generated by the same customer, who re-used y to allow the vendor to link them; (ii) the customer who generated one token leaked y to the customer who generated the other token. If the latter leakage is prevented by technical means or discouraged with appropriate incentives (see discussion in Sect. 5.8 below), then two tokens containing the same y can be linked by the vendor as corresponding to the same customer.

4   Generalization of Purchase Histories

To implement our protocol, a vendor must use a publicly available taxonomy for the products he offers. This taxonomy $\mathcal{T}$ is modeled as a tree, being its root node a generic identifier such as *Product*, and each leaf a specific product in the set of products $P = \{p_1, \ldots, p_n\}$ on sale. The inner nodes of the tree are the subsequent categories to which the products belong: the closer to the leaf nodes, the more specific categories are. A generalization function $g : \mathcal{T} \rightarrow \mathcal{T}$ returns the parent of a node. Applying the generalization function m times will be denoted as g^m. As an example, for the product $p_i = Inception$, its generalizations might be $g(p_i) = ActionMovie$, $g^2(p_i) = Movie$, $g^3(p_i) = DigitalMedia$ and $g^4(p_i) = Product$. For simplicity and ease of implementation, it is desirable that all leaves be at the same depth, that is, that the path from the root to any leaf be of the same length.

Customers in our loyalty program protocol will receive a list of anonymous tokens, each issued as described in the previous section, for every product they purchase. This list contains a receipt for the specific product and receipts for all of its generalizations in the path up to the root of the taxonomy (generalization path). When a customer decides to submit her purchase history, she chooses the level of generalization she wants for each purchase. Then the customer sends for each purchase the tokens in the purchase generalization path from the chosen generalization level up to the root of the taxonomy. Following the movie example above, a customer who wants to submit her purchase generalized to level 2 will submit the tokens *Movie*, *DigitalMedia* and *Product*. Forcing customers to send all tokens from the selected generalization level to the root prevents them from using tokens in the generalization path of a purchase to falsely claim other purchases.

5   Privacy-Preserving Loyalty Program Construction

Our proposed solution for privacy-preserving loyalty programs builds on the anonymous tokens with controlled linkability we described in Sect. 3 and the generalization of purchase histories described in Sect. 4. As introduced in Sect. 2, our construction consists of the following protocols: SETUP, VENDORSETUP, ENROLL, USE, SUBMIT, ISSUE and REDEEM.

5.1   Setup

The setup phase is run by a certification authority to generate the public parameters pms of the anonymous token with controlled linkability construction described in Sect. 3. The system parameters are made public to every $\mathcal{V}$ offering loyalty programs and to every $\mathcal{C}$ intending to participate in them.

5.2   VendorSetup

Each vendor $\mathcal{V}$ publishes a product taxonomy $\mathcal{T_V}$ as described in Sect. 4. Then, $\mathcal{V}$ obtains a key pair built as described in the key generation procedure in Sect. 3. Finally, $\mathcal{V}$ publishes his public key.

5.3   Enroll

Customers obtain the public parameters of the system and some means to communicate with the system, namely a smartcard or a smartphone application. Furthermore, customers enrolling to a loyalty program from a particular vendor obtain the vendor's public key and his taxonomy of products. This step is not mandatory, but it allows customers to check that tokens issued by vendors are valid and purchase receipt generalizations are correct.

5.4   Use

A customer $\mathcal{C}$ in a loyalty program offered by a vendor $\mathcal{V}$ purchases a product, either at a physical or online store of $\mathcal{V}$. Note that, in the case of an online store, $\mathcal{C}$ should use additional anonymization measures, such as anonymous Internet surfing, offered for example by Tor networks [15], anonymous shipping methods [9], and anonymous payment methods (*e.g.* [5,11,12] or simply prepaid scratch cards). The protocol is as follows:

1. C sends to V the name p_i of the product C wants to buy.
2. C chooses a value y to be used in the token issuance protocol, depending on her privacy preferences: if she wants the new purchase receipt to be linkable to previously obtained purchase receipts (linkability is incentivized as described in Sect. 5.8 below), she will re-use the same y that was used in those previous receipts; if she does not want this new purchase receipts to be linkable to previous receipts, she will pick a new random $y \in \mathbb{Z}_q^*$.
3. In order to produce purchase receipt tokens for product p_i and all its generalizations, V and C run the interactive protocol Issuance(V, P, p_i, y), Issuance($V, P, g(p_i), y$), Issuance($V, P, g^2(p_i), y$), etc. up to the root of the taxonomy. In this way, C obtains as many purchase receipt tokens as the depth of p_i in V's taxonomy.

5.5   Submit

At any moment, a customer can submit a list of purchase receipts (or a generalized version of them) to the vendor and obtain loyalty points. To this end, for each purchased product in her claimed purchase history, the customer sends the receipt token corresponding the level of generalization she wishes. Additionally, for each product, she also submits all tokens from the selected generalization level up to the root of the taxonomy (to make sure tokens in the generalization path cannot be later used as independent purchase receipts). The submission of each token T_i is performed according to the Verification(V, P, T_i) protocol described in Sect. 3.3.

5.6   Issue

To issue loyalty points, the vendor builds a message info that encodes an identifier of the vendor, the number of points this token is worth and an expiration date. Unlike for purchase receipts, the vendor has no legitimate interest in linking several tokens containing loyalty points; hence, the customer picks a fresh random y for each new loyalty points token she claims. Then the vendor and the customer run the interactive protocol Issuance($V, P, $info$, y$). The generated token contains the loyalty points issued to the customer.

To ensure that a loyalty points token submitted for redemption cannot be linked with an issued loyalty points token, the number of loyalty points associated to a single token should be limited to a small set of possible values, similar to the limited denominations of bank notes. There is an efficiency toll to be paid for this caution, as issuing a certain amount of loyalty points can require running the Issuance protocol several times (several tokens may be needed to reach the required amount).

5.7   Redeem

A participant C who wants to redeem a loyalty points token T previously earned at a vendor V's in exchange for some benefits runs the interactive protocol Verification(V, P, T).

It is possible to simultaneously redeem several loyalty points tokens by using the aggregation of signatures described in Sect. 3.3.

5.8   Incentives Related to Purchase Receipts Submission

Vendors can establish strategies to incentivize or discourage certain customer behaviors:

- To encourage customers to use little or no purchase receipt generalization (and hence to renounce some of their privacy), the amount of loyalty points awarded per receipt token should depend on the chosen level of generalization: more loyalty points awarded to less generalized purchase receipts.
- If the customer submits unlinkable receipts, she should just get enough loyalty points to reward her as a returning customer. To encourage customers to allow linkage of purchase receipt tokens by the vendor (and hence customer profiling), a customer should get more loyalty points if she submits $n_1 + n_2$ tokens with the same y value than if she submits n_1 tokens with one y value and then n_2 tokens with a different y value (*superlinear reward*). Furthermore, the vendor may require that the list of linkable receipt tokens for which reward is claimed correspond to purchases made within a certain time window (if linking purchases very distant in time is uninteresting for profiling).
- Two or more customers might be tempted to share their y values in order to submit a longer list of linkable receipts and thereafter share the superlinear number of loyalty points they would earn. As long the reward is only *slightly* superlinear, customer collusion is discouraged if the customer C who submits the list of linkable tokens is required by V to actually show all the actual linkable tokens (and not just a reference to them): colluders different from C may not like to pay the privacy toll of disclosing their purchase receipts to C.

6   Performance Analysis

We count here the number of operations required by the Issuance and Verification protocols described in Sect. 3.

The Issuance protocol requires the computation by the vendor of 1 exponentiation in G_1; also, 1 hash, 1 addition and 1 inversion in $\mathbb{Z}_q^*$. The customer computes 2 exponentiations in G_1 and 1 inversion in $\mathbb{Z}_q^*$. The Verification protocol requires the computation by the vendor of 1 exponentiation, 1 multiplication and 1 hash in G_1; also, 1 hash in $\mathbb{Z}_q^*$ and 2 pairings.

We used the jPBC library [7] to test times to compute each of the operations. We generated a symmetric pairing constructed on the curve $y^2 = x^3 + x$ with characteristic a 512-bit prime and embedding degree 2, *i.e.*, the Type A pairings suggested in [10]. The order of $\mathbb{G}_1$ over the curve is a prime of 160 bits, elements in $\mathbb{G}_1$ are 512 bits long and elements in $\mathbb{Z}_q^*$ 160 bits long.

With the above technology choices, a multiplication of points in $\mathbb{G}_1$ takes $0.09\,\mathrm{ms}$, an exponentiation in $\mathbb{G}_1$ takes $17.2\,\mathrm{ms}$, an exponentiation in $\mathbb{G}_1$ (with precomputation) takes $2.48\,\mathrm{ms}$, a pairing takes $20.8\,\mathrm{ms}$, and a pairing (with precomputation) takes $10.76\,\mathrm{ms}$.

7   Conclusions and Future Work

In our privacy-preserving alternative to traditional loyalty programs, the customers are granted the power to decide what private information they want to disclose, and how precise that information is. We have described a privacy-preserving protocol suite that still offers the two main features of loyalty programs: reward returning customers and make customer profiling possible.

Future research will involve hiding the y values to technically deter customer collusions in purchase receipt submission. Also, in the context of a Google Faculty Research Award that partially funds this work, we plan to implement our solution using smartphones on the customer's side and test a demonstrator to show its practical feasibility.

Acknowledgments. We thank Dr Qiang Tang for useful discussions on an earlier version of this paper. The following funding sources are acknowledged: Google (Faculty Research Award to the second author), Government of Catalonia (ICREA Acadèmia Prize to the second author and grant 2014 SGR 537), Spanish Government (project TIN2011-27076-C03-01 "CO-PRIVACY"), European Commission (FP7 projects "DwB" and "Inter-Trust") and Templeton World Charity Foundation (grant TWCF0095/AB60 "Co-Utility"). The authors are with the UNESCO Chair in Data Privacy. The views in this paper are the authors' own and do not necessarily reflect the views of Google, UNESCO or the Templeton World Charity Foundation.

References

1. Abe, M., Fujisaki, E.: How to date blind signatures. In: Kim, Kee-cheon, Matsumoto, Tsutomu (eds.) ASIACRYPT 1996. LNCS, vol. 1163, pp. 244–251. Springer, Heidelberg (1996)
2. Camenisch, J.L., Lysyanskaya, A.: An efficient system for non-transferable anonymous credentials with optional anonymity revocation. In: Pfitzmann, B. (ed.) EUROCRYPT 2001. LNCS, vol. 2045, pp. 93–118. Springer, Heidelberg (2001)
3. Camenisch, J.L., Lysyanskaya, A.: Signature schemes and anonymous credentials from bilinear maps. In: Franklin, M. (ed.) CRYPTO 2004. LNCS, vol. 3152, pp. 56–72. Springer, Heidelberg (2004)
4. Chaum, D.: Blind signatures for untraceable payments. In: Chaum, D., Rivest, R.L., Sherman, A.T. (eds.) Advances in Cryptology-CRYPTO 1982, pp. 199–203. Springer, Heidelberg (1983)
5. Chaum, D., Fiat, A., Naor, M.: Untraceable electronic cash. In: Goldwasser, S. (ed.) CRYPTO 1988. LNCS, vol. 403, pp. 319–327. Springer, Heidelberg (1990)

6. Consumers reveal privacy concerns with loyalty programs. Convenience Store Decisions (2014). www.csdecisions.com

7. De Caro, A., Iovino, V.: jPBC: Java pairing based cryptography. In: Proceedings of the 16th IEEE Symposium on Computers and Communications, pp. 850–855. IEEE (2011)

8. Dunn, C.: Loyalty programs and privacy issues: do you need to worry about providing personal information? Disney Family, 21 February 2015. family.go.com. Accessed

9. Johnson, R.C.: eDropship: methods and systems for anonymous eCommerce shipment, US Patent 7,853,481 (2010)

10. Lynn, B.: On the Implementation of Pairing-based Cryptosystems, Doctoral dissertation, Stanford University (2007)

11. Miers, I., Garman, C., Green, M., Rubin, A.D.: Zerocoin: anonymous distributed e-cash from Bitcoin. In: 2013 IEEE Symposium on Security and Privacy (SP), pp. 397–411. IEEE (2013)

12. Nakamoto, S.: Bitcoin: a peer-to-peer electronic cash system. Consulted, vol. 1, (2008). www.bitcoin.org/bitcoin.pdf

13. Neff, C.A.: A verifiable secret shuffle and its application to e-voting. In: Proceedings of the 8th ACM Conference on Computer and Communications Security, pp. 116–125. ACM, November 2001

14. Pratt, A.: Loyalty cards vs. privacy concerns, Infosec ISLAND (2011). www.infosecisland.com

15. Tor Project: Anonymity Online, 21 February 2015. www.torproject.org. Accessed

16. Tuttle, B.: A disloyalty movement? Supermarkets and customers drop loyalty card programs. TIME (2013). business.time.com

17. Zhang, F., Safavi-Naini, R., Susilo, W.: Efficient Verifiably Encrypted Signature and Partially Blind Signature from Bilinear Pairings. In: Johansson, T., Maitra, S. (eds.) INDOCRYPT 2003. LNCS, vol. 2904, pp. 191–204. Springer, Heidelberg (2003)

Secure Improved Cloud-Based RFID Authentication Protocol

Sarah Abughazalah$^{(\boxtimes)}$, Konstantinos Markantonakis, and Keith Mayes

Smart Card Centre-Information Security Group (SCC-ISG), Royal Holloway,
University of London, Egham, UK
{Sarah.AbuGhazalah.2012,K.Markantonakis,Keith.Mayes}@rhul.ac.uk

Abstract. Although Radio Frequency IDentification (RFID) systems promise a fruitful future, security and privacy concerns have affected the adoption of the RFID technology. Several studies have been proposed to tackle the RFID security and privacy concerns under the assumption that the server is secure. In this paper, we assume that the server resides in the cloud that might be insecure, thus the tag's data might be prone to privacy invasion and attacks. Xie et al. proposed a new scheme called "cloud-based RFID authentication", which aimed to address the security and privacy concerns of RFID tag's data in the cloud. In this paper, we showed that the Xie et al. protocol is vulnerable to reader impersonation attacks, location tracking and tag's data privacy invasion. Hence, we proposed a new protocol that guarantees that the tag's data in the cloud are anonymous, and cannot be compromised. Furthermore, the proposed protocol achieves mutual authentication between all the entities participating in a communication session, such as a cloud server, a reader and a tag. Finally, we analysed the proposed protocol informally, and formally using a privacy model and CasperFDR. The results indicate that the proposed protocol achieves data secrecy and authentication for RFID tags.

Keywords: RFID · Cloud server · Privacy · Security protocol · Privacy model · CasperFDR

1 Introduction

Radio Frequency IDentification (RFID) is a wireless technology that uses radio signals to identify tags attached to objects [1]. A typical RFID system is composed of three main components, namely a tag, a reader and a backend server. The reader broadcasts radio frequency (RF) signals to power, send and receive data from passive RFID tags without physical contact. The RFID tag is an identification device attached to an item that transmits stored information to the nearby reader(s) through the RF channel. The reader sends the tag's data to the backend server, which stores data about the RFID tags it manages [1].

There are increasing concerns around the security and privacy of the RFID systems [2]. Communication between the reader and tag is vulnerable to interception, modification, fabrication and replay attacks. Therefore, there are extensive

© Springer International Publishing Switzerland 2015
J. Garcia-Alfaro et al. (Eds.): DPM/SETOP/QASA 2014, LNCS 8872, pp. 147–164, 2015.
DOI: 10.1007/978-3-319-17016-9_10

studies attempting to achieve a mutual authentication between all the parties involved in an RFID communication session. Some of these studies can be found in [3–11].

In [11], the authors divided the proposed RFID mutual authentication studies into two approaches:

– Server-based RFID mutual authentication [3,4,6,7,9]: In this approach, the tag and reader depend on the backend server to be authenticated. When the reader receives a message from the tag, it forwards the tag's message to the server to be processed. The server stores secret data related to the tags. The researchers in this scheme assume that the server is secure, and their main focus is to secure the data transmission between the tags and the readers.
– Server-less RFID mutual authentication [5,8,10]: This approach takes into account an offline authentication, where the reader authenticates the tag offline without the need to contact the server. This is based on tag authentication credentials previously stored in the reader. For instance, the reader contacts the Certification Authority (CA) during the initialisation phase to retrieve a list of legitimate tags' data.

A new approach, where the RFID tags' data can be stored in a remote server residing in the cloud, has gained increasing attention. The tags' data stored in the cloud might be vulnerable to data breach and/or privacy invasion by a malicious attacker or internal employees. Therefore, while integrating RFID into the cloud, the security and privacy of the RFID tags must be considered.

To this end, the authors in [11] proposed a new scheme called "cloud-based RFID authentication". In this scheme, the authors aimed to address the security and privacy concerns of RFID tag's data in the cloud. Three entities participate in this scheme, namely a tag, a reader and a cloud server. This scheme is shown in Fig. 1. The reader is connected to the tag through a wireless channel, while the communication between the reader and the cloud server uses a Virtual Private Network (VPN). The authors assumed that the tag's and reader's data are stored in an encrypted hash table in an untrusted cloud server. The authors proposed an RFID authentication protocol that preserves the reader's and tag's privacy against an untrusted cloud server. Improvements to this study will be the focus of this paper. The protocol details can be found in Sect. 2.

Fig. 1. The cloud-based RFID authentication approach

The authors in [11] claimed that their proposed protocol resists reader impersonation attacks as only the legitimate reader can compute the authentication messages. Furthermore, they also claimed that their protocol preserves privacy by hashing the tag's data with a random number, which provides communications with confidentiality and freshness.

In this paper, we examined the cloud-based RFID authentication protocol [11], and we discovered the following:

1. An attacker is able to impersonate the reader without compromising the secret data shared with the tag, thus causing the tag to be updated with the wrong values and permit tracking the tag's location.
2. By using a privacy model, we found that the attacker can confirm that two sessions are related to the same tag, thus allowing unauthorised tracking.
3. By using CasperFDR, we found that the tag's secret data is not protected as the attacker can perform man-in-the-middle attacks and obtain the secret data at the end of the protocol session.

Hence, we propose a new protocol that uses some of the notations in [11] while utilising new notions that improve the cloud-based RFID authentication protocol. We called our protocol "improved cloud-based RFID authentication".

The rest of this paper is organised as follows: in Sect. 2, we demonstrate the cloud-based RFID authentication protocol. In Sect. 3, we discuss the detailed attacks on the cloud-based RFID authentication protocol. In Sect. 4, we show the improved cloud-based RFID authentication protocol in detail. In Sect. 5, we analyse the proposed protocol with respect to informal analysis, performance analysis, mechanical formal analysis (using CasperFDR) and a privacy model. In Sect. 6, we offer concluding remarks.

2 Review of the Cloud-Based RFID Authentication Protocol

This section reviews the cloud-based RFID authentication protocol as proposed in [11].

2.1 Notations

The notations are defined as follows:

R: denotes the identity of an RFID reader
T: denotes the identity of an RFID tag
S: denotes the number of authentication sessions between a reader and a tag, with bit length L
M: denotes the last number of sessions between a reader and a tag
Nr: denotes a random number generated by a reader
Nt: denotes a random number generated by a tag
PRNG(): denotes the Pseudo Random Number Generation (PRNG) function
H(): denotes a secure one-way hash function with output length L, that is, H(): $\{0,1\}^* \rightarrow \{0,1\}^L$

E(): denotes an encryption function using a symmetric algorithm with a reader secret key

D(): denotes a decryption function using a symmetric algorithm with a reader secret key

$\oplus$: denotes the XOR operation

||: denotes the concatenation operation stop

2.2   The Cloud-Based RFID Authentication Protocol

During the registration phase, the reader encodes the tag with three secret values, namely R, T and S. The reader also adds unique initialised records, i.e. {H(R||T||S) and E(R||T||S)} into the cloud server. The authors assume that the registration is secure and performed in a "closed" environment. The protocol works as follows:

- The tag generates H(R||T||S) as an authentication request and sends it to the reader.
- The reader retrieves E(R||T||S) from the cloud by sending the index H(R||T||S) to the server. Then, the reader decrypts D(E(R||T||S)), verifies R and obtains T and S.
- The reader generates a random number Nr as a challenge to the tag, and sends Nr to the tag.
- The tag calculates H(R||T||Nr) as a response and generates a random number Nt as a challenge to the reader.
- The reader verifies the tag's response, and if valid, the next step is started; otherwise, the protocol is terminated.
- The reader tries to read the next record indexed by H(R||T||(S + 1)) from the cloud server and checks the integrity. If there is a valid record, this implies that the tag has been desynchronized. The reader attempts to read the $S + 2^{th}$ record indexed by H(R||T||(S + 2)), until finding the last valid record.
- The reader writes E(R||T||M') with the index H(R||T||M') into the cloud server, where M' = M + 1.
- The cloud sends H(R||T||M') $\oplus$ H(E(R||T||M')) to the reader to confirm that the update process has been successful.
- The reader sends the authentication messages H(R||T||Nt) $\oplus$ M', and H(T||R|| M') to the tag.
- The tag calculates H(R||T||Nt) XORed with the received H(R||T||Nt) $\oplus$ M' to obtain M', and then it calculates and verifies H(T||R||M'). If successful, this implies that M' is not modified by an attacker, and subsequently synchroni- sation is achieved again by updating S=M' on the tag. Moreover, the validity of M' also means that the reader is authenticated by the tag.

3   Weaknesses of the Cloud-Based RFID Authentication Protocol

In this section, we show the main weaknesses found in the cloud-based RFID authentication protocol.

3.1   Reader Impersonation Attack

In [11], the authors claim that their proposed protocol achieves mutual authentication between the tag and the reader, as only the legitimate reader knows the data (R, T, M) and can compute the authentication messages. However, we found that the attacker can impersonate a legitimate reader and be successfully authenticated by the tag without compromising the internal tag's data. The scenario for accomplishing this attack is as follows:

- The tag starts a normal session with the reader and sends $H(R\|T\|S)$.
- The reader sends Nr to the tag.
- The tag generates Nt and sends $H(R\|T\|Nr)$, and Nt to the reader.
- After the reader authenticates the tag, it asks the tag to update its value by sending $N = H(R\|T\|Nt) \oplus M$, and $G = H(T\|R\|M)$.
- The attacker blocks N and G from reaching the tag and obtains N and G for further use. As a result, the tag will not update the S value.
- Since the tag did not update the S value, the attacker will track the tag's location.
- The tag starts a new session with the reader, and sends $H(R\|T\|S)$ to the reader.
- The reader sends Nr' to the tag.
- The tag generates Nt' and sends $H(R\|T\|Nr')$, and Nt' to the reader.
- After the reader authenticates the tag, it asks the tag to update its value by sending $N' = H(R\|T\|Nt') \oplus M'$, and $G' = H(T\|R\|M')$, where $M' = S + 1$.
- The attacker obtains N' and G', and calculates the following:
  1. Since $M' = M + 1$, the attacker changes the 2 least significant bits (LSB) of N to be compatible with N' when it is incremented by 1 and assigns the result to N''. In other words, if for example N is 111000 and N' is 101011, the attacker changes N to $N'' = 111010$.
  2. $N'' \oplus N' = H(R\|T\|Nt) \oplus M \oplus H(R\|T\|Nt') \oplus M'$
  3. $(N'' + 1) \oplus N' = (H(R\|T\|Nt) \oplus M + 1) \oplus H(R\|T\|Nt') \oplus M'$. Note that $M + 1 = M'$.
  4. $(N'' + 1) \oplus N' = H(R\|T\|Nt) \oplus H(R\|T\|Nt')$
  5. $((N'' + 1) \oplus N') \oplus N = (H(R\|T\|Nt) \oplus H(R\|T\|Nt')) \oplus H(R\|T\|Nt) \oplus M$
  6. $((N'' + 1) \oplus N') \oplus N = H(R\|T\|Nt') \oplus M$
- The attacker impersonates the reader and sends $H(R\|T\|Nt') \oplus M$ and the obtained G, i.e. $G = H(T\|R\|M)$ to the tag.
- The tag calculates $H(R\|T\|Nt')$ XORed with the received $H(R\|T\|Nt') \oplus M$ to obtain M, then calculates and verifies $H(T\|R\|M)$; if successful, the tag authenticates the attacker not the legitimate reader.

3.2   Location Tracking (Privacy Analysis)

The researchers have proposed a number of privacy models to evaluate the privacy of the RFID protocols. In this paper, we will focus on a well-known and frequently cited privacy model proposed in [12]. The authors developed an untraceable privacy (UPriv) model that demonstrates how the attacker can trace a tag's location. Their model is summarised as follows: An adversary (A) controls the communication channel between a tag (T) and a reader (R) by interacting either passively or actively with them. The adversary can run the following queries:

– Execute (R, T, i) query: The adversary can passively eavesdrop on a session (i) and obtain access to the exchanged messages between R and T.
– Send (V, U, m, i) query: The adversary can perform active attacks by impersonating an entity such as U ∈ T and sends a message (m) to entity V ∈ R during session (i). Also, the adversary can alter or block the exchanged message(s).
– Corrupt (T, K) query: The attacker can physically access the tag's memory T and read the tag's secret value (K).
– Test (T, i) query: When this query is invoked for session (i), depending on a randomly chosen bit $b \in \{0, 1\}$, A is given T_b from the set $\{T_0, T_1\}$. A succeeds if it can guess the bit b.

Untraceable privacy (UPriv) is defined as a game (g) played by the adversary (A) and the reader and tag instances. The game consists of three phases:

1. Learning phase: A can send the Execute, Send, and Corrupt queries to any random T_0 and T_1 tags.
2. Challenge phase: A is given a tag $T_b \in \{T_0, T_1\}$, and sends any Execute, Send and Corrupt queries to T_b.
3. Guess phase: A terminates the game and outputs a bit b', which is its guess of the value of b. The success of A in winning g and thus breaking the notion of UPriv is quantified in terms of A's advantage in distinguishing whether A received T_0 or T_1, i.e. it correctly guesses b.

We evaluated the privacy of the cloud-based RFID authentication protocol using this model, and we found that the adversary can correlate two sessions to the same tag, thus allowing the tag's location tracking as shown below:

1. Learning phase: A impersonates a reader R and sends the Send (R, T_0, Nr, $i+1$) query in the session $(i+1)$ by sending Nr to tag T_0 and thus obtains $H(R \parallel T_0 \parallel Nr)$, Nt_{T_0}.
2. Challenge phase: A chooses two fresh tags T_0, T_1 to be tested and sends a Test $(i+1, T_0, T_1)$ query. Depending on a randomly chosen bit $b \in \{0, 1\}$, A is given a tag T_b from the set $\{T_0, T_1\}$. A sends the Send (R, T_b, Nr, $i+1$) query in the session $(i+1)$ by sending the same random number (Nr) to tag T_b and thus obtains $H(R \parallel T_b \parallel Nr)$, Nt_{T_b}.
3. Guess phase: A terminates the game if:
   $T_b = T_0$, then $H(R \parallel T_b \parallel Nr) = H(R \parallel T_0 \parallel Nr)$
   Hence, it is highly likely that this is the same tag where the adversary had initially eavesdropped, i.e. $T_b = T_0$. Else $T_b = T_1$.
   Therefore, the attacker successfully correlates two sessions to the same tag, and thus allowing unauthorised tracing.

3.3 Analysing Data Secrecy in the Cloud-Based RFID Authentication Protocol Using CasperFDR

We used CasperFDR to formally analyse the cloud-based RFID authentication protocol between the reader and the tag. CasperFDR is a compiler developed by Gavin et al. [13], which takes a high-level description of the protocol and analyses the protocol description against the stated specification (goals) to show whether the protocol meets the main requirements. CasperFDR has been used to model communication and security protocols and verify the authentication and secrecy requirements of the protocol, which are the main goals of the Xie et al. protocol. CasperFDR has confirmed its capability to find vulnerabilities in many protocols such as in [14–16].

We prepared a CasperFDR script. In the script, we assume that the reader knows about the tag's data. The communication between the reader and server is secure, therefore we did not check the protocol in this area. In the #Free variables Section, the reader (R) and tag (T) are defined as Agent; the random numbers Nr and Nt are defined as Nonce; and TID (tag identifier), RID (reader identifier), S, and M are defined as Data.

#Free variables
T, R: Agent
Nr: Nonce
Nt: nonce
TID, RID, S, M: Data
h: HashFunction
InverseKeys = (h, h)

As mentioned in Sect. 2, the main goals of the cloud-based RFID authentication protocol are authenticating the reader to the tag, and vice versa, and verifying that the data, such as R, T, S and M remain secret between the reader and tag. These goals are shown in the script in the #Specification Section, where data secrecy is depicted as Secret, such as Secret(R, M, [T]), which means that M should be a secret between R and T. The goal predicate authentication takes the form of Agreement, such as Agreement(T, R, [TID, RID]), which means that the tag is authenticated to the reader, and both parties agreed on the data values TID and RID.

#Specification
Agreement(T, R, [TID, RID])
Secret(R, M, [T])
Secret (T, S, [R])
Secret (T, TID, [R])
Secret(T, RID, [R])

In addition, in the #Intruder information Section, the intruder is defined to be Mallory, who can take full control of the session; he can impersonate any entity in the protocol, read the messages transmitted in the network, intercept, analyse, and/or modify messages.

After compiling the CasperFDR script and feeding the output to the verifier tool called Failure-Divergence Refinement (FDR), a man-in-the-middle attack is found. It states that the attacker will recover the value of M, which should be a secret value. We used the Casper compiler to analyse the attack found by FDR. The attack is illustrated below:

1. $T \rightarrow$ Mallory : $H(R \parallel T \parallel S)$
2. Mallory $\rightarrow R$: $H(R \parallel T \parallel S)$
3. $R \rightarrow$ Mallory : Nr
4. Mallory $\rightarrow T$: Nr
5. $T \rightarrow$ Mallory : $H(R\|T\|Nr), Nt$
6. Mallory $\rightarrow R$: $H(R\|T\|Nr), Nr$
7. $R \rightarrow$ Mallory : $N = H(R\|T\|Nr) \oplus M, G = H(T\|R\|M)$

The attacker performs a man-in-the-middle attack and eavesdrops on a session between the tag and the reader. The attacker impersonates the reader to obtain the tag's messages and then impersonates the tag to send the tag's messages to the reader. Casper shows that the attacker can replace the tag's random number (Nt) with the reader's generated random number (Nr), and at the end of the protocol run the attacker can calculate $M = H(R\|T\|Nr) \oplus N$ and obtain M.

As a result, in Sect. 4, we propose a new improved cloud-based RFID authentication protocol.

4   The Improved Cloud-Based RFID Authentication Protocol

In this section, we explain the proposed protocol in detail.

4.1   Goals of the Proposed Protocol

The proposed protocol aims to protect the tag's data from being revealed by any entity except the legitimate reader. The privacy of the reader is beyond the scope of the paper. The proposed protocol should meet the following goals:

– Mutual authentication: The protocol should provide mutual entity authentication, where the communication should take place between valid tag, reader and cloud server. The readers should authenticate the cloud server before making any further process. At the end of the protocol, the tag should receive a message from the reader that confirms the legitimacy of the reader.
– Tag data anonymity: The RFID tag should support a mechanism for concealing the tag's data from any entity except the legitimate readers.
– Untraceability: If the data being sent from the tag to the reader is static or linked to data sent previously, the tag holder's location could be tracked. Therefore, the RFID tag's responses should be anonymous and unlinkable in order to prevent such an attack.

- Resistance to replay attacks: An adversary can eavesdrop on the communication between the reader and tag, reuse the data and send it repeatedly. Therefore, the generated messages should be fresh to the protocol session.
- Resistance to desynchronisation attacks: An adversary can eavesdrop on the communication between the reader and tag, modify the flow of data and prevent messages from reaching their target. Therefore, the server should store the old and new values of the tag in order to authenticate the tag and reach synchronisation even if the attacker blocks the exchanged messages.
- Resistance to impersonation attacks: An attacker can respond to a reader query and can claim that this response is coming from a legitimate tag, and this fabrication enables the attacker to masquerade as a legitimate tag. Similarly, an attacker may impersonate the legitimate reader and attempt to obtain access to the tag's data. Hence, to prevent such attacks, the tag's data should be protected during transmission.

4.2   Assumptions

We present an improved cloud-based RFID authentication protocol, which operates under the following assumptions:

- The reader contacts the tag through a wireless channel that is susceptible to attacks.
- The communication channel between the reader and the cloud server is secure.
- There are multiple readers in the system, so a tag can be read in many different locations.
- This scheme only supports readers that are tamper-resistant, for example, they have a secure memory and a rigid access control mechanism.
- The tag's data are stored in non-volatile memory, such as EEPROM or Flash memory, where they can be updated.
- All the operations in the tag are atomic, i.e. either all of the operations or none are processed. Although this operation might be expensive to implement, it will defend the tags if the attacker kills the electromagnetic field between the reader and the tag or simply the tag moves from the reader's signal.
- The cloud server is not trusted, it might reveal the tag's data to intruders.

4.3   Protocol Behaviour

The main protocol features are discussed below:

- Tags are capable of computing XOR, generating a pseudo-random number and calculating hash functions.
- The reader can compute XOR, generate a pseudo-random number, calculate hash functions and perform symmetric operations.
- The proposed protocol uses random numbers in an attempt to prevent location tracking and replay attacks.
- After a successful authentication between the cloud server and tag, both parties update their values to be used in the next transaction.

– The cloud server does not store the tag's ID and tag's secret key; it stores the hash of the tag's ID and the encryption of the tag's ID and tag's secret key to provide confidentiality and anonymity to the tag's data.
– The cloud server stores both the old and the new tag's data in order to prevent desynchronization attacks.
– Additional tag memory is necessary in our protocol to store a list of random numbers received from previous queries, which can be done by adding extended on-chip non-volatile memory on the RFID tags.
– Each legitimate reader contains a master key used for a symmetric encryption.
– The reader does not store any data related to the tags.
– The system operator is responsible for managing the system. The system operator encodes the RFID tag's data into the tags and the cloud server, and assigns the master key to all the readers it manages during the initialisation phase.

4.4   Notation

The notation used in the proposed protocol are presented below:

1. The notation related to the tag is:
   – ID_i: The ith tag's ID
   – K_i: The ith tag's secret key
2. The notation related to the reader is:
   – r_n: The nth reader in the system
   – MK: The master key shared by all the legitimate readers used for a symmetric encryption and decryption
3. The notation related to the cloud server is:
   – $H(ID_{new})$: A unique hash of the updated ID
   – $E_{MK}(ID_{new} \parallel K_{new})$: The updated data ($ID_{new}$, K_{new}) associated with the ith tag encrypted with the master key
   – $H(ID_{old})$: A unique hash of the old ID
   – $E_{MK}(ID_{old} \parallel K_{old})$: The old data ($ID_{old}$, K_{old}) associated with the ith tag encrypted with the master key
4. Other notation used in the proposed protocol is:
   – x: The value kept as either new or old to show whether the tag uses the old or new values of ID and K
   – R1: A pseudo-random number generated by the reader
   – R2: A pseudo-random number generated by the tag and serving as a temporary secret for the tag
   – $E_k(M)$: A message M encrypted with a key
   – A ← B: The value of A is updated to that of B
   – J: The transaction number
   – i: The number of the tag in the system

Table 1. The proposed improved cloud-based RFID mutual authentication protocol (successful run)

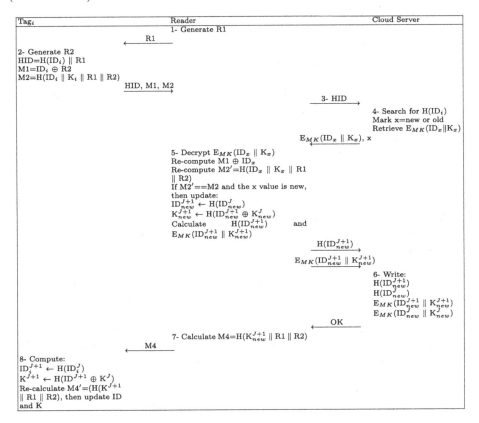

4.5 Protocol Description

The scheme consists of two phases, namely initialisation and authentication.

Initialisation Phase. We assume that the initialisation phase is carried out via a secure channel in a secure environment. The initialisation process is summarised below:

1. For each tag the system operator manages, the system operator assigns a unique $H(ID_i)$, which serves as an index, and $E_{MK}(ID_i \parallel K_i)$ in the cloud server.
2. For the i_{th} tag, the system operator assigns ID_i and K_i in the ith tag.
3. Initially, $H(ID_{old})$, and $E_{MK}(ID_{old} \parallel K_{old})$ in the cloud server are set to null.
4. The system operator assigns the master key in each reader the system manages.

Authentication Phase. The authentication process is shown in Table 1 and is described as follows:

1. Reader: The reader starts the session by generating a random number R1 and sending it to the tag.
2. Tag_i: The tag performs the following:
   - Generates R2 as a temporary secret for this session.
   - Computes the following messages:
     $\text{HID} = \text{H}(\text{ID}_i) \parallel \text{R1}$, which serves as an index message
     $\text{M1} = \text{ID}_i \oplus \text{R2}$
     $\text{M2} = \text{H}(\text{ID}_i \parallel \text{K}_i \parallel \text{R1} \parallel \text{R2})$, which serves as an authentication message
   - Sends HID, M1 and M2 to the reader.
3. Reader: The reader sends HID to the cloud server.
4. Cloud server: The cloud server performs the following:
   - For all the stored $\text{H}(\text{ID}_{new})$ and $\text{H}(\text{ID}_{old})$, it searches for $\text{H}(\text{ID}_i)$ until there is a match. Marks x = new or old based on the matched $\text{H}(\text{ID}_i)$.
   - Retrieves the associated data, i.e. $\text{E}_{MK}(\text{ID}_x \parallel \text{K}_x)$.
   - Sends $\text{E}_{MK}(\text{ID}_x \parallel \text{K}_x)$ and x to the reader.
5. Reader: The reader performs the following:
   - Decrypts $\text{E}_{MK}(\text{ID}_x \parallel \text{K}_x)$ using the master key, and obtains ID_x and K_x.
   - Re-computes $\text{M1} \oplus \text{ID}_x$ to obtain R2.
   - Re-computes $\text{M2'} = \text{H}(\text{ID}_x \parallel \text{K}_x \parallel \text{R1} \parallel \text{R2})$. If there is a match, the reader authenticates the tag. Furthermore, the reader confirms that the data within the server's message is correct and authenticates the cloud server.
     If M2' == M2 and the received x value is new, this implies that the tag's data are synchronised with the server's data, then the reader updates (ID and K) to be used in the next transaction (J + 1):
     $\text{ID}_{new}^{J+1} \leftarrow \text{H}(\text{ID}_{new}^{J})$
     $\text{K}_{new}^{J+1} \leftarrow \text{H}(\text{ID}_{new}^{J+1} \oplus \text{K}_{new}^{J})$
   - Calculates $\text{H}(\text{ID}_{new}^{J+1})$, and encrypts the new values, i.e. $\text{E}_{MK}(\text{ID}_{new}^{J+1} \parallel \text{K}_{new}^{J+1})$ using the master key.
   - Notifies the server to update their values by sending:
     $\text{H}(\text{ID}_{new}^{J+1})$, and $\text{E}_{MK}(\text{ID}_{new}^{J+1} \parallel \text{K}_{new}^{J+1})$
6. Cloud server: The cloud server performs the following:
   - Writes the following data in its database:
     $\text{H}(\text{ID}_{new}) \leftarrow \text{H}(\text{ID}_{new}^{J+1})$
     $\text{E}_{MK}(\text{ID}_{new} \parallel \text{K}_{new}) \leftarrow \text{E}_{MK}(\text{ID}_{new}^{J+1} \parallel \text{K}_{new}^{J+1})$
     $\text{H}(\text{ID}_{old}) \leftarrow \text{H}(\text{ID}_{new}^{J})$
     $\text{E}_{MK}(\text{ID}_{old} \parallel \text{K}_{old}) \leftarrow \text{E}_{MK}(\text{ID}_{new}^{J} \parallel \text{K}_{new}^{J})$
     Hence, the cloud server writes the new values in the new data fields ($\text{H}(\text{ID}_{new})$, $\text{E}_{MK}(\text{ID}_{new} \parallel \text{K}_{new})$), and writes the old entries in the old data fields ($\text{H}(\text{ID}_{old})$, $\text{E}_{MK}(\text{ID}_{old} \parallel \text{K}_{old})$).
   - Sends an OK message to notify the reader that the update process has been successful.
7. Reader: The reader performs the following:
   - If the reader received the OK message from the cloud server, the reader notifies the tag to update its data such as (ID_i, K_i) by calculating $\text{M4} = \text{H}(\text{K}_{new}^{J+1} \parallel \text{R1} \parallel \text{R2})$ using the updated tag's secret key.

- Sends M4 to the tag.

8. Tag_i: The tag performs the following:
    - Computes $\text{ID}_i^{J+1} \leftarrow \text{H}(\text{ID}_j^J)$ and $\text{K}_i^{J+1} \leftarrow \text{H}(\text{ID}_i^{J+1} \oplus \text{K}_i^J)$.
    - Re-calculates M4' $= (\text{H}(\text{K}_i^{J+1} \parallel \text{R1} \parallel \text{R2})$, and if it is equal to the received value of M4, then it authenticates the reader and updates ID and K to:
      $\text{ID}_j^{J+1} \leftarrow \text{H}(\text{ID}_j^J)$
      $\text{K}_i^{J+1} \leftarrow \text{H}(\text{ID}_i^{J+1} \oplus \text{K}_i^J)$

If M2' $==$ M2 and the received value of x is old, the reader still authenticates the tag but this implies that the tag's data has been desynchronised, thus the reader does not update the current values of ID and K. It sends no update to the server and sends M4 $= \text{H}(\text{K}_{new}^J \parallel \text{R1} \parallel \text{R2})$ to the tag using the current value of the tag's secret key. Then, the tag re-computes M4 using the current values. If there is a match with the received M4, the tag authenticates the reader and updates its data, as shown in the previous step.

If there is no match with the received M4 using the current or new values of ID_i and K_i, then the tag does not authenticate the reader and will not update its data.

5   Protocol Analysis

5.1   Informal Analysis of the Improved Cloud-Based RFID Authentication Protocol

Our proposed protocol meets the following requirements:

- Mutual authentication: If the reader successfully calculates the tag's responses M1 and M2, it authenticates the tag, as only the legitimate tag can calculate such responses. Similarly, if the tag calculates M4 and it finds a match with the received M4, it confirms that the reader is legitimate and authenticates it. Furthermore, the reader decrypts the server's message $(\text{E}_{MK}(\text{ID}_x \parallel \text{K}_x))$, and if the tag's messages M1 and M2 are authenticated, this means that the cloud server sends legitimate data within the message, and hence the reader authenticates the server.
- Tag data anonymity: The tag stores two values, namely ID and K that are supposed to be secret and that are not revealed to any entity except the legitimate readers. The tag's data are not sent in the clear, as they are protected using fresh random numbers (HID, M1 and M2) and sent within the hash function (HID and M2). Therefore, only the legitimate reader can extract these values. Furthermore, if the cloud server is a malicious entity, this will not affect the tag's data privacy, as the cloud server stores the hash of the tag's ID and the encrypted tag's data; and without the master key, the cloud server cannot disclose the tag's data.
- Tag location privacy (untraceability): In the proposed protocol, the tag's responses are changed in each session using the updated tag's values and fresh random numbers (R1 and R2), and thus the attacker will obtain new

responses every time he eavesdrops on a session. Moreover, if the previous authentication session failed, the tag's responses will change due to the existence of new fresh random numbers.

However, in case that the tag did not update its values due to desynchronisation attacks or any other means of interruption, the attacker can track the location of the tag as the tag always replies with H(ID), which remains the same until the tag interacts with a legitimate reader and updates its data.

- Resistance to replay attacks: The proposed protocol utilises a challenge-response scheme, in which each party maintains a set of random numbers that it encountered from a previous protocol run in order to avoid repeated random numbers. Therefore, if the tag received an already used random number it ignores the query.
- Resistance to desynchronisation attacks: In the proposed protocol, the desynchronisation attack is avoided by storing the previous values of the tag's data in the cloud server, and hence it achieves synchronisation. For instance, if the attacker blocks M4 more than once, the tag will not update its data. In the next session, the reader contacts the desynchronised tag and sends the tag's HID message to the cloud server, then the cloud server will find a match with the tag's old data and send $E_{MK}(ID_{old} \parallel K_{old})$ and x = old, as HID matches $(H(ID_{old}))$; and thus synchronisation is still achieved.
- Resistance to tag and reader impersonation attack: To impersonate the tag, the attacker must be able to compute a valid response (HID, M1 and M2) to a reader query. However, it is hard to compute such responses without knowledge of ID and K. Similarly, the attacker needs to be in possession of ID, K and R2 to impersonate the legitimate reader and send M4.
- Compromising the reader: The only risk that the system may encounter is compromising the reader; hence the attacker will gain the master key. However, in the Assumption Sect. 4.2, we assumed that the proposed protocol only supports readers that are tamper-resistant, for example, they have a secure memory and a rigid access control mechanism.

Table 2 shows how our proposed protocol provides more security and privacy features than the cloud-based RFID authentication protocol. Based on the discovered weaknesses, we found that the cloud-based RFID authentication protocol is vulnerable to reader impersonation attacks; hence mutual authentication is not achieved. Moreover, we used CasperFDR to analyse the cloud-based RFID authentication protocol, and it showed that an attacker can discover the secret value (M); hence the tag data anonymity is compromised. In addition, we used a privacy model to analyse the tag location privacy in the cloud-based RFID authentication protocol, and we found that the attacker can successfully correlate two sessions to the same tag, which allows unauthorised tracing.

5.2 Performance Analysis

In this section, we conduct a comparative analysis of the performance cost regarding storage cost, and communication cost.

Table 2. Comparison between the cloud-based RFID authentication protocol and our proposed protocol

RFID system main requirements	Cloud-based protocol	Our proposed protocol
Tag data anonymity	No	Yes
Tag location privacy	No	Yes under assumption that the tag has updated its values
Resistance to replay attack	Yes	Yes
Resistance to desynchronisation	Yes	Yes
Resistance to tag impersonation	Yes	Yes
Resistance to reader impersonation	No	Yes
Mutual authentication	No	Yes

- Storage cost: Due to the limitation of tag memory, the tag should store a minimum amount of data. In the proposed protocol, the tag stores two values in a rewritable flash memory namely (ID, K), as they change in different authentication sessions, each of which has a length of 224 bits. Since the tag's memory can store 1 Kilobyte of data, in our protocol the tag securely stores $224 * 2 = 448$ bits in the memory. Additional tag memory is necessary in our protocol to store a list of random numbers received from previous queries, for example by adding extended on-chip non-volatile memory on the RFID tags.
- Communication cost: In the proposed protocol, the tag sends three messages (HID, M1 and M2) in order to be successfully authenticated. A total of 896 bits are sent over the channel. Hence, it provides a relatively low communication cost.

5.3 Analysing Data Secrecy and Authentication in the Proposed Protocol Using CasperFDR

To formally analyse the proposed protocol and confirm that the secrecy and authenticity between the reader and tag are achieved, we used CasperFDR [13].

We prepared a CasperFDR script. In the script, we assume that the reader knows about the tag's data. The communication between the reader and server is secure, therefore we did not check the protocol in this area. In the #Free variables Section, the tag (T) and reader (R) are defined as Agent; the random numbers R1 and R2 are defined as Nonce; and ID (tag identifier), K (tag key) are defined as Data.

```
#Free variables
T, R: Agent
R1: Nonce
R2: nonce
ID, K: Data
h: HashFunction
InverseKeys = (h, h)
```

As mentioned in Sect. 4.1, the main goals of our protocol are authenticating the reader to the tag, and vice versa, as well as verifying that the data, such as ID, K and R2 are secure. These goals are shown in the script in the #Specification Section as shown below:

#Specification
Agreement(T, R, [ID, K, R2])
Secret (T, ID, [R])
Secret (T, K, [R])
Secret(T, R2, [R])

In addition, in the #Intruder information Section, the intruder is defined as Mallory, who can take full control of the session; he can impersonate any entity in the protocol, read the messages transmitted in the network, intercept, analyse and/or modify messages.

After compiling the CasperFDR script and feeding the output to FDR, CasperFDR did not find any feasible attack, which means that mutual authentication is achieved successfully between the reader and the tag, and the tag's data are protected and transfered securely.

5.4   Privacy Analysis

We deployed the same privacy model described in [12] to evaluate the privacy of the proposed protocol. We found that the adversary cannot invade the privacy of the tag and trace its location as shown below:

– Learning phase: The adversary eavesdrops on a valid session between R and T_0. He sends the Execute command and then maintains the following values:
R1, $HID = H(ID_0) \parallel R1$
$M1 = ID_0 \oplus R2$
$M2 = H(ID_0 \parallel K_0 \parallel R1 \parallel R2)$
– Challenge phase: A is given a tag $T_b \in \{T_0, T_1\}$ randomly. He starts a new session with T_b by impersonating the reader, sends R1 to T_b within the Send query and terminates the session. T_b responses can be:
$HID = H(ID_b) \parallel R1$
$M1 = ID_b \oplus R2$
$M2 = H(ID_b \parallel K_b \parallel R1 \parallel R2)$

A will not be able to guess the correct tag (bit b), as the received messages M1 and M2 contain a random number (R2) generated by the tag, which changes in every session and is not known to the adversary. Moreover, regarding the HID message, if the tag encounters a repeated random number, such as R1, it will terminate the session.

6   Conclusion

In this paper, we examined the cloud-based RFID authentication protocol, and we found that the protocol is prone to reader impersonation attacks, and location tracking. Moreover, we formally analysed the cloud-based RFID authentication protocol using CasperFDR, which demonstrated that the secrecy of the protocol is not protected as the attacker can perform a man-in-the-middle attack and obtain the secret data. Therefore, we proposed an improved cloud-based RFID authentication protocol that is based on the strengths in the cloud-based RFID authentication protocol while avoiding its security and privacy issues. The proposed protocol has been analysed informally, and we showed that it is more immune to reader impersonation attack and location tracking attacks than the Xie et al. protocol. Furthermore, it can resist other forms of attacks, such as reply attacks, desynchronisation attacks, and impersonation attacks. Also, we illustrated that the tag data anonymity is preserved, and hence the cloud server and the attackers will not be able to obtain the tag's data. In addition, the communication session between the reader and the tag was formally analysed using CasperFDR, and it did not find any feasible attack. Finally, we showed that the proposed protocol can comply with the required tag's memory storage cost and communication cost.

Acknowledgment. Sarah Abughazalah is supported by the Ministry of Higher Education and King Khaled University in Saudi Arabia.

References

1. Finkenzeller, K.: RFID Handbook: Fundamentals and Applications in Contactless Smart Cards and Identification, 2nd edn. John Wiley & Sons Inc, New York (2003)
2. Juels, A.: RFID security and privacy: a research survey. IEEE J. Sel. Areas Commun. **24**(2), 381–394 (2006)
3. Chien, H., Chen, C.: Mutual authentication protocol for RFID conforming to EPC Class 1 Generation 2 standards. Comput. Stand. Interfaces **29**(2), 254–259 (2007)
4. Song, B., Mitchell, C.: RFID authentication protocol for low-cost tags. In: Proceedings of the First ACM Conference on Wireless Network Security, pp. 140–147. ACM (2008)
5. Tan, C., Sheng, B., Li, Q.: Secure and serverless RFID authentication and search protocols. IEEE Trans. Wirel. Commun. **7**(4), 1400–1407 (2008)
6. Poulopoulos, G., Markantonakis, K., Mayes, K.: A secure and efficient mutual authentication protocol for low-cost RFID systems. In: International Conference on Availability, Reliability and Security, ARES 2009, pp. 706–711. IEEE (2009)
7. Li, J., Wang, Y., Jiao, B., Xu, Y.: An authentication protocol for secure and efficient RFID communication. In: 2010 International Conference on Logistics Systems and Intelligent Management, vol. 3, pp. 1648–1651. IEEE (2010)
8. Chun, J., Hwang, J., Lee, D.: RFID tag search protocol preserving privacy of mobile reader holders. IEICE Electron. Express **8**(2), 50–56 (2011)
9. Yoon, E.: Improvement of the securing RFID systems conforming to EPC Class 1 Generation 2 standard. Expert Syst. Appl. **39**(1), 1589–1594 (2012)
10. Lee, C.F., Chien, H.Y., Laih, C.S.: Server-less RFID authentication and searching protocol with enhanced security. Int. J. Commun. Syst. **25**(3), 376–385 (2012)
11. Xie, W., Xie, L., Zhang, C., Zhang, Q., Tang, C.: Cloud-based RFID authentication. In: 2013 IEEE International Conference on RFID (RFID), pp. 168–175. IEEE (2013)

12. Ouafi, K., Phan, R.C.-W.: Privacy of recent RFID authentication protocols. In: Chen, L., Mu, Y., Susilo, W. (eds.) ISPEC 2008. LNCS, vol. 4991, pp. 263–277. Springer, Heidelberg (2008)
13. Lowe, G.: Casper: a compiler for the analysis of security protocols. In: Proceedings of 10th IEEE Computer Security Foundations Workshop, pp. 18–30 (1997)
14. Alshehri, A., Briffa, J.A., Schneider, S., Wesemeyer, S.: Formal security analysis of NFC m-coupon protocols using casper/fdr. In: 2013 5th International Workshop on Near Field Communication (NFC), pp. 1–6. IEEE (2013)
15. Aiash, M., Mapp, G., Phan, R.W., Lasebae, A., Loo, J.: A formally verified device authentication protocol using Casper/FDR. In: 2012 IEEE 11th International Conference on Trust, Security and Privacy in Computing and Communications (TrustCom), pp. 1293–1298. IEEE (2012)
16. Kumari, V.V., Raju, K.K.: Formal verification of IEEE 802.11w authentication protocol. Procedia Technology **6**, 716–722 (2012). 2nd International Conference on Communication, Computing and Security [ICCCS-2012]

Autonomous and Spontaneous Security

Environment–Reactive Malware Behavior: Detection and Categorization

Smita Naval[1]([⊠]), Vijay Laxmi[1], Manoj S. Gaur[1], Sachin Raja[1],
Muttukrishnan Rajarajan[2], and Mauro Conti[3]

[1] Malaviya National Institute of Technology, Jaipur, India
{smita.710,vlgaur,gaurms,sachinraja13}@gmail.com
[2] City University of London, London, UK
r.muttukrishnan@city.ac.uk
[3] University of Padova, Padua, Italy
conti@math.unipd.it

Abstract. Present malicious threats have been consolidated in past few years by incorporating diverse stealthy techniques. Detecting these malwares on the basis of their dynamic behavior has become a potential approach as it suppresses the shortcomings of static approaches raised due to the obfuscated malware binaries. Additionally, existing behavior based malware detection approaches are resilient to zero–day malware attacks. These approaches rely on isolated analysis environment to monitor and capture the run–time malware behavior. Malware bundled with environment–aware payload may degrade detection accuracy of such approaches. These malicious programs detect the presence of execution environment and thus inspite of having their malicious payload they mimic a benign behavior to avoid detection. In this paper, we have presented an approach using system–calls to identify a malware on the basis of their malignant and environment–reactive behavior. The proposed approach offers an automated screening mechanism to segregate malware samples on the basis of aforementioned behaviors. We have built a decision model which is based on multi–layer perceptron learning with back propagation algorithm. Our proposed model decides the candidacy of a sample to be put into one of the four classes (clean, malignant, guest–crashing and infinite–running). Clean behavior denotes benign sample and rest of the behaviors denote the presence of malware sample. The proposed technique has been evaluated with known and unknown instances of real malware and benign programs.

1 Introduction

Widespread use of the Internet and communication technologies has leveraged the malicious attackers to carry out their evil intentions. These malware generated threats disrupt our system services, sensitive information and communication infrastructure. Distribution of these threats makes our system a source of infection spread. To avoid these infections, security researchers across the globe have developed numerous malware detection techniques which rely on signatures

© Springer International Publishing Switzerland 2015
J. Garcia-Alfaro et al. (Eds.): DPM/SETOP/QASA 2014, LNCS 8872, pp. 167–182, 2015.
DOI: 10.1007/978-3-319-17016-9_11

or pattern matching (either static or dynamic). The dynamic behavior–based malware detection (DBMD) approaches have an upper hand as compared to static signature based techniques [1]. The behavior based approaches are capable of capturing the polymorphic, metamorphic, obfuscated and packed variant of known malware. Also, these techniques allow to detect unseen malware attacks [10]. A standard procedure is adopted to monitor the run–time behavior of malware in the most of these DBMD approaches. During the monitoring process, a safe and isolated environment set–up is established to protect the host from any malware generated side–effects. Variety of sandboxing, virtualization and emulator based tools are available to create such set–ups. These controlled environments imitate a real runtime environment. But a full imitation of real system cannot be achieved as these environments differ in CPU semantics (CPU semantic attacks) and in instruction execution time (timing attacks) as compared to uninstrumented host [1]. The detection–aware malware exploits these variations and ensures that it is being analyzed. Rutkowska developed a technique Red Pill [22] which shows that incorporating CPU semantic attack using SIDT (Store Interrupt Descriptor Table) is an effortless task. On the other hand, the timing attacks are deployed using TSC (Time Stamp Counter) register. In virtual machines, the instruction execution time is more than the real machines and this difference can be captured using TSC. Thus, by employing these attacks malware senses the existence of non–real environments and portrays an incorrect picture of itself. Existing plethora of DBMD techniques [10,18,21] do not address this category of malware. These techniques rely on run–time traces and perform the analysis on acquired logs. This form of analysis is not sufficient to alleviate the current environment–aware malware threats. There is a need of an automated approach which can infer the strand of malware infection from their environment–reactive behavior. These observed behaviors can be used to detect and categorize the unknown detection–aware malware instances.

Environment–Reactive Malware Behaviors: Present detection–aware malware carries multiple payloads to remain invisible to any protection system and to persist for longer period of time. The environment–aware payloads determine originality of running environment, if environment is not real then the actual malicious payload is not delivered. After detecting the presence of virtual or emulated environment, malware either terminates its execution or mimics a benign/unusual behavior. In literature, different terms have been utilized to address this category of malware such as environment–sensitive, environment–resistant, environment–aware and split–personality. We have used environment–reactive term for the same. Malware with environment–reactive behavior incorporates two activities (1) sensing the presence of virtual environment and (2) responding to this environment sensing by showing an unusual behavior. We closely monitored these environment–reactive behaviors and labeled each malware binary during training phase. These behaviors are discussed in Sect. 3.

Contributions: In this paper, we have proposed a multi–class model which can identify the environment–reactive behavior of malware binaries. The focus of our proposed approach is to predict the behavior class of a test sample by neural network based learning algorithm. We have also considered the execution logs of malware and benign executables which do not encapsulate environment–reactive behavior. Using these behavior traits, we have discriminated between clean and malicious applications. Following are the contributions of our proposed approach:

(a) Devised a mechanism which transforms the manual behavior screening into the automated one. Our proposed approach exploits malware's tactics of evading detection to predict its reactive and malicious behavior under a host–based virtualized environment (Ether [7]). Though the proposed approach is specific to a given monitoring environment but can be generalized by applying same methodology with other environments also.
(b) Construction of input vector that is best suited for our learning model. The input vector consists of transition probabilities of two consecutive system–calls.
(c) Creation of an unbiased neural–network based multi–class decision model. We have constructed four networks based on multi–layer perceptron learning algorithm with back propagation. Each network is trained and tested in parallel to reduce the performance overhead.
(d) Our experimental results indicate that the proposed model is capable of (1) finding the known and unknown instances of malware binaries which are environment–reactive (2) improving the monitoring mechanism of Ether by analyzing the detected binaries.

The rest of the paper is organized as follows. Section 2 briefly outlines the related work in analysis–aware malware detection. Section 3 outlines the basic building blocks of our approach. The experimental setup and results are explained in Sect. 4. Section 5 explores the limitations of our approach. Finally, the concluding remarks are presented in Sect. 6.

2   Related Work

The desirable property of any malware detector is that it must be capable of detecting unknown malicious attacks. Modern malware is analysis–aware therefore it contains various other payloads which try to evade the existing detection mechanism. To remain undetected, these malware apply various checks during their execution prior to delivery of the actual payload. Techniques have been illustrated in literature that address the detection of analysis–aware malware.

2.1   Feasibility of Analysis–Aware Malware

Bethencourt et al. [3] have demonstrated the feasibility of PIR (Private Information Retrieval)–based malware (specifically worms). The authors discussed that these malicious programs are analysis–resistant and bundled with crpto–computing techniques. They have shown that these malicious codes covertly retrieve the sensitive information from infected computing nodes while hiding their presence from any analysis environments.

2.2 Behavior Divergence Due to Analysis Environment

Chen *et al.* have proposed an approach in [5] to identify the malware behavior under three different environment (virtual, debugger and real). They have compared the behavior of a sample using linear least squares fitting and Mean Squared Error (MSE) to capture malware having anti–debugging and anti–virtualization behavior. Similar work has been proposed in [14,24]. In former approach, the authors have detected the malware which employ anti–VM technique. They have calculated the behavioral distance of a sample using Levesthein distance. The calculated distance depicts the divergence in malware behavior in real and virtual environments. The authors in latter approach have proposed a tool DISARM, to detect the malware with evasive behavior. They have shown that same sample does not constitute similar behavior if executed in different environments. They have calculated a distance score using Jaccard index to explore the change in malware behavior in four different sandboxing environments. Balzarotti *et al.* [2] and Kang *et al.* [11] have analyzed the difference in execution traces of a malware in different analysis. In [2], authors have described the split–personality behavior of malware in virtual and uninstrumented reference host. Any sample having non–similar system–call traces in these two environments are termed as split–personality malware. Kang *et al.* [11] have compared the behavior difference of run–traces of malware in real and emulated environments to detect malware with anti–emulation techniques.

Our proposed approach differs from existing approaches as:

– It does not execute a sample in multiple environments which reduces our execution monitoring time and efforts. We detect the environment–reactive malware behavior from a single execution trace of malware in a single analysis environment.
– It does not incorporate any fingerprint matching or distance matching technique. We developed a multi–class behavior model which detects and categorizes the benign and malicious (Non–environment reactive and environment–reactive) program behavior.

3 Approach Overview

Main objective of our approach is to identify the malware's environment–reactive behaviors. In addition to that, our approach also discriminates the benign and malware (Non environment–reactive) executables. To achieve these objectives, we executed binaries in a virtualized environment using Ether and noted interaction of binary with Kernel in terms of system–calls. On the basis of noted behaviors, we have classified samples in four categories. Figure 1 outlines proposed classification framework details of which are as follows.

3.1 Analysis Framework

The analysis framework plays an important role in analyzing behavior of malicious binaries. It must provide an isolated and transparent environment setup

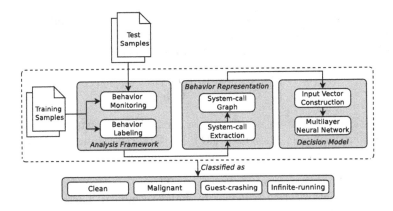

Fig. 1. Proposed classification framework

which does not relay any side–effects to host. We have used Ether as our dynamic analysis framework. It offers a complete and accurate execution sequence by utilizing native CPU instruction and out–of–the guest monitoring [19]. We preferred Ether over other platforms (BitBlaze, Anubis, CWSandbox, Cuckoo) as it has the capability of providing solutions against anti–detection attacks incorporated by malware binaries [1]. These anti–detection attacks include anti-debugging, anti–emulation, anti–sandboxing and host–modification. Our approach relies on Ether for behavior monitoring and labeling of benign and malware executables.

Behavior Monitoring: Ether [7] produces a page fault or exception to intercept the system–call made by the target application. Whenever this application requires a system service, it executes SYSENTER. The SYSENTER transfers the control from user space to kernel space where it copies the value (address) stored in a special register SYSENTER_EIP_MSR into instruction pointer (IP). Ether sets this value of SYSENTER_EIP_MSR to a default value. Accessing this value causes a page fault and in this way Ether knows that a system–call has been made. The value SYSENTER_EIP_MSR is changed back to its original value and the target application continues its execution. Ether mediates all access to the SYSENTER_EIP_MSR register and can therefore hide any modifications of the register from the analysis target [7]. To generate system–call logs, each sample is permitted to execute for 10 min. According to [20], five minute is enough duration for the execution monitoring. We doubled this execution time to capture the malware equipped with capability of carrying out time–out attacks.

Behavior Labeling: According to [7] Ether is capable of capturing execution traces of all malware and remains invisible to the target application being monitored. We have noticed that there are samples for which no logs are generated which indicate that Ether is not completely transparent. Also, Pek *et al.* [19] have shown in their approach (nEther) that Ether is prone to timing attack. In such situations, when Ether is detected by an application the acquired logs cannot be trusted. So, we applied a close manual monitoring of malware behavior of training samples and utilized these noted behavior to detect the maliciousness of an unknown sample. In training phase, we adapted following definition of clean and malicious behavior of benign and malware binaries.

$$\mathbb{P} = \begin{cases} \text{Suspicious } \{\beta \mid \beta \in \{M,\ G,\ I\}\} \\ \quad \text{Clean} \qquad \text{Otherwise} \end{cases} \tag{1}$$

A program $\mathbb{P}$ is said to be suspicious or clean if it depicts a behavior β in one of the four forms (1) Malignant (M), (2) Guest–crashing (G), (3) Infinite–running (I) and (4) Clean (C). All four are discussed as follows:

- *Malignant (Non Environment–Reactive):* This class of malware depicts the non environment–reactive behavior of malware binary. These malicious programs generate system–call logs within our specified timeframe and do not constitute any visible abnormal activity which alters the guest OS state.
- *Guest–crashing (Environment–Reactive):* Guest–crashing behavior is marked for those samples which crash the guest OS to terminate the execution–monitoring process. To incorporate such a mechanism in the malware source code is not a difficult task. The system can be crashed by causing a page fault, exception and access violation [15].
- *Infinite–running (Environment–Reactive):* We labeled a malware sample as having infinite running behavior if the target sample does not terminate in 10 min and logs show repetitions. Malware binaries eagerly wait just for a single chance of execution and if granted it will try to infect the machine as soon as possible. The infinite running behavior indicates that malware is running in an infinite loop and try to add non–malicious sequence in generated logs.
- *Clean (Non Environment–Reactive):* We marked each benign application with this behavior. The benign executables do not reflect any system crash or infinite running behavior. Our benign dataset does not include any large setup and installation files having execution time more than 10 min.

3.2 Behavior Representation

We have utilized system–calls to model program behavior during execution. System–calls are the interface by which an user application can interact with kernel to access the system services. A program behavior is speculated from the OS state. Any alternation in OS state cannot be made without using system–calls as these are non–bypassable interface [23]. In our approach, the acquired system–call sequences are transformed as system–call graph which is based on Markov model. Markov model based graph representation enables the consolidated comparisons in two dimensional space and maintains the sequential nature of data [1]. Representing system–call sequences in this way hampers malware author's aim of evading detection of any system–call based approach. As the malware authors can very conveniently re–arrange or insert irrelevant system–calls in their malware source code [13]. According to [9] and our traces, there are 284 unique system–calls that can be invoked by any running application in Windows XP.

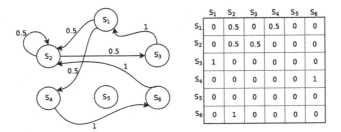

	S_1	S_2	S_3	S_4	S_5	S_6
S_1	0	0.5	0	0.5	0	0
S_2	0	0.5	0.5	0	0	0
S_3	1	0	0	0	0	0
S_4	0	0	0	0	0	1
S_5	0	0	0	0	0	0
S_6	0	1	0	0	0	0

Fig. 2. System–call graph and TPM: an example

System–Call Graph: Let ξ is an execution trace of a sample which represents the set of system–calls invoked by the sample. ξ is further transformed into weighted directed graph $G = \{V, E\}$, where V is a finite set of 284 unique system–calls and E represents set of edges in G. Every edge e_{ij} indicates a transition from node i to j with transition probability ρ_{ij}. Applying Markov property (Eq. 2), we built our Transition Probability Matrix (TPM).

$$\sum_{j=1}^{284} \rho_{ij} = \begin{cases} 0 \ if \ all \ entries \ in \ i^{th} \ row \ is \ zero \\ 1 \qquad\qquad otherwise \end{cases} \qquad (2)$$

For example, consider the execution trace $\xi = \{S_1, S_2, S_3, S_1, S_4, S_6, S_2, S_2, S_3, S_1\}$ of a program $\mathbb{P}$. Figure 2 shows the corresponding graph and matrix for this example. Here, program $\mathbb{P}$ invokes 5 unique system–calls (S_1, S_2, S_3, S_4, S_6) and call S_5 is not utilized in its execution path. The graph contains 5 connected nodes and one isolated node. Edges are directed (showing transition direction) and labeled with transition probability ρ_{ij}. The matrix representation of $\mathbb{P}$ shows a 6×6 square matrix called as TPM. Every row in TPM is summed to either 1 or 0. In our experimentation, we have constructed 284×284 TPM for each benign and malware executable. These individual TPMs are used to form a composite matrix of a dataset as shown in Eq. 3. Here, composite matrix (R.H.S.) is constructed by adding two TPMs (L.H.S.) and then dividing each cell (i, j) of resultant matrix by number of samples (2 in this case). In similar manner we have created composite matrix of our datasets which is further used to construct our input vector. Each cell in this matrix can have a value ranging from 0 to 1 which indicates the average transition from one state to other in a dataset.

$$\begin{cases} a_{11} \ a_{12} \ a_{13} \\ a_{21} \ a_{22} \ a_{23} \\ a_{31} \ a_{32} \ a_{33} \end{cases} + \begin{cases} b_{11} \ b_{12} \ b_{13} \\ b_{21} \ b_{22} \ b_{23} \\ b_{31} \ b_{32} \ b_{33} \end{cases} = \frac{1}{2} \begin{cases} (a_{11} + b_{11}) \ (a_{12} + b_{12}) \ (a_{13} + b_{13}) \\ (a_{21} + b_{21}) \ (a_{22} + b_{22}) \ (a_{23} + b_{23}) \\ (a_{31} + b_{31}) \ (a_{32} + b_{32}) \ (a_{33} + b_{33}) \end{cases} \quad (3)$$

3.3 Decision Model

We used neural network [8, 17] model to categorize the aforementioned behaviors. This model has ability of learning non–linear discriminant function and recognizing patterns in high–dimensional feature space. It can be structured using either single–layer or Multi–Layer Perceptron (MLP). Our initial experiments with single–layer perceptron indicate that our data is not linearly separable. For this reason, we adopted MLP [8] model with error back propagation algorithm for our classification methodology. We applied one–against–all (OAA) [17] pattern modeling over one–against–one (OAO) and P–against–Q (PAQ) because other two modeling methods require more number of network structures and shall result into a computational overhead. Applying OAA, our network becomes a bi–class model and therefore we developed four different networks for each of the behaviors (C vs. All, M vs. All, G vs. All and I vs. All).

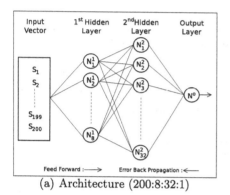

(a) Architecture (200:8:32:1)

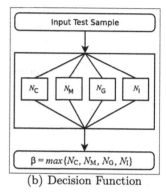

(b) Decision Function

Fig. 3. Decision model

Figure 3(a) shows our decision model (200:8:32:1). The architecture of our proposed network is described by one input vector, two hidden layers and one output layer. We constructed input vector using state transition probabilities discussed later in Sect. 4.2. The proposed classification model was designed with two hidden layers instead of one according to the findings of the work in [6]. We adopted hit and trial strategy to select the number of neurons in the hidden layer as low and high neuron count may result into under–fitting and over–fitting which further lead towards poor learning of training sets. In this quest, we performed an extensive experimentation by using neuron count from 4 to 40 at both the hidden layers. We observed best results with 200:8:32:1 in terms of accuracy and training time and hence decided for 8 neurons in the first hidden layer and 32 neurons in the second hidden layer. At the output layer, a single neuron is sufficient in our case, since for each network, we need a single value which gives a measure of how closely an input sample relates with the corresponding behavior.

Besides these structural issues there are factors which play a crucial role in designing a decision neural network. These factors are described as follows.

Activation Function: Every neuron is associated with a bias value and makes use of an activation function to transform the value of the activation level into an output signal. If the learning algorithm is back propagation, it is necessary for the activation function to be differentiable. For our model, we have selected $\frac{tanh(x)}{No.\ of\ neurons\ in\ the\ layer}$ as the activation function as (i) it is highly differentiable and leads to good gradient descend on error, (ii) it requires less mathematical computations on each neuron, and (iii) it gives output in the range -1 to $+1$. We have trained our neural network in a way that a positive value is expected for a positive class and negative value for negative class.

Learning Rate and Momentum Rate: Learning rate is a numerical factor by which weights are updated in each iteration. Lower the learning rate, finer tuned are the weights, but it requires more iterations, thereby leading to a high training time. Higher learning rate results in less overall training time with lesser accuracy of detection. Also, during the learning process a momentum factor is introduced to reduce the sensitivity of the network to a local minima with respect to weights and increases the convergence speed. For our model, we have observed good classification results and appreciable training time with 0.01 as the value of the learning rate and 0.5 as the momentum factor value.

Decision Function: When a sample is to be classified, its output from each network is generated and passed through a decision function for a final classification. A high positive output from a network indicates a close match of the input sample to the corresponding behavior. Figure 3(b) illustrates the process of determining class of a input test sample. The sample is supplied into all four networks and four output values $N_C, N_M, N_G,$ and N_I are generated in parallel with respect to each network. It is labeled with behavior β where β is the maximum value out of four generated values.

4   Experimental Setup and Results

The experiments were performed on Intel Core i7 2.30 GHz with 8 GB, 1600 MHz DDR3 RAM Macbook Pro. Implementation code is written in JAVA (eclipse IDE) and executed in JRE environment with 2.5 GB and 3.0 GB of heap space.

4.1   Dataset Preparation

We have used malware and benign executables as input. Total 1150 Benign executables are gathered from `Windows/system32` directory of freshly installed Windows system. Our proposed model relies on the system–call sequence gathered from a target binary while it is being executed in Windows XP platform. Although Microsoft abandons its support to Windows XP yet this will not affect our proposed model because (i) the target malicious binaries (win32 PE) affect the all Windows platform, (ii) system–call sequence used in Windows XP is a subset of those used in Windows 7 [9].

Our malware dataset consists of 1120 samples collected from on line sources and user agencies. All malicious samples are then applied to three different AV scanners (Norton, Quick Heal, AVG) to segregate them into their respective malware families (Worm, Trojan, Virus). The training (70 %) and known test sets (30 %) are formed from both the benign and malware datasets. The known test set consists of samples whose behavior is known but these are not used for training. We labeled each known malware and benign sample with their respective behavior. We labeled 1150 samples as Clean, 505 samples as Malignant, 329 samples as Guest–crashing and 286 samples as Infinite–running. It is clear that more than 50 % of malware samples depict environment–reactive behavior reinforcing our motive of detecting environment–reactive malware. Furthermore, we have used one unknown test set, samples of which is not labeled with any behavior to check whether our model makes an accurate behavior prediction for unknown instances.

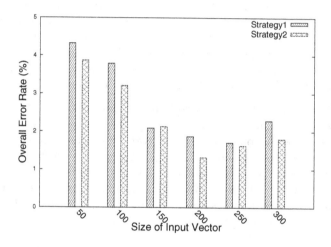

Fig. 4. Input vector construction

4.2   Input Vector Construction

Input vector plays a key role in designing a decision network which yields into a better detection accuracy. We have chosen transition states of composite matrix to be used as input in our constructed input vector. Composite matrix is a 284×284 matrix so our state space will have total 284×284 transitions. This state space is very large and applying it to our model will degrade its performance. Therefore, to decide the appropriate transition states and size of the input vector we adopted following two strategies.

1. Construct *four* input vectors w.r.t. each behavior network using four composite matrices corresponding to each of the behavior datasets. (Strategy 1)
2. Construct *one* input vector for all four behavior networks using one composite matrices created from training samples of all behavior datasets. (Strategy 2)

We selected top 50, 100, 150, 200, 250 and 300 transition states for both the strategies. After this, we applied TPMs of our samples and trained all four networks for fixed 10000 iterations with these strategies. The main aim of this experiment is to select the suitable strategy and size for our input vector. Figure 4 shows results of this experiment in terms of overall error rate with respect to each of the 12 (two strategies and six sizes) experiments. We found that Strategy 2 outperforms the Strategy 1 as the individual choice of input vector trains the model for relevant behavior class and ignores the global knowledge. Though, there is a marginal difference in the error rate but for any malware detection system this difference cannot be avoided. Therefore, we considered Strategy 2 for our experimentation. The minimum error rate is obtained at input size 200 for Strategy 2. We observed that the error rate increases as we increase the input size. Because adding more state to our input vector will also increase the noise in the data and as a result it will lead to poor detection accuracy. Also, we observed that the training time is directly proportional to input size. But, we decided to sacrifice training time over detection accuracy and fixed the input vector size as 200.

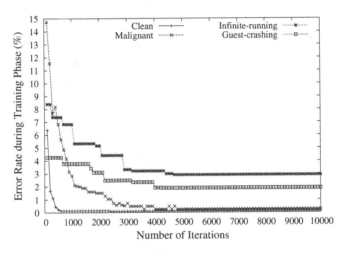

Fig. 5. Number of iteration selection

4.3   Training Results

In training phase, we randomized samples after each epoch to avoid the biasness in the adjusted weights. Figure 5 shows the plot of error rate vs. number of iterations. This figure indicates that our model has been trained in just 5000 iterations as the overall error rate get stabilized from this point onwards. It will allow us to fix the number of iterations to 5000 for our testing phase. As discussed earlier, the training time increases as we increase the number of iterations therefore selecting low number of iteration for our model will improve the running performance of the model. But, this selection cannot assure an accurate decision model as the error stability is must in such type of networks. We can ignore the training time as it is one time cost to achieve higher detection accuracy for unknown test samples.

We evaluated our proposed model's performance using TPR, FPR, TNR, FNR, Accuracy and Error [25]. Table 1 illustrates performance of constructed trained neural networks. A high value of TPR and low value of FPR indicates that developed model is performing well. Our model discriminates the clean and malignant behavior with higher accuracy of 99.9 % and 99.24 %. The false-alarm rate in these cases is negligible which indicates that our selected input vector is significantly diverse in identifying samples with clean and malignant behavior. Remaining two behavior classes indicate the categorization within a malware class, so here we expected the overlapping. The infinite–running and guest–crashing are two environment–reactive behaviors which do not reflect its malicious behavior instead these categories of malware try to mimic the clean behavior. Therefore, we are observing a false–alarm rate in these two cases.

Table 1. Performance evaluation with training and known test datasets

Dataset	Network	TPR	FPR	TNR	FNR	Accuracy
Training	C vs All	99.8	0	100	0.2	99.9
	M vs All	98.56	0.09	99.91	1.44	99.24
	I vs All	95.12	0.92	99.08	4.88	97.1
	G vs All	97.01	0.24	99.76	2.99	98.39
Test	C vs All	97.22	3.4	96.6	2.78	96.91
	M vs All	97.12	1.59	98.41	2.88	97.76
	I vs All	95.56	3.04	96.96	4.44	96.26
	G vs All	92.8	5.53	94.47	7.2	93.64

4.4 Testing Phase

We conducted testing for our known and unknown test datasets. As illustrated earlier, the known test samples are labeled with their respective behavior but are not utilized during the training phase. Table 1 shows the results of our known test dataset. We observed that the testing results are quite similar to the training results. There is a tolerable difference in detection accuracy of our training and test datasets because of our model is trained with less number of guest–crashing and infinite–running samples as compared to benign samples. We have observed that overall testing accuracy of 96.125 %.

Table 2 shows our testing results with unknown test set. We supplied this set to verify the correctness of proposed model with unknown unlabeled instances of binaries. From statistics, we can deduce that our model is capable in categorizing the unknown instances. We confirmed the assigned behavior labels of unknown test samples by monitoring these samples in Ether. With an error rate of 4.6 %, we found that designed model automates our manual behavior labeling process. This proves that the proposed model can determine the environment–reactive behavior of unknown instances also.

Table 2. Detection accuracy with unknown test dataset

Behavior class	# Samples	# Correct instances	# Incorrect instances
Clean	265	258	7
Malignant	103	102	1
Guest–crashing	36	34	2
Infinite–running	19	17	2

4.5   Performance Evaluation

To evaluate the performance of the proposed supervised learning model we considered three factors. These factors are described as follows.

Detection Rate: The detection rate determines the accuracy of a proposed model. The proposed model addresses the malware detection problem which categorizes the malware instances according to their suspicious (Non–environment–reactive and environment–reactive) behavior. This detection problem is sensitive therefore the high true positive rate and low false positive rate is desirable. We obtained high TPR and low FPR in Table 1.

Generality: Generality determines how well the trained model performs on test data. According to [17] we cannot achieve the generality with smaller (as in our case) and imbalanced datasets. However, our experimental results contradict this and indicate significant uniformity in testing and training results. For instance the FNR value with both training and test samples tables are more as compared to FPR. The reasons for this achieved generality are that (i) our constructed input vector includes such patterns which can identify the diversity in all four behavior classes and (ii) our dataset is not completely imbalanced. To check whether the dataset is balanced or not we applied an imbalance measure derived in [17]. Let Ω be an imbalance measure for OAA. Equation 4 decides the value of Ω. Here $K = 4$ denotes the number of classes and n_i is the total number of samples in i^{th} class. If Ω tends to zero means the dataset is imbalanced and the maximum value for Ω will be $1/(K-1)$ which denotes that the dataset is balanced. In our case, Ω is 0.15 which indicates that our training set is not completely imbalanced and thus we have achieved uniformity in training and testing results.

$$\Omega = min\left\{ \frac{n_i}{\sum_{j=1,\ i \neq j}^{k} n_j} \ \middle| \ i = 1, \ldots , K \right\} \qquad (4)$$

Training Time: We created neural networks equal to the number of behaviors to be detected, which in our case is 4. In order to achieve a high efficiency with respect to training time, we trained all these four networks in parallel by making use of JAVA threads. Hence, training of each network occurs in parallel and the overall training time becomes equal to the maximum value of the time taken by all four networks. We obtained training time in the range of 17–1096 s for 100–10000 iterations respectively with heap space 3 GB. We also trained the designed model with heap space 2.5 GB (training time ranges from 22 to 1536 s) and observed a significant speed up (1.45 for 5000 iterations) with the former. This speedup is achieved due to the lower execution frequency of the JAVA garbage collector in higher heap space. The obtained training time is not a big issue to be considered. But when our proposed method applied with larger datasets this time will increase drastically. To reduce the training time with larger dataset we can increase the heap space memory of the system and can acquire a significant speed up without making any modifications into our developed model.

5   Limitations

We have shown that our approach can detect real unknown malware on the basis of their environment–reactive behavior. Also we have observed that most of the current malware depicts these behaviors. However, malware portraying behavior other than malignant, guest–crashing and infinite cannot be detected by our decision model. To overcome this, the proposed model can be trained again to detect the new behavior as well. In this section, we describe cases which restrict our detection and categorization approach.

Tracing and behavior screening of malware binaries completely depend on Ether. So, the limitations associated with Ether are inherited into our approach. The malware with root privileges can detect Ether framework as it utilizes the emulated version of Bochs virtual machine [12] for BIOS data strings. Our proposed model does not deal with these obscure malware as Ether cannot generate their execution logs. Second, analyzing executables from Ether is a time consuming task. Ether uses exceptions whenever a running application makes a system–call to access system service. These exceptions result into significant performance overhead.

Our approach does not consider multiple execution paths of running binaries. Exploring multiple execution path of a single sample can detect the trigger–based malware. The trigger–based malware delivers its malicious payload only if certain trigger conditions are met. These triggers include certain system state, timestamp (a particular date, day or even time), URL and certain keywords [4,16]. Our single–execution path based approach may miss this category of malware. However, our approach can detect a fraction of these trigger–based malware which prefer environment–sensitive payload over trigger–based payload in its execution path. Also, our experimental results deduce that a single execution path of an executable is sufficient to detect its benign or malignant nature.

6   Conclusion

Emerging malicious threats are detection–aware therefore the current DBMD approaches are in getting out–of–date. New generation of malware can detect the presence of analysis–environment and do not reflect malignant behavior. Ether which is a hardware–based virtualization framework can also be detected by these new–generation malware samples. In our proposed approach, we developed a decision model for identifying and categorizing the behavior of a sample during its execution in virtualized environment. The proposed model automates our behavior screening and labeling process and captures the environment–reactive and non–environment–reactive behavior of malware. It makes use of execution sequence generated in a single analysis environment and this log sequence is used to predict the behavior class of malware. We evaluated our proposed model with known and unknown real instances and discovered that the proposed model is effective in detecting these instances.

Acknowledgments. Mauro Conti is supported by a Marie Curie Fellowship funded by the European Commission under the agreement No. PCIG11-GA-2012-321980. This work is also partially supported by the TENACE PRIN Project 20103P34XC funded by the Italian MIUR, and by the Project "Tackling Mobile Malware with Innovative Machine Learning Techniques" funded by the University of Padua.

References

1. Anderson, B., Quist, D., Neil, J., Storlie, C., Lane, T.: Graph-based malware detection using dynamic analysis. J. Comput. Virol. **7**(4), 247–258 (2011)
2. Balzarotti, D., Cova, M., Karlberger, C., Kirda, E., Kruegel, C., Vigna, G.: Efficient detection of split personalities in malware. In: Proceedings of the Network and Distributed System Security Symposium, NDSS, San Diego, California, USA, pp. 1–16 (2010)
3. Bethencourt, J., Song, D., Waters, B.: Analysis-resistant malware. In: Proceedings of the Network and Distributed System Security Symposium, NDSS, San Diego, California, USA, pp. 1–13 (2008)
4. Brumley, D., Hartwig, C., Liang, Z., Newsome, J., Song, D., Yin, H.: Automatically identifying trigger-based behavior in malware. In: Lee, W., Wang, C., Dagon, D. (eds.) Botnet Detection. Advances in Information Security, vol. 36, pp. 65–88. Springer, New York (2008)
5. Chen, X., Andersen, J., Mao, Z., Bailey, M., Nazario, J.: Towards an understanding of anti-virtualization and anti-debugging behavior in modern malware. In: Dependable Systems and Networks With FTCS and DCC, DSN, pp. 177–186, June 2008
6. Chester, D.L.: Why two hidden layers are better than one. In: Proceedings of the International Joint Conference on Neural Networks, IJCNN 1990, Washington, DC (1990)
7. Dinaburg, A., Royal, P., Sharif, M., Lee, W.: Ether: Malware analysis via hardware virtualization extensions. In: Proceedings of the 15th ACM Conference on Computer and Communications Security, CCS 2008, pp. 51–62. ACM, New York (2008)
8. Hornik, K., Stinchcombe, M., White, H.: Multilayer feedforward networks are universal approximators. Neural Netw. **2**(5), 359–366 (1989)
9. J00ru: Windows win32k.sys system call table, April 2014
10. Jacob, G., Hund, R., Kruegel, C., Holz, T.: Jackstraws: picking command and control connections from bot traffic. In: Proceedings of the 20th USENIX Conference on Security, SEC 2011, pp. 29–48. USENIX Association, Berkeley (2011)
11. Kang, M.G., Yin, H., Hanna, S., McCamant, S., Song, D.: Emulating emulation-resistant malware. In: Proceedings of the 1st ACM Workshop on Virtual Machine Security, VMSec 2009. ACM, New York, pp. 11–22 (2009)

12. Kevin, L., Bryce, D., David, G., Volker, R., Christophe, B.: Bochs user manual (2010)
13. Kolbitsch, C., Comparetti, P.M., Kruegel, C., Kirda, E., Zhou, X., Wang, X.: Effective and efficient malware detection at the end host. In: Proceedings of the 18th Conference on USENIX Security Symposium, SSYM 2009, pp. 351–366. USENIX Association (2009)
14. Lindorfer, M., Kolbitsch, C., Milani Comparetti, P.: Detecting environment-sensitive malware. In: Sommer, R., Balzarotti, D., Maier, G. (eds.) RAID 2011. LNCS, vol. 6961, pp. 338–357. Springer, Heidelberg (2011)
15. Mark, R., David A, s., Alex, L.: Windows internal part 2
16. Moser, A., Kruegel, C., Kirda, E.: Exploring multiple execution paths for malware analysis. In: Proceedings of the 2007 IEEE Symposium on Security and Privacy, SP 2007, Washington, DC, pp. 231–245 (2007)
17. Ou, G., Murphey, Y.L.: Multi-class pattern classification using neural networks. Pattern Recogn. 40(1), 4–18 (2007)
18. Park, Y., Reeves, D.S., Stamp, M.: Deriving common malware behavior through graph clustering. Comput. Secur. 39, 419–430 (2013)
19. Pék, G., Bencsáth, B., Buttyán, L.: nEther: in-guest detection of out-of-the-guest malware analyzers. In: Proceedings of the Fourth European Workshop on System Security, EUROSEC 2011, pp. 3:1–3:6. ACM, New York (2011)
20. Quist, D., Liebrock, L., Neil, J.: Improving antivirus accuracy with hypervisor assisted analysis. J. Comput. Virol. 7(2), 121–131 (2011)
21. Rieck, K., Holz, T., Willems, C., Düssel, P., Laskov, P.: Learning and classification of malware behavior. In: Zamboni, D. (ed.) DIMVA 2008. LNCS, vol. 5137, pp. 108–125. Springer, Heidelberg (2008)
22. Rutkowska, J.: Red pill... or how to detect vmm using (almost) one cpu instruction
23. Srivastava, A., Lanzi, A., Giffin, J.T.: System call API obfuscation (extended abstract). In: Lippmann, R., Kirda, E., Trachtenberg, A. (eds.) RAID 2008. LNCS, vol. 5230, pp. 421–422. Springer, Heidelberg (2008)
24. Sun, M.K., Lin, M.J., Chang, M., Laih, C.S., Lin, H.T.: Malware virtualization-resistant behavior detection. In: Proceedings of the 17th International Conference on Parallel and Distributed Systems (IEEE), ICPADS 2011, Washington, DC, USA, pp. 912–917 (2011)
25. Vinod, P., Laxmi, V., Gaur, M.S.: REFORM: relevant feature for malware analysis. In: Proceedings of Sixth IEEE International Conference of Security and Multimodality in Pervasive Environment (SMPE 2012), pp. 26–29. Fukuoka Institute of technology (FIT), Fukuoka, Japan (2012)

Metric for Security Activities Assisted by Argumentative Logic

Tarek Bouyahia[(✉)], Muhammad Sabir Idrees, Nora Cuppens-Boulahia,
Frédéric Cuppens, and Fabien Autrel

Telecom Bretagne, 2 Rue de la Châtaigneraie, Cesson Sévigné, France
tarek.bouyahia@telecom-bretagne.eu

Abstract. Recent security concerns related to future embedded systems make enforcement of security requirements one of the most critical phases when designing such systems. This paper introduces an approach for efficient enforcement of security requirements based on argumentative logic, especially reasoning about activation or deactivation of different security mechanisms under certain functional and non-functional requirements. In this paper, the argumentative logic is used to reason about the rationale behind dynamic enforcement of security policies.

Keywords: Argumentative logic · Reasoning · Complex attack · Reaction policies

1 Introduction

Designing a secure system has always been a complex exercise. In practice, much of the focus for designers and developers being on delivering a working system in the first place; on the other hand, security concerns have long been considered only in retrospect, especially after serious flaws are discovered. Security experts are thus generally confronted with an existing system, whose architecture might actually hamper the deployment of security mechanisms that would prevent the occurrence of the attacks they envision. On the contrary, the challenges of modern security tools is to keep the system in a safe state while maintaining the best possible level of performance and quality of service. From the embedded system viewpoint, enforcement of security requirements becomes even more challenging and more critical. These challenges stem from the tight relationship between architecture design and its functional, and non-functional requirements as well as their impact on one another. For instance, if the system architecture design changes or evolves, these requirements should meet the new architecture design objectives and choose the best countermeasure that can be applied in this specific context or situation. This is especially true in safety-critical systems such as automotive systems [6,13], where attacks may be devastating, but where security functions overhead may also result in an absolutely useless system. In such a context, designing a secure system has always been a complex exercise. Indeed, security is a functionality that is difficult to specify and implement because it is

J. Garcia-Alfaro et al. (Eds.): DPM/SETOP/QASA 2014, LNCS 8872, pp. 183–197, 2015.
DOI: 10.1007/978-3-319-17016-9_12

not modular: modifications to one part of an application may interact strongly with the security properties of other parts of the same application.

In this paper, we present an approach that solves these problems. This approach is driven by argumentative logic (AL) [8]. It describes a structured collaboration and interrelationship between the system architecture design and security requirements to support the long-term needs of the system. The purpose of security activities assisted by argumentative logic is to bring into focus the key areas of concern, highlighting the decision criteria and security context for each system aspect that has direct or indirect value for a stakeholder. We also claim that the security analysis should also play an important role with respect to convincing the designer of increasingly complex embedded systems of the consistency and exhaustivity of his reasoning and selection of security measures, at least with respect to the identified threats. The use of argumentative logic driven reasoning engine can help in dynamic enforcement of security mechanisms through the introduction of non-monotonic reasoning capabilities. This capability opens up the door to the dynamic selection and enforcement of security mechanisms performed statically only today.

The paper is organized as follows: Sect. 2 introduces a case study from an automotive domain we use throughout the paper. Section 3 goes around works already done within the scope of this paper. Section 4 explains our approach for dynamic enforcement of security requirements assisted by argumentative logic. We show deployment scenario highlighting how an argumentative logic driven reasoning engine, which makes it easier to dynamically enforce security mechanisms in Sect. 5. Section 6 concludes the paper and outlines future work.

2   Motivation Example for Efficient Security Enforcement

In order to give an example of potential need for dynamic enforcement of security requirements to control different security activities, we consider the following abstract example of automotive on-board system. A modern automotive on-board network interconnects a hundred of microcontrollers, termed Electronic Control Units (ECUs) organized into application-specific domains bridge by gateways, as shown in Fig. 1. Attacks have been shown to be quite feasible [9] by bypassing the filtering performed between domains or by brute-forcing ECU cryptography-based protection mechanisms. Such attacks may in practice originate from the Internet connection increasingly available in vehicles or even from the Bluetooth pairing of a compromised mobile phone to the vehicle on-board network. Further attacks are anticipated in upcoming Car2X applications, which will feature vehicle-to-vehicle or vehicle-to-infrastructure communications. Many security attacks and vulnerabilities are due to the fact that either security policy is not well specified and enforced or system-wide security policies (dependencies between different security policies) are too weak. Automotive on-board architectures do not only rely on the simple enforcement of security rules but also involve multiple enforcement points, especially when the underlying platforms and infrastructures are providing services themselves, like HSM, or middleware layers. For instance,

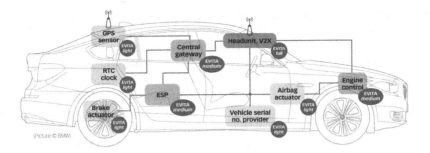

Fig. 1. Automotive on-board network architecture [11]

the security policy to be applied in a vehicle is the combination of an invariant policy for the usage control of cryptographic credentials of Electronic Control Units (ECU), and a flexible networking security policy. The credential usage control policy is enforced by the HSM and possibly through the virtualization of the ECUs if applications on the same ECU have to be segregated. In contrast, the networking security policy is enforced by all network elements. Moreover, the access control architecture must also allow enforcement of rules that limit the traffic on the buses under consideration, based on trusted authentication or other security mechanisms like traffic filtering or secure logging. However, as highlighted in the previous section, the enforcement of these different security mechanisms depends on a specific event or situation. For instance, while communicating with external entities like vehicle-to-infrastructure, it is preferable to apply the traffic filtering rules to limit the computation load on the HSM, which is responsible for the verification of cryptographic operations. Applying such rules will eventually increase the performance of on-board system. However, always applying such kind of rules is not desirable, as the enforcement of rules requires that the vehicle is in a specific context as well as a specific security event is active. To dynamically enforce these different sets of security policies, we call these policies as reaction policies [3]. In an on-board architecture, we need a system in which policy enforcement decisions are based on specific arguments in order to attain more fine grained enforcement of security policies.

3   Related Work

Based on the general idea of the platform in [8], the authors in [5] use the logical argumentation to support generation of the low-level rules from high-level policies. In [4] the authors treat the problem of resolving the possible anomalies in firewall policies using Argumentation for Logic Programming with Priorities (LPP). The use of this framework allows preferences to be encoded, thus allowing complex reasoning over the relative priorities between rules. The framework presented by Applebaum in [2] differentiates itself from these last two references through the introduction of the rationales behind each argument in the policy. Applebaum propose to resolve conflictual situations in firewall policies by defining a potential ordering of the rationales behind each argument (rule). Firewall can then resolve anomalies and conflictual rules through this order of priorites. In [2] Applebaum defines a static order of priorities for the rationales behind the firewall rules. However, administrators can decide in specific cases to change the order of rationales priority. For instance, giving "allow legitimate senders" rationale a higher priority than "allow programs". In this case, firewall adminstrators are obliged to update the firewall configuration for each required change in order priorities. Argumentation has also received attention in the community of multi-agent systems in recent years, with a particular interest in the use of argumentative models from the informal logic viewpoint such as that by Walton and Krabbe [12,15]. Additionnaly, Bench-Capon introduces the value-based framework in [7], and he extends it in [10] to provide meta-arguments to reason about preference levels. However, current AL approaches target the system from the static viewpoint, while ignoring any dynamic change in the system state or security event, during system evolution.

4   Argumentative Logic-Driven Reasoning Engine

In our approach, we design an argumentative framework allowing the automation of adapting priorities order, according to the current security situation and building the security metric. To achieve this goal, our approach can be summarized in the following three steps:

- For each security event, we define the rationale behind each possible counter-measure.
- According to the contextual values and depending on security events, we build the security metric which define the order between rationales.
- In case of conflict between countermeasures, we reason about the risk analysis to decide which countermeasure is more important to apply.

In this section, we will define the role of different parts involved in the architecture described in Fig. 2 and the relations between them.

4.1   Security Policies

We start by defining the reaction policies, which presents the knowledge base of security policies defined by the target organization. The reasoning module performs the mapping between the collected information and security policies in order to identify the rules that match. Reaction security policies are presented as sets of rules in which we define the list of possible countermeasure for possible security events that may occur in system evolution. We present in Table 1 some examples of countermeasures for some security events according to automotive system case [1]. The functional experts are responsible for giving rationales for different countermeasure introduced in the security policy. These rationales are defined to express the result of the application of each countermeasure on the system. In the Policy Administration Point (PAP) part, we assign to each rule defined in the policy, the rationale behind it. For instance, we attribute "performance" as a rationale for the countermeasure "Reduce frequency of beaconing and other repeated

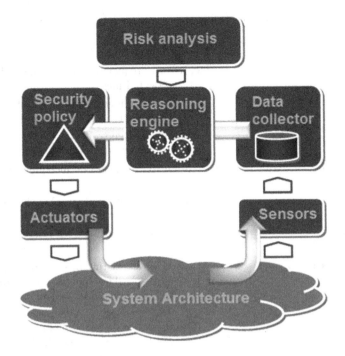

Fig. 2. Architecture of system detection & reaction

messages" when "message saturation" threat occurs. According to the contextual values and depending on security events, we build in the PAP the security metric which defines the priorities order between rationales. According to the security and contextual information collected by the data collection part, the Policy Decision point (PDP) refers to the reasoning module to choose, among the rules introduced into security policies, the suitable rule to apply(e.g., if "performance" rationale has the highest priority in the context on which the "message saturation" threat was executed, the PDP choose "Reduce frequency of beaconing and other repeated messages"). Finally, the decision will be applied at the level of the Policy Enforcement Point (PEP) of the targeted system component. In complex system, the PEP is integrated in all the system components, to enforce the reasoning engine decision in the relevant component.

4.2   Reasoning Engine

In order to ensure system security, policy reactions must maintain a certain level of intelligence and dynamicity. Those properties allow security systems, according to a specific security situation, to choose the best countermeasures to apply from the security metric. At the same time, the system enforces security conditions and a better efficiency of execution. Many approaches use argumentative logic (AL) [2] to provide rationales behind security policies. However, current AL

Table 1. Potential security countermeasures to threats in an ITS system [1]

Threats	Countermeasure
Message saturation	Reduce frequency of beaconing and other repeated messages
	Add source identification (IP address equivalent) in V2V messages
	Limit message traffic to V2I/I2V and implement station registration
Manipulation of relayed ITS messages en route	Plausibility checks on incoming messages
	Include a non-cryptographic checksum of the message in each message sent
	Remove requirements for message relay in the ITS BSA
Wormhole attacks	Use INS or existing dead-reckoning methods (with regular - but possibly infrequent - GNSS corrections) to provide positional data
	Implement differential monitoring on the GNSS system to identify unusual changes in position
	Use broadcast time (Universal Coordinated Time - UTC - or GNSS) to timestamp all messages

approaches typically target the system from the static viewpoint and developed the metric of arguments, while ignoring any dynamic change in the system state or security event, during system evolution. To do this, security tools must have intelligent reasoning capabilities as the one of the human brain. To develop an approach for dynamic policy reactions, we inspire from the human way of arguing. Argumentation has been shown to be a useful framework for formalizing non-monotonic reasoning. It is a branch of logic that enables reasoning about the arguments to resolve inconsistencies in logic theory.

Argumentative Logic. An argumentation system is a way for an agent to manage conflicting information and draw conclusions. In an abstract argumentation system, the basic information is a set of abstract arguments, which may for example represent a given proposal, and conflicts between arguments are represented by a binary relation on the set of arguments. For two arguments A and B, the meaning of attacks(A,B) is that A represents an attack on B. We also say that a set of arguments S attacks an argument B if B is attacked by an argument in S. We rely on the Dung's [6] definition of an argumentation logic, which states that:

Definition 1:
An argumentation framework is a pair AF = < AR, attacks >
Where AR is a set of arguments and attacks is a binary relation on AR, i.e.
attacks ⊆ ARXAR.

Dung introduces also the notion of acceptability of arguments. An accepted argument, in a set of arguments, is the one that every attack on it is rebutted by an accepted argument form the set.

Definition 2:
An argument $A \in AR$ is acceptable with respect to set of arguments S (acceptable(A,S)), if:
$(\forall x)((x \in AR)\&(attacks(x, A)) \rightarrow (\exists y)(y \in S)\&attacks(y, x)$.

In security policies, we consider that each attack on a rule implemented in the policy is rebutted by itself because attack relation is considered as symetric from reaction security point of view. Thus, each security rule implemented in security policy is accepted. To adapt the argumentation system to the security requirements, we consider security policies as arguments. In addition, we define a relation of attack between arguments (rules), two or more different possible countermeasures that can be applied for a specific security event. For instance, in the automotive case, three different countermeasures are presented according to the "Message saturation" security threat as shown in Table 1. Based on the above mentioned Definition 1, these countermeasures represent two arguments that attack each other because we are in a conflicting situation and we need to choose the suitable countermeasure among them. In our approach, we define the conflict between independent countermeasures according to a specified threat as following:

Definition 3:
$\forall A \in T, \forall X_1, X_2 \in C_A$
$conflict\_independent(X1, X2) \leftarrow countermeasure(X1) \land countermeasure(X2)$.
Where T present the set of all the threats and C_A is the set of possible countermeasures according to threat A.

Attack relation may also occur between two or more different arguments, according to different threats, that the system is unable to apply at the same time as described in Sect. 5.1. We define the conflict between dependent countermeasures according to two threats as following:

Definition 4:
$\forall A, B \in T, \forall X_1 \in C_A$ and $\forall X_2 \in C_B$
$conflict\_dependent(X1, X2) \leftarrow countermeasure(X1) \land countermeasure(X2) \land$
$dependent(X1, X2)$.

Where T present the set of all the threats, C_A is the set of possible countermeasures according to threat A, C_B is the set of possible countermeasures according to threat B, and $dependent(X1, X2)$ is the predicate that inform the system about the dependence between countermeasures.

4.3 Risk Determination

The purpose of this risk assesment is to assess whether the threats or security vulnerabilities are relevant according to the security level specified by the security goals. In our approach, we estimate the security risks based on the relevant threats, their likelihood/impact [13] that the threats will materialize as real attacks, any potential consequences on the system assets or possible severity of an attack for the stakeholders, and the resulting impact of that adverse event on the organization. We also consider the weakness that may occur when we apply a specific countermeasure. In the case of a complex attack, we are always facing conflicting situations where applying a countermeasure for a security event can deactivate the application of other countermeasures. In our approach, we are interested in the likelihood and the impact of each security threat. The likelihood depends on five factors that we affect range and value as shown in Table 2 (e.g., an attack that affect a standard equipment is more likely to occur than an attack that affect a specialized one, attackers can be better familiarized with standard than specialized equipment). The "likelihood" value is calculated from the sum of the five factors values. The threat group likelihood is evaluated through the sum obtained, likelihood increases with the decrease of the sum. For instance, for a sum belonging to the interval [0,3] the likelihood value is considered the most important "likely".

4.4 System Architecture

The system architecture shows the composition of the system in terms of components and interconnections between them. Through sensors and intrusion detectors installed in the various components of the system, data collection part is able to acquire security information as attack notifications and contextual data. Each component in the system architecture is linked by a sensor to detect all malicious activities that may occur, and actuators to apply different actions taken by the PDP. From the automotive viewpoint, the system architecture is composed of several components interlinked. The components of automotive system architecture are equipped by a hardware security module (HSM) that provides means to protect the plateform by protecting critical assets of the architecture. Once the reasoning module has taken the right decision to respond to an attack, the PEP is responsible for applying the countermeasure taken at the relevant component in the architecture. The information in complex system is distributed in all the system. Thus, in order to have a global view of all the security data, we need a data collector in our architecture which collects information from all components sensors.

4.5 Data Collection

Data collection is the process of combining and associating information regarding one or more entities considered in a knowledge framework. The aim of data collector is to improve capability for detection, identification and characterization of that entity. In modern decision support systems, information coming

Table 2. Risk determination in an ITS system [13]

Threat Group	Attack				Impact
	Factor	Range	Value	Likelihood	
Acquisition of personal information	Time	< = 1 day	0	2(Possible)	3(Medium)
	Expertise	Proficient	2		
	Knowledge	Restricted	1		
	Opportunity	Moderate	4		
	Equipment	Standard	0		
Acquisition of behavioural	Time	< = 1 day	0	1(Possible)	2(Medium)
	Expertise	Proficient details	2		
	Knowledge	Restricted	1		
	Opportunity	Difficult	12		
	Equipment	Specialized	3		
Denial of transmission	Time	< = 1 day	0	3(Likely)	1(Low)
	Expertise	Layman	0		
	Knowledge	Public	0		
	Opportunity	Easy	1		
	Equipment	Standard	0		
Denial of receipt	Time	< = 1 day	0	3(Likely)	2(Low)
	Expertise	Layman	0		
	Knowledge	Public	0		
	Opportunity	Easy	1		
	Equipment	Standard	0		

from several sensors is fused in order to overcome the uncertainty in a case. The main purpose of collection is to provide an overall picture of the significance of the information collected by different platforms to classify/identify the target entities and to have a new data set containing the meaningful data. Data collection part notifies the reasoning module when security events occur (individual or complex attacks) and the contextual information on which they were produced.

Security Events. Security events present all the types of attacks that may occur on a system and harm its evolution in safety conditions. Nowadays attacks are becoming more and more complex which complicate the task of security tools to prevent them. And it becomes even more difficult in the case of coordinated attacks. A coordinated attack is the collaboration of several attacking sources to achieve a common goal. In order to achieve this goal, attacking sources, controlled by one or several attacking entities, may cooperate by resource sharing, task allocation, synchronization,etc. Many works focus on complex attack and the way to design them as in [14] where the authors define a formal description of individual and coordinated attacks.

Contextual Information. Data collector collects contextual information describing the circumstances in which the attacks occurred. Those information are extracted by the reasoning module that used it to reason and take the decision that best fits the context. From the automotive point of view, we distinguish in this paper three types of context:

- In-car
- V2V (Vehicule to Vehicule)
- V2I/I2V (Vehicule to Infrastructure / Infrastructure to Vehicle).

5 Dynamic Deployment of Security Policies

We present in this section the deployment of our approach, described in the last section. The security data (i.e., security event and contextual information) are collected, by the data collector, through the sensors integrated at different layer of system architecture. These data are extracted by the reasoning engine and compared by the security rules defined in the security policies, to identify the possible countermeasures to apply.

5.1 Evaluation of Countermeasures

In some cases, the PDP can make the decision to apply two or more countermeasures (especially in the case of complex attack) where one of them prevents the execution of another countermeasure, or reduces the efficiency of its application as described in Sect. 5.4. Each countermeasure taken by the system, may have one or several weakness points that can affect the reaction process and the maintenance of the system in security conditions. We present in Table 3 some of the weaknesses of the potential countermeasures that may degrade the overall security and safety of the system. Complex systems such as automotive on-board system arhictecture are more vulnerable to coordinated and complex attacks, due to the complexity of its components and the distributed nature of the system. The attackers try to damage the system through the intrusion to one or many components of the system.

5.2 An Example of Complex Attack in Automotive System

The coordinated attack described below requires a minimum number of Group of Coordinating Attackers (GCA), and it inflicts damage to automotive ITS system by executing two different attacks (Message Saturation (MS) and Manipulation of Relayed ITS messages in route (MR)): A part of attackers saturates the ITS server by sending a huge number of requests at the same time. While the ITS system is unable to process all the incoming messages, the other part of attackers captures those messages as an ITS server and manipulates them. We use the modelisation of complex attacks described in [14] to define an example of complex attack in automotive system (CXA) corresponding to the type "Coordinated Attack with Load Accumulation – CALA". CALA is defined in [14] as a

Table 3. Security countermeasures and their limitations [1]

Security Countermeasure	Limitations
Reduce frequency of beaconing and other repeated messages	Safety-critical messages may not be received quickly enough by affected vehicles
Add source identification (IP address equivalent) in V2V messages	The desired principles of anonymity within ITS are breached
	May not be available in the existing stack
Limit message traffic to V2I/I2V when infrastructure is available and implement message flow control and station registration	The coverage of the ITS infrastructure would have to be extensive
	The speed of response to an incident would deteriorate (however, response times would be deterministic)
	Current IEEE 802.11 technologies do not support flow control

coordinated attack in which attackers accumulate their capabilities. This offers execution of the attack in a distributed and simultaneous way.

$(CALA) : CALA\_ComplexAttack(GCA_{CXA}, ITS)$
$min_{CXA} = 17$
$A_{CXA} = \{network\_access(attackerID, ITS)\}; A'_{CXA} = \{\}$
$B_{CXA} = \{knows(attackerID, is\_on(ITS))\}; B'_{CXA} = \{MS(ITS)))\}$
$\Gamma_{CXA} = \{is\_on(ITS, MS(ITS))\}; \Gamma'_{CXA} = \{MS(ITS), MR(ITS)\}$

A_{CXA}, B_{CXA} and Γ_{CXA} present the precondition predicates that have to be satisfied to allow the action execution. A'_{CXA}, B'_{CXA} and Γ'_{CXA} present the postcondition predicates that become true after the action execution. The min_{CXA} value is obtained from the sum of the opportunity values of the threats involved in the complex attack. Automotive experts define the opportunity value for attacks as the number of attackers required to achieve the attack. In this case, we have two different attacks (MS and MR) with the opportunity values of each one is 12 and 5, the resulting min_{CXA} value is 17.

5.3   System Reaction and Inconsistency Resolution

To mitigate this complex attack, we apply the approach defined in Sect. 4:

– We start by defining, for each security event, the rationale behind each possible countermeasure as presented in Table 4, where we have defined the priorities for "Message saturation" threat, we start with the "in-car" context then "V2V" context, and finally "V2I/I2V" context:

Table 4. Priority order between reasons for message saturation threat

Context	Rule	Countermeasure	Reason	Attack
In-car	1	Reduce frequency of beaconing and other repeated messages	Performance	2,3
	2	Add source identification (IP address equivalent) in V2V messages	Data-source authenticity	1,3
	3	Limit message traffic to V2I/I2V and implement station registration	Filtering	1,2
V2V	2	Add source identification (IP address equivalent) in V2V messages	Data-source authenticity	1,3
	1	Reduce frequency of beaconing and other repeated messages	Performance	2,3
	3	Limit message traffic to V2I/I2V and implement station registration	Filtering	1,2
V2I/I2V	3	Limit message traffic to V2I/I2V and implement station registration	Filtering	1,2
	2	Add source identification (IP address equivalent) in V2V messages	Data-source authenticity	1,3
	1	Reduce frequency of beaconing and other repeated messages	Performance	2,3

These requirements are defined in a formal way as following:

$rule1 : countermeasure(reduce\_frequency) \leftarrow threat(message\_saturation)$
$rule2 : countermeasure(add\_source) \leftarrow threat(message\_saturation)$
$rule3 : countermeasure(limit\_traffic) \leftarrow threat(message\_saturation)$

We include the incompatibility predicate defined in Definition 3 to ensure that different countermeasure cannot be part of the same acceptable argument:

$conflict\_independent(countermeasure(reduce\_frequency),$
$countermeasure(add\_source)) \wedge conflict\_independent(countermeasure$
$(limit\_traffic), countermeasure(reduce\_frequency)) \wedge conflict\_$
$independent(countermeasure(limit\_traffic), countermeasure(add\_source)).$

This conflict is resolved through the priority predicate which define the rationale priority order:

$priority(1, rule1, incar, performance) :$
$rule1 \leftarrow threat(message\_saturation) \wedge context(incar)$
$priority(2, rule2, incar, authenticity) :$
$rule2 \leftarrow threat(message\_saturation) \wedge context(incar)$
$priority(3, rule3, incar, filtering) :$
$rule3 \leftarrow threat(message\_saturation) \wedge context(incar)$

– According to the complex attack (CXA), we present in the Table 5, the best countermeasure to apply corresponding to the reason having the higher priority, and depending to the context in which the security event was produced (In-car).

Table 5. Default countermeasures configuration for complex attack

Security event	Countermeasure	Reason	Weakness	Likelihood/ impact
MS	Reduce frequency of beaconing and other repeated messages	Performance	Safety-critical messages may not be received quickly enough by affected vehicles	(1,3)
MR	Include a non-cryptographic checksum of the message in each message sent	Availability	A subverted legitimate ITS-S possess all of the necessary algorithms to compute a valid checksum for a maliciously modified message	(2,3)

When the system applies the "Reduce frequency of beaconing and other repeated messages" countermeasure, the safety-critical messages may not be received quickly enough by affected vehicles. Thus, the system is not able to include a non-cryptographic checksum of the message in each message sent, which is the countermeasure for "Manipulation of relayed ITS messages in route" threat. The weakness of the "Message saturation" countermeasure affects the treatment of the second security event which can be detected through conflict_dependent predicate defined in Definition 4:

$conflict\_dependent(countermeasure(reduce\_frequency), countermeasure$
$(checksum))$

To resolve this conflict, the reasoning engine refers to the risk analysis part to identify which security threat has the greatest likelihood/impact value.

$prefer(threat(manipulation\_ITS\_messages), threat(message\_saturation) \leftarrow$
$like\_impact(manipulation\_ITS\_messages) > like\_impact(message\_saturation)$

The prefer predicate inform the reasoning engine about the most important threat from the threats having conflictual countermeasures. The processing of the "Manipulation of relayed ITS messages in route" is more important than the "Message saturation" thread because of the likelihood/impact values. We are confronted here to a conflict between two countermeasures. Applying the best countermeasure for each security event is impossible, that is why we refer to Table 4 and we pass to the second possible countermeasure for "Message saturation" which

Table 6. Countermeasures adopted for complex attack

Security event	Countermeasure	Reason	Weakness	Likelihood/impact
MS	Add source identification (IP address equivalent) in V2V messages	Data-source authenticity	The desired principles of anonymity within ITS are breached	(1,3)
MR	Include a non-cryptographic checksum of the message in each message sent	Availability	A subverted legitimate ITS-S possess all of the necessary algorithms to compute a valid checksum for a maliciously modified message	(2,3)

ensures Data-source authenticity. We present in Table 6 the configuration of countermeasures adopted by the reasoning engine to mitigate the complex attack.

As we can see in Table 6, the application of each countermeasure of MS and MR does not affect the execution of the other one. We consider this configuration as the best that system can apply to maintain the system in safe conditions and offer better performance.

6   Conclusion and Future Work

In order to protect system from modern attacks, it is necessary to have a dynamic and intelligent enforcement of security policies. We consider the argumentative logic driven system the most appropriate to achieve this objective. In this work we showed how to improve the existing argumentation framework, we proposed a new approach that allows us to consider the context of security situations in order to take the suitable and dynamic decisions. We are currently working to include the case of dependancies between system components and other functional and non functional requirements of the system. More specifically, we are designing an approach that consider the system dependancies in reasoning while considering other requirements such as performance, cost, etc.

References

1. Etsi tr 102 638: "intelligent transport systems (its); vehicular communications; basic set of applications; definitions"
2. Applebaum, A., Levitt, K.N., Rowe, J., Parsons, S.: Arguing about firewall policy. In: Verheij, B., Szeider, S., Woltran, S. (eds.) COMMA, Frontiers in Artificial Intelligence and Applications, vol. 245, pp. 91–102. IOS Press, Graz (2012)

3. Autrel, F., Cuppens-Boulahia, N., Cuppens, F.: Reaction policy model based on dynamic organizations and threat context. In: Gudes, E., Vaidya, J. (eds.) Data and Applications Security XXIII. LNCS, vol. 5645, pp. 49–64. Springer, Heidelberg (2009)
4. Bandara, A.K., Kakas, A.C., Lupu, E.C., Russo, A.: Using argumentation logic for firewall policy specification and analysis. In: State, R., van der Meer, S., O'Sullivan, D., Pfeifer, T. (eds.) DSOM 2006. LNCS, vol. 4269, pp. 185–196. Springer, Heidelberg (2006)
5. Bandara, A.K., Kakas, A.C., Lupu, E.C., Russo, A.: Using argumentation logic for firewall configuration management. In: Integrated Network Management, pp. 180–187. IEEE (2009)
6. Bar-El, H.: Intra-vehicle information security framework. In: Proceedings of the 7th Escar Conference, Düsseldorf, Germany (2009)
7. Bench-Capon, T.J.M.: Persuasion in practical argument using value-based argumentation frameworks. J. Log. Comput. **13**(3), 429–448 (2003)
8. Dung, P.M.: On the acceptability of arguments and its fundamental role in non-monotonic reasoning, logic programming and n-person games. Artif. Intell. **77**(2), 321–358 (1995)
9. Koscher, K., Czeskis, A., Roesner, F., Patel, S., Kohno, T., Checkoway, S., McCoy, D., Kantor, B., Anderson, D., Shacham, H., Savage, S.: Experimental security analysis of a modern automobile. In: 2010 IEEE Symposium on Security and Privacy (SP), pp. 447–462, May 2010
10. Modgil, S., Bench-Capon, T.J.M.: Integrating object and meta-level value based argumentation. In: Besnard, P., Doutre, S., Hunter, A. (eds.) COMMA, Frontiers in Artificial Intelligence and Applications, vol. 172, pp. 240–251. IOS Press, Graz (2008)
11. E. Project. E-safety Vehicle InTrusion protected Applications. http://www.evita-project.org
12. Reed, C.: Dialogue frames in agent communication. In: Demazeau, Y. (ed.) ICMAS, pp. 246–253. IEEE Computer Society (1998)
13. Ruddle, A., Ward, D., Weyl, B., Idrees, M.S., Roudier, Y., Friedewald, M., Leimbach, T., Fuchs, A., Gürgens, S., Henniger, O., Rieke, R., Ritscher, M., Broberg, H., Apvrille, L., Pacalet, R., Pedroza, G.: Security Requirements for Automotive On-Board Networks based on Dark-side Scenarios. Technical report 2.3, EVITA Project (2010)
14. Samarji, L., Cuppens, F., Cuppens-Boulahia, N., Kanoun, W., Dubus, S.: Situation calculus and graph based defensive modeling of simultaneous attacks. In: Wang, G., Ray, I., Feng, D., Rajarajan, M. (eds.) CSS 2013. LNCS, vol. 8300, pp. 132–150. Springer, Heidelberg (2013)
15. Walton, D., Krabbe, E.: Commitment in Dialogue: Basic Concepts of Interpersonal Reasoning. G - Reference, Information and Interdisciplinary Subjects Series. State University of New York Press, New York (1995)

Quantitative Aspects
in Security Assurance

Calculating Adversarial Risk from Attack Trees: Control Strength and Probabilistic Attackers

Wolter Pieters[1,2](✉) and Mohsen Davarynejad[1,3]

[1] Technology Policy and Management, ICT, Delft University of Technology,
Delft, The Netherlands
w.pieters@tudelft.nl, mohsen@davarynejad.com
[2] EEMCS, Services, Cybersecurity and Safety, University of Twente,
Enschede, The Netherlands
[3] Department of Radiation Oncology, Erasmus Medical Center,
Daniel den Hoed Cancer Center, Rotterdam, The Netherlands

Abstract. Attack trees are a well-known formalism for quantitative analysis of cyber attacks consisting of multiple steps and alternative paths. It is possible to derive properties of the overall attacks from properties of individual steps, such as cost for the attacker and probability of success. However, in existing formalisms, such properties are considered independent. For example, investing more in an attack step would not increase the probability of success. As this seems counterintuitive, we introduce a framework for reasoning about attack trees based on the notion of control strength, annotating nodes with a function from attacker investment to probability of success. Calculation rules on such trees are defined to enable analysis of optimal attacker investment. Our second result consists of the translation of optimal attacker investment into the associated adversarial risk, yielding what we call adversarial risk trees. The third result is the introduction of probabilistic attacker strategies, based on the fitness (utility) of available scenarios. Together these contributions improve the possibilities for using attack trees in adversarial risk analysis.

Keywords: Adversarial risk analysis · Attack trees · Attacker models · Control strength · Fitness functions · Security metrics · Simulation

1 Introduction

Attack trees [8,9,15] are a well-known formalism for analysing cyber attacks consisting of multiple steps and alternative paths. It is possible to derive properties of the overall attacks from properties of individual steps, such as cost for the attacker, probability of success, and probability of detection. In existing formalisms, such properties are considered independent. For example, investing more in an attack step would not increase the probability of success. This even holds for more complicated schemes in which multiple parameters are considered simultaneously [4].

© Springer International Publishing Switzerland 2015
J. Garcia-Alfaro et al. (Eds.): DPM/SETOP/QASA 2014, LNCS 8872, pp. 201–215, 2015.
DOI: 10.1007/978-3-319-17016-9_13

Although such approaches have definitely shown their value in both theoretical and practical respect, there are several issues. Firstly, assuming that an attack step always costs the same in any situation seems counterintuitive. An attacker who wants to be really sure that a particular step succeeds may invest more time and/or money, thereby increasing the likelihood of success (and maybe reducing the likelihood of detection). Secondly, analysis tools are available which work precisely with a relation between investment (time) and likelihood of success [1]. To enable the attack tree paradigm to take full advantage of such methods, they need to support suitable annotations (i.e. dependent parameters).

To address these issues, this paper proposes a framework for reasoning about attack trees based on the notion of control strength, which is a function from attacker investment to probability of success. Calculation rules on such trees are defined to enable analysis of optimal attacker investment, in the context of a two-step game where the attacker can choose the optimal attack after the defender has placed his controls. The key application of this approach is in adversarial risk assessment. Whereas traditional attack trees were not directly connected to the notion of risk, our approach enables their use in calculating adversarial risk in terms of threat, vulnerability, and impact, where vulnerability describes the relation between attacker investment and probability of success, and threat describes the optimal attacker strategy based on vulnerability and impact.

In Sect. 2, we provide definitions for parameters of interest and analysis of attack trees with dependent parameters, based on optimal attacker investment. Section 3 shows an example including simulations. In Sect. 4, we illustrate how to factor in time, to calculate risk based on optimal attacker investment. In Sect. 5, we extend the approach with probabilistic attackers, assuming that limited knowledge and limited rationality will lead attackers to not always choosing the optimal scenario, creating a different risk picture for the defender. In Sect. 6, we discuss related work, and we conclude in Sect. 7.

2 Definitions

2.1 Preliminaries

Factor Analysis of Information Risk (FAIR). To define our concepts (the same as in [13,14]), we use the risk definitions provided by The Open Group [16]. In this taxonomy, risk-related variables are defined starting from the notions of assets and threat agents acting against these assets, potentially causing damage. A threat event occurs when a threat agent acts against an asset, and a loss event occurs when this causes damage. For example, a storm may occur at the location of a power line (threat event), and this may or may not damage the power line (loss event).

Like many other approaches, The Open Group distinguishes between what they call Loss Event Frequency (LEF) and Probable Loss Magnitude (PLM). The former represents the expected number of loss events of a particular type per unit of time (often referred to as likelihood), and the latter represents the expected damage per loss event of that type (often referred to as impact).

Risk can be seen as expected damage due to a certain type of loss event within a given time frame, and it can then be calculated as LEF · PLM.

Within LEF and PLM, The Open Group makes further distinctions. We will not discuss PLM here, but focus on LEF. First of all, the Loss Event Frequency can be separated in Threat Event Frequency (TEF) and Vulnerability (V). TEF denotes the expected frequency of occurrence of a particular threat (seen as a threat agent acting against an asset; a storm at the location of a power line), and V specifies the likelihood of the threat inflicting damage upon the asset. The value for LEF can then be calculated as TEF · V. The Open Group defines the Vulnerability V based on Threat Capability (TC) and Control Strength (CS). In this definition, TC denotes some ability measure of the threat agent, and CS a resistance (or difficulty of passing) estimate of the control. We have discussed this relation in detail in [14]. Note that the term vulnerability is used as probability of success here, not as a software bug causing a security weakness. To avoid ambiguity, we will only use the term probability of success in this paper.

Attack Trees. Attack trees [15] describe attacks by means of a tree structure, in which attacker goals are refined by means of AND-nodes (all subgoals have to be achieved) and OR-nodes (only a single subgoal has to be achieved). In the end, attack trees represent a set of possible attack paths [9]. Figure 1 shows a simple attack tree for obtaining secret data. The tree consists of four leaves. The left branch is an AND-node; the other two non-leaf nodes are OR-nodes.

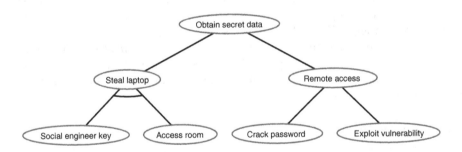

Fig. 1. An attack tree for obtaining secret data by laptop theft or remote access in ADTool [7]. The bottom left non-leaf node is an AND-node, the other non-leaf nodes are OR-nodes.

Attack trees can be annotated with all kinds of values, such as probability of success, cost for the attacker, required time, etc. Many calculations are possible on such trees, from simple bottom-up value aggregation from leaves to root, to complicated calculations made feasible by genetic algorithms. An extensive literature review of work to date on attack trees is provided in [8]. Some dependency between variables is taken into account in [4], in the sense that the probability of detection depends on whether the attack step succeeded or failed. However, the cost of an attack step is still fixed.

2.2 Contributions

Our innovation lies in the explicit use of control strength and threat capability in the analysis of attack trees. This separates system properties and attacker properties. In addition, we distinguish between static attacker properties (skill) and dynamic attacker properties (investment). The former are pre-defined and constant over the duration of the attack; the latter can be strategically chosen by the attacker.

In particular, we consider control strength (also called difficulty) as a function from threat capability to probability of success. By defining difficulty in this way, we enable the use of separate, explicit attacker profiles, that can contain static properties (skill) and rules for dynamic properties (investment strategy). In this paper, we assume only a single investment strategy, namely the (rational) one that maximises utility for the attacker. However, we do take account probabilistic deviations from optimal selection of scenarios (Sect. 5). The question on how to define the difficulty function has been treated elsewhere [14], and we will not repeat this issue here. The definition of difficulty as a function also implies that attacker investment (cost) and probability of success cannot be treated as independent properties, like in existing formalisms. This adaptation seems intuitive, as the more an attacker invests in trying to get in, the more likely he will be able to succeed. Thus, the existing assumption of fixed costs and a fixed probability of success for an attack step is lifted.

To be able to calculate attacker utility, we assume there is a certain value for the attacker associated with the goal represented in the root node of the attack tree. For example, achieving the root goal would provide a utility of € 1,000 to the attacker. We will not address the question how to define this value in the present work. The model presented here is a *parallel model* [4] in which all atomic attacks $x_1, \ldots, x_n$ take place simultaneously; e.g. the adversary chooses a subset of atomic attacks and executes them in parallel independent of success or failure of some of attack steps.

2.3 New Definitions

Definition 1. *The* probability of success *of an attack step or composite attack is a value in the range [0,1], indicating how likely the attack (step) is to succeed when executed. The probability of success can also be interpreted as an expectation value of the success variable, when failure is 0 and success is 1.*

Note that this is different from what is generally referred to as likelihood in risk assessment, as that likelihood refers to probability (frequency) of occurrence, not probability of success.

Definition 2. *A* control strength function *is a function $c : T \rightarrow [0,1]$, indicating the relation between threat capability and probability of success. T can be any partially ordered set suitable for representing capability (in its simplest form {Low, Medium, High}, but could also be money). It is assumed that c is monotonic: a higher threat capability will lead to a higher or equal probability of success.*

Definition 3. *A* threat capability function *is a function* $t : S \times I \to T$, *indicating the relation between attacker skill, attacker investment, and threat capability. S could again be for example {Low, Medium, High}. I is typically expressed in terms of money. It is assumed that t is monotonic in both parameters: a higher skill or a higher investment will lead to a higher or equal threat capability.*

Definition 4. *An* investment function *is a function* $f : I \to [0,1]$, *indicating the relation between attacker investment and probability of success. It is assumed that f is monotonic: a higher investment will lead to a higher or equal probability of success.*

An investment function f can be expressed in terms of a control strength function c, a threat capability function t, and an attacker skill s as $f(i) = c(t(s,i))$. If both c and t are monotonic, f will be monotonic as well. Nodes in attack trees can now be annotated with control strength functions rather than simple values. For non-leaf nodes, the functions represent the results for the associated subtree. If no explicit attacker profiles (e.g. skill) are considered, an annotation with investment functions suffices.

2.4   Analysis

The analysis is based on the formalisation of attack trees by Mauw and Oostdijk [9], in which the semantics of an attack tree is the corresponding set of attacks C, which are multisets of attack steps. It determines what constitutes the optimal investment for the attacker (maximum utility), by finding out how to distribute resources as investments over attack steps. To this end, we first need to determine how the investment function of AND- and OR-nodes can be derived from those of their children. The calculation rule for the investment function f of an AND-node with children x_1 and x_2 with investment functions f_1 and f_2 is:

$$f(j) = max\{f_1(i_1)f_2(i_2) \mid i_1 + i_2 \le j\} \tag{1}$$

Note that, under the assumption that f_1 and f_2 are monotonic, the maximum will always occur when $i_1 + i_2 = j$. The calculation rule for the investment function f of an OR-node with children investment functions f_1 and f_2) is:

$$f(j) = max\{f_1(i_1) + f_2(i_2) - f_1(i_1)f_2(i_2) \mid i_1 + i_2 \le j\} \tag{2}$$

In this equation, it is assumed that the attacker can invest in multiple branches of the OR-split in order to maximise his probability of success. In practice, the attacker may first try one branch and base his further investment upon the result. We do not discuss such "sequential OR-nodes" in this paper, but they would be relevant for future studies.

In addition to combining the investment functions of the children into one, the analysis would need to keep track of the distribution of investment over the subtrees associated with the maximum probability of success (the argmax). As can be seen from the definitions, the functions will get increasingly complicated when moving towards the root node (at least in the general case). For each branch of the tree, the function definition could be split in two separate domain intervals. In practice, one will not do these calculations before a specific question has been asked on the tree. In particular, the question of the optimal attack from the attacker perspective is relevant here.

In this paper, we assume that an attacker only gains utility if he achieves the root goal. The optimal balance between investment and probability of success depends on how much utility the root node provides. The higher this utility, the more important the probability of success becomes, compared to the investment.

3   Examples and Simulations

In this section we provide a number of examples to illustrate the theoretical properties of investment trees. The examples provided here are small; they are meant for illustrative purposes. This means that we can exhaustively enumerate the possible attack paths and their utilities, which is useful for explaining the intuitions. In these examples the cumulative distribution functions (CDFs) of logistic distributions are adopted to mathematically represent the probability of success as a function of investment (according to Definition 4). There are two reasons for choosing logistic distributions: (1) logistic distributions provide a strong analogy with difficulty metrics in other domains [14], and (2) the logistic distribution reflects the fact that with little investment, the probability of success is low, whereas there is a certain critical point around which the probability of success increases rapidly with higher investment. There are three parameters of interest: the mean μ of the distribution, the scale s, and the maximum success probability c. The latter reflects the fact that a probability of success of almost 1 is not always achievable, not even with nearly infinite resources.

Figure 2 shows an example of such a function with $\mu = 33$, and $s = 0.15$ (blue dash curve) or $s = 0.44$ (dot-dash red curve). The units are not specified here, but investment can be thought of as units of time or money the attacker invests in an attack step. In all the simulation results provided below the assumption is that the attacker is rational, so s/he launches multi-stage attacks to achieve his/her goals. Other distributions like Rayleigh CDF might be also suitable for particular cases, but the essentials remain the same. In an ideal scenario these functions can be estimated from empirical evidence like penetration tests [2].

Example 1. Suppose that the attacker goal is to steal a laptop, which will yield a gain (positive utility) of 1000 for the attacker, and a damage (negative utility) of 5000 to the defender (e.g. replacement plus data loss). The attacker can invest in two branches of an AND-split. The first branch x_1 has an investment function f with a logistic CDF form with $\mu_1 = 33$ and $s_1 = 0.15$. The second branch x_2 has exactly the same investment function as x_1 with the exception of $s_2 = 0.44$. Figure 2 shows the investment function and Fig. 3a the profit landscape. Each black asterisk represents the optimal investment in each attack step when the sum of resources j is limited. In this example j is set at 0 and increases to 300 with step size of 2.

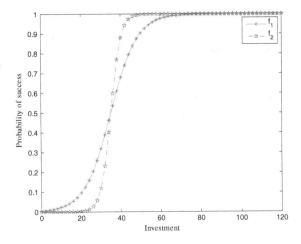

Fig. 2. Investment function f_1 with $\mu_x = 33$, $s_x = 0.15$, and f_2 with $\mu_y = 33$, $s_y = 0.44$ (Color figure online)

Example 2. Suppose that the attacker goal is to steal a laptop, where she can invest in two branches of an OR-split. The first branch has an investment function f_1 similar to that of the first branch of Example 1 and the second branch x_2 has exactly the same investment function as that of the second branch of Example 1. Then the profit landscape is shown in Fig. 3b. Here again each black asterisk represents the optimal investment in each attack step when the sum of resources j is limited. In this example j is set at 0 and increases to 300 with step size of 2. The maximum resources the attacker can spend is the same as in the first example. Because the attacker can choose between two alternatives with different investment functions, the optimum jumps from one alternative to the other depending on the amount the attacker can invest.

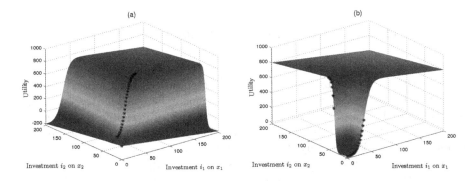

Fig. 3. Profit landscape for (a) the AND-node example, (b) the OR-node example.

Example 3. Now consider the attack tree from Fig. 1, with leaf node investments labelled i_1, i_2, i_3, i_4, from left to right. In this example f_1 and f_2 (left branch) are the same as what we have described in previous examples. The μ_3 and μ_4 (right branch) are both set at 75 and s_3 and s_4 are set at 0.15 and 0.4 respectively (Fig. 4). The optimal investment on each attack step for a number of values of j is reported in Table 1. When the attacker's maximum investment j is less than 56, then the empty strategy (i.e. not playing at all) is optimal.

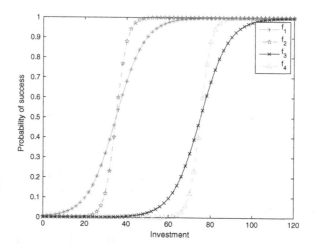

Fig. 4. Investment functions for the complete example attack tree.

These examples show how to use control strength in attack tree calculations, optimising the relation between investment and probability of success from the point of view of the attacker. However, this does not directly provide information about adversarial risk.

4   From Optimal Investment to Risk

Many papers on security risk assessment end with the analysis of optimal investments, without considering time. We take one step further here, and try to align security risk assessment with safety risk assessment by considering attack frequencies, based on a profile of the attacker in terms of available resources and investment strategy. As in the previous sections, we choose the Factor Analysis of Information Risk taxonomy [16] as the risk assessment framework. We choose this taxonomy because it explicitly relates threat capability (investment), control strength, and probability of success, similar to our extended attack trees. In this framework, vulnerability is synonymous to probability of success, and this vulnerability is dependent on both threat capability and control strength. From the point of view of the attacker, the control strength (strength of the defense)

Table 1. Optimal investment on each attack step when j is incremented from 50 to 100 with step size of 4.

j	Optimal investment on each attack step				Utility	Total investment
	i_1	i_2	i_3	i_4		
50	0	0	0	0	0.013011	0
54	0	0	0	0	0.013011	0
58	21.2594	36.7406	0	0	17.3807	58
62	24.9633	37.0367	0	0	63.8835	62
66	0	0	66	0	139.8704	66
70	0	0	70	0	250.8213	70
74	0	0	74	0	388.5702	74
78	0	0	0	78	690.5278	78
82	0	0	0	82	860.6766	82
86	0	0	0	86	901.8717	86
90	0	0	0	89.9661	907.5276	89.9661
94	0	0	0	89.9661	907.5276	89.9661
98	0	0	0	89.9661	907.5276	89.9661

is fixed, and vulnerability can thus be expressed as a function from investment (in threat capability) to probability of success (vulnerability).

As risk is expressed as threat event frequency (likelihood) times vulnerability times impact, we need to address the missing item, which is the frequency. To this end, we need to extend the analysis from a single point in time decision by the attacker to longitudinal, by limiting the attacker income (and thereby his resources) as a function of (continuous) time. In this paper, we choose the discrete event model from [13] for the analysis of risk, based on attack trees endowed with control strength annotations for optimal investment analysis. In the discrete event model, attackers save resources and attack with the accumulated resources at a single point in time. After the attack, the damage is assumed to be repaired, the attacker resources are reset to zero, and the same process will be repeated. Whereas [13] only discusses atomic attacks, we apply the analysis to attack trees here. In addition, we extend the analysis with non-zero-sum situations, as well as probabilistic attacker strategies. The mapping from optimal investment to risk, via time, proceeds as follows [13]. Attackers can, at each point in time, choose to launch an attack with the resources they have built up until that point ($R(t)$). Attackers will also have a skill level s, and the threat magnitude m is a function of the skill and the available resources:

$$m(t) = f(s, R(t)) \tag{3}$$

Attackers will not attack, but rather wait and save resources, if they can gain higher expected average utility by launching an attack with more resources later.

If they cannot improve their average utility by waiting, they will execute the scenario with the highest expected utility given their current resources.

The vulnerability (probability of success) V of an attack step/scenario c depends on the threat magnitude m. The expected utility $U_c(m)$ for each threat capability level m and for each attack scenario c is:

$$U_c^A(m) = V_c(m) \cdot G_c^A \tag{4}$$

where G_c^A is the utility (gain) for the attacker upon *success* of scenario c.

The maximum utility for a given threat capability level m is specified by

$$\hat{U}^A(m) = \max_{c \in C} U_c^A(m) \tag{5}$$

The optimal scenario to execute is then $\underset{c \in C}{\operatorname{argmax}}\, U_c^A(m)$.[1]

We can therefore calculate the maximum expected utility at each point in time, $\hat{U}^A(t) = \hat{U}^A(m(t))$, and also the maximum average utility over the elapsed time, which we denote S for *success*, $\hat{S}^A(t) = \hat{U}^A(m(t))/t$. Assuming an attacker who wants to maximise his average gain per unit of time, the attacker will thus attack at the time $\hat{t}$ when $\hat{S}^A(t)$ reaches its maximum. The scenario that will be executed is

$$\hat{c} = \underset{c \in C}{\operatorname{argmax}}\, U_c^A(m(\hat{t})) \tag{6}$$

Assuming instant repair, the expected threat event frequency can be determined as $h_{\hat{c}} = 1/\hat{t}$. For all other scenarios, the threat event frequency is zero. The loss event frequency for scenario $\hat{c}$ is $\lambda_{\hat{c}} = V_{\hat{c}}/\hat{t}$. From the loss event frequency, we can calculate the risk (negative success) S^D as annual loss expectancy, by filling in the utility for the defender rather than the attacker of a successful scenario c. Note that both $U_{\hat{c}}^D$ and S^D are negative.

$$S^D = h_{\hat{c}} \cdot U_{\hat{c}}^D \tag{7}$$

Example 4. Consider the attack tree of Example 3. We assume that the skill level is irrelevant here, and we therefore assume that $m(t) = R(t)$. The attacker has income density function $\frac{dR}{dt} = 1$, i.e. the attacker will earn 1 resource unit per unit of time, or $m = t$. Up to $t = 1$, the attacker will thus be able to invest 1 unit. In Fig. 5, the resulting optimal utility function $\hat{S}^A(t)$ is shown.

Note that in the discrete model, it is required that $V(0) = 0$. Otherwise, the expected risk (damage per unit of time) for very small t would be very high (up to infinite with t approaching 0), and the attacker would simply launch loads of "mini-attacks" with almost zero effort. For logistic vulnerability models where V is not zero as t approaching 0 additional considerations are required. In this study, this property of logistic vulnerability models is handled by setting the step size of change in t to a value bigger than 1.

---

[1] Note that picking argmax may involve nondeterministic choice if multiple arguments produce the maximum. This is one of the issues that the probabilistic attackers in this paper (Sect. 5) help to solve.

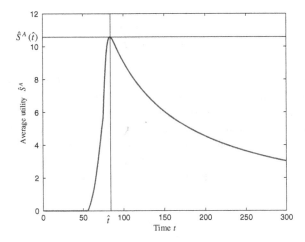

Fig. 5. A simulation of attacker success (utility per unit of time) as a function of attack time for the laptop theft scenario (Example 3). Initially, it does not make sense to invest at all. From $t = 58$, utility increases rapidly (see also Table 1), but success (utility per unit of time) starts to decline when marginal utility decreases.

5   Probabilistic Attackers

When evaluating the effect of countermeasures, an optimising attacker model implies that defenses that are not on the critical (optimal) path will have no effect. This is not very realistic. In reality, attackers have only limited information and need not be fully rational. To account for attackers not always choosing the optimal attack, we introduce probabilistic attacker strategies. In such a strategy, the probability of selecting a particular scenario is based on the fitness of that scenario, expressed as the utility it provides to the attacker per unit of time. For now, we assume that the attacker will always execute a chosen scenario at the optimal point in time. This is still a worst-case approximation, but it does not matter that much for defender decisions on effectiveness of countermeasures. Our probabilistic attacker is *not* meant to model a strategic attacker that knows everything, but chooses less optimal scenarios to evade defender actions. It is only meant to represent uncertainty on the part of the attacker.

Our proposal for assigning selection probability P_c to attack scenario c has its roots in genetic algorithms. The higher the utility of an attack scenario S_c^A, the higher its probability of being selected. This represents an attacker optimising his selection while possessing limited information about the fitness of the scenarios. In order to differentiate between levels of knowledge and understanding of the system, we use Boltzmann selection [10], which defines selection probabilities in the form of Boltzmann canonical distributions. It has been shown that the Boltzmann distribution can be derived from maximizing the Shannon entropy under proper constraints [11]. The selection probability is assigned as follows:

$$P_c = \frac{exp(-T/f_c)}{\sum\limits_{c \in C} exp(-T/f_c)} \qquad (8)$$

where $T \in \mathbb{R}^+$ represents the level of knowledge and understanding of attacker concerning the system. The higher T, the higher the knowledge of the attacker, which results in better identification of high utility attack scenarios. In contrast, lower T represents a poor understanding of the system for the attacker, which results in poor distinction between high- and low-profit attack scenarios. This poor understanding results in higher uncertainty and insignificant difference in probability of selection of attack scenarios. In Eq. (8) f_c is described as:

$$f_c = \frac{S_c^A}{\sum\limits_{c \in C} S_c^A} \cdot |C| \qquad (9)$$

Example 5. We take the attack tree presented in Example 3 (Fig. 1). This attack tree has three attack scenarios: $\{x_1, x_2\}$, $\{x_3\}$, and $\{x_4\}$. The optimal attack time $\hat{t}$ for each of these attack scenarios and their respective success values at optimal attack time $S_c^A(\hat{t})$ and $S_c^D(\hat{t})$ are reported in Table 2.

Table 2. Attack scenario selection probability.

c	$\hat{t}$	$S_c^A(\hat{t})$	$S_c^D(\hat{t})$	T, attacker knowledge level			
				$T = 0.1$	$T = 1$	$T = 10$	$T = 100$
$\{x_4\}$	84	10.59	-56.94	0.3375	0.3761	0.7512	1.0000
$\{x_3\}$	92	09.08	-49.41	0.3326	0.3247	0.1728	0.0000
$\{x_1, x_2\}$	96	08.04	-46.03	0.3299	0.2991	0.0760	0.0000
Attacker $\bar{S}^A$				9.3168	9.3944	10.1260	10.5881
Defender $\bar{S}^D$				-50.5810	-50.9381	-54.3882	-56.9407

The analysis proceeds as follows:

1. Calculate fitness (attacker success S_c^A) for all attack scenarios, assuming optimal time of attack $\hat{t}$; also calculate defender success (risk);
2. Assign probabilities P_c to scenarios based on their fitness in accordance with Eq. (8);
3. Calculate expected attacker success and defender succeess by weighted average.

The calculation of the weighted average is:

$$\bar{S}^A = \frac{\sum\limits_{c \in C} P_c U_c^A}{\sum\limits_{c \in C} P_c t_c} \qquad (10)$$

The assumption is that the attacker chooses a scenario first based on the assigned probabilities, and then spends the associated time executing that scenario. This means that the time spent on a particular scenario is dependent on both the probability of selecting that scenario, and the time taken to execute the scenario. The expected utility of the whole strategy (all scenarios, weighted by probability), can then be divided by the expected time spent to find the average utility per unit of time. Replacing U_c^A with U_c^D, the same equation can be used to calculate the expected (negative) utility for the defender.

6   Related Work

Many of the annotations on attack trees, including time, cost and probability, are dependent both on properties of the system (e.g. resistance) and properties of the attacker (e.g. skill). In the TREsPASS project, we are looking for attacker-independent metrics, such that different attacker profiles can be used on the same attack tree. The idea of using control strength as a metric stems from the Factor Analysis of Information Risk framework, included in the Risk Taxonomy of The Open Group [16]. This idea was further developed in [2,14]. In this paper, we define control strength as function from attacker investment to probability of success.

In [1], a time-dependent analysis of attack trees is provided, relating time and success probability. However, investment (cost) is not considered, and the results are not linked to risk. The approach is also not focused on attacker decisions (in which step to invest). Because an exponential distribution is assumed, *the best choice never depends on the available time*, as the corresponding time-probability (cumulative probability) curves never intersect. For an OR-node, simply the fastest subtree is chosen; for an AND-node, both are started in parallel; for the additional sequential SEQ-node, the first subtree has to succeed first.

Several authors have considered return on attack as a security metric [3,6]. The lower the return on attack, the more secure the system. The return on attack complements the return on security investment from the defender's point of view. Several game-theoretic approaches have tried to relate the two. In this paper, we used the minimax approach suggested in [5], which optimises the defender investments under the assumption that the attacker will optimise his return on attack in the next step.

7   Conclusions

In this paper, we provided a new type of analysis on attack trees, namely the analysis of optimal attacker investment, under the assumption that the investment in an attack step influences the probability of success for that step. The formalisation in terms of control strength (difficulty) as a function from threat capability to probability of success was inspired by the Risk Taxonomy of The Open Group [16]. This constitutes an innovation beyond traditional formalisms, which considered attacker cost and probability of success as independent parameters. In addition, we showed how the analysis of optimal investment can be used to define adversarial risk in the context of attack trees, by limiting attacker resources in time (income). Finally, we showed how probabilistic attacker models, based on fitness evaluation of different scenarios, can improve the risk analysis, in particular when it comes to evaluation of countermeasures. The approach can be used to enhance existing security metrics, such as for example weakest link [12], adversarial risk, and return on security investment.

In this paper, we assume that the attacker makes his investment decisions upfront. In future work, we will investigate how the framework changes if the attacker can adapt his investment decisions on the fly, and how cooperation between multiple attackers influences the results. Also, we may consider the situation where other nodes than the root node would provide positive utility to the attacker upon success, and the situation in which the attacker invests his gain in new attacks. In addition, the probability of detection and punishment may be included next to the probability of success. Finally, case studies could provide further insights into the behaviour of the simulations.

Acknowledgements. The research leading to these results has received funding from the European Union's Seventh Framework Programme (FP7/2007–2013) under grant agreement number ICT-318003 (TREsPASS). This publication reflects only the authors' views and the Union is not liable for any use that may be made of the information contained herein.

References

1. Arnold, F., Hermanns, H., Pulungan, R., Stoelinga, M.: Time-dependent analysis of attacks. In: Abadi, M., Kremer, S. (eds.) POST 2014 (ETAPS 2014). LNCS, vol. 8414, pp. 285–305. Springer, Heidelberg (2014)
2. Arnold, F., Pieters, W., Stoelinga, M.I.A.: Quantitative penetration testing with item response theory. In: 2013 Proceedings of Information Assurance and Security (IAS). IEEE (2013)
3. Bistarelli, S., Fioravanti, F., Peretti, P.: Defense trees for economic evaluation of security investments. In: 2006 The First International Conference on Availability, Reliability and Security, ARES 2006 (2006)
4. Buldas, A., Laud, P., Priisalu, J., Saarepera, M., Willemson, J.: Rational choice of security measures via multi-parameter attack trees. In: López, J. (ed.) CRITIS 2006. LNCS, vol. 4347, pp. 235–248. Springer, Heidelberg (2006)
5. Cox Jr, L.A.: Game theory and risk analysis. Risk Anal. **29**(8), 1062–1068 (2009)
6. Cremonini, M., Martini, P.: Evaluating information security investments from attackers perspective: the return-on-attack (ROA). In: 4th Workshop on the Economics on Information Security (2005)
7. Kordy, B., Kordy, P., Mauw, S., Schweitzer, P.: ADTool: security analysis with attack–defense trees. In: Joshi, K., Siegle, M., Stoelinga, M., D'Argenio, P.R. (eds.) QEST 2013. LNCS, vol. 8054, pp. 173–176. Springer, Heidelberg (2013)
8. Kordy, B., Piètre-Cambacédès, L., Schweitzer, P.: DAG-based attack and defense modeling: don't miss the forest for the attack trees. Comput. Sci. Rev. **13–14**, 1–38 (2014)

9. Mauw, S., Oostdijk, M.: Foundations of attack trees. In: Won, D.H., Kim, S. (eds.) ICISC 2005. LNCS, vol. 3935, pp. 186–198. Springer, Heidelberg (2006)

10. de la Maza, M., Tidor, B.: An analysis of selection procedures with particular attention paid to proportional and Boltzmann selection. In: Proceedings of the 5th International Conference on Genetic Algorithms, pp. 124–131 (1993)

11. Nulton, J.D., Salamon, P.: Statistical mechanics of combinatorial optimization. Phys. Rev. A **37**(4), 1351–1356 (1988)

12. Pieters, W.: Defining "the weakest link": comparative security in complex systems of systems. In: 2013 IEEE 5th International Conference on Cloud Computing Technology and Science (CloudCom), vol. 2, pp. 39–44, December 2013

13. Pieters, W., Lukszo, Z., Hadžiosmanović, D., Van den Berg, J.: Reconciling malicious and accidental risk in cyber security. J. Internet Serv. Inf. Secur. **4**(2), 4–26 (2014)

14. Pieters, W., Van der Ven, S.H.G., Probst, C.W.: A move in the security measurement stalemate: elo-style ratings to quantify vulnerability. In: Proceedings of the 2012 New Security Paradigms Workshop, NSPW 2012, pp. 1–14. ACM (2012)

15. Schneier, B.: Attack trees: modeling security threats. Dr. Dobb's J. **24**(12), 21–29 (1999)

16. The Open Group. Risk taxonomy. Technical report C081, The Open Group (2009)

Analysis of Social Engineering Threats with Attack Graphs

Kristian Beckers[1], Leanid Krautsevich[2], and Artsiom Yautsiukhin[2(✉)]

[1] Paluno – The Ruhr Institute for Software Technology,
University of Duisburg-Essen, Duisburg, Germany
kristian.beckers@paluno.uni-due.de
[2] Istituto di Informatica E Telematica, Consiglio Nazionale Delle Ricerche,
Via G. Moruzzi 1, 56124 Pisa, Italy
{leanid.krautsevich,artsiom.yautsiukhin}@iit.cnr.it

Abstract. Social engineering is the acquisition of information about computer systems by methods that deeply include non-technical means. While technical security of most critical systems is high, the systems remain vulnerable to attacks from social engineers. Social engineering is a technique that: (i) does not require any (advanced) technical tools, (ii) can be used by anyone, (iii) is cheap.

While some research exists for classifying and analysing social engineering attacks, the integration of social engineering attackers with other attackers such as software or network ones is missing so far. In this paper, we propose to consider social engineering exploits together with technical vulnerabilities. We introduce a method for the integration of social engineering exploits into attack graphs and propose a simple quantitative analysis of the graphs that helps to develop a comprehensive defensive strategy.

Keywords: Social engineering · Threat analysis · Attacker modelling · Attack graph

1 Introduction

A study[1] of 2011 from Dimensional Research considered 853 IT professionals from United States, United Kingdom, Canada, Australia, New Zealand, and Germany concluded that: (i) 48 % of large companies and 32 % of small companies were victims of 25 or more social engineering attacks in the past two years, (ii) an average cost per incident is over \$25 000 and (iii) 30 % of large companies even cite a per incident cost of over \$100 000. In addition, the SANS institute report in a white paper[2] about social engineering that cyber attacks cost U.S.

---

[1] Dimensional Research Study about Social Engineering http://www.checkpoint.com/press/downloads/social-engineering-survey.pdf.

[2] SANS Institute InfoSec Reading Room http://www.sans.org/reading-room/whitepapers/engineering/threat-social-engineering-defense-1232.

© Springer International Publishing Switzerland 2015
J. Garcia-Alfaro et al. (Eds.): DPM/SETOP/QASA 2014, LNCS 8872, pp. 216–232, 2015.
DOI: 10.1007/978-3-319-17016-9_14

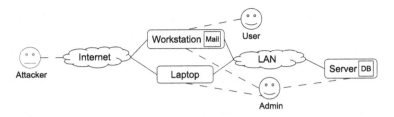

Fig. 1. An infrastructure model

companies $266 million every year and that 80 % of all attacks are caused by authorised users that are either disgruntled employees or non-employees that have established some form of trust within a company. The study also cites Kevin Mitnick a famous hacker, who stated in a BBC interview: "The biggest threat to the security of a company is not a computer virus, an unpatched hole in a key program or a badly installed firewall. In fact, the biggest threat could be you. What I found personally to be true was that it's easier to manipulate people rather than technology. Most of the time organizations overlook that human element." Thus, we can conclude that social engineering is still an important security issue to address.

Social engineering threats have been classified and analysed in the past [1–4]. Research into social engineering, e.g., [5], showed that the attacks often follow a simple process: gather information about the target, develop and exploit a trust relationship, and utilise the gathered information. Possible countermeasures are organisational rules in the form of security policies and staff training to recognise and prevent social engineering attacks, so-called awareness training.

One of the problem with tackling the social engineering threat is that security analysis of social engineering attackers is often isolated c.f. [1,3,6] from a technical security analysis, e.g., network vulnerability analysis. In this work, we investigate how social engineering exploits may completely or partially substitute technical vulnerabilities in an attack. We aim at enhancing our existing threat analysis methodology [8] with a social engineering threat analysis. Our methodology uses a detailed attack graph that represents systems as connected sets of vulnerabilities and that helps to analyse what steps the attacker needs to execute in order to achieve his goal. We focus on the integration of social engineering exploits into a combined attack graph for a further quantitative security analysis.

Our main contributions are: (i) formalisation of social engineering threats using threat patterns; (ii) (semi-automatic) identification of the existing social engineering vulnerabilities for a concrete system using access control rules and some information about the system; (iii) consolidation of social engineering vulnerabilities with network vulnerabilities in a combined attack graph; (iv) quantitative analysis of possible attacks considering the combined attack graph.

The remainder of the paper is structured as follows: Sect. 2 shows our research gap with respect to the related work. Section 3 describes several types of social engineering threats. Our methodology is shown in Sects. 4 and 5 concludes our paper and provides directions for future research.

Running example. We consider the Huntsville Consortium that sells energy to customers (see [8] for more details). There is an infrastructure which is responsible for storage of the metering data and issuing bills (see Fig. 1). The information is stored on a server serv, which runs under FreeBSD OS, in a database db (Oracle MySQL). The operator (user) uses a workstation ws, which runs under Windows OS, to process the data from the database. There is also an administrator adm of the network who uses a laptop lap to manage the server and the workstation. The laptop runs under Linux OS. The internal firewall allows access to a server from the workstation and the laptop only through LAN. The workstation and the laptop are connected to the Internet. The operator and the administrator have access to e-mail for interaction with clients and between themselves. Finally, this organisation is located in the same building without (properly) guarded access into it. The aim of the attacker is to change the data in the database to avoid paying for electricity.

2   Related Work

The only work we are aware of that tries to combine social engineering attackers with network attackers in a threat analysis is Kvedar et al. [7]. The authors used social engineering techniques successfully in a case study to acquire knowledge about network vulnerabilities as part of training exercise in the U.S. military. In contrast to our work the authors do not consider social engineering as separate exploits, but use it simply as a mean to acquire domain knowledge, e.g., firewall configurations. To show this gap in research we provide an overview of existing work in the areas of social engineering threat taxonomies and countermeasures for social engineering. We use attack graph analysis to analyse threats to provide an overview of this field as well.

Analysing Social Engineering Threats. Krombholz et al. [6] and Ahmadi et al. [9] presented overviews of social engineering threats, the communication channels used to conduct these attacks, e.g., social networks or instant messaging. Mills [10] focused on the problem of social networking offers with regard to the risk of information leakage. Chitrey et al. [11] conducted a survey using a questionnaire with IT practitioners in India with the aim of understanding the awareness of practitioners of social engineering threats. Furthermore, Laribee et al. [4] created models to describe social engineering threats in general. While Algarni and Xu [2] described two different attacker models for the domain of social networking sites. In addition, Dimkov et al. [3] contributed methodologies and guidelines for physical penetration testing using social engineering.

Countermeasures against Social Engineering Attacks. Severals works proposed social engineering countermeasures that include security awareness trainings, policies, incident reporting systems, and penetration testing. Winkler et al. [12] and Mitnick [5] described a large number of attacks and showed how to mitigate them using their catalogs of countermeasures. Peltier [1] and Gonzales et al. [13] based their collections of countermeasure on human behavioural patterns, which can be exploited by social engineering attackers. Twitchell [14] provided recommendations of how to teach people about social engineering threats and countermeasures in security training courses. Moreover, social engineering is also considered in security standards. The ISO 27001 [15] international standard contains a list of countermeasures that includes for example Control A.7.2.2. information security awareness, education and training, and A.5.1.1 policies for information security. Similar controls can be found in national guidelines, e.g., the German Grundschutzhandbuch IT [16].

Attack Graph Analysis. An attack graph is a technique for security modelling and analysis of a system which specifies states, related to the privileges the attacker may have, and transitions between them. There are two types of attack graphs in the literature. The first type denotes every state as a set of all privileges the attacker possesses at a certain stage of an attack [17]. The graph in this case is acyclic if we assume that an attacker cannot loose her privileges. The advantage of this model is that such type of analysis as Markov Decision Process (MDP) may be applied to it [18,19]. The main drawback of this model is the state-explosion problem. The second type is proposed by Noel and Jajodia [20] who represented nodes as atomic privileges. An attacker possesses several privileges at some stage of an attack, "owns" several nodes, i.e., the privileges she has are the union of the privileges assigned to these vertices. A transition requires "owning" certain vertices and leads to new privileges. This model is free from the state explosion problem, but has cycles and cannot be used for analysis with MDP.

3   Social Engineering Exploits

We summarise several common social engineering exploits identified by Krombholz et al. [6]. We choose all possible exploits for which we could define pre and post conditions. For example, we excluded the waterholing exploit in which an attacker compromises a website that is likely to be of interest for an employee. Formulating the "likely interest" is rather difficult and requires a deeper understand of psychological sciences.

Phishing refers to masquerading as a trustworthy entity and using this trust to acquire information or manipulating somebody to execute an action.
Shoulder Surfing means to obtain information from a display by being physically close to it and reading the information on the screen.
Dumpster Diving is the act of analysing the documents and other things in a garbage bin of an organisation to reveal sensitive information.
Reverse Social Engineering is to create a problem for a victim and to offer help to the victim for solving the problem. This way the attacker establishes trust, which is used to exploit the victim for sensitive information.
Baiting is to leave a storage medium (e.g., a USB stick) inside a company location that contains a malicious software (e.g., a key logger). The malicious software is executed automatically when the stick is inserted in a computer.

Table 1. Social engineering exploits

ID	Name	Precondition	Postcondition
SEE-0001	Phishing	☒Communication Channel ☐Physical Access	☒Credentials ☐ Access
SEE-0002	Shoulder Surfing	☐Communication Channel ☒Physical Access	☒Credentials ☐ Access
SEE-0003	Dumpster Diving	☐Communication Channel ☒Physical Access	☒Credentials ☐ Access
SEE-0004	Reverse Social Engineering	☒Communication Channel ☒Physical Access ☒Physical Access	☒Credentials ☒Access
SEE-0005	Baiting	☐Communication Channel ☒Physical Access	☒Credentials ☒Access

We derived pre and post conditions for these exploits (see Table 1) and recognised that social engineering exploits are possible using different communication channels such as: Telephone, VoIP, In person, Email, Fax, Instant messaging, and Social networks. For simplicity's sake, we do not distinguish between them in this work. Note that in all pre conditions the attacker has to be in possession of domain knowledge about the target, e.g., the attacker has to know how to use a communication channel to contact employees. Moreover, an attacker often needs physical access to the target organisation, for example in order to distribute USB sticks in the baiting exploit. Note that in some exploits technical access might also be required, e.g., in the Reverse Social Engineering exploit to create a technical problem with a machine.

Social engineering exploits often result in an attacker (illegally) obtaining credentials of a user of an organisation, e.g., a username and password combination. This combination can be used by an attacker to authenticate herself as the user. Moreover, a user can be compromised to provide access to an operating system to an attacker, e.g., via being asked to run a malicious program on the attacker's behalf or to perform some operation for the attacker. In summary, we consider credentials and access as possible outcomes of social engineering exploits and state them as post conditions in Table 1.

4   Analysis of Social Engineering Threats with Attack Graphs

We propose a combined analysis of a system against social engineering attackers and attackers with technical skills. We show the possible interactions of these attackers in an attack graph. The graph aims at finding sequences of low-level actions that an attacker needs to execute in order to achieve her high-level goals. Figure 2 shows our security analysis method. Further in this section we describe the steps of our approach in details.

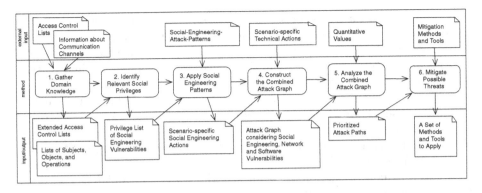

Fig. 2. An overview of our method for integrating social engineering threats in attack graphs

4.1 Step 1. Gather Domain Knowledge

Input: access control lists and information about communication channels.

Output: extended access control lists, lists of subjects, objects, allowed operations.

The first step in our methodology is gathering knowledge about the system. In particular, we will need access control information for different domains, existing communication channels (e.g., e-mail service, phone, skype, etc.), information about physical access and segregation of networks. Our goal is to create a model of the system.

Let S be a set of all subjects in the system plus an attacker att, O be a set of all objects, and OP be a set of all possible operations over objects. This information can be retrieved from existing access control lists used in the considered organisation. In the sequel, we consider only three types of operations: (R)ead, (W)rite, and (M)odify, but this list can be extended if needed. The real meaning of these operations depends on the type of the object. In this paper, we use "R" when a user may only read information (e.g., displayed on the computer), "W" when the user may interact with the object (e.g., execute the installed programs), and "M" when the user may modify the behaviour of the object (e.g., install programs on the computer).

Next, we need all access control lists themselves for different domains used in the considered organisation. By an access control list ACL we mean a set of access control rules expressed as triples $acl = (s, o, op)$, $s \in S$, $o \in O$, $op \in OP$, and $acl \in ACL$. Every access control list specifies access to a specific domain, i.e., the guarded set of objects. Therefore, we consider a set of such lists $\mathbb{ACL}$. We assume that $\mathbb{ACL}$ could be derived even if such systems as RBAC or ABAC are used in the system.

We sometimes need specific classes of subject and object. In other words, a class is a set of subjects or objects. Let CL be a set of classes $cl \in CL$ defined for the system, where domain of cl is $S \times O$. For example, we may have a class of administrators, class of workstations or class of network channels. The meaning of the required classes is specified by the social engineering exploits to be considered. We also assume that system analysts are able to specify which subjects and objects are contained in these classes using supporting information (e.g., business model, network model, etc.).

We need information about existing communication and physical channels. A channel is any means of human interaction used in the system. Let CH be a set of all possible channels in the system. We consider channels as objects, from which the users may receive messages ("R"), write messages to ("W"), and modify the channel ("M").

We also extend the notion of channels with channels for different networks. Social engineering attacks often lead to acquisitions of knowledge required for accessing some part of the system (e.g., login and password pair). On the other hand, next to the knowledge the attacker needs the possibility to use the knowledge (e.g., access to the internal network). Only having the knowledge *and* the possibility the attacker is able to execute her attack. Since, such channels are established between parts of the system (e.g., some objects) then we extend the S set with such objects.

Example 1. In our running example we consider two channels: e-mail ch^m and physical access ch^{phy}. Physical access channel refers to physical access to different parts of the system. In our example, we have only one unguarded building, i.e., there is only one physical channel in the system. Next to these social channels we have two network channels: internal LAN access ch^{lan}, and the Internet access ch^{int}. The internal access channel refers to the access to LAN between the workstation, laptop and server, when external access channel is available between the workstation, laptop and the Internet.

For specifying ACL we need a set of possible users $S = \{user, adm, att, ws, lap, serv, db\}$ and a set of objects is $O = \{ws, lap, serv, db, ch^m, ch^{phy}, ch^{int}, ch^{lan}\}$. Please, note, that the same entity can be both in the set of users and objects. This happens because the entity can either be accessed by another object or access another object itself depending on a scenario. A set of operations are: $OP = \{R, W, M\}$. Moreover, we need a class of computers $cl^{comp} = \{ws, lap, serv\}$, a class of network channels $cl^{net} = \{ch^{int}, ch^{lan}\}$, a class of separate physical areas: $cl^b = \{ch^{phy}\}$ and a class of e-mail channels $cl^m = \{ch^m\}$. In general, $CL = \{cl^{comp}, cl^{net}, cl^b, cl^m\}$.

Table 2 shows the access control lists that exist in the system. In fact, we have 4 access control lists for accessing the workstation, laptop, database and server. We also have access control lists for mail and physical channels and two lists for network access channels. We combine some access control rules by writing operations separated by "/".

There are a couple of simplifications in the model. First, the access to the e-mail channel can also be done through a client software installed on the user's computer. Access to this client is not guarded (as the login and password are stored by the client) and, thus, the only guard in this case is the access control mechanism of the workstation. Also the database is considered as having access

Table 2. Access control lists for our running example.

ACL^{ws} :	ACL^{lap} :	ACL^{db} :	ACL^{serv} :
$(user, ws, R/W/M)$	$(adm, lap, R/W/M)$	$(user, bd, R/W)$	$(adm, serv, R/W/M)$
$(adm, ws, R/W/M)$	$(adm, ch^{m}, R/W)$	$(adm, bd, R/W/M)$	$(adm, ch^{lan}, R/W)$
$(user, ch^{m}, R/W)$	$(adm, ch^{lan}, R/W)$	$(adm, ch^{lan}, R/W)$	
$(user, ch^{lan}, R/W)$	$(adm, ch^{int}, R/W)$	$(user, ch^{lan}, R/W)$	
$(user, ch^{int}, R/W)$			
$(adm, ch^{lan}, R/W)$			
$(adm, ch^{int}, R/W)$			
ACL^{lan} :	ACL^{int} :	ACL^{m} :	ACL^{phy} :
$(ws, ch^{lan}, R/W)$	$(ws, ch^{int}, R/W)$	$(adm, ch^{m}, R/W)$	$(user, ch^{phy}, R/W)$
$(lap, ch^{lan}, R/W)$	$(lap, ch^{int}, R/W)$	$(user, ch^{m}, R/W)$	$(adm, ch^{phy}, R/W)$
$(serv, ch^{lan}, R/W)$			
$(bd, ch^{lan}, R/W)$			

to the internal network. In fact, it accesses the network only though the server, but we skip these details for the sake of simplicity. We are going to work on a more strict model in the future.

4.2   Step 2. Identify Relevant Social Privileges

Input: extended access control lists, lists of subjects, objects, allowed operations.

Output: privilege list for social engineering vulnerabilities.

We define all privileges in a similar way as access control rules. Although, the way of defining access control rules and privileges are similar, their semantics is slightly different. In contrast to network attacks, for modelling social engineering attacks it is not enough for the attacker simply to receive credentials for accessing an object. The attacker needs also to have a channel to reach an object before she is able to use it. Thus, we would like to underline that *a privilege is a combination of credentials and an existing channel*. For example, assume, that an attacker was able to get credentials for a computer of an employee by deceiving him. An attacker needs a channel connecting her computer and the computer of the user to be able to access it (or have physical access).

Let P be a set of all possible privileges in a system and $\mathbb{P}(P)$ be a powerset of this set. In this work, we will split the whole set of privileges considered for the system into two sets: $P^N \cup P^{SE} = P$, where P^N is a set of privileges used for usual network attacks and P^{SE} are specific privileges for social engineering attacks. Although, similar ways of defining elements of these sets is not strictly required for consistency of the proposed approach, we assume that the privileges look similar for simplicity. Here, we focus on P^{SE} and only assume that some intersection between the sets can be established.

All possible privileges can be seen as a triple $\mathbb{P}(P^{SE}) = \{att\} \times O \times OP$ and every privilege $p \in P^{SE} \subseteq \mathbb{P}(P^{SE})$ can be seen as $p = (att, o, op)$. We assume, that an attacker, in theory, is able to get any privilege existing in the system to define P^{SE}:

$$P^{SE} = \{(att, o, op) | \exists s \in S, (s, o, op) \in ACL, ACL \in \mathbb{ACL}\} \tag{1}$$

Next to the possible privileges of an attacker (i.e., P^{SE}) we also need privileges of the system (P^{SYS}). We assume, that all access control rules have corresponding channels for realising the access for the users. This is a valid assumption, because otherwise the system is not configured correctly. P^{SYS} are needed only for the specification of applicable social engineering attacks and do not intersect with P. Therefore, we will ignore them when all social engineering exploits for a concrete system are identified.

The privileges for the system can be received by aggregating all entries of $\mathbb{ACL}$:

$$P^{SYS} = \{(s, o, op) | \exists ACL, (s, o, op) \in ACL, ACL \in \mathbb{ACL}\} \tag{2}$$

Example 2. In our running example the P^{SE} is:

$$\begin{aligned} P^{SE} = \{&(att, ws, R/W/M), (att, lap, R/W/M), (att, serv, R/W/M), \\ &(att, sb, R/W/M), (att, ch^{int}, R/W), (att, ch^{lan}, R/W), \\ &(att, ch^m, R/W), (att, ch^{phy}, R/W)\} \end{aligned} \tag{3}$$

4.3   Step 3. Apply Social Engineering Patterns

Input: social engineering patterns (techniques), access control lists, sets of privileges.

Output: a set of scenario specific social engineering actions.

Now we need to find the set of the exploits available for an attacker. In order to execute an exploit an attacker has to have some initial privileges (for example, access to a computer via LAN). Successful execution of a vulnerability provides the attacker with some additional privileges, e.g., root privileges on the targeted node. The sets of initial and ending privileges are determined on the basis of system configuration and identified vulnerabilities.

Let every action of an attacker $a \in Act$ be a single exploit of a vulnerability where Act is a set of possible actions for this system. Then, we may see actions as transitions from one set of privileges to a wider set:

$$Act \subseteq \mathbb{P}(P) \times \mathbb{P}(P) \wedge \forall a = (P^b, P^e) \in Act . P^b \subset P^e \tag{4}$$

where P^b is a minimal set of privileges required to perform the action and P^e is the resulting set of privileges. We also use two special functions: fst and snd, which return the first and the second element of a Cartesian product, i.e., $fst\ a = P^b$ and $snd\ a = P^e$ for $a = (P^b, P^e)$. Please, note that we make the usual assumption for attack graphs that privileges once gained remain until the end of an attack [17].

The set of network exploits is usually defined using different network scanning tools (e.g., Nessus, OpenVAS, etc.). The result of a scan is a set of vulnerabilities. These vulnerabilities are supported by pre- and postconditions, which help to identify the list of network actions for an attacker Act^N. We do not consider Act^N in this article, since this has already been done before (e.g., [21]) and focus on social engineering exploits Act^{SE}, $Act = Act^N \cup Act^{SE}$.

We propose to define social engineering patterns and apply them to the considered system in order to find the set of social engineering exploits. The social engineering patterns can be defined in the following way:

Pattern name	$< Name >$
Free Variables	$< List\ of\ variables >$
Pre-conditions	$P^b \cup P^s\ .\ P^b \subseteq P^{SE}\ \wedge\ \cup P^s \in Privs^{SYS}\ \wedge$
	$< Constraints\ B >$
Post-conditions	$P^e = P^b \cup P'\ .\ P' \in P^{SE} \bigwedge$
	$< Constraints\ E >$

The *constraints* B and E are the boolean logical expression, which can be written with any logic suitable for expressing constraints. In this work we use the first order logic. In the logical constraint we use only the finite sets defined earlier S, O, OP, $\mathbb{ACL}$, CL and free variables specified in the beginning. Free variables are the members of these sets and are unique for the whole pattern. A usual example for social engineering patterns is the subject the attacker decides to deceive. The free variables will be instantiated when a pattern is applied to a concrete system.

The *constraint* B restricts free variables and defines the initial set P^b of privileges the attacker must have to start the attack and the required set P^s of privileges the system must have. The *constraint* E does the same for a set P' of privileges gained by the attacker after successful execution of the attack.

When a pattern is applied to a system it is required to find all such combinations of free variables which satisfy the specified initial constraints. For construction of attack graph we will need only the privileges of attacker (since, the attack graph describes the evolution of attacker's privileges). Thus, privileges of the system are needed only to check whether the pattern is applicable. Every single set of privileges found applicable for the system uniquely defines an action (and its post conditions) in a set Act^{SE}.

Example 3. First, lets consider the baiting attack type as an example pattern. In this pattern an attacker needs to leave a flash key near the working place of the user and wait when the user will try to read it and a special program will install a key logger granting access privileges to the attacker. Thus, the initial conditions are (1) a physical access to the building, where the user is working, (2) the ability of the user to run a program on a computer, and (3) existence of a network channel between the attacker and the targeted computer of the user. We use $\bigwedge$ to highlight the separation of the requirements. The result is the access to all privileges of the user within the compromised domain.

Pattern name	$Baiting: SEE-05$
Free variables	$s_1 \in S, o_1 \in cl^{comp}, o_2 \in cl^b, o_3 \in cl^{net}$
Pre-conditions	$P^b \cup P^s . P^b \subseteq P^{SE} \wedge P^s \subseteq P^{SYS} \bigwedge$
	$P^b = \{(att, o_2, op_1), (att, o_3, op_3)\} \bigwedge$
	$P^s = \{(s_1, o_2, op_2), (s_1, o_1, op_4), (o_1, o_3, op_5)\} \bigwedge$
	1) $op_1 = W \wedge op_2 = W \bigwedge$
	2) $op_4 = M \bigwedge$
	3) $op_3 = W \wedge op_5 = R$
Post-conditions	$P^e = P^b \cup P' . P' \in P^{SE} \bigwedge$
	$P' = \{(att, o', op') | \exists ACL' \in \mathbb{ACL} \wedge (s_1, o_1, op) \in ACL' \wedge$
	$op = M \wedge (s_1, o', op') \in ACL'\}$

Note, that the privileges received by the attacker are limited by the privileges of the user s in the access control list ACL'. This is because once the attacker (by)passed the access control check she is able to access any object, which the deceived user can access within this access control domain.

Example 4. For instantiation of the baiting pattern $Baiting(s, o_1, o_2, o_3)$ we need to find possible free variables, satisfying the *constraint B* specified in earlier examples. For subject $s_1 =$ user, o_1 could be only ws, since user has execution access right only on ws. In the system we have only one channel o_2 of type building - ch^{phy}. There are two possible networks (o_3) through which the attacker may access the workstation ws: ch^{lan} (through a previously compromised lap or serv) and ch^{int} (directly from the Internet). Then, the baiting pattern for the user can be instantiated as the following possible actions of the attacker:

Pre-conditions	$\{(att, ch^{phy}, W), (att, ch^{int}, W), \overline{(user, ws, M), (user, ws, M), (ws, ch^{int}, M)}\}$
Post-conditions	$\{(att, ch^{phy}, W), (att, ch^{int}, W), (att, ws, M), (att, ch^m, R/W), (att, ch^{lan}, R/W)\}$

Pre-conditions	$\{(att, ch^{phy}, W), (att, ch^{lan}, W), \overline{(user, ws, M), (user, ws, M), (ws, ch^{lan}, M)}\}$
Post-conditions	$\{att, ch^{phy}, W), (att, ch^{lan}, W), (att, ws, M), (att, ch^m, R/W), (att, ch^{int}, R/W)\}$

The administrator in our example has modify access rights on all 3 computers in the system. Thus, we get 5 additional instances of this pattern for the administrator adm (i.e., 3 instances for ch^{lan} and 2 for ch^{int}), which are formed using the same strategy.

4.4   Step 4. Construct the Combined Attack Graph

Input: set of technical actions, set of social engineering actions.

Output: an attack graph considering social engineering and technical attackers.

In this section we briefly recall how an attack graph could be formally defined and constructed. More details could be found in our previous work [8].

For the construction we need a set of privileges P and a set of actions Act. Both these sets consist of network and social engineering privileges or actions, but the construction of the graph does not depend on origin of privileges and actions.

Definition 1. *Let P be a set of all possible privileges and Act be a set of all possible attacker actions relevant for the system. Then, the attack graph $G \subseteq \mathbb{P}(\mathbb{P}(P) \times Act \times \mathbb{P}(P))$ associated to P and Act is defined as follows:*

$$G := \{(P^b, a, P^e) \in \mathbb{P}(P) \times Act \times \mathbb{P}(P)| \tag{5}$$

$$1)\; fst\; a \subseteq P^b;\; 2)\; P^e = P^b \cup snd\; a;\; 3)\; snd\; a \setminus fst\; a \not\subseteq P^b\}$$

In words, the attack graph is defined as a set of edges, which relate to actions and allow an attacker to move from one set of privileges to a wider set. A vertex in the attack graph is defined by a set of privileges. The attack graph defined in Definition 1 is a directed acyclic graph (DAG).

The graph specifies all possible attacks on the system. In most cases, the administrators and security staff are interested in protection against a specific type of attacker (e.g., an outsider) which would like to achieve some goal (e.g., get access to the database). Formally, this means that we should consider only a part of the graph which is formed by all paths from a vertex with initial privileges of the attacker to the vertices containing goal privileges.

Example 5. The analyst in our example would like to consider how an outsider can get access to the data of the database. This attacker initially has access to the Internet and physical access to the premises of the organisation. Thus, the attacker starts with the set of privileges $P^0 = \{(att, ch^{int}, W), (att, ch^{phy}, W)\}$ and would like to get the privilege: $P^f = \{(att, db, W)\}$.

In order to construct the attack graph we need a set of combinations of privileges (states) and a set of available actions (transitions). An attack graph usually is a huge, interconnected structure. Here *we concentrate only on a part of this graph* to exemplify the effect of using social engineering exploits on the combined attack graph. In other words, we consider only a subgraph formed by some paths from the initial set of privileges to the sets which contain the desired privilege.

For the construction of the subgraph we need the combinations of privileges shown in Table 3 and a set of actions listed in Table 4. The resulting subgraph is shown in Fig. 3.

Table 3. Privileges corresponding to the vertices of the considered subgraph.

Node	Relevant combinations of privileges
v_0	$\{(att, ch^{int}, W/R), (att, ch^{phy}, W/R)\}$
v_1	$v_0 \cup \{(att, ws, M/W/R), (att, ch^{lan}, W/R), (att, ch^m, W/R)\}$
v_2	$v_1 \cup \{(att, ch^m, W/R), (att, serv, M/W/R)\}$
v_3	$v_1 \cup \{(att, db, W/R)\}$
v_4	$v_2 \cup \{(att, db, M/W/R)\}$

Table 4. Actions available for the attacker.

CVE code	Target	Initial privileges	Resulting privileges
CVE-2011-3108	Chrome	$\{(att, ch^{int}, W/R)\}$	$\{(att, ws, M/W/R), (att, ch^m, W/R),$ $(att, ch^{lan}, W/R), (att, ch^{int}, W/R)\}$
CVE-2011-4862	FreeBSD	$\{(att, ws, M/W/R),$ $(att, ch^{lan}, W/R)\}$	$\{(att, ws, M/W/R), (att, ch^{lan}, W/R),$ $(att, serv, M/W/R)\}$
CVE-2012-0114	MySQL	$\{(att, serv, M/W/R)\}$	$\{(att, serv, M/W/R), \{(att, db, M/W/R)\}$
SEE-04	Employee	$\{(att, ws, M/W/R),$ $(att, ch^m, W/R)\}$	$\{(att, ws, M/W/R), (att, ch^m, W/R),$ $(att, db, W/R)\}$
SEE-05	Employee	$\{(att, ch^{int}, W/R),$ $(att, ch^{phy}, W/R)\}$	$\{(att, ch^{int}, W/R), (att, ws, M/W/R),$ $(att, ch^{lan}, W/R), (att, ch^m, W/R)\}$

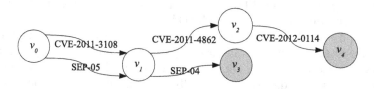

Fig. 3. A subgraph with social engineering and network exploits.

In Fig. 3 there are four possible paths from initial v_0 to one of the combinations of privileges which contain the desired privilege v_3 or v_4.

$$\pi_1 = \langle CVE\text{-}2011\text{-}3108, CVE\text{-}2011\text{-}4862, CVE\text{-}2011\text{-}0114 \rangle, \qquad (6)$$
$$\pi_2 = \langle CVE\text{-}2011\text{-}3108, SEE\text{-}04 \rangle,$$
$$\pi_3 = \langle SEE\text{-}05, SEE\text{-}04 \rangle,$$
$$\pi_4 = \langle SEE\text{-}05, CVE\text{-}2011\text{-}4862, CVE\text{-}2011\text{-}0114 \rangle$$

Path π_1 is purely technical. First, a vulnerability in Chrome browser CVE-2011-3108 is exploited remotely, then the attacker exploits the vulnerability in the server via LAN (CVE-2011-4862) and, finally, compromises the database (CVE-2012-0114). Path π_3 consists only of social engineering attacks. The attacker uses baiting (SEP-05) throwing a USB stick in the building of the targeted company. The employee plugs in the stick to the workstation thus the attacker obtains access to the the workstation, LAN of the company and the e-mail of the employee. Then the attacker applies reverse social engineering (SEP-04) disabling the access to the database from the workstation and asking for the credentials of the user by e-mail on the behalf of the administrator "to solve the issue". There are also two hybrid paths (π_2 and π_4) for the attacker which contain mixed sets of used exploits.

4.5 Step 5. Analyse the Combined Attack Graph

Input: attack graph, quantitative input parameters.

Output: prioritised attack paths.

Social engineering attacks do not require much technical knowledge and may be executed by an inexperienced attacker. Moreover, many organisations pay much attention to hardening the technical security of their network underestimating the danger of social attacks [5]. On the other hand, social engineering attacks often require a direct contact with people working in the organisation and physical penetration into the premises of the organisation. Such actions rise the risk of detection and the risk to be caught.

Let π be a path in an attack graph G. We can see this path as a sequence of $(P_i^b, a_i, P_i^e) = x_i$, $i = \{1, 2, ..., n\}$, such that P_1^b is equal to the initial sets of privileges and P_n^e contains the goal privileges of the attacker. Let the probability of successful execution of an action a_i be $\mathbf{pr}_i^e$ and the probability to be caught be $\mathbf{pr}_i^c$. In general, it is far not every time the attacker is caught, when an attack fails, therefore $\mathbf{pr}_i^c \leq 1 - \mathbf{pr}_i^e$. Let also the benefit the attacker aims to get after successful execution of the attack be c_{succ}, when the loss in case of capture (e.g., cost of the lawyers or a fine) is c_{loss}. Then, we may identify the path, which is more profitable for the attacker:

$$Benefit = c_{succ} \times \prod_{i=1}^{n} \mathbf{pr}_i^e; Loss = c_{loss} \times (1 - \prod_{i=1}^{n}(1 - \mathbf{pr}_i^c)); \quad (7)$$

$$Profit = Benefit - Loss$$

Example 6. The probabilities of the successful execution of actions and the probabilities for the attacker to be caught are in Table 5. Suppose also in case of successful attack attacker obtains $c_{succ} = 10$ (thousands of \$) and in case the attacker fails her loss is $c_{loss} = 20$ (thousands of \$). Profits of the attacker for paths are correspondingly $Profit(\pi_1) = -1.5$, $Profit(\pi_2) = 2.1$, $Profit(\pi_3) = -2.4$, and $Profit(\pi_4) = -4.56$. We see, that nevertheless, the pure social engineering attack (π_2) is relatively beneficial for the attacker (3.2) the potential probability to be caught is high and so are the potential loss (5.7). Thus, the most dangerous path according to the analysis is π_2 and the analyst should put high priority to mitigate this attack.

Table 5. Probabilities of success and possible capture for the considered actions.

a	$\mathbf{pr}^e$	$\mathbf{pr}^c$
CVE-2011-3108	0.70	0.08
CVE-2011-4862	0.60	0.05
CVE-2011-0114	0.50	0.06
SEE-05	0.40	0.20
SEE-04	0.80	0.10

4.6   Step 6. Mitigate Possible Threats

Input: prioritised attack paths, set of mitigation methods/tools.

Output: a set of methods/tools to apply.

We propose to establish the following countermeasures for social engineering attacks, as introduced by Mitnick [5]. The first action should be (i) to design clear and easily understandable security policies. Strict constraints on length and technical language have to be imposed on these policies to achieve this goal. The second action is (ii) data classification, e.g., in the four basic categories: confidential, private, internal and public. This distinction clearly defines data that employees should guard carefully and get suspicious if someone aims to get access them. Then the administrator should establish (iii) verification and authorisation procedures that include the use of caller ID, callback, shared secret, etc. to prevent unauthorised access to confidential, private, or internal data. (iv) Simple and repeated security awareness training with seminars and reminders, e.g., via messages on screensavers is also a useful countermeasure. The fifth action is (v) penetration testing for social engineering attacks and a reward system for employees that prevent the attacks. Finally, (vi) an alert system for social engineering attacks where employees can report possible attacks.

Example 7. The most important attack to be mitigated is the reverse social engineering (SEE-05), since it belongs to π_3. Security awareness training should provide the user with the ability to get suspicious and trigger a security check for the requesting person.

5   Conclusions

We contributed a structured threat analysis method for combining the analysis of social engineering attackers and technical attackers (e.g., network attackers) using attack graphs. In contrast to current research in attack graph analysis, which focuses solely on technical attackers. Our methodology relies on access control lists and communication diagrams of a company to identify relevant actors that can become victims of a social engineering attacker. We have shown how social engineering patterns could be defined and instantiated for a specific organisation. Once the model of a system (i.e., access control lists, sets of objects and subjects and required classes) is defined, the actions required for attack graph construction and the construction itself can be done (semi)automatically. Finally, the proposed quantitative analysis specifies not only the most beneficial path for the attacker, but also takes into account the possibility of the attacker to be caught.

One direction for the future work is a more rigorous specification of the system model. Currently, we rely a lot on an analyst that aggregates the existing information and models the system. We will also consider not only access control lists and communication channels, but also organisational charts that illustrate the hierarchies in companies, detailed network topologies that illustrate the flow of digital information, and system architecture diagrams that explain the relation of all information.

Acknowledgements. This paper was partially supported by ARTEMIS Joint Undertaking SESAMO project, POR-CREO 2007-2013 Secure! regional project, PRIN Security Horizons project and the Ministry of Innovation, Science, Research and Technology of the German State of North Rhine-Westphalia and EFRE (Grant No. 300266902).

References

1. Peltier, T.R.: Social engineering: concepts and solutions. Inf. Syst. Secur. **15**(5), 13–21 (2006)
2. Algarni, A., Xu, Y., Chan, T., Tian, Y.C.: Social engineering in social networking sites: Affect-based model. In: Proceedings of the 8th International Conference on Internet Technology and Secured Transactions, pp. 508–515. IEEE (2013)
3. Dimkov, T., van Cleeff, A., Pieters, W., Hartel, P.: Two methodologies for physical penetration testing using social engineering. In: Proceedings of the 26th Annual Computer Security Applications Conference, pp. 399–408. ACM (2010)
4. Laribee, L., Barnes, D., Rowe, N., Martell, C.: Analysis and defensive tools for social-engineering attacks on computer systems. In: Proceedings of the Information Assurance Workshop, pp. 388–389. IEEE (2006)
5. Mitnick, K.D., Simon, W.L.: The Art of Deception. Wiley, Indianapolis, Indiana (2009)
6. Krombholz, K., Hobel, H., Huber, M., Weippl, E.: Social engineering attacks on the knowledge worker. In: Proceedings of the 6th International Conference on Security of Information and Networks, pp. 28–35. ACM (2013)
7. Kvedar, D., Nettis, M., Fulton, S.P.: The use of formal social engineering techniques to identify weaknesses during a computer vulnerability competition. J. Comput. Sci. Coll. **26**(2), 80–87 (2010)
8. Beckers, K., Heisel, M., Krautsevich, L., Maritnelli, F., Yautsiukhin, A.: Considering attacker motivation in attack graphs analysis in a smart grid scenario. In: Proceedings of the Second Open EIT ICT Labs Workshop on Smart Grid Security, Springer (2014, To appear)
9. Ahmadi, N., Jazayeri, M., Lelli, F., Nesic, S.: A survey of social software engineering. In: Workshop Proceedings of the 23rd IEEE/ACM International Conference on Automated Software Engineering, pp. 1–12. IEEE (2008)

10. Mills, D.: Analysis of a social engineering threat to information security exacerbated by vulnerabilities exposed through the inherent nature of social networking websites. In: Proceedings of the Information Security Curriculum Development Conference, pp. 139–141. ACM (2009)
11. Chitrey, A., Singh, D., Singh, V.: A comprehensive study of social engineering based attacks in india to develop a conceptual model. Int. J. Inf. Netw. Secur. 1(2), 45–53 (2012)
12. Winkler, I.S., Dealy, B.: Information security technology?...don't rely on it: a case study in social engineering. In: Proceedings of the 5th Conference on USENIX UNIX Security Symposium, p. 1–1. USENIX Association (1995)
13. Gonzalez, J.J., Seasick, A.: A framework for human factors in information security. In: Proceedings of WSEAS International Conference on Information Security (2002)
14. Twitchell, D.P.: Social engineering in information assurance curricula. In: Proceedings of the 3rd Annual Conference on Information Security Curriculum Development, pp. 191–193. ACM (2006)
15. International Organization for Standardization (ISO), International Electrotechnical Commission (IEC): Information technology - Security techniques - Information security management systems - Requirements. ISO/IEC 27001 (2013)
16. BSI: Grundschutzhandbuch IT. Bundesamt für Sicherheit in der Informationstechnik (BSI) (2007). http://www.bsi.bund.de/gshb/index.htm
17. Jha, S., Sheyner, O., Wing, J.: Two formal analyses of attack graphs. In: Proceedings of the Computer Society Security Foundations Workshop. IEEE (2002)
18. Krautsevich, L., Martinelli, F., Yautsiukhin, A.: Towards modelling adaptive attacker's behaviour. In: Garcia-Alfaro, J., Cuppens, F., Cuppens-Boulahia, N., Miri, A., Tawbi, N. (eds.) Foundations and Practice of Security. LNCS, vol. 7743, pp. 357–364. Springer, Heidelberg (2013)
19. LeMay, E., Ford, M.D., Keefe, K., Sanders, W.H., Muehrcke, C.: Model-based security metrics using adversary view security evaluation (advise). In: Proceedings of the 8th International Conference on Quantitative Evaluation of SysTems, pp. 191–200. IEEE (2011)
20. Noel, S., Jajodia, S.: Managing attack graph complexity through visual hierarchical aggregation. In: Proceedings of the Workshop on Visualization and Data Mining for Computer Security. ACM (2004)
21. Sheyner, O., Haines, J., Jha, S., Lippmann, R., Wing, J.M.: Automated generation and analysis of attack graphs. In: Proceedings of the 2002 IEEE Symposium on Security and Privacy. IEEE (2002)

Introducing Probabilities in Controller Strategies

Jerry den Hartog[1]([⊠]) and Ilaria Matteucci[2]

[1] Technische Universiteit Eindhoven, Eindhoven, The Netherlands
J.d.Hartog@tue.nl
[2] National Research Council, Istituto di Informatica e Telematica (IIT), Pisa, Italy
Ilaria.Matteucci@iit.cnr.it

Abstract. In this paper we propose a basic framework to merge security controllers with probabilistic concepts. This framework provides a first step towards quantitative security achieved by probabilistic controllers. It extends the framework for specification, analysis, and automatic generation of security controllers provided in [21,23] by considering probabilistic aspects of the behaviour of both the target process and the controller. Controllers may actively try to influence the choice of action of the target system or only passively react to actions the target system tried to perform. In a non-probabilistic setting both active and passive controllers can be expressed by the same model. In a probabilistic setting, however, these two types of controllers can differ. We respectively use the notions of generative and reactive processes to capture this distinction and discuss the different behaviours obtaining in the different settings.

Keywords: Security controller · Probability · Reactive · Generative

1 Overview

The importance of securing software and systems needs little argument in our ever more connected and information saturated world. Indeed, the security of systems is one of the main challenges of the last decades in computer science. With ubiquitous information gathering and sharing of huge amounts of valuable sensitive data on the Internet and all its connected devices the importance of security is only growing. Nowadays, each of us is using on a daily bases, devices, such as smart-phones, that exposes most of the functionalities of a networked personal computer. The wide range of users, including many with less (security) skills, adds risks to security. Furthermore, smart-phones are used for multiple purposes, both for work and leisure activities, exposing the users to a wide range of attacks that may *e.g.,* leak private data.

This work has been partially supported by the Italian TENACE PRIN Project (#20103P34XC), ARTEMIS J.U. SESAMO (#295354) and EU FP7 Marie Curie project MEALS (#295261).

J. Garcia-Alfaro et al. (Eds.): DPM/SETOP/QASA 2014, LNCS 8872, pp. 233–249, 2015.
DOI: 10.1007/978-3-319-17016-9_15

Our increasingly complex devices containing ever more (personal) data incorporate software and components with differing levels of trustworthiness, such as different apps running on a smart-phone. Mechanisms to monitor and enforce security policies are thus essential in guaranteeing secrecy, confidentiality, and integrity of our (private) information. Different approaches, *e.g.*, [4,6,7,22,26] therefore, aim to formally define and automatically generate enforcement mechanisms able to guarantee the satisfaction of security policies on systems and devices. In particular, from a formal perspective, starting from Schneider's seminal work [26], a lot of effort has been spent on the characterization the kind of policies can be monitored and enforced at runtime. This leads to the clear identification of basic concepts, such as security policy, target (or monitored system), execution traces, enforcement mechanisms. Initially, this strand of work only considered blocking of the system as a possible countermeasure but it has since then been refined by considering several approaches for the correction of execution traces. The kind of security policies that can be enforced with these models have been extensively studied leading to precise characterization of what can be enforced with a certain class of enforcement mechanisms and under which conditions.

Another research strand related to this work addresses the adoption of formalisms such as automata [7,18] or process algebras [22,23], to better define the interactions between target and enforcement mechanism as well as enforcement capabilities. A main advantage of these approaches is their well studied properties and associated procedure and results. For instance, it is possible to formalize the behaviour of a security automata through process algebra operators. By combining process algebra techniques with concepts from temporal logic, it is possibly to study the problem of automatically synthesizing enforcement mechanisms for (parts of) targets and policies expressed in logic. The framework presented in [23], which is based on process algebras, partial model checking, and satisfiability techniques for logic, finds mechanisms that enforce global security policies on a system by considering the target as only a subcomponent of this system, thus enabling the possibility to project global security policies onto local ones.

In those approaches security is often regarded as a binary concept. Behaviour is either good or bad. Good behaviour is either enforced or not. Thus they focus on what we call *qualitative* enforcement, *i.e.*, finding a "good" enforcement mechanism for a security policy, if possible. However, in many cases perfect enforcement is not possible or *e.g.*, more costly than the value you are trying to protect. For instance, if the target system is an airplane, halting it is just not an option; it may cause failures and deaths (a *safety* violation). In case like this, we have to consider more aspects than just two security values. Reality is much more complex and may force us to consider several *quantitative* aspects that play a role in the design and evaluation of enforcement strategies. For example, a controller may only be *likely* able to enforce a policy or can *cost* less than another one in enforcing a specific security policy, or the *benefits* of enforcing a specific policy may fail to counter-balance the disadvantages. We can also consider the more challenging problem, that we are going to name hereafter *quantitative enforcement*, to find the "best" enforcement mechanism for a security policy and a target, in accordance to some quantitative criteria such as the probability of attack, its cost or precision of enforcement. Quantitative enforcement could be also seen as an optimization problem to find the best among all good enforcement mechanisms. It would, thus, be useful to be able to rank controllers based on different quantitative aspects such as cost.

However, many controllers are incomparable if we do not know the likely behaviour of the target; often some (possibly unlikely) target behaviour can be found for which one controller will be more expensive than the other and vice versa. By taking into account the likely behaviour of a target, such controllers can be compared by looking at the expected cost of the enforcement. This means that we have to consider probabilistic behaviour of the target. Similarly a probabilistic controller strategy will be more powerful than a deterministic strategy and more readily analysed than a purely non-deterministic strategy. Thus also for the controller probabilistic behaviour should be considered.

The main goal of this paper is to take a first step towards a formal framework that enables automated generation of probabilistic security controllers by providing a way for specifying the probabilistic behaviour of such controllers. In particular, we consider that both controller and target processes behave in a probabilistic way in order to define probabilistic controlling strategies. In [14], the authors introduce different models for probabilistic processes, including *reactive* and *generative* processes. Starting from these notions, this paper analyses the different combination of these probabilistic models for both the target and the controller process. In particular, we consider four types of controls; *Acceptance, Suppression*, and *Insertion* operators. According to the behaviour of the considered target, a controller can apply one of these methods. The application of different rules depends on the probabilistic behaviour of the target and on the nature of both processes, *i.e.*, whether they are reactive or generative. In the end, we obtain a complete view of all the cases. This helps us in the next step of our research stream for the synthesis of the optimal (if any) probabilistic controlling strategy.

The remainder of this paper is organized as follows: The next section provides some basic notions about probabilistic process algebra operators and reactive and generative processes. Section 3 presents semantics definitions of probabilistic controller operators. In this section, we also discuss different resulting behaviours that can be obtained by considering reactive/generative controller processes that control reactive and/or generative target systems. Section 4 compares our approach with respect to related literature. Section 5 draws the conclusion of the paper and presents some further directions.

2   Basic Probabilistic Process Algebra

In order to analyse how probability affects the interaction between a controller and a target, hereafter we consider a minimal language that is still sufficient to address the effect of different types of probabilistic choice on the controller and target process behaviour. This minimal language contains only actions, probabilistic choice, recursion and the controller process which keeps interpretation of the processes simple. For practical use this is clearly too restrictive thus we plan to extend this with *e.g.*, non-deterministic and parallel operators as future work.

We start from a set of actions Act, ranged over by $a, b, c, \ldots$. We extend this set with silent action τ and so called control actions $CAct = \{\ominus a \mid a \in Act\} \cup \{\oplus a.b \mid a, b \in Act\}$. We use ζ to range over this extended action set $EAct = Act \cup \{\tau\} \cup CAct$. A probability ρ is added to obtain probabilistic action $\rho \cdot \zeta$; i.e., $PAct = [0, 1] \times EAct$.

For the processes given below, we define transition systems with steps between processes labelled with probabilistic actions. For equivalence of processes we consider probabilistic bisimulation [14] for reactive processes and weak probabilistic bisimulation [3] for generative processes. We assume it is clear how these can be derived from the semantic rules we provide. Below we introduce the syntax of our processes and then in turn explain the different types of processes along with their semantics.

$$P ::= 0 \mid \sum_{i \in I} \rho_i \cdot \zeta_i.P_i \mid \sum_{i \in I} \zeta_i \cdot \rho_i.P_i \mid X \mid P \rhd_K P \qquad (1)$$

A process P can be the empty process 0. This process has no transitions. It can also be a probabilistic choice between actions ζ_i followed by a corresponding process P_i (referred to as the continuation of the process). We omit the $\sum$ symbol if there is only one option and also use $+$ as an alternate notation. We consider both generative and reactive probabilistic choice as explained below.

In a *generative* choice, denoted by $\sum_{i \in I} \rho_i \cdot \zeta_i.P_i$, the sum of all the probabilities of all possible actions ($\sum_{i \in I} \rho_i$) is one. This corresponds to an "active" probabilistic choice; it probabilistically chooses which action to execute next.

In a *reactive* choice, denoted by $\sum_{i \in I} \zeta_i \cdot \rho_i.P_i$, the sum of probabilities per action is one (for the actions present). This type of choice can be seen as passive; it waits for one of the offered actions to be selected and then probabilistically chooses how to continue after that. To emphasise this we place the probability after the action in the notation of this choice. The choice may also be seen as being only partially specified; the relative likelihood of actions is omitted. Control actions $\ominus a$ and $\oplus a.b$ and counted together with the action a. For this we define $\sim$ as the smallest equivalence relation on $EAct$ that contains $\ominus a \sim a$ and $\oplus a.b \sim a$ for all actions a, b. The requirement for a reactive choice thus is that $\sum_{j \in J, \zeta_i \sim \zeta_j} \rho_j$ is one for each $i \in I$.

Both generative choice $\sum_{i \in I} \rho_i \cdot \zeta_i.P_i$ and reactive choice $\sum_{i \in I} \zeta_i \cdot \rho_i.P_i$ can take a step $\xrightarrow{\rho_i \cdot \zeta_i}$ to reach P_i for each $i \in I$. A technical complication in probabilistic transition systems is that when exactly the same transition is obtained from different branches in a probabilistic choice, as for e.g., $\frac{1}{2} \cdot a.0 + \frac{1}{2} \cdot a.0$, their multiplicity becomes important. This can be solved e.g., by counting (turning the transition relation into a multiset) or by turning the transitions into one transitions by adding their probabilities. To not clutter the presentation, we ignore this issue here and implicitly assume equal steps are combined by adding their probabilities. Thus we obtain $\frac{1}{2} \cdot a.0 + \frac{1}{2} \cdot a.0 \xrightarrow{1 \cdot a} 0$.

For the remainder of this paper, we assume that a process will not alternate reactive and generative choices. (This could be relaxed by defining a notion of similarity for such alternating processes. We could then even combine both types of options in one choice if we indicate which options are generative and which reactive, for example by splitting actions in reactive and generative ones. See also Example 1). Formally we thus require a process to be either a reactive or a generative process which are defined by: 0 is a reactive process, a reactive choice $\sum_{i \in I} \zeta_i \cdot \rho_i.P_i$ is a reactive process when P_i is a reactive processes for each $i \in I$, a process variable X is a reactive process if its body is and $P \triangleright_K P'$ is a reactive process when both P and P' are reactive processes. In turn 0 is a generative process, a generative choice $\sum_{i \in I} \rho_i \cdot \zeta_i.P_i$ is a generative process if P_i is a generative process for each $i \in I$, a process variable X is a generative process if its body is and $P \triangleright_K P'$ is a generative processes when P or P' is a generative process and the other is either a generative or a reactive process. (The reason for this typing of the control process will be clarified in the next section).

A process variable X is also a process and its steps are those of its body. We use guarded equations to specify the body associated to a process variable, *e.g.*, $X = 1 \cdot a.X$ defines X to be a process that produces an infinite sequence of a actions.

In [22,23] the definition of possible security *controller process algebra operator*, denoted by $\triangleright$, has been provided. We also use this operator in our processes, writing $C \triangleright_K F$ for controller process C controlling target process F according to some strategies denoted by K. The parameter K ranges over $\{A, S, I\}$, *i.e.*, *Acceptance* operator, *Suppression* operator, and *Insertion* operator. These operators describe three possible strategies that can be applied in order to control the behaviour of (possibly untrusted) target components by a control program. The intuition behind of the definition of these three operator is the following one: the acceptance operator behaves as a synchronous composition, the suppression operator models communication through synchronizations, and insertion operator works as an asynchronous composition made in an asymmetric way.

The semantics of the controller processes is treated in the next section. We extend the original definition of the operators as it has been provided in [22] to create a probabilistic version of the controller operators. The informal interpretation of Acceptance, Suppression, and Insertion operators is as follows:

Acceptance Operator (A) constrains the controller and the target to perform the same action, in order for it to be observed in the resulting behaviour. Given two processes C and F, the semantics of acceptance operator is equivalent to that of CSP-style parallel composition [16] of C and F, where synchronisation is forced over all actions of the two processes.

Suppression Operator (S) allows the controller to hide actions of the target. The target *wants to* perform the action, but the action is not performed by the controlled entity and the observed result is a τ action.

Insertion Operator (I) describes the capability of correcting some bad behaviour of the target, by inserting another action in its execution trace. It is worth noting that the target does not perform any action, but rather stays in its current state, as in [7].

Remark 1. The main difference between the controller operators treated here and the ones reported in [22] is that we do not consider *blocking* controllers which prevent the target from performing an action at all. A classical example of a blocking controller is the *truncation* operator which stops the target to perform actions upon attempting a disallowed action. The acceptance controller that we do treat, while disallowing some actions, always allows the process to select one of the allowed actions. In our setting a process is thus either equivalent to 0 or it will always perform some action. To model blocking controllers one could add a notion of failure δ though truncating can also be modelled as suppression of the action followed by no allowed behaviour (0).

Note that a controller only controls actions (see the rules in the next section) not *e.g.*, control actions in $CAct$ of the form $\ominus a$ or $\oplus a.b$. Thus a controller C will typically not control another controller C', *e.g.*, $(C \triangleright_K C') \triangleright_K F$ is usually not meaningful (if C' is a simple acceptance controller it would technically be possible), though C may control a process F already controlled by another controller C' as in $(C \triangleright_K (C' \triangleright_K F))$.

3   Controlling Probabilistic Processes

In this section, we provide the semantics for the controllers in a probabilistic setting. Recall that reactive choice models process behaviour which is guided by the outside such as input to the process; the user selects one of the offered actions. Generative choice models active process behaviour, where the selection of an option is driven by the process itself; for example the output generated by the process. When considering a target process F controlled by a controller C we can consider both types of choice for either the target and the controller. Below we treat each of the four combinations for all the three controller operators giving some intuition on how such processes can be interpreted and thus what type of systems they may be able to model. First we focus on the interpretation of reactive and generative choice in the controller and the target process by considering a probabilistic version of a basic type of controller; the acceptance controller. Next we extend the discussion by introducing probabilistic versions of the other types of controllers: the suppression and insertion controllers.

3.1   Probabilistic Acceptance Controller

The acceptance controller specifies which actions a target system is allowed to take. Any other action along with its continuation is blocked.

The semantics of the probabilistic version of the acceptance operator is given by:

$$\frac{C \xrightarrow{\rho \cdot a} C' \quad F \xrightarrow{\sigma \cdot a} F'}{C \triangleright_A F \xrightarrow{\rho\sigma/n_A \cdot a} C' \triangleright_A F'} \qquad \frac{C \xrightarrow{\rho \cdot \tau} C'}{C \triangleright_A F \xrightarrow{\rho/n_A \cdot \tau} C' \triangleright_A F} \qquad \frac{F \xrightarrow{\sigma \cdot \tau} F'}{C \triangleright_A F \xrightarrow{\sigma/n_A \cdot \tau} C \triangleright_A F'}$$

where normalization factor n_A is 1 if $C \triangleright_A F$ is a reactive process (*i.e.*, both C and F are reactive) and otherwise $n_A = \sum_{C \xrightarrow{\rho \cdot a} C', F \xrightarrow{\sigma \cdot a} F'} \rho\sigma + \sum_{C \xrightarrow{\rho \cdot \tau} C'} \rho + \sum_{F \xrightarrow{\sigma \cdot \tau} F'} \sigma$. This semantics rule states that if F performs action a and this action is allowed by controller C then $C \triangleright_A F$ performs action a. The probability of performing action a is determined by the probabilities for a in C and F and the type of choice (reactive or generative). Both the controller and the target system can independently perform a silent action τ.

For a generative controlled process $C \triangleright_A F$, we use normalization to ensure the resulting process is again generative; the total probability sums up to one. The interpretation of this is that if the controller prevents an action selected through a probabilistic choice from occurring, the system will attempt the choice again (with the same probabilities). This eventually results in one of the allowed options being chosen according to the normalized probabilities or in no behaviour at all (equivalent to the 0 process), in case none of the options are allowed. Below we illustrate the interpretation of a controlled process for the four possible combinations of reactive or generative target system and controller.

Reactive target system, reactive controller. Consider the following system: a building with two doors, one leading to the elevator (door a) and one leading to the stairs (door b). The simple system that keeps the doors open can be modelled by reactive process $F_1 = a \cdot 1.F_1 + b \cdot 1.F_1$

Suppose we want to protect the elevator from overload. A strategy to do this could be to place a guard who closes the elevator door with probability $\frac{1}{2}$ whenever someone enters the elevator and opens it again once someone uses the stairs. This controller can be modelled by (reactive) process C_1 that satisfies:

$$C_1 = a \cdot \tfrac{1}{2}.C_1 + a \cdot \tfrac{1}{2}.C_1' + b \cdot 1.C_1 \qquad (2)$$
$$C_1' = b \cdot 1.C_1 \qquad (3)$$

Using controller C_1 to control process F_1, resulting in process $C_1 \triangleright_A F_1$, will here actually result in exactly process C_1 because at each stage all options allowed by C_1 are offered by F_1. Of course this does not have to be the case. Take for example:

$$F_2 = a \cdot \tfrac{1}{2}.F_2 + a \cdot \tfrac{1}{2}.0 + b \cdot \tfrac{1}{3}.F_2 + b \cdot \tfrac{2}{3}.0 \qquad (4)$$
$$C_2 = b \cdot \tfrac{1}{2}.C_2 + b \cdot \tfrac{1}{2}.0 \qquad (5)$$

The process $C_2 \triangleright_A F_2$ will only perform b steps and after every b step there is a five in six chance the process stops; only if both F and C decide to continue will the process be able to take further steps.

As can be seen from examples given above, a reactive target system controlled by a reactive controller acts as one may expect; the enabled actions are those allowed by both the system and the controller and, after selection of one of those controlled actions, the system and controller independently (probabilistically) choose their strategy for which future actions are offered/allowed. Thus a reactive controller may disallow certain steps and probabilistically determines its strategy for future control based on the action that it sees. It, however, does not interfere with the strategy of the target system in choosing its next state for the actions that are allowed. The probabilities for allowed actions are unaffected, the others become zero. The combined process is reactive: the user selects from the enabled actions, *i.e.*, those offered by the target system and allowed by the controller. The controller observes the actions that users execute on the system and decides its control strategy accordingly by disallowing or enabling certain future actions.

Generative target system, reactive controller. If the system we are trying to control is actively making (probabilistic) choices we need to use a generative model to be able to describe this. Consider, for example, users of the building from the example above. These users will actively decide which door to take, for example by randomly selecting one of them. The building and the users together may be modelled by generative process $F_3 = \frac{1}{2} \cdot a.F_3 + \frac{1}{2} \cdot b.F_3$.

Our controller has remained reactive; it only responds to the actions the users of the building execute. Still, because the users drive the choice of actions, the controlled process will still actively choose the actions; it is generative. Consider process $C_1 \rhd_A F_3$. The users will randomly select a door. If it is the stairs nothing changes. If it is the elevator (a), the controller may react by disabling that door. Then, the next user may try the elevator door but will find it blocked so in the end will have to take the other door (b) with probability 1. The controller will react to this action by re-enabling door a.

The intuitive interpretation of a generative-reactive combination is also clear; the generative target process drives the selection of actions amongst those that are allowed. The reactive controller simply observes which actions the target system executes and updates its strategy.

Generative target system, generative controller. So far we have considered a "passive", reactive controller that can only react to choices being made by updating its strategy for future actions. However, what if we consider a controller that actively tries to influence also the current action. Consider, for example, the guard at the door; the guard knows that taking the stairs is both healthier and cheaper, so would prefer more people taking the stairs. When people arrive at the building the guard tries to convince them that taking the stairs is much better. These actions and preference of the guard (combined with how successful she is in convincing users) can be captured by a generative process, for example; $C_3 = \frac{1}{3} \cdot a.C_3 + \frac{2}{3} \cdot b.C_3$.

Now, if again the users randomly select a door (F_3), the guard trying to convince users to take the stairs will influences the overall probability, resulting in a two third probability of taking the stairs. If, on the other hand, users in a wheelchair arrive who cannot use the stairs; $(F_4 = 1 \cdot a.F_4)$ then the preference of the guard will be ignored; the result will be action a with probability 1. These cover the two extreme cases for the users; no preference at all or only having one of the options. In general the preferences of the guard and the user are combined. For instance, if the users have a preference for the stairs already, it will be further strengthened by the preference of the guard.

A generative target and a generative controller combined yield a generative overall system. The target system still drives the choice of the next action among those allowed by the controller but now the controller is also actively involved in this choice. The controller can indicate preferences which will influence the choice of the target system.

Reactive target system, generative controller. If the target system is reactive, it has not specified a preference for any of the actions. A generative controller can by itself determine the likelihood of next action. As an example, we can consider the model for the building (without its users) and an active guard that opens only one door for each user that arrives. As seen above, a generative process can also indicate 'no preference' by giving equal likelihood to each action. When controlled by a generative controller, a reactive target system, indeed, behaves exactly the same as such a generative system without preferences. This combination can thus be seen as a special case of the generative-generative combination.

This intuition for the different controller-target system combinations also translates to the other types of controller automata. However, the other types of controller automata include actions that are inherently generative which posses some restrictions on the processes that can be used. In the next section we discuss how these controllers can be extended to a probabilistic setting as well as the required restrictions.

3.2   Probabilistic Suppression, Insertion, and Edit Controllers

The Suppression, Insertion, and Edit controllers enable additional control strategies. Suppression controllers are able to hide target actions to an external observer; Insertion controllers aim at correcting wrong execution traces by inserting actions before not allowed action; Edit controllers combine both the functionalities in such a way to be able to hide actions and correct execution traces.

In order to extend the definitions above with probabilistic versions of these controllers, we have to consider again the reactive versus the generative choice. Recall that a reactive process passively reacts to external actions, only probabilistically choosing the continuation after an action. It can also be interpreted as an incompletely specified choice. A generative process, on the other hand, actively makes a probabilistic choice between actions to execute.

According to the example of probabilistic acceptance controller, both reactive and generative choices are useful for modelling different types of target systems and controllers. However, some types of actions are inherently generative. The silent τ action, for example, is used to model a change in the system state which is not (directly) observable by the user. Such an action can obviously not be "chosen by the user". The system has to actively choose to execute it.

We may need to deal with inherently generative actions in a reactive setting. The Suppression controller, for example, may cause an action to be replaced by silent action τ. In [1], the syntax of the hiding operation, which also replaces actions by τ, is extended with an additional (probability) label to allow its use in a reactive setting. The label p determines the generative probability of τ if a reactive action is hidden and is ignored if a generative action is hidden. This thus uses the 'not fully specified choice' interpretation of reactive choice and provides the added specification in the syntax in case it is needed. Here we follow a similar approach; we require that probabilities for inherently generative actions are fully specified. A choice involving such actions is interpreted as always first making an active choice between either executing one of the generative actions or, if present, offering the choice between the reactive options.

Example 1. Suppose we add an additional label to the syntax; *e.g.*, let $\frac{1}{2}a$ denote a reactive action a that will be selected with probability $\frac{1}{2}$ when suppressed. If a reactive process with additional label $\frac{1}{2}a \cdot 1.p_1 + b \cdot 1.p_2 + c \cdot 1.p_3$ is controlled by a reactive controller that suppresses action a and allows actions b and c the result is a choice of the form: $\frac{1}{2} \cdot \tau.p_1 + \frac{1}{2} \cdot (b \cdot 1.p_2 + c \cdot 1.p_3)$. Note that this is a choice between processes rather than between actions or continuations after actions; as such it is not a (generative or reactive) process as defined in this paper but rather a stratified choice [14].

We actually do not need to add additional labels to our syntax to model this; a generative choice has exactly the same expressiveness as a reactive choice with additional labels. The labels are determined by the relative probabilities of the first action.

Example 2. The labelled reactive process of the previous example is expressed by generative process $a \cdot \frac{1}{2}\tau.p_1 + b \cdot \frac{1}{4}.p_2 + c \cdot \frac{1}{4}.p_3$. When this process is controlled by a reactive controller that suppresses action a and allows actions b and c, the result is generative process: $\frac{1}{2} \cdot \tau.p_1 + \frac{1}{4} \cdot b.p_2 + \frac{1}{4} \cdot c.p_3$.

We can informally write this as a stratified choice $\frac{1}{2} \cdot \tau.p_1 + \frac{1}{2} \cdot (\frac{1}{2} \cdot b.p_2 + \frac{1}{2} \cdot c.p_3)$ which, by reversing the interpretation from generative probability back to 'additional labels' on the actions b and c, results in the choice $\frac{1}{2} \cdot \tau.p_1 + \frac{1}{2} \cdot (\frac{1}{2}b \cdot 1.p_2 + \frac{1}{2}c \cdot 1.p_3)$. Note that this choice is exactly the same as the result in the previous example. The 'additional labels' for b and c are included but these are ignored when not needed.

The example above illustrates that generative processes can be used rather than labelled reactive ones without changing expressiveness or the semantics. Also, as already seen in the previous section, a uniform generative choice, *i.e.*, one which assigns equal probability to all initial actions, behaves like a reactive choice. Thus, having to give a probability to all actions, rather than to only those that may be suppressed, is not a real restriction; we can ignore/omit the probabilities if they are equal and the actions are not suppressed. Finally, by using the interpretation above we can restrict ourselves to generative processes rather than needing to consider stratified choices.

Probabilistic Suppression Controller. The probabilistic suppression controller operator is an extension of the acceptance operator. We require that at least one of the controller or the target is generative. The probabilistic suppression operator inherits the three rules given for the acceptance operator and, additionally, has the following rule:

$$\frac{C \xrightarrow{\rho \cdot \ominus a} C' \quad F \xrightarrow{\sigma \cdot a} F'}{C \triangleright_S F \xrightarrow{\rho\sigma/n_S \cdot \tau} C' \triangleright_S F'}$$

with $n_S = n_A + \sum_{C \xrightarrow{\rho \cdot \ominus a} C', F \xrightarrow{\sigma \cdot a} F'} \rho\sigma$. The inherited semantics rules allow F, as with the acceptance operator, to perform the action $a \neq \tau$ if also performed by the controller, *i.e.*, if F performs action a and C performs the same action a, then $C \triangleright_S F$ performs action a. The inherited rules allow both the controller C and the target F to independently perform τ actions. The new rule states that the controller is able to hide a possible incorrect action to an external observer by relabelling a to τ. The normalization factor n_S is updated to include this final possibility to ensure probabilities still add up to 1.

As the action is hidden from outside, a choice involving it clearly has to be made by the system itself. Hence, it needs to be generative. As such the rule does not work in the case both controller and target are reactive. In particular, the rule then does not properly work in the following two cases:

- when the target performs internal action τ;
- when the controller suppresses more that one action.

In these cases a choice has to be made between actions while their relative probabilities are not known. The following example illustrates this point. (For an example of use of suppression in a generative controller see controler C_S in Sect. 3.3.)

Example 3. Consider again the building example used above. We consider a basic system that allows one entry but through either door. A guard in front of the doors hides the choice of the user:

$$F = a \cdot 1.0 + b \cdot 1.0 \tag{6}$$

$$C = \ominus a \cdot 1.0 + \ominus b \cdot 1.0 \tag{7}$$

For this simple system the above rule would give for $C \triangleright_S F$:

$$C \triangleright_S F = \tau \cdot 1.0 + \tau \cdot 1.0 = \tau \cdot .2.0 \tag{8}$$

The total probability is more than 1. We cannot scale this probability without knowing the relative probability to use between the two options.

Probabilistic Insertion Controller. Sometimes actions are not forbidden per se but they need to be prepared for, *e.g.*, you are allowed to enter the building but only if a security guard is present in the building. In this case a controller may want to insert an action (send in guard) before allowing your action (enter building). The insertion controller operation is used to express this control strategy. The special action $\oplus a.b$ is used to express that the controller inserts action b before allowing action a. Also insertion operator inherits the rules of acceptance operators. In addition to those rules, it has the following key semantic rule:

$$\frac{E \xrightarrow{\rho \cdot \oplus a.b} E' \quad F \xrightarrow{\sigma \cdot a} F'}{E \triangleright_I F \xrightarrow{\rho \sigma / n_I \cdot b} E' \triangleright_I F}$$

(Note that if F can chose among multiple a transitions the resulting steps of the controlled process are the same. As mentioned we implicitly assume these steps are combined by adding their probabilities together.) The normalization factor is adapted as before to also consider $\oplus a.b$ action; $n_I = n_A + \sum_{C' \xrightarrow{\rho \cdot \oplus a.b} C', F \xrightarrow{\sigma \cdot a} F'} \rho \sigma$. In this rule we assume that the users/controlled systems can change their mind;

after inserting the action b, F again gets to make its choice for which action to execute. It is thus very well possible that action a in the end does not actually happen (*e.g.*, you do not enter the building after the guard has been sent in.)

Insertion of an action has, like the τ action, an inherent generative nature; it is the system that decides to insert the action. This rule thus is not valid when both the controller and target are both reactive processes and the target is able to perform the same action that the controller has inserted.

Example 4. Coming back to the building example with a target that leaves both doors open. Consider a reactive controller that always lets the user open the door to the stairs (b) but if the user tries to take the elevator (a), it blocks her and first opens the door for the stairs in order to convince her to take the stairs instead of the elevator.

$$F = b \cdot 1.0 + a \cdot 1.0 \tag{9}$$

$$C = b \cdot 1.0 + \oplus a.b \cdot 1.0 \tag{10}$$

Hence, $C \triangleright_I F$ always leaves the stairs door open and hermetically closes the stairs one. The resulting probabilistic process is as follows:

$$C \triangleright_I F = b \cdot 1.0 + b \cdot 1.0 = b \cdot 2.0 \tag{11}$$

The total probability is more than 1 and we miss the information needed to normalize.

Probabilistic Edit Controller operator. It is possible, as is done in the quantitative case, to combine the functionalities of suppression and insertion in a single probabilistic controller, a *probabilistic Edit controller*. The Edit controller thus inherits the two semantic rules above along with their restrictions on processes that can be used.

The non-probabilistic Edit controller operators apply suppression and insertion rules in a mutual exclusive way, *i.e.*, the set of action that can be suppressed is disjoint from the one of actions that are prevented to be made by inserting something before. This assumption has been made in order to be able to deterministically apply one rule or the other. For the probabilistic controller we do not need this assumption; we can use the relative probabilities of controlling actions $\ominus a$ and $\oplus a$. For instance consider in the building with users scenario that a check should be made upstairs before using the elevator. A guard lets people take the stairs (b) but if they try to take the elevator (a) he either simply forbids this or sends someone upstairs to make the check: $C = b \cdot 1.C + \ominus a \cdot \frac{3}{4}.C + \oplus a.b \cdot \frac{1}{4}.C'$ If a user tries to take the elevator then with probability $\frac{3}{4}$ they will be forbidden and with probability $\frac{1}{4}$ someone will be sent up the stairs first (with C' presumably upon confirmation that it is safe allowing use of the elevator.)

3.3   Comparing Probabilistic Operators

Let us consider again the example of the building with two doors, one for the elevator (door a) and one for the stairs (door b). We have already seen the example of the guard that tries to persuade users to take the stairs expressed with the probabilistic Acceptance operator: $C_A = \frac{1}{3} \cdot a.C_A + \frac{2}{3} \cdot b.C_A$ When people arrive at the building the guard tries to convince them that taking the stairs is much better. Note that simple locking the elevator door $C'_A = 1 \cdot b.C'_A$ is not an option as the whole system would block when a user unable to use the stairs arrives.

Guard C_A only tries to persuade the user. We can also consider a guard that wants to force users to not use the elevator. One possible strategy, expressed using the Suppression operator is $C_S = \ominus a \cdot 1.C_S + b \cdot 1.C_S$; the guard allows anyone to take the stairs but anyone trying to take the elevator is sent away. This can be combined with persuasion as in $C'_S = \frac{1}{3} \cdot \ominus a.C'_S + \frac{2}{3} \cdot b.C'_S$; the guard tries to convince users to take the stairs. Those that choose the elevator anyway are sent away.

We can extend any base strategy $(C_I^{(0)})$ with a guard that will always allow users to take the stairs but will first send them back a number of times when they try to use the elevator: $C_I^{(i)} = \oplus a.\tau \cdot 1.C_I^{(i-1)} + b \cdot 1.C_I$ Only users determined to take the elevator (e.g., because they cannot take the stairs) will reach the base strategy.

Adding probability to the system description as well as the controller operators improves the ability to compare different controller strategies and to select the one with the best (expected) results. To illustrate this we add another feature to our example as a first glance to our future work. Users can only take the elevator when an operator is present. Action c expresses deploying the operator for that day. A controller could choose to insert action c at some point. We want to allow as many users as possible to enter but deploying the operator incurs some cost. The result (traces) of the system can thus be quantified by considering these costs and benefits. While formalizing cost and benefit is part of future work we consider a basic example in order to show this idea.

Both C'_S above and C_c below which inserts an operator as soon as needed achieve the security property that the elevator is not used without an operator.

$$C_c = \oplus a.c \cdot 1.C'_c + b \cdot 1.C_c \tag{12}$$

$$C'_c = a \cdot 1.C'_c + b \cdot 1.C'_c \tag{13}$$

If n users arrive without preference for a door, $F^{(n)} = \frac{1}{2} \cdot a.F^{(n-1)} + \frac{1}{2} \cdot b.F^{(n-1)}$, $F^{(0)} = 0$ the guard C'_S will convince two thirds of the users to take the stairs. One third is sent away. Guard C_c on the other hand will allow all users to enter but with high probability $(1 - \frac{1}{2}^n)$ will incur the cost of c. Thus if $(1 - \frac{1}{2}^n) \cdot cost(c)$ is less than $\frac{1}{3} \cdot benefit(a)$ the later strategy is superior in this scenario. If also users in a wheelchair arrive who cannot use the stairs; $(F = 1 \cdot a.F')$ then C'_S will not be able to convince them to take the stairs; such a scenario thus more quickly favors strategy C_c.

Besides allowing comparison of operators that guarantee a deterministic property, we can also consider probabilistic requirements, e.g., a limit on the probability that the elevator is used. To sum up; adding probability to controller operator introduces a new parameter according to which it is possible to refine and to optimize controlling strategies in order to satisfy the system requirement as well as possible, and, sometimes in the *best* way.

4   Related Work

Security and, more specifically, its evaluation, are important topics that have been receiving a lot of attention in recent years. However, controlling systems and formally measuring and evaluating (quantitative) security aspects of the system remains a challenging subject which seems to have received limited study compared to its importance.

Caravagna *et al.* consider in [10] the notion of lazy controllers, which only control the security of a system at some points in time, and based on a probabilistic modelling of the system, quantify the expected risk. Basin *et al.* consider in [5] the case where some actions are uncontrollable (*i.e.*, cannot be stopped), and define what policies can then be enforced, by modelling a controller as a Deterministic Turing Machine.

In the context of access control, Molloy *et al.* use a machine learning approach to predict the decision for a given request [25], and balance the risk of error against the cost of contacting the real mechanism to get the actual decision.

In a recent approach [20], the authors deal with probabilistic cost enforcement based on input/output automata to model complex and interactive systems. Associating to each execution trace a probability and a cost measure, it is possible to evaluate the expected cost of the monitor and of the monitored systems. Even though Input/output automata are similar to our reactive processes, our work goes beyond [20] by also considering generative processes as both controller and target. Furthermore, it uses a process algebraic specification of the controllers which we hope will allow for the automatic generation of controller automata as in [23]. Also, in [12], a notion of cost to compare correct enforcement mechanisms (defined as state machines) with different strategies.

Easwaran *et al.* in [13] aim at finding an optimal control strategy in the context of software monitoring. A system is represented as a Directed Acyclic Graph and rewards and penalties with correcting actions are taken into account. Dynamic programming is then used to find the optimal solution. Similarly, an encoding of access control mechanisms using Markov Decision Process is proposed in [24], where the optimal policy can be derived by solving the corresponding optimisation problem. Markov chains are used in PRISM [17] in order to evaluate and validate systems in a quantitative and probabilistic way. From a different perspective, Bielova and Massacci propose in [8] a notion of distance among traces, thus expressing that if a trace is not secure, it should be edited to a secure trace close to the non-secure one, thus characterizing enforcement strategies by the distance from the original trace they create.

In [9], Buchholz and Kemper propose a *generalized process algebra* in which each operators has been extended with the notion of cost modelled through a semiring. In [11], the authors present a framework for quantitative evaluation of controller strategies. This framework is based on process algebra to model the behaviour of the process and on semirings to model different measures. Probability is not considered as an evaluation metric since it cannot be easily modelled through a semiring.

5 Conclusion and Future Work

In this paper we take a first step towards automated generation of optimal quantitative controller strategies. This step consists of classifying probabilistic controller strategies for probabilistic systems. The classification of the strategy considers reactive and generative processes for both the controller and target processes. In particular, focusing on a simplified process algebra with only probabilistic choice and a controller operator as its main components, we consider three possible corrective actions (acceptance, suppression, and insertion) that can be performed by the controller process. We provide a definition of probabilistic controlling strategies based on these actions and we analyse the different behaviours according to the reactive and generative nature of both controller and target processes.

The use of a probabilistic language allows modelling a wide range of strategies applied to different situations. Also many strategies which are incomparable in a possibilistic analysis can be compared probabilistically. When we want to compare controllers across multiple systems or we do not know the (exact) probabilities for certain choices (as will often be the case in realistic complex systems) having a notion of non-determinism in conjunction with probability would be useful.

To have a language powerful enough for specifying a realistic, complex system we aim to extend the basic process language considered here with more advanced controllers, non-deterministic choice and parallelism. We will then also need to extend our classification by considering different models for the combination of nondeterminism and probability, e.g. [2,15,19,27].

Another extension of this work that we plan to investigate is the combination with the notion of cost. In particular, we aim to be able to choice the best control strategy finding a trade-off between maintaining a security property and the cost of attack.

References

1. Aldini, A., Gorrieri, R.: Security analysis of a probabilistic non-repudiation protocol. In: Hermanns, H., Segala, R. (eds.) PROBMIV 2002, PAPM-PROBMIV 2002, and PAPM 2002. LNCS, vol. 2399, pp. 17–36. Springer, Heidelberg (2002)
2. Andova, S.: Process algebra with probabilistic choice. In: Katoen, J.-P. (ed.) AMAST-ARTS 1999, ARTS 1999, and AMAST-WS 1999. LNCS, vol. 1601, pp. 111–129. Springer, Heidelberg (1999)
3. Baier, C., Hermanns, H.: Weak bisimulation for fully probabilistic processes. In: Grumberg, O. (ed.) Computer Aided Verification. LNCS, pp. 119–130. Springer, Heidelberg (1997)

4. Bartoletti, M., Degano, P., Ferrari, G.L.: Policy framings for access control. In: Proceedings of the 2005 Workshop on Issues in the Theory of Security, pp. 5–11. ACM (2005)
5. Basin, D., Jugé, V., Klaedtke, F., Zălinescu, E.: Enforceable security policies revisited. In: Degano, P., Guttman, J.D. (eds.) Principles of Security and Trust. LNCS, vol. 7215, pp. 309–328. Springer, Heidelberg (2012)
6. Bauer, L., Ligatti, J., Walker, D.: More enforceable security policies. In: Cervesato, I. (ed.) Foundations of Computer Security: proceedings of the FLoC 2002 workshop on Foundations of Computer Security, pp. 95–104. DIKU Technical Report (2002)
7. Bauer, L., Ligatti, J., Walker, D.: Edit automata: enforcement mechanisms for run-time security policies. Int. J. Inf. Secur. 4(1–2), 2–16 (2005)
8. Bielova, N., Massacci, F.: Predictability of enforcement. In: Erlingsson, Ú., Wieringa, R., Zannone, N. (eds.) ESSoS 2011. LNCS, vol. 6542, pp. 73–86. Springer, Heidelberg (2011)
9. Buchholz, P., Kemper, P.: Quantifying the dynamic behavior of process algebras. In: de Alfaro, L., Gilmore, S. (eds.) Proceedings of the Joint International Workshop on Process Algebra and Probabilistic Methods, Performance Modeling and Verification. LNCS, vol. 2165, pp. 184–199. Springer, Heidelberg (2001)
10. Caravagna, G., Costa, G., Pardini, G.: Lazy security controllers. In: Jøsang, A., Samarati, P., Petrocchi, M. (eds.) STM 2012. LNCS, vol. 7783, pp. 33–48. Springer, Heidelberg (2013)
11. Ciancia, V., Martinelli, F., Ilaria, M., Morisset, C.: Quantitative evaluation of enforcement strategies: position paper. In: Danger, J.-L., Debbabi, M., Marion, J.-Y., Garcia-Alfaro, J., Heywood, N.Z. (eds.) FPS 2013. LNCS, vol. 8352, pp. 178–186. Springer, Heidelberg (2014)
12. Drábik, P., Martinelli, F., Morisset, C.: Cost-aware runtime enforcement of security policies. In: Jøsang, A., Samarati, P., Petrocchi, M. (eds.) STM 2012. LNCS, vol. 7783, pp. 1–16. Springer, Heidelberg (2013)
13. Easwaran, A., Kannan, S., Lee, I.: Optimal control of software ensuring safety and functionality. Technical report MS-CIS-05-20, University of Pennsylvania (2005)
14. Glabbeek, R.V., Smolka, S., Steffen, B.: Reactive, generative and stratified models of probabilistic processes. Inform. Comput. 121, 130–141 (1990)
15. den Hartog, J.I., de Vink, E.P.: Mixing up nondeterminism and probability: a preliminary report. Electr. Notes Theor. Comput. Sci. 22, 88–110 (1999)
16. Hoare, C.: Communicating Sequential Processes, vol. 178. Prentice-hall, Englewood Cliffs (1985)
17. Kwiatkowska, M., Norman, G., Parker, D.: PRISM 4.0: verification of probabilistic real-time systems. In: Gopalakrishnan, G., Qadeer, S. (eds.) CAV 2011. LNCS, vol. 6806, pp. 585–591. Springer, Heidelberg (2011)
18. Ligatti, J., Bauer, L., Walker, D.W.: Enforcing non-safety security policies with program monitors. In: di Vimercati, S.C., Syverson, P.F., Gollmann, D. (eds.) ESORICS 2005. LNCS, vol. 3679, pp. 355–373. Springer, Heidelberg (2005)
19. Lowe, G.: Representing nondeterminism and probabilistic behaviour in reactive processes. Technical report PRG-TR-11-93, Oxforf University Computing Laboratory (1993)
20. Mallios, Y., Bauer, L., Kaynar, D., Martinelli, F., Morisset, C.: Probabilistic cost enforcement of security policies. In: Accorsi, R., Ranise, S. (eds.) STM 2013. LNCS, vol. 8203, pp. 144–159. Springer, Heidelberg (2013)
21. Martinelli, F.: Analysis of security protocols as open systems. Theor. Comput. Sci. 290(1), 1057–1106 (2003)

22. Martinelli, F., Matteucci, I.: Through modeling to synthesis of security automata. Electr. Notes Theor. Comput. Sci. **179**, 31–46 (2007)
23. Martinelli, F., Matteucci, I.: A framework for automatic generation of security controller. Softw. Test. Verif. Reliab. **22**(8), 563–582 (2012)
24. Martinelli, F., Morisset, C.: Quantitative access control with partially-observable markov decision processes. In: Proceedings of CODASPY 2012, pp. 169–180. ACM (2012)
25. Molloy, I., Dickens, L., Morisset, C., Cheng, P.C., Lobo, J., Russo, A.: Risk-based security decisions under uncertainty. In: Proceedings of CODASPY 2012, pp. 157–168. ACM (2012)
26. Schneider, F.B.: Enforceable security policies. ACM Trans. Inf. Syst. Secur. **3**(1), 30–50 (2000)
27. Segala, R.: Modeling and verification of randomized distributed real-time systems. Ph.D. thesis, Massachusetts Institute of Technology (1995)

Automatically Calculating Quantitative Integrity Measures for Imperative Programs

Tom Chothia[1]([⊠]), Chris Novakovic[1], and Rajiv Ranjan Singh[2]

[1] School of Computer Science, University of Birmingham, Birmingham, UK
T.Chothia@cs.bham.ac.uk
[2] Department of Computer Science, Shyam Lal College, University of Delhi,
New Delhi, India

Abstract. This paper presents a framework for calculating measures of data integrity for programs in a small imperative language. We develop a Markov chain semantics for our language which calculates Clarkson and Schneider's definitions of data contamination and suppression. These definitions are based on conditional mutual information and entropy; we present a result relating them to mutual information, which can be calculated by a number of existing tools. We extend a quantitative information flow tool (CH-IMP) to calculate these measures of integrity and demonstrate this tool with examples based on error correcting codes, the Dining Cryptographers protocol and the attempts by a number of banks to influence the Libor rate.

1 Introduction

Data integrity is an important issue for programs, but this does not mean that programs must guarantee that all good data is perfectly preserved, or that no bad data can affect a program's output in any way. It is often the case that a good service can be provided with a small but acceptable loss in the integrity of data. Therefore, there is a need for a framework in which the level of integrity a system provides can be accurately measured.

Qualitative integrity has been well-studied (see e.g. the work of Birgisson et al. [3], who provide a unified framework for qualitative integrity policies), but quantitative integrity measures have received far less attention. An exception to this is the work of Clarkson and Schneider, which defines the data integrity measures of "contamination" and "suppression" [8,9]. In this paper, we extend these measures to a small imperative language, give this language a Markov chain semantics, and show how these measures of integrity can be calculated for programs with multiple trusted and untrusted inputs and outputs. We extend an existing quantitative information flow (QIF) tool, CH-IMP [6], to use this semantics to automatically calculate these measures.

Clarkson and Schneider's definitions are based on conditional mutual information and entropy. Existing QIF tools can calculate the mutual information between a system's secret values and observable outputs; we investigate whether mutual information can be used to calculate conditional mutual information.

© Springer International Publishing Switzerland 2015
J. Garcia-Alfaro et al. (Eds.): DPM/SETOP/QASA 2014, LNCS 8872, pp. 250–265, 2015.
DOI: 10.1007/978-3-319-17016-9_16

We find that for secrecy, in which the public inputs of a system must be unrelated to the secret inputs, conditional mutual information can be calculated using mutual information (and therefore that existing QIF tools can calculate conditional mutual information-based definitions of secrecy by simply appending a program's public inputs to its public outputs). However, for integrity, the trusted data is considered to be public, and so the untrusted data sent to a system may depend on it, so conditional mutual information must be calculated explicitly.

The semantics we present makes it possible to calculate the integrity between multiple trusted and untrusted inputs and outputs. In doing so, we pay particular attention to what data is recorded by the semantics, and thus the probability distributions used to calculate the integrity measures. These decisions define the attacker model: CH-IMP models an attacker that wishes to learn anything they can about the secret values (including, e.g., the order in which they occur) and can only observe certain outputs from the system. For integrity, we consider a model in which we are only concerned that data is correctly preserved as it flows between variables. Thus, because of the different attacker models, the calculation of quantitative integrity is not the dual of the calculation of quantitative secrecy.

The contributions of this paper are:

- An extension of the CH-IMP semantics that can calculate the integrity measures defined by Clarkson and Schneider for multiple trusted and untrusted inputs and outputs in a simple imperative language.
- Showing that, when trusted/public inputs are unrelated to untrusted/secure inputs, measures based on conditional mutual information can be calculated in terms of mutual information.
- A software tool — the first of its kind — that automatically quantifies measures of integrity, and example programs.

In Sect. 2 we review related work, including the integrity definitions of Clarkson and Schneider and the CH-IMP framework. In Sect. 3 we show that definitions based on conditional mutual information can be rewritten in terms of mutual information, and can therefore be calculated more easily. In Sect. 4 we extend the CH-IMP semantics to calculate quantitative integrity for imperative programs. We implement this semantics and give some example programs in Sect. 5. Finally, we conclude in Sect. 6.

Our tool and a number of example programs are available on our website [14].

2   Background

2.1   Information Theory

The entropy (see e.g. [10]) of a random variable X with a probability mass function p is defined as

$$H(X) = - \sum_{x \in X} p(x) \log_2 p(x)$$

and is the average number of bits required to describe the result of the random variable. This extends to joint distributions in the obvious way: $H(X,Y) = -\sum_{x\in X}\sum_{y\in Y}p(x,y)\log_2 p(x,y)$.

The conditional entropy gives the amount of information required to describe the value of a random variable X if the value of a second random variable Y is known:

$$H(X|Y) = \sum_{x\in X}\sum_{y\in Y} p(x,y)\log_2 \frac{p(x)}{p(x,y)}$$

A natural extension of this is to define $H(X|Y,Z) = \sum_{x,y,z} p(x,y,z)\log_2 \frac{p(x)}{p(x,y,z)}$.

Mutual information is a measure of the information that one random variable contains about another:

$$I(X;Y) = H(X) - H(X|Y) = \sum_{x\in X}\sum_{y\in Y} p(x,y)\log_2 \frac{p(x,y)}{p(x)p(y)}. \tag{1}$$

Finally, conditional mutual information tells us how much information a random variable X contains about another random variable Y, given knowledge of a third random variable Z:

$$I(X;Y|Z) = H(X|Z) - H(X|Y,Z). \tag{2}$$

2.2 Quantification of Information Leakage and CH-IMP

QIF systems measure how much information an attacker learns about the high-level secret values in a system by observing low-level public values. Clark et al. [7] propose a standard model in which a system has high and low inputs and outputs, as depicted in Fig. 1. The information leakage in the system is then defined using conditional mutual information:

$$\text{Leakage} = I(H_{in}; L_{out}|L_{in})$$

i.e., the information the system leaks is the amount of information that an attacker (who knows the public inputs to the system) can learn about the high-level secret inputs to a system by observing the low-level public outputs.

More recently, a number of QIF tools have been developed that calculate the leakage from programs of varying sizes and complexities (e.g., [2,6,12]). However these tools calculate the simpler leakage measure of $I(H_{in}; L_{out})$; i.e., they do not explicitly model the attacker's knowledge of low inputs to the system.

Another popular measure of QIF is min-entropy leakage [13], which is given by $\log_2(\Sigma_l \max_h p(h,l)) - \log_2(\max_h p(h))$. This measure describes a system's resistance to correct guesses of the secret value in a single attempt. In this paper, we use definitions based on mutual information, but much of this work also applies to min-entropy-based definitions of integrity.

In previous work [6], we generalised the standard model of information leakage to allow secrets and observables to occur at any point in a program, and

Fig. 1. Information leakage model of a program

$$
\begin{aligned}
C ::= \ &\text{new } V := \rho \\
| \ &V := \rho \\
| \ &\text{if } (B) \ \{ \ C \ \} \ \text{else} \ \{ \ C \ \} \\
| \ &\text{while } (B) \ \{ \ C \ \} \\
| \ &C; \ C \\
| \ &\text{start} \\
| \ &\text{end} \\
| \ &\text{secret } V \\
| \ &\text{observe } V
\end{aligned}
$$

Fig. 2. The syntax of CH-IMP

we developed a tool (CH-IMP) to automatically calculate the leakage from a program.

The syntax of the CH-IMP language is given in Fig. 2. It is a simple imperative language with loops, variable declaration and assignment, and scope. It is a probabilistic language: the ρ in declaration and assignments is a probability distribution on expressions. The novel features of this language are the secret and observe commands,[1] which are used to tag high-level secret data and low-level observable data respectively. CH-IMP calculates how much information an attacker learns about the values tagged with secret by inspecting the values tagged with observe.

The semantics of CH-IMP are defined as a discrete-time Markov chain (DTMC) with states of the form $(C, \sigma, \mathcal{S}, \mathcal{O})$, where C is the program to be executed, σ is the current environment (mappings of variables to values), $\mathcal{S}$ are the secret variable mappings observed so far, and $\mathcal{O}$ is a list of the observed values. In order to support scope, an environment is a stack of sets of variable mappings, and the start and end commands push and pop elements onto and from this stack respectively.

The DTMC for a program C has the initial state $(C, \langle \rangle, \langle \rangle, \langle \rangle)$ and a probability transition matrix defined by the rules in Fig. 3. $s \xrightarrow{p} s'$ denotes the existence of a transition from state s to state s' with probability p, and $\sigma \oplus \{V \mapsto n\}$

---

[1] For simplicity, we write secret and observe as commands in the language but, as they have no effect on the state or control flow of a program, they may more accurately be considered annotations.

$$(\text{new } V := \rho; \ C, o :: \sigma, \mathcal{S}, \mathcal{O}) \xrightarrow{\rho(n)} (C, (\{V \mapsto n\} \cup o) :: \sigma, \mathcal{S}, \mathcal{O})$$

$$(\text{secret } V; \ C, \sigma, \mathcal{S}, \mathcal{O}) \xrightarrow{1} (C, \sigma, \mathcal{S} :: (V \mapsto \llbracket V \rrbracket \sigma), \mathcal{O})$$

$$(\text{observe } V; \ C, \sigma, \mathcal{S}, \mathcal{O}) \xrightarrow{1} (C, \sigma, \mathcal{S}, \mathcal{O} :: \llbracket V \rrbracket \sigma)$$

$$(V := \rho; \ C, \sigma, \mathcal{S}, \mathcal{O}) \xrightarrow{\rho(n)} (C, \sigma \oplus \{V \mapsto n\}, \mathcal{S}, \mathcal{O})$$

$$\frac{\sigma(B) \rightarrow \textbf{true}}{(\text{if } (B) \ \{ \ C_T \ \} \text{ else } \{ \ C_F \ \}; \ C, \sigma, \mathcal{S}, \mathcal{O}) \xrightarrow{1} (\text{start}; \ C_T; \ \text{end}; \ C, \sigma, \mathcal{S}, \mathcal{O})}$$

$$\frac{\sigma(B) \rightarrow \textbf{false}}{(\text{if } (B) \ \{ \ C_T \ \} \text{ else } \{ \ C_F \ \}; \ C, \sigma, \mathcal{S}, \mathcal{O}) \xrightarrow{1} (\text{start}; \ C_F; \ \text{end}; \ C, \sigma, \mathcal{S}, \mathcal{O})}$$

$$\frac{\sigma(B) \rightarrow \textbf{true}}{(\text{while } (B) \ \{ \ C_W \ \}; \ C, \sigma, \mathcal{S}, \mathcal{O}) \xrightarrow{1} (\text{start}; \ C_W; \ \text{end}; \ \text{while } (B) \ \{ \ C_W \ \}; \ C, \sigma, \mathcal{S}, \mathcal{O})}$$

$$\frac{\sigma(B) \rightarrow \textbf{false}}{(\text{while } (B) \ \{ \ C_W \ \}; \ C, \sigma, \mathcal{S}, \mathcal{O}) \xrightarrow{1} (C, \sigma, \mathcal{S}, \mathcal{O})}$$

$$(\text{start}; \ C, \sigma, \mathcal{S}, \mathcal{O}) \xrightarrow{1} (C, \{\} :: \sigma, \mathcal{S}, \mathcal{O})$$

$$(\text{end}; \ C, o :: \sigma, \mathcal{S}, \mathcal{O}) \xrightarrow{1} (C, \sigma, \mathcal{S}, \mathcal{O})$$

Fig. 3. The semantic rules of CH-IMP.

denotes the replacement of the mapping for V with $V \mapsto n$ in the narrowest scope in σ already containing a mapping for V. The novel rules in the semantics are the rules for secret and observe; these rules record the high and low values that occur along a particular path of execution of the program.

A subtlety of the language is that it records variable mappings for secrets, but only the values of the public observables. This reflects our attacker model, in which the attacker wishes to learn *any* information about how the secret data is processed — in particular, if an attacker learns which secret variables are used (or in which order), but does not learn the values of those variables, then we consider that they have learnt some information about the secrets; the variable name must therefore be recorded in $\mathcal{S}$. However, the attacker only sees the values outputted by the program (not where or how these values were produced), so only the values of the observables are recorded in $\mathcal{O}$.

Fig. 4. Integrity measurement model of a program

The final states of the DTMC of a terminating program give the probability distribution $p(\mathcal{S}, \mathcal{O})$ from which the information leakage measure $I(\mathcal{S}; \mathcal{O})$ can be calculated. The CH-IMP tool, source code and a range of examples are available at [14].

2.3 Quantification of Integrity

Clarkson and Schneider's work on the quantification of integrity [8,9] provides three definitions of integrity, although they do not address how to compute these definitions for programs. Their framework considers a program which has both trusted and untrusted inputs and outputs, as depicted in Fig. 4. Their intuition is that the untrusted data is bad data that an attacker may have added to the system, whereas the trusted input is the good data added by an honest party. A good system should minimise the effect that the untrusted inputs have on the trusted outputs, while at the same time preserving as much of the information from the trusted inputs as possible.

Clarkson and Schneider's first definition is *data contamination*, which they define as the amount of untrusted input data which can be learnt from the trusted output:

Definition 1 (Contamination). *The contamination in a system with untrusted input U_{in}, trusted input T_{in} and trusted output T_{out} equals $I(U_{in}; T_{out}|T_{in})$.*

We note that the measure $I(U_{in}; T_{out})$ would tell us how much information about the untrusted inputs is carried over to the trusted outputs; however, using this measure would produce misleading results in cases where the untrusted inputs were based on the trusted inputs. For instance, if the untrusted input was always an exact copy of the trusted input, and the trusted output was an exact copy of the trusted input, we would not consider that contamination was occurring.

The second measure Clarkson and Schneider define is *data suppression*; their intuition here is that the amount of data suppressed is the amount of data from the trusted inputs that the receiver cannot learn from the trusted outputs.

Definition 2 (Suppression). *The suppression in a system with trusted input T_{in} and trusted output T_{out} equals $H(T_{in}|T_{out})$.*

Their third measure, *program suppression*, compares a program's outputs to a specification of a program, and is beyond the scope of this paper. We note that none of these measures uses the untrusted outputs of a program, as these should not be taken into account when determining a program's integrity.

None of these measures make use of the untrusted output, which is included in Fig. 4 for completeness. This indicates that, when considering the integrity of a system, the value of any output of a system that we do not trust is irrelevant.

Clarkson and Schneider's work only provides the definitions of quantification of integrity; they do not address how the measures can be calculated for programs, and they only give single-line examples with single trusted and untrusted values in which the probability distributions on the trusted and untrusted values are clear, and so do not need to be calculated.

3   Using Mutual Information to Calculate Conditional Mutual Information and Entropy

CH-IMP, along with several other QIF tools (e.g. [2,6,12]), can calculate the mutual information between the input and output values of a program. In the next section, we consider how the models of integrity and secrecy differ for complex programs, but setting this aside it is natural to ask if these other tools can be used to calculate integrity measures directly; i.e., given a tool to calculate $I(X;Y)$, can we calculate contamination or suppression?

With regard to suppression ($H(T_{in}|T_{out})$), we note that Eq. 1 gives us:

$$H(T_{in}|T_{out}) = H(T_{in}) - I(T_{in};T_{out}).$$

If the distribution of the trusted inputs is known, which we would expect, then $H(T_{in})$ can be calculated directly; we could then tag the trusted inputs to a program as secrets and the trusted outputs as observables, run the tool to calculate $I(T_{in};T_{out})$, and subtract this from $H(T_{in})$ to calculate suppression.

Contamination ($I(U_i;T_o|T_i)$) presents us with more of a problem. However, we note that:

$$\begin{aligned}
I(U_i;T_o|T_i) &= H(U_i|T_i) - H(U_i|T_o,T_i) & \text{by Eq. 2} \\
&= H(U_i) + H(U_i|T_i) - H(U_i|T_o,T_i) - H(U_i) & \text{+ and - } H(U_i) \\
&= H(U_i) - H(U_i|T_o,T_i) - (H(U_i) - H(U_i|T_i)) & \text{rearrange terms} \\
&= I(U_i;T_o,T_i) - I(U_i;T_i) & \text{by Eq. 1.}
\end{aligned}$$

If the untrusted inputs U_i and the trusted inputs T_i are completely unrelated then $I(U_i;T_i) = 0$, which in turn means that $I(U_{in},T_{out}|T_{in}) = I(U_{in};T_{in},T_{out})$; i.e., contamination in this case could be calculated by appending the trusted inputs to the trusted outputs and calculating the mutual information between this and the untrusted inputs. We state this as a theorem:

Theorem 1. *Contamination* = $I(U_i;T_o|T_i)$ = $I(U_i;T_i,T_o) + I(U_i;T_i)$, *and, in the case that the untrusted inputs are independent of the trusted inputs, contamination* = $I(U_i;T_i,T_o)$.

$$C ::= \text{new } V := \rho$$
$$| \quad V := \rho$$
$$| \quad \text{if } (B) \{ C \} \text{ else } \{ C \}$$
$$| \quad \text{while } (B) \{ C \}$$
$$| \quad C; C$$
$$| \quad \text{start}$$
$$| \quad \text{end}$$
$$| \quad \text{untrustedin } V$$
$$| \quad \text{trustedin } V$$
$$| \quad \text{trustedout } V$$

Fig. 5. The syntax of CH-IMP with integrity quantification (CH-IMP-IQ)

However, the attacker's untrusted inputs may depend on the trusted inputs. There is no assumption of secrecy for the trusted values, and attacks on the integrity of a system may rely on an attacker sending carefully-crafted untrusted inputs based on the trusted inputs; e.g., the attacker might pick an input which, when combined with a trusted input, causes an overflow. In this case, $I(U_i; T_i, T_o)$ overestimates contamination by an amount equal to the amount of information about the untrusted inputs contained in the trusted inputs.

When calculating information leakage from a system, on the other hand, we explicitly require that the attacker does not know the value of the secret inputs $(High_{in})$, and therefore the attacker cannot pick low values (Low_{in}) based on these; i.e., $I(High_{in}; Low_{in}) = 0$. So, for secrecy, the conditional form with low inputs can be calculated directly by existing QIF tools:

Corollary 1. *When calculating information leakage, for which we have $I(H_{in}; L_{in}) = 0$, the standard measure of information leakage, $I(H_{in}; L_{out}|L_{in})$ is equal to $I(H_{in}; L_{in}, L_{out})$.*

Thus, existing QIF tools that calculate $I(High_{in}; Low_{out})$ can calculate the conditional mutual information measurement of leakage by simply appending the low-level inputs to the low-level outputs used to calculate leakage.

4   A Language for Integrity Checking

CH-IMP-IQ Syntax. The syntax of CH-IMP with integrity quantification (CH-IMP-IQ) is given in Fig. 5. V ranges over variable names, B ranges over Boolean expressions (i.e., evaluating to one of $\{\mathbf{true}, \mathbf{false}\}$), and ρ ranges over probability distributions on arithmetic expressions: variables, integers, or the result of evaluating two variables or integers with one of the standard arithmetic operations $\{+, -, *, /, \mathsf{mod}, \mathsf{xor}\}$.

The key new commands are untrustedin, trustedin and trustedout. These are used to label variables; we note that there is no label for untrusted outputs, as these are not needed to calculate contamination or suppression. An input in CH-IMP-IQ is not concrete; instead, it is selected from a probability distribution.

For instance, Clarkson and Schneider use a one-line example program in their paper — $o_T := i_T$ xor j_U — in which o_T is the trusted output, i_T is the trusted input, and j_U is the untrusted input (i_T and j_U are chosen to be 0 or 1 uniformly). This example is equivalent to the following CH-IMP-IQ program:

$$
\begin{aligned}
&\text{new } i_T := \{\ 0 \mapsto 0.5,\ 1 \mapsto 0.5\ \}; \\
&\text{trustedin } i_T; \\
&\text{new } j_U := \{\ 0 \mapsto 0.5,\ 1 \mapsto 0.5\ \}; \\
&\text{untrustedin } j_U; \\
&\text{new } o_T := i_T \text{ xor } j_U; \\
&\text{trustedout } o_T;
\end{aligned}
$$

The CH-IMP-IQ Model. The CH-IMP-IQ semantics calculates the probability distributions on the (un)trusted inputs and outputs. Furthermore, we would like to be able to analyse programs with many (un)trusted inputs and outputs, so we must consider which probability distributions should be calculated, and in particular whether we should consider the values of the variables (as CH-IMP does with observables) or the distribution on the mapping of variable names to values (as CH-IMP does with secrets). We illustrate this with the following example program (we use the shorthand trusted[in|out] new $V := \rho$ to mean new $V := \rho$; trusted[in|out] V):

$$
\begin{aligned}
&\text{trustedin new } in1 := \{\ 0 \mapsto 0.5,\ 1 \mapsto 0.5\ \}; \\
&\text{trustedin new } in2 := \{\ 0 \mapsto 0.5,\ 1 \mapsto 0.5\ \}; \\
&\text{new } coin := \{\ 0 \mapsto 0.5,\ 1 \mapsto 0.5\ \}; \\
&\text{if (coin = 1) \{} \\
&\quad \text{trustedout new } out1 = in1+1; \\
&\quad \text{trustedout new } out2 = in2+1; \\
&\text{\} else \{} \\
&\quad \text{trustedout new } out2 = in2+1; \\
&\quad \text{trustedout new } out1 = in1+1; \\
&\text{\}}
\end{aligned}
$$

This program has two trusted inputs and it adds 1 to each of them. The order in which the inputs are incremented and marked as trusted outputs is decided by a random coin flip. We argue that this program does not suppress the integrity of its inputs: the order in which the outputs are declared should not matter, so the suppression of this program should be 0. However, if we consider only the values of the valuables marked as trusted outputs, we obtain the probability transition matrix on the left-hand side below, which implies a suppression value greater than 0.

	11	12	21	22		{out1=1, out2=1}	{out1=1, out2=2}	{out1=2, out2=1}	{out1=2, out2=2}
00	1	0	0	0	{in1=0,in2=0}	1	0	0	0
01	0	0.5	0.5	0	{in1=0,in2=1}	0	1	0	0
10	0	0.5	0.5	0	{in1=1,in2=0}	0	0	1	0
11	0	0	0	1	{in1=1,in2=1}	0	0	0	1

$$(\text{trustedin } V; C, \sigma, \mathcal{T}_{in}, \mathcal{U}_{in}, \mathcal{T}_{out}) \xrightarrow{1} (C, \sigma, \mathcal{T}_{in} \oplus (V \mapsto \mathcal{T}_{in}(V) :: [\![V]\!]\sigma), \mathcal{U}_{in}, \mathcal{T}_{out})$$

$$(\text{untrustedin } V; C, \sigma, \mathcal{T}_{in}, \mathcal{U}_{in}, \mathcal{T}_{out}) \xrightarrow{1} (C, \sigma, \mathcal{T}_{in}, \mathcal{U}_{in} \oplus (V \mapsto \mathcal{U}_{in}(V) :: [\![V]\!]\sigma), \mathcal{T}_{out})$$

$$(\text{trustedout } V; C, \sigma, \mathcal{T}_{in}, \mathcal{U}_{in}, \mathcal{T}_{out}) \xrightarrow{1} (C, \sigma, \mathcal{T}_{in}, \mathcal{U}_{in}, \mathcal{T}_{out} \oplus (V \mapsto \mathcal{T}_{out}(V) :: [\![V]\!]\sigma))$$

Fig. 6. The integrity quantification semantics of CH-IMP-IQ

To capture the behaviour we want, we need to consider mappings from the variables to the values taken by those variables as the elements of the probability distribution, as in the matrix on the right-hand side. This means that the model of integrity in CH-IMP-IQ is not *exactly* the dual of the model of secrecy in CH-IMP, because the different systems use different attacker models. For secrecy, we consider an attacker that only sees the output values of a program, and who would like to learn *any* information about the secrets, including the order in which they occur. For integrity, the observer should know which values relate to which trusted variables, and is only interested in the integrity of these values.

CH-IMP-IQ Semantics. The semantics of a CH-IMP-IQ program C is defined as a DTMC (as with CH-IMP programs) with states describing the current path of execution, annotated with the information needed to compute integrity. They are of the form $(C, \sigma, \mathcal{T}_{in}, \mathcal{U}_{in}, \mathcal{T}_{out})$, where C, σ are the commands to be executed and the program state respectively, $\mathcal{T}_{in}$ is a set of mappings from variables to lists of values that have been marked as trusted inputs (indicated with the trustedin command), $\mathcal{T}_{out}$ is a set of mappings from variables to lists of values that have been marked as trusted outputs (indicated with the trustedout command), and $\mathcal{U}_{in}$ is a set of mappings from variable names to lists of values that have been marked as untrusted inputs (indicated with the untrustedin command).

The semantic rules for the new commands are given in Fig. 6; they track the values of the variables marked as containing trusted input, untrusted input and trusted output by appending their current values to the lists $\mathcal{T}_{in}$, $\mathcal{U}_{in}$ and $\mathcal{T}_{out}$ respectively. The rules for the remaining CH-IMP commands are unchanged from Fig. 3. The DTMC for a program C has the initial state $(C, \langle\rangle, \{\}, \{\}, \{\})$, and a probability transition matrix defined by these rules.

Calculating Integrity. The final states of a terminating program[2] give us the probability distribution $p(t_{in}, u_{in}, t_{out})$. To calculate suppression, we calculate $p(t_{in}, t_{out}) = \sum_{u \in U_{in}} p(t_{in}, u, t_{out})$ and $p(t_{in}) = \sum_{t \in T_{out}} p(t_{in}, t)$, then, using the formula for conditional entropy:

$$H(T_{in}|T_{out}) = \sum_{t_i \in T_{in}} \sum_{t_o \in T_{out}} p(t_i, t_o) \log_2 \frac{p(t_i)}{p(t_i, t_o)}.$$

---

[2] We only consider terminating programs in this paper; however, simpler methods than the ones we presented in [6] could be used to extend our definitions to non-terminating programs.

To calculate contamination, we calculate $p(u_i, t_i) = \sum_{t \in T_{out}} p(t_{in}, u_i, t)$ and then use Bayes' Theorem to expand the definition of conditional mutual information to give:

$$I(U_{in}, T_{out}|T_{in}) = \sum_{t_i \in T_{in}} \sum_{t_o \in T_{out}} \sum_{u_i \in U_{in}} p(u_i, t_o, t_i) \log_2 \frac{p(t_i)p(u_i, t_o, t_i)}{p(u_i, t_i)p(t_o, t_i)}.$$

5   Implementation and Examples

We have implemented the CH-IMP-IQ semantics to calculate contamination and suppression using approximately 1,000 lines of ML code (about two-thirds of which are shared with the CH-IMP implementation). This implementation calculates the measures precisely, modulo any rounding errors made by ML's floating point arithmetic.

The implementation builds the DTMC defined by the semantics, so its run-time is proportional to the state space. While the exact run-time will depend on the program being analysed, for a typical example the tool can analyse programs with 2^{12} states in seconds, and programs with 2^{22} states overnight. The source code and all of the examples from this section are available at [14].

Error Correcting Code. Our first example considers two simple error correction strategies. We first consider a program that broadcasts a 2×2 matrix in which each cell is either 1 or 0 with a probability of 0.5. However we assume that, for each cell, there is a probability that an error will occur and that the cell's value will be incremented by 1. In this case, the trusted inputs are the original cell values, the untrusted inputs are the occurrences of the errors, and the trusted outputs are the (possibly incremented) cell values.

The values of contamination and suppression for this program, with different probabilities of error, are graphed in Fig. 7(a) (where the dashed line is suppression and the solid line is contamination). We see that both the contamination and suppression values increase as the probability of an error increases, but as an error becomes more certain (and therefore predictable), they both decrease. This is because if we can be certain that an error will take place, we can treat a 2 as a 1, and a 1 as a 0, and the original information in the matrix is maintained.

In this example, a 2 as the final value in one of the cells clearly indicates that an error has occurred; we could therefore attempt to correct for this error by replacing all 2 s with 1 s.

Running CH-IMP-IQ again, for a range of different probabilities of error, we find the values of suppression and contamination graphed in Fig. 7(b). We find that this error correction has decreased the contamination; i.e., the error value has a smaller effect on the result. However, the suppression value has increased, and indicates that now almost no useful data is received for high error rates. This is because the output of the system now contains less information: previously a cell value of 2 indicated that the original value was 1 and that an error had occurred. This error correction could therefore be considered counterproductive.

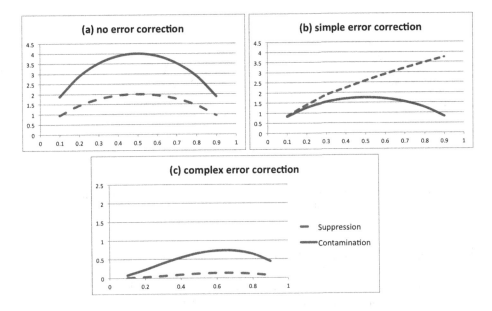

Fig. 7. Integrity measures for the cell errors

Finally, we consider a more complex error correction method that calculates the sum for each row or column, and then uses these sums to check for errors. After the errors, we add code that tries to correct the cell values based on the checksums. This code checks the post-error cell values and a correction is applied if one of the cells does not match the sum for the row and column. Again, the suppression and contamination measures for this code are graphed in Fig. 7(c) (note the different scale for this graph). Errors now only go uncorrected if they occur in pairs, so both suppression and contamination are much lower but still non-zero. We see that the information integrity of the data actually increases for high-error probabilities, again because errors become predictable and the information is preserved.

The Dining Cryptographers Protocol. Reference [4] is a popular example in the information flow literature. The protocol is motivated by the story of three cryptographers who, at the end of a meal, discover that the bill has been paid. They suspect that it was either anonymously paid by one of them, or that it was paid by the NSA. Not wanting to accept money from an organisation that may be performing mass surveillance, they need a protocol that allows one of them to communicate the fact that they paid, without revealing their identity. The protocol runs as follows: each adjacent pair of cryptographers flips a coin that only they see. The cryptographers therefore each see two coins, and they then publicly announce whether the coins agree or disagree — except for the payer (if any), who negates their answer. As the cryptographers are essentially computing the XOR of the coins, if there is an odd number of "disagree" announcements

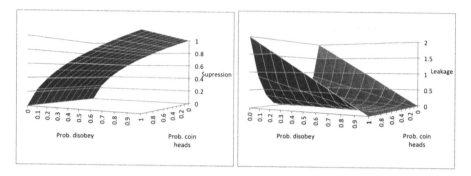

Fig. 8. Comparison of information leakage (via biased coins) and integrity loss (via payer disobedience) in the Dining Cryptographers protocol

then one of the cryptographers paid, but if there is an even number of "disagree" announcements then the NSA paid.

The secrecy of the payer's identity in this protocol relies on the fairness of the coins. A popular example for QIF tools is to show that secrecy of the payer's identity decreases as the coins become more biased; however, the effect that biased coins have on the *integrity* of the protocol has not been studied. A CH-IMP-IQ model of this protocol is available on our website [14]. In this model, a variable *nsapaid* indicates whether the NSA is the payer; we tag this variable as the trusted input. The trusted outputs are the announcements by the cryptographers, and the untrusted inputs are the (possibly biased) coins. We can also calculate secrecy for this program using CH-IMP. Previous analysis of this protocol has shown that biased coins lead to the payer's identity being leaked, so we also consider how probabilistically disobeying the protocol may protect the payer: we introduce a probabilistic variable *obey*, and if this equals zero the payer will disobey the protocol and announce the true results of their coins.

We tested the secrecy and integrity of this system for a range of biased coins and probabilities of the payer disobeying the protocol; the results are shown in the surface plots in Fig. 8. The left-hand subfigure shows the suppression (a suppression of 0 bits means that the payer's identity is always correctly communicated). We see that making the coins biased has no effect on this value; i.e., biased coins do not affect integrity. On the other hand, as the probability of the payer disobeying the protocol increases, the amount of information suppressed rapidly increases.

The right-hand subfigure shows the amount of information leaked about the payer's identity when the probability of disobeying the protocol is zero: a small bias has little effect, but the leakage increases exponentially as the bias increases, leading to a total loss of anonymity for completely biased coins. We also see that disobeying the protocol increases the payer's anonymity, but only at a linear rate. This suggests that probabilistically disobeying the protocol is a poor defence for the payer.

Banks Fixing Libor. Our final example is inspired by the attempts of certain banks to influence the London Interbank Offered Rate (Libor) [1]. Libor is an estimate of the rate at which London banks lend money to each other. This measure is calculated by asking each bank to estimate the rate it would expect and averaging the responses. The rate affects payments on mortgages, student loans and other financial products; thus, any bank that can anticipate its value can make a lot of money. Problems with Libor were first spotted in 2008 [11] and it became evident in 2012 that some banks were constantly trying to fix Libor by under- or over-reporting their estimates [1].

We model a number of different strategies that a corrupt bank could use to fix Libor. Our model makes a number of simplifying assumptions: we assume there is a true rate, modelled as a CH-IMP-IQ variable *rate* (the trusted input) with an integer value selected uniformly between 1 and 4. We also assume that there are four banks that will estimate this value either exactly, or ± 1, with equal probability. Each of the four banks report their estimated rates, which can then be used to calculate Libor (the trusted output).

Perhaps the biggest simplifying assumption we make is that there is only one dishonest bank: one of the four banks will be randomly chosen as the corrupt bank, and a random variable will be used to decide if the bank will try to push the rate up or down; this variable is the untrusted input to the system. We write four different CH-IMP-IQ programs to reflect four ways in which the bank might try to affect the rate (all of which are available on our website):

1. No fixing: the bank does not make any changes, giving us a baseline to see how well the process estimates the true rate.
2. Maximum fixing: the bank will either set its rate to 1 or 4 depending on whether it is trying to increase or lower the rate.
3. ± 1: the bank will change its estimated rate by just 1 point within the range 1 to 4.
4. Average-based: the bank will follow the ± 1 strategy except when this would make the banks reported rate more than 1 point away from the average of the other bank's rates, in which case the corrupt bank will report its true rate.

As well as calculating the integrity of the reported rate, we declare the identity of the corrupt bank as secret and the reported rates as observable, and calculate how much information about the identity of the corrupt bank could be computed from the rates. The results are shown in the following table:

	No fixing	Max. fixing	± 1	Average-based
Suppression	0.487	1.083	0.687	0.648
Contamination	0	0.789	0.222	0.171
Leakage	0	1.32	0.153	0.108

We see that the "maximum fixing" strategy allows the bank to have a large effect on the rate, but the high leakage value indicates that the bank's actions will be obvious. The "± 1" strategy has a smaller effect and a smaller leakage value, indicating that it would be harder to spot than the "maximum fixing" strategy. The "average-based" strategy avoids the cases where the corrupt bank's estimate is suspiciously high or low, so we see a much lower leakage, with only a slightly smaller effect on the rate.

The strategy the dishonest banks actually employed was closest to the "± 1" strategy. In 2008, the Wall Street Journal spotted that banks were reporting rates that, at times, seemed too high or too low [11], and started the investigation into the Libor-rigging scandal. Our analysis suggests that if the banks had instead followed the "average-based" strategy it would have been much harder for reporters to have spotted their actions, and only have had a minor decrease in the affect they had over Libor.

6   Conclusion and Further Work

We have presented a framework that makes it possible to calculate quantitative measures of integrity from imperative programs. We have extended Clarkson and Schneider's definitions of data contamination and suppression to a semantics for a small imperative language, and we have implemented this language to produce the only currently available tool that can be used to quantify integrity.

As further work, we are interested in developing Clarkson and Schneider's definition of integrity with respect to specifications for imperative programs. This would involve a framework in which a user could write a specification program in CH-IMP-IQ, along with a more complex implementation program. The integrity of the implementation program would then be checked against the specification. While we have used Shannon entropy measures in this paper, most of this work would also apply to min-entropy-based measures, and as min-entropy leakage has proven to be a good measure of information leakage [13], it is worth investigating whether it also provides a good measure of integrity.

Due to their complexity and typical state space size, it would be difficult to extend the semantics we present in this paper to real programming languages, such as Java. However, in other work, we have investigated how statistical methods can be used to estimate information leakage measures from large, complex Java programs [5]; we would also like to investigate whether similar techniques can be used to estimate integrity in Java and other languages.

References

1. BBC: Libor scandal: Seven banks face us questioning. BBC News, 16 August 2012
2. Biondi, F., Legay, A., Traonouez, L.-M., Wasowski, A.: QUAIL: a quantitative security analyzer for imperative code. In: Sharygina, N., Veith, H. (eds.) CAV 2013. LNCS, vol. 8044, pp. 702–707. Springer, Heidelberg (2013)
3. Birgisson, A., Russo, A., Sabelfeld, A.: Unifying facets of information integrity. In: Jha, S., Mathuria, A. (eds.) ICISS 2010. LNCS, vol. 6503, pp. 48–65. Springer, Heidelberg (2010)

4. Chaum, D.: The dining cryptographers problem: unconditional sender and recipient untraceability. J. Cryptology **1**, 65–75 (1988)
5. Chothia, T., Kawamoto, Y., Novakovic, C.: LeakWatch: estimating information leakage from java programs. In: Kutyłowski, M., Vaidya, J. (eds.) ICAIS 2014, Part II. LNCS, vol. 8713, pp. 219–236. Springer, Heidelberg (2014)
6. Chothia, T., Kawamoto, Y., Novakovic, C., Parker, D.: Probabilistic point-to-point information leakage. In: Proceedings of the 26th IEEE Computer Security Foundations Symposium (CSF 2013), pp. 193–205. IEEE Computer Society, June 2013
7. Clark, D., Hunt, S., Malacaria, P.: Quantified interference for a while language. Electron. Notes Theor. Comput. Sci. **112**, 149–166 (2005)
8. Clarkson, M.R., Schneider, F.B.: Quantification of integrity. In: 2010 23rd IEEE Computer Security Foundations Symposium (CSF), pp. 28–43. IEEE (2010)
9. Clarkson, M.R., Schneider, F.B.: Quantification of integrity. Math. Struct. Comput. Sci. **25**, 207–258 (2014)
10. Cover, T.M., Thomas, J.A.: Elements of information theory. Wiley, New York (2012)
11. Mollenkamp, C., Whitehouse, M.: Study casts doubt on key rate. Wall Street J., 29 May 2008
12. Mu, C., Clark, D.: A tool: quantitative analyser for programs. In: Proceedings of the 8th Conference on Quantitative Evaluation of Systems (QEST) (2011)
13. Smith, G.: On the foundations of quantitative information flow. In: de Alfaro, L. (ed.) FOSSACS 2009. LNCS, vol. 5504, pp. 288–302. Springer, Heidelberg (2009)
14. University of Birmingham: CH – IMP – IQ. http://www.cs.bham.ac.uk/research/projects/infotools/chimp/iq

Risk-Aware Information Disclosure

Alessandro Armando[1,2]($\boxtimes$), Michele Bezzi[4],
Nadia Metoui[2,3], and Antonino Sabetta[4]

[1] DIBRIS, University of Genova, Genova, Italy
armando@dist.unige.it
[2] Security and Trust Unit, FBK-Irst, Trento, Italy
[3] DISI, University of Trento, Trento, Italy
[4] Product Security Research, SAP Labs, Sophia-Antipolis, France

Abstract. Risk-aware access control systems grant or deny access to resources based on some notion of risk. In this paper we propose a model
that considers the risk of leaking privacy-critical information when querying, e.g., datasets containing personal information. While querying databases containing personal information it is current practice to assign
all-or-nothing access to avoid the disclosure of sensitive information. Using
our model, access-control decisions are based on the disclosure-risk associated with a data access request and, differently from existing models, we
include adaptive anonymization operations as risk-mitigation methods.
By applying these operations, a request that would otherwise be rejected,
is permitted after reducing the risk associated with the returned dataset.

1   Introduction

The increasing availability of large and diverse datasets (*Big Data*, such as customer data, transactions, demographics, product ratings) helps businesses to get
insights on their markets and their customers' needs, and predict what is next.
It is also boosting the creation of new *data monetization* businesses, where companies package their data and sell them to other organizations. According to
IDC [17] the market for Big Data business will reach 16.9 billion USD by 2015,
up from 3.2 billion USD in 2010.

The full exploitation of big data raises various issues on the possible disclosure
of sensitive or private information. In particular, big data often contain a large
amount of personal information, which is subject to multiple and stringent regulations (EU data protection directive, HIPAA[1], etc.). These regulations impose
strong constraints on the usage and transfer of personal information, which make
their handling complex, costly, and risky from a compliance point of view. As a
consequence, personal data are often classified as confidential information, and
only a limited number of business users (e.g., high level managers) have access
to them, and under specific obligations (e.g., within the perimeter of the company network, no transfer to mobile devices, etc.). As a matter of fact, because

---

This work has been partly supported by the EU under grant 317387 SECENTIS
(FP7-PEOPLE-2012-ITN).
[1] HIPAA: Health Insurance Portability and Accountability Act.

© Springer International Publishing Switzerland 2015
J. Garcia-Alfaro et al. (Eds.): DPM/SETOP/QASA 2014, LNCS 8872, pp. 266–276, 2015.
DOI: 10.1007/978-3-319-17016-9_17

of the difficulty of dealing with the potential privacy implications in an efficient and systematic way, an *all-or-nothing* decision is often followed; by using this approach, many business users are just prevented from retrieving data from databases as soon as these databases contain, even if only in few specific tables, some personal information. However, many business applications (e.g., business analytics and reporting, recommendation systems) do not need all the personal details on specific individuals, and an *anonymized version* of the dataset is still an asset of significant value that can address the business requirements in most cases.

Anonymization methods can be applied to obfuscate the personal identifiable information, such as suppressing part of or entire records; generalizing the data, i.e., recoding variables into broader classes (e.g., releasing only the first two digits of the zip code) or rounding numerical data; replacing identifiers with random values (e.g., replacing a real name with a randomly chosen one), randomly swapping some attributes in the original data records, applying permutations or perturbative masking, i.e., adding random noise to numerical data values.

To assess the level of anonymity, several metrics have been proposed in the literature (see [3,8] for a review). These metrics differ in a number of ways, but they all express the risk of disclosing personal-identifiable information when releasing a given dataset. Based on these metrics, several anonymization methods have also been put forth [7]. These methods increase protection by lowering the privacy risk and by enabling a wider exploitation of the data, but they assume the accepted risk level is statically given. In practice the accepted risk level may depend on a number of factors that can only be computed at run-time, e.g., the trustworthiness or the competence of the user or the quality of the security context used to issue the query.

In this paper we propose an access control model for risk-aware information disclosure. In our model access-control decisions are based on the disclosure-risk associated with a data access request and, differently from existing models, we include adaptive anonymization operations as risk-mitigation methods. By applying these operations, a request that would otherwise be rejected, is permitted after reducing the risk associated with the returned dataset.

Structure of the paper. In the next section we provide a representative, real-world scenario that illustrates the motivation for risk-aware information disclosure. In Sect. 3 we recall some background notions on risk-aware access control and privacy preserving information disclosure. In Sect. 4 we present our access control model for risk-aware information disclosure and in Sect. 5 we illustrate its application on the scenario introduced in Sect. 2. In Sect. 6 we discuss the related work. We conclude, in Sect. 7, with some final remarks.

2   Scenario

Employee surveys are a widely used instrument for organizations to assess job satisfaction, quality of management, people motivation, etc. Considering the possible sensitiveness of data, surveys should be anonymous, meaning that the organization and management should not be able to identify how a specific employee responded. Usually, the organization – say, a large company – conducting the survey outsources the data collection to a third-party. When processing the data, the third-party has access to individual-level information, whereas this data is not accessible to the company. To protect the anonymity of the survey, the company can access the data under the condition that *(i)* identifiers are removed and *(ii)* the number of respondents is larger than a certain thresholds (usually between 10 and 25). Different splits of data can be requested (e.g., per organization, per job profile, etc.), but data are accessible only if the query results contains a number of respondents that is larger than the fixed thresholds. On top of that, additional access control rule can be enforced, e.g., a manager would only see data referring to his/her team or department (provided that conditions *(i)* and *(ii)* are also fulfilled); an employee would be allowed to see overall (company results) only. As an example, consider a question like "Do you respect your manager as a competent professional?" with a five points scale (1 to 5). A manager could see the response of his/her team if at least, say, 10 people answered to it. If the manager decides to refine the analysis asking for data related to the people in his/her team AND with a "developer" role, again the response should be made available only if at least 10 respondents with that role answered to the question.[2] Current systems typically do not provide any data if the number of respondents is below the defined thresholds (for the specific role). In other words, in order to avoid the risk of disclosing too much information, an overly conservative approach is taken and problematic queries are not permitted altogether. Ideally, the access control system should be able to provide the largest possible amount of information (still preserving anonymity) for any query. In practice, in presence of queries that might cause anonymity issues (i.e., not enough respondents, or more generally, too small result set), the system should be able to quantify the disclosure risk associated with the query and compare it with whatever risk level has been set as the acceptable threshold. If the threshold is exceeded, the system could apply, for example, a "generalization" operation (making the query less specific), thus increasing the cardinality of the result set and reducing the risk of disclosing the identity of respondents. Of course, applying such operation would not yield the *exact* data set the user asked for, but this method would: (1) provide some relevant (i.e., as close as possible to the original query) information to the user, and (2) preserve anonymity according to some pre-defined disclosure-risk levels (possibly linked to the requestor trust or role).

In the next section, we discuss how to implement such a system using risk-based access control, and anonymization mitigation strategies.

3 Background

In this section, we present a Risk Aware Access Control model introduced in earlier work by Chen et al. [4,5]. We also present some privacy concepts and

---

[2] In real surveys single records are actually never shown, but just percentages, in this example it would be something like 10 % answered 1, 25 % answered 2, etc. Since the number of respondents is known, in practice, for one question, this equivalent of getting the data with no identifiers.

the "k-anonymity" model for preserving privacy [18], since it is the mostly used metrics for anonymity for surveys.

3.1 Risk-Aware Access Control

We provide a brief presentation of the formal model for Risk-Aware Access Control (RAAC) that has been introduced in [5]. We use this model as the basis of our access control model for risk-aware information disclosure that is presented in Sect. 4.

Formally, a RAAC consists of the following components:

- a set of users U;
- a set of permissions P, usually representing action-object pairs;
- a set of access requests Q, modeled as pairs of the form (u, p) for $u \in U$ and $p \in P$;
- a set of *risk mitigation methods* $\mathcal{M}$, i.e., actions that are required to be executed to mitigate risk;
- a function π mapping permissions into *risk mitigation strategies*, i.e., lists of the form $[(l_0, M_0), (l_1, M_1), \ldots, (l_{n-1}, M_{n-1}), (l_n, M_n)]$, where $0 = l_0 < l_1 < \cdots < l_{n-1} < l_n \leq 1$ and $M_i \in \mathcal{M}$ for $i = 0, \ldots, n$;
- a set of *states* Σ, i.e., tuples of the form (U, P, π, τ) where τ abstracts further specific features of the state; for instance, in the Risk-Aware Role-Based Access Control (R^2BAC) model [4], τ comprises the set of roles R, the user-role assignment relation $UA \subseteq U \times R$, the role-permission assignment relation $PA \subseteq P \times R$, the role hierarchy $\succeq \subseteq R \times R$, and the user trustworthiness $\alpha : U \to (0..1]$, the user-role competence function $\beta : U \times R \to (0..1]$, and the role-permission appropriateness function $\gamma : R \times P \to (0..1]$;
- a *risk function risk* : $Q \times \Sigma \to [0..1]$ such that $risk(q, \sigma)$ denotes the risk associated to granting q in state σ;
- an *authorization decision function Auth* : $Q \times \Sigma \to D \times 2^{\mathcal{M}}$ with $D = \{\text{allow}, \text{deny}\}$ such that if $q = (u, p)$ and $\pi(p) = [(l_0, M_0), \ldots, (l_n, M_n)]$, and σ the current state, then

$$Auth(q, \sigma) = \begin{cases} (d_i, M_i) & \text{if } risk(q, \sigma) \in [l_i, l_{i+1}), i < n, \\ (d_n, M_n) & \text{otherwise} \end{cases}$$

where $d_i \in D$. Intuitively, if the risk associated with access request (u, p) is l, then *Auth* returns an authorization decision and a set of risk mitigation methods corresponding to the interval containing l.

3.2 Privacy Preserving Information Disclosure

From a data privacy standpoint, the data stored in database tables and the columns (data attributes) of the tables can be classified as follows.

- *Identifiers.* These are data attributes that can uniquely identify individuals. Examples of *identifiers* are the Social Security Number, the passport number, the complete name.

– *Quasi-identifiers (QIs) or key attributes* [9]. These are the attributes that, when combined, can be used to identify an individual. Examples of *quasi-identifiers* are the postal code, age, job function, gender, etc.
– *Sensitive attributes*. These attributes contain intrinsically sensitive information about an individual (e.g., diseases, political or religious views, income) or business (salary figures, restricted financial data or sensitive survey answers).

Various anonymity metrics have been proposed so far (see [3,8] for a review). In this paper we concentrate on a very popular metric, k-Anonymity [18]. Other metrics are presented in Sect. 6. k-Anonymity condition requires that *every* combination of quasi-identifiers is shared by at least k records in the anonymized dataset. A large k value indicates that the anonymized dataset has a low identity privacy risk, because, at best, an attacker has a probability $1/k$ to re-identify a record (i.e., associate the sensitive attribute of a record to the identity of a person).

4   Risk-Aware Information Disclosure

We now refine the RAAC model of Sect. 3.1 into our model for Risk-Aware Information Disclosure. Let P be a set of database views (or virtual tables). If p is a view, then $|p|$ denotes the anonymity of p according to some given metrics (e.g. k-anonymity). The higher is the value of $|p|$, the smaller is the risk to disclose sensitive information by releasing p. Thus, for instance, we can define *the (privacy) risk of disclosing p* to be $1/|p|$ and *the (privacy) risk of disclosing p to u in $\sigma = (U, P, \pi, \tau)$* to be

$$risk((u,p), \sigma) = \begin{cases} 1 & \text{if not } granted_\tau(u,p) \\ 1/|p| & \text{otherwise} \end{cases}$$

where $granted_\tau(u,p)$ holds if and only if u is granted access to p according to τ. For instance, if τ is an RBAC policy $(U, R, P, UA, RA, \succeq)$, then $granted_\tau(u,p)$ holds if and only if there exist $r, r' \in R$ such that $(u, r) \in UA$, $r \succeq r'$, and $(p, r') \in PA$.

When the risk associated to the disclosure of a certain view p is greater than the maximal accepted risk t, we can use obligations for obfuscating or redacting the view and thus bring the risk below t. In this paper we consider k-anonymization functions $\phi_k : P \to P$ for $k \in \mathbb{N}$ as risk mitigation methods, but functions based on other metrics can be used as well. Clearly $|\phi_k(p)| \geq k$ for all $p \in P$. We then consider risk mitigation strategies of the form $\pi(p) = [(0, \iota), (t, \phi_{\lceil 1/t \rceil}(\cdot))]$, where $\iota : P \to P$ is the identity function (i.e. such that $\iota(p) = p$ for all $p \in P$) and the following authorization decision function:

$$Auth((u,p), \pi) = \begin{cases} (\text{allow}, \iota) & \text{if } risk(u,p) < t, \\ (\text{allow}, \phi_{\lceil 1/t \rceil}(\cdot)) & \text{if } risk(u,p) \geq t \end{cases}$$

that always grants access but yields an anonymized version of the requested view if the risk is greater that the maximal accepted risk t. In other words, if user

u asks to access p, then access to p is granted unconditionally if $risk(u, p) < t$, otherwise an anonymized version of p, say $\phi_{\lceil 1/t \rceil}(p)$, is computed and returned to u.

Example 1. To illustrate assume Alice asks for a view p_1 such that $|p_1| = 4$ and that $\pi(p_1) = [(0, \iota), (t, \phi_{\lceil 1/t \rceil}(.))]$ with $t = 0.1$, i.e. $\pi(p_1) = [(0, \iota), (0.1, \phi_{10}(.))]$. It is easy to see that $risk(Alice, p_1) = 0.25$ and that $Auth((Alice, p_1), \pi) = \phi_{10}(p_1)$.

Alice then asks for a view p_2 such that $|p_2| = 20$ and that $\pi(p_2) = \pi(p_1) = [(0, \iota), (t, \phi_{\lceil 1/t \rceil}(.))]$ with $t = 0.1$, i.e. $\pi(p_2) = [(0, \iota), (0.1, \phi_{10}(.))]$. It is easy to see that now $risk(Alice, p_2) = 0.05$ and therefore that $Auth((Alice, p_2), \pi) = \iota(p_1) = p_1$.

The following results state that the risk of disclosing the view returned by our authorization decision function is never greater than the maximum accepted risk.

Proposition 1. *Let* $(D, M) = Auth((u, p), \pi)$. *Then* $risk(u, M(p)) \leq t$.

In many situations of practical interest, we want the risk of a query $q = (u, p)$ to depend also on the trustworthiness of the user u. This can be done by (re)defining the risk function as follows:

$$risk((u, p), \sigma) = \begin{cases} 1 & \text{if not } granted_\tau(u, p) \\ \max\{0, \frac{1}{|p|} - \alpha(u)\} & \text{otherwise} \end{cases} \tag{1}$$

where $\alpha : U \to (0..1]$ is a function that assigns a trust value to users.

When roles correspond to job functions, it is natural to assign trust to roles and to derive the trust of a user from the trust assigned to the roles assigned to that user in the following way:

$$\alpha(u) = \max\{\alpha(r') : (p, r') \in PA \text{ and } \exists r \succeq r' \text{ s.t. } (u, r) \in UA\}.$$

5   Application of Risk-Aware Role-Based Access Control

We now show how our risk-aware information disclosure model can be used to support the scenario of Sect. 2. This will be done by setting appropriate values to the parameters occurring in the definition of the risk function (1).

For sake of simplicity we consider a small company, with 8 employees and one manager. The company runs an employee survey, with one single question with answer ranging in a five points scale (from 1 to 5) (*sensitive attribute*, cf. Sect. 3.2), and collecting user names[3] (the *identifiers*), as well as the job title and the location of the office (the *quasi-identifiers*). The actual dataset is in Table 1(a). To preserve privacy we set the maximal acceptable risk to $t = 0.125$.

The outsourcing company collecting the data is considered fully trusted and will therefore have access to all the information. We model this by setting the

---

[3] In real cases they are typically user IDs.

Table 1. The Employee Survey Example

(a) Original dataset

Survey Administrator view $|p_{all}| = 1$			
Name	Job	Location	**Answer**
Timothy	SeniorDeveloper	Houston	4
Alice	Support	Houston	5
Perry	JuniorDeveloper	Rome	5
Tom	Admin	Rome	3
Ron	SeniorDeveloper	London	4
Omer	JuniorDeveloper	London	4
Bob	Support	Houston	5
Amber	Admin	Houston	3

(b) Anonymized version: *identifiers* and *quasi-identifiers* are suppressed

Employee View $|p_{supp}| = 8$			
Name	Job	Location	**Answer**
***	***	***	4
***	***	***	5
***	***	***	5
***	***	***	3
***	***	***	4
***	***	***	4
***	***	***	5
***	***	***	3

trust of the admin role to 1, i.e. $\alpha(\texttt{admin}) = 1$. Thus, an administrator can access the original dataset, say p_{all} with anonymity $|p_{all}| = 1$ (i.e., all distinct values, see Table 1(a)), since $\alpha(\texttt{admin}) = 1$ and the risk value is smaller than the threshold, i.e., $1 - 1 = 0 < 0.125$. If we set the trust value of the manager role to 0.21, i.e. $\alpha(\texttt{manager}) = 0.21$ (corresponding to access views with anonymity $k \geq 3$), than a manager cannot access p_{all} as is, since $1 - 0.21 > 0.125$ and some anonymization, as risk mitigation strategy, must be carried out on the data to decrease the risk. For example, if we suppress the identifier attribute (*Name*) and the quasi-identifiers (*Job* and *Location*), we obtain the view p_{supp} shown in Table 1(b). The view p_{supp} corresponds to an anonymity level $|p_{supp}| = 8$ and since $0.125 - 0.21 < 0.125$, access is granted to the manager.[4]

The manager can also ask for more granular views of the results. For example, if she wants to know the distribution of the answers in one location, say Houston, $|p_{Houst}| = 4$, the risk $0.25 - 0.21 = 0.04$ is still smaller than $t = 0.125$. On the other hand, if she asks for the result in Rome, $|p_{Rome}| = 2$, then the risk associated with the view for the manager is $0.5 - 0.21 > 0.125$ and the access is granted only if appropriate anonymization is performed. In this case, location could be generalized from Rome to EMEA (so including London workforce), as shown in Table 2(b). The resulting view has anonimity $|p_{EMEA}| = 4$ and since the risk is smaller than $t = 0.125$, then the manager is allowed to see the view.

Similarly, if the manager wants to see the results per location and per job function (say in Rome for JuniorDeveloper only, see Table 3(a)), the anonymity level is low, $|p_{Rome+JuniorDeveloper}| = 1$, and the associated risk is greater than $t = 0.125$. Again, instead of simply denying access, the system can perform generalization on both the quasi-identifiers, *Job* (generalized to the job family

---

[4] In real surveys the result will appear as a report like: 37.5 % answered 5, 37.5 % answered 4 and 25 % answered 3. For a single question this is equivalent to the view in Table 1(b).

Table 2. Views of the employee survey for the Rome location

(a) Before generalization.

View: Location=Rome, $|p_{Rome}| = 2$			
Name	Job	Location	**Answer**
***	***	Rome	5
***	***	Rome	3

(b) After generalization

View: Location=Rome Anonymized $|p_{EMEA}| = 4$			
Name	Job	Location	**Answer**
***	***	EMEA	5
***	***	EMEA	3
***	***	EMEA	4
***	***	EMEA	4

Table 3. Views of the employee survey for Rome and JuniorDeveloper

(a) Before generalization of location and job

Loc=Rome AND Job=JuniorDeveloper $|p_{Rome+JuniorDeveloper}| = 1$			
Name	Job	Location	**Answer**
***	JuniorDeveloper	Rome	5

(b) After generalization of location and job

View Loc=Rome AND Job=JuniorDeveloper Anonymized $|p_{EMEA+Dev}| = 3$			
Name	Job	Location	**Answer**
***	Dev	EMEA	5
***	Dev	EMEA	4
***	Dev	EMEA	4

developer) and *Location*, thereby increasing the anonymity ($|p_{EMEA+Dev}| = 3$) and decreasing the risk ($risk(manager, p_{EMEA+Dev}) = 0.123$) to an acceptable level for a manager (see Table 3(b)).

Finally, employees should have access to the global results only. The trust value is therefore set to $\alpha(\texttt{employee}) = 0.125$ and the only view permitted is with suppression of all identifiers and quasi-identifiers, which has $|p_{supp}| = 8$, see Table 3(b).

6 Related Work

Risk-aware access control (see, e.g., [4–6,10,19]) has received a growing attention in the last few years. However, little attention is given to privacy aspects. The approaches that address privacy (see, e.g., [14,16]) do so by adding privacy policy enforcement on top of the access control evaluation process. In our approach privacy risk as well as access risk are evaluated for every access request.

Risk Aware Access Control Models generally determine the risk as a function of the likelihood of a permission misuse and the cost of the permission authorized and misused. The likelihood of misuse can depend on the user trustworthiness and competence [4], the user behavior [1], and the uncertainty of the access decision [15]. The quantification of the cost of permission misuse has been addressed by several researches. Cheng et al. [6], in their assign a sensitivity label to every resource. The value of a resource is then determined according to its sensitivity. The cost of a misused permission depends on the resource's value. Molloy et al. [15] and Baracaldo et al. [1] propose to evaluate the cost in term of financial gain and damage. Chen and Crampton [4] do not explicitly calculate the permission misuse cost in their model, but mention that the cost of misuse is valued and used to define risk thresholds and risk mitigation strategies for every permission. In our model the risk results from the likelihood of identity disclosure which depends on the sensitivity of the requested information and the requestor trustworthiness.

Chen et al. [5,12] propose to use, both user and system obligations as risk mitigation methods. An obligation describes some actions that have to be fulfilled by the subject, the system or a third part (e.g.an administrator), in a specific time window. In the literature we can distinguish between two categories of obligations: *provisions* or *pre-obligations* [2] are actions that must be executed prior to making an authorization decision; *post-obligations* are actions that must be fulfilled after the authorization decision is made. Unlike Chen et al. models that use post-obligations, monitor the fulfillment of these obligations after granting access and reward or punish users according to whether they have succeed or not to fulfill the required action, in our model we use provisions to enforce the risk mitigation strategy at run-time.

In this paper we consider only k-anonymity as anonymity metrics, but alternative metrics do exist. A group (with minimal size of k records) sharing the same combination of quasi-identifiers could also have the same sensitive attribute, so even if the attacker is not able to re-identify the record, he can discover the sensitive information (attribute disclosure). To capture this kind of risk ℓ-diversity was introduced [13]. The ℓ-diversity condition requires that for *every* combination of key attributes there should be at least ℓ values for each confidential attribute. Although, ℓ-diversity condition prevents the possible attacker from inferring exactly the sensitive attributes, he may still learn a considerable amount of probabilistic information. More specifically, if the distribution of confidential attributes within a group sharing the same key attributes is very dissimilar from the distribution over the whole set, an attacker may increase his knowledge on sensitive attributes (*skewness attack*, see [11] for details). To overcome the problem, t-closeness [11] estimates this risk by computing the distance between the distribution of confidential attributes within the group and in the entire dataset. These measures provide a quantitative assessment of the different risks associated to data release, and each of them (or a combination thereof) can be applied to estimate privacy risk depending on the use case at hand.

7   Conclusions

We have presented a model for information disclosure where access-control decisions are based on the risk associated with a data access request. Anonymization operations are used as risk-mitigation methods to compute views satisfy the accepted level of risk. This allows for granting access to requests that would otherwise be rejected. Our model leverages existing modes for Risk-Aware Access Control (most notably [4,5]) but it also shows how they can be adapted so to support the controlled disclosure of privacy-sensitive information.

References

1. Baracaldo, M., Joshi, J.: A trust-and-risk aware rbac framework: tackling insider threat. In: Proceedings of the 17th ACM Symposium on Access Control Models and Technologies, SACMAT 2012, pp. 167–176, ACM, New York (2012)
2. Bettini, C., Jajodia, S., Sean Wang, X., Wijesekera, D.: Provisions and obligations in policy management and security applications. In: Proceedings of the 28th International Conference on Very Large Data Bases, VLDB 2002, pp. 502–513. VLDB Endowment (2002)
3. Bezzi, M.: An information theoretic approach for privacy metrics. Trans. Data Priv. 3(3), 199–215 (2010)
4. Chen, L., Crampton, J.: Risk-aware role-based access control. In: Meadows, C., Fernandez-Gago, C. (eds.) STM 2011. LNCS, vol. 7170, pp. 140–156. Springer, Heidelberg (2012)
5. Chen, L., Crampton, J., Kollingbaum, M.J., Norman, T.J.: Obligations in risk-aware access control. In: Cuppens-Boulahia, N., Fong, P., García-Alfaro, J., Marsh, S., Steghöfer, J.-P. (eds.) PST, pp. 145–152. IEEE (2012)
6. Cheng, P.-C., Rohatgi, P., Keser, C., Karger, P.A., Wagner, G.M., Reninger, A.S.: Fuzzy multi-level security: an experiment on quantified risk-adaptive access control. In: IEEE Symposium on Security and Privacy, pp. 222–230. IEEE Computer Society (2007)
7. Ciriani, V., De Capitani di Vimercati, S., Foresti, S., Samarati, P.: Theory of privacy and anonymity. In: Atallah, M., Blanton, M. (eds.) Algorithms and Theory of Computation Handbook, 2nd edn. CRC Press (2009)
8. Clifton, C., Tassa, T.: On syntactic anonymity and differential privacy. Trans. Data Priv. 6(2), 161–183 (2013)
9. Dalenius, T.: Finding a needle in a haystack-or identifying anonymous census record. J. Official Stat. 2(3), 329–336 (1986)
10. Dickens, L., Russo, A., Cheng, P.-C., Lobo, J.: Towards learning risk estimation functions for access control. In: Snowbird Learning Workshop (2010)
11. Li, N., Li, T., Venkatasubramanian, S.: t-closeness: Privacy beyond k-anonymity and l-diversity. In: IEEE 23rd International Conference on Data Engineering, ICDE 2007, pp. 106–115 (April 2007)
12. Timothy, J., Chen, N.L., Gasparini, L.: XACML and risk-aware access control, Technical report (2013)
13. Machanavajjhala, A., Gehrke, J., Kifer, D., Venkitasubramaniam, M.: l-diversity: Privacy beyond k-anonymity. In: ICDE 2006: Proceedings of the 22nd International Conference on Data Engineering (ICDE 2006), p. 24. IEEE Computer Society, Washington, DC (2006)
14. Martino, L.D., Ni, Q., Lin, D., Bertino, E.: Multi-domain and privacy-aware role based access control in ehealth. In: Second International Conference on Pervasive Computing Technologies for Healthcare, PervasiveHealth 2008, pp. 131–134 (January 2008)
15. Molloy, I., Dickens, L., Morisset, C., Cheng, P.-C., Lobo, J., Russo, A.: Risk-based security decisions under uncertainty. In: Proceedings of the Second ACM Conference on Data and Application Security and Privacy, CODASPY 2012, pp. 157–168, New York (2012)
16. Ni, Q., Trombetta, A., Bertino, E., Lobo, J.: Privacy-aware role based access control. In: Proceedings of the 12th ACM Symposium on Access Control Models and Technologies, SACMAT 2007, pp. 41–50. ACM, New York (2007)

17. IDC Report. Worldwide big data technology and services 2012–2015 forecast. IDC Report (2012)
18. Samarati, P.: Protecting respondents' identities in microdata release. IEEE Trans. Knowl. Data Eng. **13**(6), 1010–1027 (2001)
19. Shaikh, R.A., Adi, K., Logrippo, L.: Dynamic risk-based decision methods for access control systems. Comput. Secur. **31**, 447–464 (2012)

Probabilistic Modelling of Humans in Security Ceremonies

Christian Johansen[(⊠)] and Audun Jøsang

Department of Informatics, University of Oslo,
Blindern, P.O. Box 1080, 0316 Oslo, Norway
{cristi,audun}@ifi.uio.no

Abstract. We are interested in formal modelling and verification of security ceremonies. Considerable efforts have been put into verifying security protocols, with quite successful tools currently being widely used. The relatively recent concept of security ceremonies, introduced by Carl Ellison, increases the complexity of protocol analysis in several directions: a ceremony should include all relevant out-of-bad assumptions, should compose protocols, and should include the human agent. Work on modelling human agents as part of IT systems is quite limited, and the few existing studies come from psychology or sociology. A step towards understanding how to model and analyse security ceremonies is to integrate a model of human agents with models for protocols (or combination of protocols). Current works essentially model human agent interaction with a user interface as a nondeterministic process.

In this paper we propose a more realistic model which includes more information about the user interaction, obtained by sociologists usually through experiments and observation, and model the actions of a human agent as a probabilistic process. An important point that we make in this paper is to separate the model of the human and the model of the user interface, and to provide a "compilation" operation putting the two together and encoding the interaction between the human and the interface. We base our work on a recently proposed model for security ceremonies, which we call the Bella-Coles-Kemp model.

1 Introduction

The motivation for analysing security ceremonies is well articulated in [10,31] with convincing examples. Technically, security ceremonies are meant to extend security protocols by including human agents in the formalization, and by explicitly including aspects of the environment and potential attackers. A ceremony may also combine protocols. In consequence, a formalism for security ceremonies is expected to be expressive enough to include existing formalisms for protocols as special cases. Such a formalism should offer the possibility to model human behavior related to the ceremony.

This work was partially supported by the project OffPAD with number E!8324 part of the Eurostars program funded by the EUREKA and European Community.

J. Garcia-Alfaro et al. (Eds.): DPM/SETOP/QASA 2014, LNCS 8872, pp. 277–292, 2015.
DOI: 10.1007/978-3-319-17016-9_18

With the risk of appearing pedantic to some readers, we give some motivation for using formal techniques for security protocol analysis. Arguably, for security systems perfection and assurance of perfection are highly important, since bugs cannot be considered "features". For a security system one often wants to be provided with guarantees that some expected security properties are met. This can be even more difficult to achieve for security ceremonies, which are more complex, composing protocols, including hidden assumptions, and human agent models. In case of security protocols one can hardly rely on testing to provide assurance; and experience has shown that protocols that are thoroughly tested in practice for years turn out to contain serious flaws, where an infamous example is [21].

The need to eliminate hidden flaws in security protocols is the motivation for developing mathematical models and theories for studying security protocols. The practical results of such efforts are the formal tools based on the underlying mathematical theories. These tools offer the ability to have a (semi-)automated way of ensuring security properties. Examples of tools include model checkers like Murphi [22,38] or FDR [13] which are push-button tools with yes/no answers; or theorem provers, which often need interaction with expect users but which achieve stronger results than model checkers do, with examples like ProVerif [6] for the symbolic (process calculi) approach, CryptoVerif [7] for the computational approach, or Isabelle/HOL [25].

We are interested in formal models for security ceremonies, and our work is inspired by the rather limited, recent literature on this topic [8,10,26,27, 29,31]. Because of the complexity of the problem, this paper focuses only on the aspect of integrating the human agent into the ceremony, together with a user interface. Therefore, in this paper we concentrate on the human-computer interaction, which forms the layer III in the Bella-Coles-Kemp model [3] for security ceremonies. This is a general/abstract model introduced with similar purposes as the Dolev-Yao model. In fact, the Dolev-Yao model [9] could form the first layer of the Bella-Coles-Kemp model, i.e., the layer of the network communication protocols. But for ceremonies, many other factors need to be considered, including social factors, and this is what the Bella-Coles-Kemp model tries to identify. This model has also been used by [11]. One of our purposes is to extend the work of [3], where layer III was modeled as a nondeterministic process, to the more general probabilistic setting here.

A security ceremony involves a user interface to collect any needed input, like passwords, from the human participant in the ceremony. Generally speaking, several different user interfaces can be available to the same human user; and there can be user interfaces for several of the components of the ceremony, like for the different protocols involved. But for simplicity we restrict our discussion for now to a single user interface, which is supposed to provide the required input information to a security protocol.

The few studies on modelling human interacting with a user interface using formal methods [3,33] are based on a nondeterministic approach. Our intention in this paper is to extend these approaches to a *probabilistic* model. Moreover,

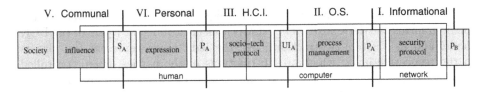

Fig. 1. The Bella-Coles-Kemp model (BCK model) for security ceremonies. (Picture taken from [3, Fig. 1])

these approaches usually provide one model that captures the total human-computer interaction. We split this into: one probabilistic model for the human, using the notion of "persona" from user-centred design, one model for the user interface, and a notion of "compilation" which puts the two models together and captures the interactions between the human and the user interface.

The structure of this paper is as follows: we explain the Bella-Coles-Kemp model in Sect. 2, introduce probabilistic models of humans and their interaction with the user interface in Sect. 3, and investigate ways of putting together the human model with the UI model, which we call "compilation" in Sect. 4.

2   The Bella-Coles-Kemp Model

We refer to the model introduced in [3] as "the Bella-Coles-Kemp model" and sometimes use the abbreviation BCK model. This is a rather abstract model for security ceremonies, which provides a good common basis for formal analysis by offering a framework of reference for defining models, attackers, and reasoning tools. The BCK model, pictured in Fig. 1, extends and includes standard models for analysing security protocols, like the Dolev-Yao model [9]. The standard security protocols would form only the layer I of the BCK model.

When explaining the BCK model it is good to make correlations with the existing approaches for analysing security protocols, usually based on the Dolev-Yao assumptions, and using specification languages like the spi calculus [2] or applied pi-calculus [1]. Usually, security protocols are formed of the parties (or players) and the interaction medium they use for communication (or any other exchange of information). The parties are usually honest, whereas the intruder (attacker) controls the interaction medium. More than two parties can be involved in the protocol, but the standard protocols consist of two honest parties, Alice and Bob. Third parties, usually dishonest, appear due to the ability of the intruder to disguise as a party in any number of protocol runs. The Dolev-Yao model defines the powers that the attacker has over the interaction medium, like power to delete, change, or insert messages, to and from any other party. As there exist many kinds of security protocols (e.g., with multiple honest parties, with different attacker possibilities, etc.) we will confine our presentation here to the basic definitions which can be carried over to the BCK model.

In the BCK model the parties form the light boxes, whereas the interaction medium forms the dark boxes. The parties appear at different layers of the BCK model and in different abstractions; i.e., the light boxes represent the players in the respective layer, which are abstractions of the parties or are controlled by the parties. In the layer I (also called "Informational") we encounter the processes p_A and p_B controlled by Alice respectively Bob, which are running the computers of Alice and Bob, communicating through the network, i.e., the dark box. This layer I would thus be subject to the standard Dolev-Yao assumptions.

In BCK other players appear at the other layers: at layer II (also called "Operating System") *the user interface UI_A* associated to Alice, which interacts with the computer process p_A, e.g., by sending information taken from the user required by the security protocol run by p_A, like a password or biometrics. The same UI_A interacts at layer III (also called "Human-Computer Interaction") with a *"persona" P_A* of Alice for this particular ceremony. The persona has interaction at layer IV (also called "Personal") with *the self S_A* of Alice, which in turn is influenced by the Society through various social protocols at layer V.

Players may interact only as part of a layer, and one layer may involve players pertaining to different users. Important to note is that in BCK one player usually is involved in two (adjacent) layers.

Research in computer science until now has mostly focused on layer I, and largely ignored layers II–V. We see layer II as pertaining also to the technological community, the same as layer I has been until now; whereas layer V would pertain to the sociology community. Layer IV would be investigated more by the psychology researchers. Layer III on the other hand is at the interaction between technological and social sciences, with a rapidly evolving field, having terminology s.a.: HCI, user-centred design [4], interaction design [32], etc.

The usefulness of the BCK model is also to make obvious the need of collaboration between these fields of social, psychology, and technology, in order to tackle the complexities of the security ceremonies. One can very well focus on individual layers, but the BCK model brings the isolated results into the general picture which eventually needs to be handled in order to claim security results of practical use.

The BCK model is abstract and general, and we see works in the future detailing on all the new layers II–V, the same as has been done until now with the layer I. The interaction medium, the dark box, can be split into more fine-grained divisions, and each division would have its protocol and assumptions. For layer II it is more easy for computer scientists to bring their knowledge of operating systems design and see that a UI could consist of a screen and its driver, a display client like a browser displaying an input form, a keyboard with its drivers, and the many other components that transport the information between these many UI components and the end process p_A. The same in the social protocols of layer V, where various means of social manipulation exist, and quantitative and qualitative measures could be devised for analysing their usefulness in terms of power to influence, e.g., depending on the social scale or training level of the users, i.e., the self S_A.

In this paper we take the stand that layer III has not so many division possibilities, and think of the possible interactions in the dark box as rather simplistic, like matching of actions on the persona and UI sides. But various kinds of interactions can be thought of, and we capture them with a notion of *compilation*. Various compilation operations can be devised for various kinds of simple interactions between personas and UIs, and we detail on these in Sect. 4. Compilation would put together the model for the persona and the model for the UI, to form a single model for the whole layer III, which would include the two players and the dark box. This model would be representing a new player which interacts in the layer II and layer IV.

Attacks can be thought at all the layers of the BCK model [11]:

Layer I attacks: The classic attacks like snooping, brute-force, or involving any of the Dolev-Yao assumptions.

Layer II attacks: The bank account number is typed and seen at UI_A by Alice but is not the same as the one used by p_A in the security interaction with the Bank process p_B.

Layer III attacks: The expressed interaction of P_A is not properly captured by UI_A, e.g.:
  - User types digit 0 but the UI discards it;
  - User types digit 8 but the UI receives and displays digit 3.

Such attacks can be observed by the persona or not, and detecting them and quantifying the observational possibilities is a problem for models and techniques pertaining to analyses of layer III.

Layer IV attacks: The user is tricked into being *trusting instead of cautious*; which can be done by the attacker through clever use of the colours, logos, security symbols, etc.

3   Probabilistic Modelling of Humans

Some formal models have been proposed for analysing human agents and their behavior when interacting with a user interface. We are inspired by work in the cognitive sciences [23,33] which has also been used to analyse security breaches in [34]; as well as by work from the social sciences [3,20], with a good reference being [36]. We adopt the notion of *persona* to characterize a user in a socio-technical interaction situation. We define a persona to be a set of social and cognitive attributes of a human, including emotions, senses, or memory.

Definition 3.1 (Persona). *An attribute is represented as a predicate in some logic (usually propositional logic or first-order logic). A persona is defined as a finite set of attributes.*

This definition of persona is related to the one in [36, Lemma 2] in the sense that the attribute predicates can be represented as a computer data structure and thus stored in the digital world (whereas the actual user resides in the physical world). In [36] a persona is a representation of a user from the physical world into the digital world.

We will mostly use attributes as propositional predicates, like *cautious* or *confident*, which are either true or false. But more complex attributes, like memory, may require more expressive logics. It is interesting and certainly useful to investigate deeper the kinds of logics needed to express various persona attributes, but this is outside the scope of this paper, and the work of Blandford et al. [34], which uses first-order logic to model the human involvement in a security protocol, is a good start for such investigations. Also useful would be works on applying first-order dynamic logic to model memory in computer programs, e.g., [15, Part III].

For the layer III that we are concerned with here, a persona is an abstract representation in the digital world of a physical user. Personas represent the user (usually class of users with the same expected qualities) in different particular situations (in our case, w.r.t. the UI), e.g. the user as a: citizen (when accessing her social services) or an employee (when accessing corporate networks).

A user may exhibit different personas at different points in time, and may change from one persona to another depending on the interaction with the user interface. For the same user, we may be interested in different personas for different aspects of the user interface.

Therefore, we will be working with *personas models*, which may contain several personas connected by actions. The actions are the way we model the *change factor*, i.e., that which makes the human exhibit a different persona. Without a change factor there would be no change in the persona. An action can be thought of many things, from passage of time, to interaction with the user interface, to social change coming from the social context, i.e., from the outside of the human-computer interaction system. Examples of actions can be high-level s.a.: "fill-in-form", "provide-explanation", or "make-query"; or concrete s.a.: "press-submit-button", "type-password", "abort". A formalism for actions should be used, like algebras [14] or logics [28,35], but we do not go into this detail here, and keep our presentation simple. Introducing such an action formalism would complicate the models.

Definition 3.2 (Ideal Personas Model). *Consider a countable set of actions Λ and a set of attributes Φ. A personas model is a tuple $PM = (Q, T, \Lambda, \Phi)$ with:*

- *$Q \subseteq 2^{\Phi}$ a finite set of personas, and*
- *$T \subseteq Q \times \Lambda \times Q$ a transition relation labeled by actions between personas, with the restriction that T is a partial function between $Q \times \Lambda \to Q$ (meaning that for each action it is determined how it changes a persona).*

Notation 3.3. *The following notation will be useful. In a personas model $PM = (Q, T, \Lambda, \Phi)$, for some set of transitions $T' \subseteq T$, define $Q[T'] \stackrel{def}{=} \{q \in Q \mid \exists (q, \alpha, q') \in T' \text{ or } \exists (q', \alpha, q) \in T'\}$; i.e., the set of those personas entering some transition from T'. For some set Λ (of actions usually), we denote by $\Lambda_* \stackrel{def}{=} \Lambda \cup \{*\}$, where $* \notin \Lambda$ is a special symbol not part of any action set. We sometimes denote transitions from T as $q \stackrel{\alpha}{\longrightarrow} q'$.*

A minimal non-trivial personas model has no transitions and one single persona. Other simple personas models can be defined with one single persona and one transition to itself for each action.

Personas models would usually be studied in general settings by sociologists and psychologists, and include many and various actions. But for a specific user interface only a subset of these actions is of interests. Therefore, restrictions of these general personas models would be needed before compiling with the user interface. One way to define such restrictions is as follows, using what we call an *action restriction operation*.

Definition 3.4 (Action Restriction Operation). *For a personas model* $PM = (Q, T, \Lambda, \Phi)$ *and a set of actions* Λ', *an* action restriction operation *would take an actions map* $f : \Lambda \to \Lambda'_*$, *and return a new personas model* $PM|_{\Lambda'} = (Q|_{\Lambda'}, T|_{\Lambda'}, \Lambda', \Phi)$ *with:*

- $T|_{\Lambda'} \stackrel{def}{=} \{(q, f(\alpha), q') \mid (q, \alpha, q') \in T \text{ and } f(\alpha) \neq *\}$,
- $Q|_{\Lambda'} \stackrel{def}{=} Q[T|_{\Lambda'}]$.

A simple instance of the action restriction operation is when the action map f is a partial identity function that maps any action from $\Lambda \cap \Lambda'$ into itself and any other into $*$. The restricted personas model would thus keep only those transitions that are labelled by actions from $\Lambda \cap \Lambda'$ and discards the rest of the model. But the above definition is open to more possibilities, like when the personas model works with more fine-grained actions, which in the user interface model would be collapsed (i.e., through a specific definition of f) into a single, more abstract, action.

The personas model from above is *deterministic*, meaning that it is completely known how an action changes a persona. This is also why we called it "ideal". But in reality this is not the case because we never have complete information. We are unsure of how an action may change a persona, but empirical studies do give some information. We introduce probabilities to capture the existing knowledge in a more meaningful way. Probabilities allow the model to carry more knowledge, usually accumulated from social studies. Our model extends the existing non-deterministic models in which it is assumed that there is no knowledge about how an action changes a persona (except for the fact that the new persona is part of some restricted subset of possible personas).

Definition 3.5 (Probabilistic Personas Model). *A probabilistic personas model extends an ideal personas model* $PM = (Q, T, \Lambda, \Phi)$ *by not restricting the transition relation, and by adding a probability mapping function* $P : T \to [0, 1]$, *attaching probabilities to transitions, with the property that*

$$\forall q \in Q, \alpha \in \Lambda : \Sigma_{q \xrightarrow{\alpha} q' \in T} P(q, \alpha, q') = 1.$$

The way we defined our probabilistic model has been studied under the name of *reactive* probabilistic models in [12,19], where the Markov decision processes would fit, as opposed to *generative* models [12]. To explain the difference we first need some notation, taken from [37].

Notation 3.6. *A discrete probability distribution over some set Ω is a function* $\mu : \Omega \rightarrow [0,1]$ *such that the (support) set* $\{x \in \Omega \mid \mu(x) > 0\}$ *is finite and* $\sum_{x \in \Omega} \mu(x) = 1$. *We denote by* $\mathcal{D}(\Omega)$ *the set of all such distributions over* Ω.

Our probabilistic personas model $PM = (Q, T, \Lambda, \Phi, P)$ can be seen as assigning to each persona $q \in Q$ and action $\alpha \in \Lambda$ a probability distribution μ_q^α over the set of personas Q as follows: for each transition $q \xrightarrow{\alpha} q' \in T$ starting from q and labelled by α, assign its particular probability $\mu_q^\alpha(q') = P(q \xrightarrow{\alpha} q')$; for all other personas not reachable from q by α use the probability 0, i.e., μ_q^α resolves to 0. The restrictions in Definition 3.5 ensure that what we just defined as μ_q^α is a discrete probability distribution. This is essentially the definition of a *reactive probabilistic model*, i.e., which assigns to each $q \in Q$ a function from $\mathcal{D}(Q)^\Lambda$, i.e., which attaches to each action a distribution over Q. On the other hand, a generative probabilistic model assigns to each $q \in Q$ a distribution μ_q over the set $\Lambda \times Q$.

Intuitively, the generative models treat the actions as *output* of the probabilistic system, whereas the reactive models treat the actions as *input*. A reactive model takes as input an action from the environment and then probabilistically chooses the next state; whereas a generative model probabilistically chooses the next state and assigns an action to this transition, which is visible to outside.

The intuitive reason for the personas models being reactive in nature is that we want to model the knowledge that we have about how an action changes a persona. In an ideal world this should be completely determined, i.e., knowing with certain probability 1 that from a persona q an action α will result in some other persona q', i.e., for which $\mu_q^\alpha(q') = 1$. In the real world it is not so clear, but some evidence exists, and is encoded in the probabilities. Thus, from a persona, some action may result in reaching one of several personas, each with some probability. The input action can either be done intentionally by the persona, like clicking the button on the interface, or unintentional, like when being transmitted information through the adds on the metro.

On the other hand, the personas models do not capture the likelihood of some actions being taken by a persona when faced with a state of a user interface. These likelihoods will be made part of the user interface models in the next section, and will be coupled with personas through the compilations. In this way we can capture the two kinds of probabilistic information (about likelihood of changing a personas and the likelihood of choosing some action) in a single probabilistic model.

Example 3.7. In Fig. 2 we pictured a toy example of a user interface for a popup in case a certificate is not automatically validated by the browser, which offers the manual choices of *accept* and *reject*. This in turn would give access to the online service or disallow access. It is possible that the certificate is malicious, in which case acceptance may compromise the user's assets. The respective probabilities are drawn on the arrows.

The personas model studies three personas, given by the attributes in the picture (i.e., *cautious*, *indifferent*, and *aware*), and how three actions affect these

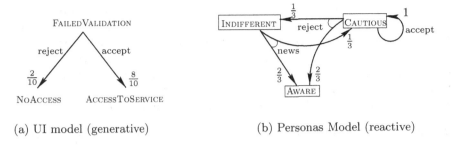

(a) UI model (generative)   (b) Personas Model (reactive)

Fig. 2. Personas model and UI model.

personas (i.e., *accept, reject,* or *news* reading). Many other personas could be introduced in the model, like being both cautious and aware.[1]

Empirical studies may show that rejecting a certificate validation notice may make the person indifferent or more aware, each with its respective probability. Whereas reading news about some recent cyberattack done through invalid certificates may make the person more aware. Acceptance of an invalid certificate always makes someone cautious.

3.1 Models for User Interfaces

A simple model of a user interface is that of a deterministic state machine with labels on transitions denoting the options that are offered by the interface to the user in each state. The determinism is necessary because the user interface is assumed to be a piece of code running on some digital device. This code responds to the input from the user by transmitting the choice (probably in some processed form) to the back-end program and then providing a new list of choices. One can imagine this simple interface as a machine equipped with lighted buttons. The buttons that are lit are enabled, i.e., possible interaction choices for the user. Pressing a lighted button makes that the whole buttons interface changes its lighting configuration. Whereas pressing a dark button makes no change.

The above view is of a discrete nature, where interaction happens in steps, one button press at a time. But more complex interfaces can be identified, which have also forms of continuous interactions; like a car acceleration pedal, or a game console joystick. Through such interfaces the user can have a prolonged interaction with, e.g., a button, and the observable response from the interface changes with time during the user interaction. The response from the user interface is determined by the amount of time the button is pressed. Such interfaces are called *hybrid* because interaction can be both discrete and continuous. We will develop our ideas using a simple model of a user interface, and postpone the more complex hybrid models for a proper study.

---

[1] We draw an angle between transitions to denote those which share the same label (like *news* and *reject*); and by definition must form a probability distribution.

But just a simple deterministic model is not enough, since we are interested in some more empirical information which the personas model is not providing. We want to know for a particular user interface which actions are more probable to be taken by a persona. But coming up with this probabilistic information for each persona is infeasible. Instead we start from assumptions made by the designer of the user interface about the probability of taking each action, and rely on later empirical social studies to update these probabilities.

Definition 3.8 (User Interface Model). *We define a* user interface model *as a* $UI = (S, \Lambda, T, P)$ *containing a set S of states, a set Λ of actions, a transition relation $T \subseteq S \times \Lambda \times S$ which is restricted to be a partial function from $S \times \Lambda \to S$, and a probability mapping function $P : T \to [0, 1]$ with the property that*

$$\forall s \in S : \Sigma_{s \xrightarrow{\alpha} s' \in T} P(s, \alpha, s') = 1.$$

If we ignore the labels, then we have just defined a Markov chain. The action labels just say which actions change the state of the user interface. The above model should not be confused with a Markov decision process. The probabilities on transitions tell for each state which action is more probable to be executed.

Our probabilistic model for a user interface $UI = (S, \Lambda, T, P)$ can be seen as assigning to each state $s \in S$ a probability distribution μ_s over the set $\Lambda \times S$ as follows: take all transitions $s \xrightarrow{\alpha} s' \in T$ starting from s, and assign their particular probabilities $\mu_s(\alpha, s') = P(s \xrightarrow{\alpha} s')$; for all other non-existing transitions we assume to have a probability 0, i.e., μ_s resolves to 0. The restrictions in Definition 3.8 ensure that we defined μ_s as a discrete probability distribution. This is essentially the definition of a generative probabilistic model, i.e., which attaches to each $s \in S$ a distribution μ_s over the set $\Lambda \times S$. User interface models can be seen as special cases of generative models where there are no two transitions labelled by the same action (i.e., deterministic).

We need to do statistical inference, from observations, for pairs of a user interface model and personas model. This would start from a UI model which is initially populated with base rate probabilities, or even with a linear distribution, i.e., completely uninformative. The result should be a probabilistic model which should be recognized as an improved approximation of the user interface model we started with. Because of this we can apply the statistical inference over and over again, thus, more observations would imply more accurate user interface model, which will reflect better the choices of the users. We will call the inference process, the *update operation*, and the coupling of the persona and the user interface, the *compilation operation*.

4   Compilation Operations

The notion of compilation is our way of capturing the interaction between personas and user interfaces. Therefore, we do not want to be restrictive in its definition, so to allow for various future forms of interactions to be defined as compilation operations.

Definition 4.1 (Compilation). *Denote by $\mathcal{U}$ the set of all user interface models (cf. Definition 3.8) and by $\mathcal{P}$ the set of all personas models (cf. Definition 3.5). The compilation operation $\odot$ is defined as $\odot : \mathcal{U} \times \mathcal{P} \to \mathcal{U}$ taking a user interface model and a personas model and returning a user interface model.*

Essentially this definition requires the compilation operation to return a new user interface. This would allow for successive compilations of the result with other personas models.

We can give a more concrete definition under the following assumptions. Consider that $\mathcal{U}$ and $\mathcal{P}$ are defined over the same set of actions Λ. This requirement can be achieved for any personas model by applying (a probabilistic version of) the action restriction operation from Definition 3.4 on the set of labels of the user interface model. Consider only those personas models which have a *total* transition function, i.e., for each persona all the actions are possible, leading to some other persona; call this a *total personas model*. We can view a general personas model as a total personas model where all those actions that do not exist in the general model are self-loops, having origin and target the same persona, and probabilities 1. A minimal total personas model consists of a single persona with a self-looping transition for each action. Other kinds of total personas models can be thought, e.g., with the missing actions added in a completely non-deterministic manner, i.e., using uniform distributions, meaning that noting is known about how these actions change the personas. But we are not concerned with these in the following definition.

Definition 4.2 (Concrete Compilation). *For a user interface model $UI = (S, \Lambda, T_U, P_U)$ and a total personas model $PM = (Q, T_P, \Lambda, \Phi, P_P)$ over the same set of actions Λ, we define $\odot_c$ as:*

$$UI \odot_c PM \stackrel{def}{=} (S', \Lambda, T', P'), \text{ where}$$

1. $S' = S \times Q$,
2. $((s_1, q_1), \alpha, (s_2, q_2)) \in T'$ *iff* $(s_1, \alpha, s_2) \in T_U \wedge (q_1, \alpha, q_2) \in T_P$,
3. $P'((s, q), \alpha, (s', q')) = P_U(s, \alpha, s') \cdot P_P(q, \alpha, q')$.

We have essentially made a synchronous product. The use of synchronous product is natural here because we consider that one action in the user interface should be actually triggered by the user, therefore the same action should be visible on the personas model. In the personas model this interaction with the user interface may trigger a change of persona, but not necessarily.

Looking more closely at the concrete compilation operation from above we can see that the transitions from the user interface model are preserved. This happens because we worked only with total personas models.

Proposition 4.3. *The compilation $\odot_c$ returns a generative probabilistic model (i.e., like a UI model). This model may contain non-determinism (i.e., several transitions with the same action) since the personas models contain these.*

Proof. This is easy to see because for each resulting pair we multiply probabilities from the reactive model, which sum up to 1 for each action, with the generative probabilities. This results in a probability distribution over the new transitions because the whole sum equals to 1.

There are drawbacks with the above concrete compilation, mainly coming from the restrictions we imposed. We cannot model interactions in the layer III where the persona does not observe actions of the UI, and thus neither changes of state in UI. Internal actions are obvious examples, but other actions may be deliberately hidden by some attacker. Also there may be actions on the personas model which we want to not be correlated with the model. Either such actions come from outside layer III, and influence it, or are actions from the persona that fail to trigger the appropriate response on the UI. A third aspect is the complete match of actions which Definition 4.2 requires. This is not usual in practice, but rather an approximation is made by the designer of the interface about what the UI actions are associated to in the mind of the user. These are not always good approximations, and could be learned from empirical studies.

Definition 4.4 (General Compilation). *For a user interface model* $UI = (S, \Lambda_U, T_U, P_U)$ *and a total personas model* $PM = (Q, T_P, \Lambda_P, \Phi, P_P)$, *and a total function* $g : (\Lambda_U \times \Lambda_P) \to \Lambda'_*$, *we define* $\odot_g$ *as:*

$$UI \odot_g PM \stackrel{def}{=} (S', \Lambda', T', P'), \text{ where}$$

1. $S' = S \times Q$,
2. $((s_1, q_1), \alpha', (s_2, q_2)) \in T'$ *iff* $(s_1, \alpha_u, s_2) \in T_U \wedge (q_1, \alpha_p, q_2) \in T_P$ *and*
   $$g(\alpha_u, \alpha_p) = \alpha' \neq *,$$
3. $P'((s, q), \alpha, (s', q')) = P_U(s, \alpha_u, s') \cdot P_P(q, \alpha_p, q')$.

The compilation $\odot_g$ is parametrized by the function g. When choosing the $g(\alpha_u, \alpha_p) = \alpha$ iff $\alpha_u = \alpha_p = \alpha$, and equals $*$ for all other cases, we find the particular definition of concrete compilation. Care needs to be taken when defining the g parameter because depending on this is whether we obtain a probabilistic system, and what kind, after the compilation. In such cases variations of the general compilation would be devised which would take into account the specific definition of g when building the probabilities.

The general compilation still has one drawback which does not have an easy solution. The fact that the personas model is compiled with a single UI model means that for each persona we would have the same actions likelihoods provided by this single UI. But in reality one persona (e.g., a cautious one) coupled with one UI would incur different likelihoods for the provided actions than would be the case for another persona (e.g., an indifferent one).

This drawback is important because it has been argued that each protocol, in our case each user interface, behaves differently when put in different contexts, in our case when coupled with different personas (i.e., not only different users, but the same user in different social and cognitive contexts). This is the purpose of security ceremonies, to analyse a protocol in all its contexts. This view is similar to how the symbolic approach to verification of security protocols is working; there, observational equivalence is used as a tool, thus allowing them to analyse a protocol w.r.t. all possible contexts definable in some protocol language. The compilation should allow for such kind of reasoning too.

For the update operation we can use a simple statistical inference method applicable to Markov chains [5] (or probabilistic automata [16,30]), like maximum likelihood estimation [39]. For a persona (or personas model) and a user interface model consider a *test* to be a finite sequence of actions part of a run of the compilation of the persona and the user interface. Several such tests form a *test set*. The update operation takes a compilation of a personas model and a user interface model, together with a test set, and applies a statistical inference method to obtain a new user interface model with the probability function updated according to the tests.

5 Conclusion and Further Work

For security ceremonies the abstract model introduced in [3] (which we called the Bella-Coles-Kemp model) provides a nice setup for developing formal models and analysing security breaches by concentrating on the different parts of a ceremony. We concentrated here on the human-computer interaction which forms layer III. In particular, we have argued for a probabilistic model of the human personas interacting with a user interface. The probabilities are supposed to be inferred from statistical tests, and should give a more realistic view on how a human provides input to (and receives information from) a security protocol through the user interface.

We have separated the model of the humans from the model of the user interface, each capturing some different information natural for the respective model. In particular, the personas model is reactive in nature, capturing the probabilistic knowledge about how an action affects the persona. Whereas the user interface model is generative in nature, capturing the probabilistic information about which choices are more probable to be taken at each state of the UI. These information are put together through compilation, resulting in a probabilistic model that can be used at both layers II and IV.

Probabilistic models are more close to reality, incorporating more knowledge usually obtained through empirical studies. A wealth of analysis techniques exist based on probabilistic models. These usually give quantitative answers (besides also standard qualitative ones). One example is model checking [24] based on probabilistic versions of temporal logics. A mature tool for this is PRISM, actively developed at Oxford [18].

Examples of probabilistic reasoning about security ceremonies using the framework we just proposed, are the subject of a different paper. But very common properties would be defined as reachability problems. Reachability gives quantitative answers to whether a particular situation is reached and with what probability. In our invalid certificate example one would be interested in what are the probabilities for whether the user would accept an invalid certificate or would reject a valid certificate (i.e., not recognized by the browser).

We have only looked at models and how they appear to capture probabilistic aspects of the human in security ceremonies. We have not looked at languages for describing such models. Such a language would be needed before being able to apply a tool like PRISM. The same as labelled finite state systems (used to model programming systems) have a wealth of process algebras as languages of varying abstraction capabilities, probabilistic models also have probabilistic process algebras [17]. Since the models we described are close to existing probabilistic automata, the best approach would be to start looking for existing probabilistic process algebras that we could use. What we might need is to add the compilation operations as operators of the process algebra.

References

1. Abadi, M., Fournet, C.: Mobile values, new names, and secure communication. In: Hankin, C., Schmidt, D. (eds.) POPL, pp. 104–115. ACM (2001)
2. Abadi, M., Gordon, A.D.: A calculus for cryptographic protocols: the spi calculus. Inf. Comput. 148(1), 1–70 (1999)
3. Bella, G., Coles-Kemp, L.: Layered analysis of security ceremonies. In: Gritzalis, D., Furnell, S., Theoharidou, M. (eds.) SEC 2012. IFIP AICT, vol. 376, pp. 273–286. Springer, Heidelberg (2012)
4. Bevan, N.: International standards for HCI and usability. Int. J. Hum. Comput. Stud. 55(4), 533–552 (2001)
5. Billingsley, P.: Statistical Inference for Markov Processes. The University of Chicago Press, Chicago (1961)
6. Blanchet, B.: Automatic proof of strong secrecy for security protocols. In: IEEE Symposium on Security and Privacy, pp. 86–102. IEEE Computer Society (2004)
7. Blanchet, B.: A computationally sound mechanized prover for security protocols. IEEE Trans. Dependable Sec. Comput. 5(4), 193–207 (2008)
8. Carlos, M.C., Martina, J.E., Price, G., Custódio, R.F.: An updated threat model for security ceremonies. In: Shin, S.Y., Maldonado, J.C. (eds.) 28th Annual ACM Symposium on Applied Computing (SAC 2013), pp. 1836–1843. ACM (2013)
9. Dolev, D., Yao, A.C.: On the security of public key protocols. IEEE Trans. Inf. Theory 29(2), 198–207 (1983)
10. Ellison, C.: Ceremony design and analysis. Cryptology ePrint Archive, Report 2007/399 (2007)
11. Ferreira, A., Giustolisi, R., Huynen, J.L., Koenig, V., Lenzini, G.: Studies in socio-technical security analysis: authentication of identities with TLS certificates. In: TrustCom/ISPA/IUCC, pp. 1553–1558. IEEE (2013)
12. van Glabbeek, R.J., Smolka, S.A., Steffen, B.: Reactive, generative and stratified models of probabilistic processes. Inf. Comput. 121(1), 59–80 (1995)
13. Goldsmith, M., Lowe, G., Roscoe, B., Ryan, P., Schneider, S.: Modelling and Analysis of Security Protocols. Pearson Education, Harlow (2000)
14. Groote, J.F., Mathijssen, A., Reniers, M.A., Usenko, Y.S., van Weerdenburg, M.: The formal specification language mCRL2. In: Methods for Modelling Software Systems (MMOSS 2006). Dagstuhl Seminar Proceedings, vol. 06351 (2007)
15. Harel, D., Tiuryn, J., Kozen, D.: Dynamic Logic. MIT Press, Cambridge (2000)
16. de la Higuera, C., Oncina, J.: Learning stochastic finite automata. In: Paliouras, G., Sakakibara, Y. (eds.) ICGI 2004. LNCS (LNAI), vol. 3264, pp. 175–186. Springer, Heidelberg (2004)

17. Jonsson, B., Larsen, K.G., Yi, W.: Probabilistic extensions of process algebras. In: Bergstra, J., Ponse, A., Smolka, S. (eds.) Handbook of Process Algebras, pp. 685–711. Elsevier, Amsterdam (2001)
18. Kwiatkowska, M., Norman, G., Parker, D.: Advances and challenges of probabilistic model checking. In: Proceedings of the 48th Annual Allerton Conference on Communication, Control and Computing, pp. 1691–1698. IEEE Press (2010)
19. Larsen, K.G., Skou, A.: Bisimulation through probabilistic testing. Inf. Comput. **94**(1), 1–28 (1991)
20. Latour, B.: Reassembling the Social - An Introduction to Actor-Network-Theory. Oxford University Press, Oxford (2005)
21. Lowe, G.: Breaking and fixing the needham-schroeder public-key protocol using FDR. Softw. Concepts Tools **17**(3), 93–102 (1996)
22. Mitchell, J.C., Mitchell, M., Stern, U.: Automated analysis of cryptographic protocols using Murphi. In: IEEE Symposium on Security and Privacy, pp. 141–151. IEEE Computer Society (1997)
23. Newell, A.: Unified Theories of Cognition. Harvard University Press, Cambridge (1990)
24. Norman, G., Parker, D., Sproston, J.: Model checking for probabilistic timed automata. Formal Meth. Syst. Des. **43**(2), 164–190 (2013)
25. Paulson, L.C.: The inductive approach to verifying cryptographic protocols. J. Comput. Secur. **6**(1–2), 85–128 (1998)
26. Pavlovic, D., Meadows, C.: Actor-network procedures: modeling multi-factor authentication, device pairing, social interactions. arXiv.org (2011)
27. Pieters, W.: Representing humans in system security models: an actor-network approach. J. Wirel. Mob. Netw. Ubiquit. Comput. Dependable Appl. **2**(1), 75–92 (2011)
28. Pratt, V.R.: Process logic. In: 6th Symposium on Principles of Programming Languages (POPL 1979), pp. 93–100. ACM (1979)
29. Prisacariu, C.: Actor network procedures as psi-calculi for security ceremonies. In: International Workshop on Graphical Models for Security. Electronic Proceedings in Theoretical Computer Science, vol. 148, pp. 63–77. Open Publishing Assoc. (2014)
30. Rabin, M.O.: Probabilistic automata. Inform. Control **6**(3), 230–245 (1963)
31. Radke, K., Boyd, C., Gonzalez Nieto, J., Brereton, M.: Ceremony analysis: strengths and weaknesses. In: Camenisch, J., Fischer-Hübner, S., Murayama, Y., Portmann, A., Rieder, C. (eds.) SEC 2011. IFIP AICT, vol. 354, pp. 104–115. Springer, Heidelberg (2011)
32. Rogers, Y., Sharp, H., Preece, J.: Interaction Design: Beyond Human-Computer Interaction, 3rd edn. Wiley, Chichester (2011)
33. Rukšėnas, R., Curzon, P., Back, J., Blandford, A.: Formal modelling of cognitive interpretation. In: Doherty, G., Blandford, A. (eds.) DSVIS 2006. LNCS, vol. 4323, pp. 123–136. Springer, Heidelberg (2007)
34. Ruksenas, R., Curzon, P., Blandford, A.: Modelling and analysing cognitive causes of security breaches. Innovations Sys. Softw. Eng. **4**(2), 143–160 (2008)
35. Segerberg, K.: Getting started: beginnings in the logic of action. Stud. Logica **51**(3/4), 347–378 (1992)
36. Semančík, R.: Basic properties of the persona model. Comput. Inform. **26**(2), 105–121 (2007)

37. Sokolova, A., de Vink, E.P.: Probabilistic automata: system types, parallel composition and comparison. In: Baier, C., Haverkort, B.R., Hermanns, H., Katoen, J.-P., Siegle, M. (eds.) Validation of Stochastic Systems. LNCS, vol. 2925, pp. 1–43. Springer, Heidelberg (2004)
38. Stern, U., Dill, D.L.: Parallelizing the Murφ verifier. In: Grumberg, O. (ed.) CAV 1997. LNCS, vol. 1254, pp. 256–278. Springer, Heidelberg (1997)
39. Teodorescu, I.: Maximum likelihood estimation for markov chains (2009). arxiv: 0905.4131

High-Level Simulation for Multiple Fault Injection Evaluation

Maxime Puys[1], Lionel Rivière[1,2]([✉]), Julien Bringer[1], and Thanh-ha Le[1]

[1] SAFRAN Morpho, Paris, France
{maxime.puys,julien.bringer,thanh-ha.le}@morpho.com
[2] Télécom Paristech, Paris, France
lionel.riviere@telecom-paristech.fr

Abstract. Faults injection attacks have become a hot topic in the domain of smartcards. This work exposes a source code-base simulation approach designed to evaluate the robustness of high-level secured implementations against single and multiple fault injections. In addition to an unprotected CRT-RSA implementation, we successfully attacked two countermeasures with the high-level simulation under the *data* fault model. We define a filtering criterion that operates on found attacks and we refine our simulation analysis accordingly. We introduce a broader fault model that consists in skipping C lines of code and exhibit benefits of such high-level fault model in term of simulation performance and attack coverage.

1 Introduction

Effects of physical attacks on secure implementations were first described in 1997. In particular, fault injection attacks aim at modifying a program's state using an external event such as laser beams, voltage glitches or electromagnetic waves. Among the numerous possibilities opened by such attacks, an attacker can perform a Differential Fault Analysis (DFA) [1,2] and retrieve secret information such as embedded cryptographic keys.

Smartcard-based products, which are widespread in the daily life, can be a profitable target for attackers. Banking or biometric credentials for instance are stored on such devices. They may be sensitive to such fault attacks and therefore require a high security certification standards such as the Common Criteria [3]. Their compliance to those standards are evaluated by governmental agencies that deliver certificates accordingly. One of the very first step of a certification process is the security code review. In order to bring out vulnerabilities, evaluators and developers perform high-level security code reviews at the source code level. Suspected points are then audited at the assembly level, but not systematically. However, mostly manual, this task is time consuming and error prone. A code reviewer could miss critical errors that might lead to a major security breach.

This work was partially funded by the French ANR E-MATA HARI Project.
M. Puys—Work done while the author was in internship at Morpho.

© Springer International Publishing Switzerland 2015
J. Garcia-Alfaro et al. (Eds.): DPM/SETOP/QASA 2014, LNCS 8872, pp. 293–308, 2015.
DOI: 10.1007/978-3-319-17016-9_19

These two reasons encourage the development of automated high-level code analysis to help evaluators and developers. Complete and exhaustive approaches are often used at the binary level where all impacts of a fault can be considered (such as code operation modification) but this takes a long time to perform. In order to rapidly point out vulnerabilities in the security evaluation process, the high-level fault simulation becomes definitely useful. It constitutes a complementary step to other following low-level simulated or practical analyses. From the research point of view, on the one hand, we must provide fault models as accurate as possible on which simulation can rely with a high level of confidence. On the other hand, a comprehensive understanding of fault properties would allow us to better analyze its impacts on software and to design more efficient countermeasures accordingly.

Contributions. We propose an efficient high-level approach to analyze source codes against multiple fault injections. To achieve this end, we built tools to exhaustively explore a data fault model defined a the C variable level. Helped by an oracle, they can for each combination of faults tell if an attack worked on the program. Thanks to the testing approach we are able to produce detailed counterexamples or state on the program's robustness with respect to the chosen fault model. We demonstrate the validity of our approach on three implementations of the CRT-RSA [4] algorithm in the signature process by performing BellCoRe attacks [1]. Moreover, we propose two attack classification criteria aiming at regrouping them, which becomes time-saving when dealing with multiple faults on realistic implementations. Finally, we study the results of the analysis with a line-skip fault model, lighter than the data fault model.

Organization of the paper. In Sect. 2, we define useful terms widely used to express several concepts and security notions. We also recall the CRT-RSA algorithm and the BellCoRe attack. Section 3 further explains the considered fault model and the approach we use to evaluate implementations. Section 4 shows the results of our tests on the three CRT-RSA implementations. Finally, Sect. 5 defines two classification criteria and discusses outcomes obtained from the three examples under the line-skip fault model.

2   State-of-the-Art and Definitions

2.1   Terminology

This section proposes succinct definitions of five notions: an attack, a fault, a security breach, a vulnerability and the fault order. We explain how these notions are related and we will refer to these definitions all along this paper.

A **security breach** is the deviation of a program from its expected behavior in terms of security. A **vulnerability** names the presence of an error or lack of security in the program that might lead to a security breach. A **fault** represents an external event changing the program's state. Effects of fault and its behavior is formalized through a fault model, which is characterized by its parameters such as the attacker *control* or the *fault persistence*. The spatial *control* parameter reflects the ability of the attacker to accurately locate its target in the source code whereas the timing *control* reflects his ability to tamper with its target at a particular moment during an ongoing computation. The *fault persistence* reflects the duration of a fault. For instance, for a given attacked variable v, the fault persistence is said transient when a single evaluation of v differs from its expected value. It is said permanent when v keeps a wrong state for each remaining evaluations. An **attack** is the exploitation of a vulnerability by a fault. In [5], authors refined this definition with the presence of a goal for the attacker. However, we will confine to the basic definition. In physical experiments, the **fault order** is the number of injections (laser pulse or electromagnetic beam for instance). However, a single physical injection can imply one or several logical changes. In a simulation experiment, the physical fault is abstracted through a fault model and the fault order corresponds to the number of occurrence of the model. Nevertheless, note that it is generally assumed that a single injection is aimed to induce one specific change during code execution.

2.2 CRT-RSA

We choose to analyze the well known asymmetrical CRT-RSA algorithm [4]. Let's say that Alice wants to send the message m to Bob. She has to sign m using her RSA private key (d, N) and then she computes the signature $S = m^d$ mod N. The idea behind the CRT algorithm is to replace the costly modular exponentiation of RSA with two sub-exponentiations with half the size of the original exponent. This roughly speeds up the computation by a factor of four.

Hence, the RSA private key d is split in two parts d_p and d_q. As shown in Table 1, we compute the inverse of q modulo p, denoted i_q in (a) and the two modular sub-exponentiations in (b):

Table 1. Inverse (a) and Sub-exponentiation(b)

(a)	(b)
$d_p = d \mod (p-1)$	$S_p = m^{d_p} \mod p$
$d_q = d \mod (q-1)$	$S_q = m^{d_q} \mod q$
$i_q = q^{-1} \mod p$	$S = S_q + q \cdot (i_q \cdot (S_p - S_q) \mod p)$

This last step *recombines* the two sub-signatures S_p and S_q in the final signature S. It can be performed using either Gauss or Garner's formula. The latter is the most used because as it provides better memory performances. This is the one we presented in the algorithm.

2.3 BellCoRe Attack on CRT-RSA

This attack has been discovered in 1997 by Boneh, DeMillo and Lipton [1] from BellCoRe (Bell Communications Research). An attacker is able to retrieve a prime factor p or q of N if he is able to inject a fault in the signature computation in order to obtain a faulty signature $\widehat{S}$ such as:

1. $|\widehat{S}| \neq |S|$
2. And $|\widehat{S} \mod p| = |S \mod p|$ or $|\widehat{S} \mod q| = |S \mod q|$

The attacker is then able to retrieve either p or q by computing $gcd(N, S - \widehat{S})$. In 1999, Joye, Lenstra and Quisquater [6] showed that this attack can use only the faulty signature $\widehat{S}$ and the message m and retrieve either p or q by computing $gcd(N, m - \widehat{S}^e)$ with an overwhelming probability.

2.4 Code Security Properties

Security metrics aim at defining quantitative and objective criteria in order to gauge various aspect of security. It can be considered in multiple ways [7] and takes several form [8,9]. In the context of smartcards implementation robustness testing against fault injection and considering a manual security code review, they are designed to facilitate decision-making and improve the code robustness. Measuring how the targeted implementation deviates from its functional specification under fault injection constitutes the *correctness* aspect of security. It is the assurance that the targeted function carries out its task precisely to the specification with the expected behavior. Another metric to assess the *efficiency* of a simulation tool is needed in order to confront specific tools.

Measurement requires realistic assumptions and inputs to attain reliable results [10]. The qualitative and quantitative properties of a security objective must be defined. In our case, the security objective is to preserve the correctness of an ongoing RSA ciphering or signature under fault injections to avoid Bell-CoRe attacks. The quantitative aspect of such an objective lies in the number of deviation from the expected behavior. According to Sect. 2.1, it corresponds to the number of security breaches. The qualitative aspect corresponds to the nature of the attack (the fault model), and the way it deviates from the reference.

The classification of deviant cases permit to define the criticality level of found attacks. Thereby, we can measure the code sensitivity or robustness of a targeted code under fault attack, and determine potential vulnerabilities according to a measurement system, a fault model and a simulation tool.

2.5 Existing Works

In [11,12], Christofi et al. propose a formal method to validate cryptographic implementations against first order fault injections relying on theorem proving. The fault targets a C variable and sets it to zero. Their studies lead them to the implementation of a *Frama-C* plugin named *TL-Face* and using the *Jessie* plugin in order to solve *weakest precondition* problems. A case study has been made on the Vigilant implementation of CRT-RSA, revealing possible BellCoRe attacks.

In [13], Rauzy et al. study the effects of a first order fault on several CRT-RSA implementations. Their fault model consists in replacing any intermediate value with either zero or a random value. No mathematical property such as co-primality or equivalent modulo is considered. Their analyses lead to the implementation of an OCaml tool testing exhaustively every possible faults. It has been used to compare an unprotected implementation of CRT-RSA with the Shamir [14] one and the Aumüller one [15]. In [16], they extend their approach on Vigilant and Coron's counter-measures and provide high-order attacks. Note that their approach targets values that are used in mathematical operations only.

In [17], Kauffmann-Tourkestansky works on a first order fault model targeting control flow in order to skip instructions (using NOP or JUMP instructions). He uses a mutation analysis of C source codes and tries to fill the gap between high-level and low-level implementations.

In [18], Heydemann et al. also focus on an instruction skip based fault model. They propose a set of counter-measures applicable to every instruction of the Thumbs2 instruction set of the ARM language [19]. They suppose that it is hard for an attacker to reproduce twice the same fault in a few cycles delay and give a way to duplicate each instruction. Finally, they prove that this mutated program (with all its instruction duplicated) has the same behavior than the original using the Vis model-checking tool [20].

In [21], Berthier et al. propose a brand new approach for evaluating smart-cards security against first order fault injection. It consists in embedding the fault simulator itself directly on the smartcard. This way, faults are tested on the final product, which is more reliable than on a software model. Moreover, it also enables the possibility to study the behavior of the card after injections using side-channel analysis. Their fault model targets byte skipping of an arbitrary length. They put it into practice on an implementation of a DES cipher, revealing for instance a fault that skip a function call, which compromised the security of the implementation.

In [5], Potet et al. study the effects of a test inversion based fault model. The analysis is objective guided, in term of reaching or not basic blocks. The fault model is exhaustively explored by a mutation approach. Moreover, in order to take into account higher order faults, that would cause path explosion (and in their case, mutants number explosion), they only create one higher-level mutant. It embeds on its own the *possibility* of injecting each possible fault or not. The paths are then covered by the concolic execution tool Klee [22].

Those existing works emphasize the importance of considering both data and control flow fault models in secure implementation robustness evaluation. With our high-level fault simulation approach presented in the next section, we consider both models while ensuring a very efficient detection and high performances.

3 High-Level Simulation Approach

Section 3.1 defines two reachable fault models considered with fault simulator, namely the data and the line-skip fault models. Section 3.2 defines the testing protocol used to evaluate implementations.

3.1 Mechanisms

The fault simulator operates at the source code level, considered fault models are defined with this granularity accordingly.

Granularity:	: C variable
(Spatial | temporal) control	: Complete | Limited
Persistence:	: Permanent or transient
Multiplicity:	: First order or higher
Type:	: Set to 0 or 1

FAULT MODEL 1: Data

This model is a subset of the one proposed in [13, 23]. Both of them allow the attacker to perform permanent and transient faults on every variable and intermediate values. On the opposite, our model only allow permanent faults on variable and transient faults on intermediate values, which is more realistic. It also assumes that an attacker can not modify the secret key, the message to sign or the signature, which should pass integrity checks at any time.

The *instruction-skip* fault model is explored in previous works [21, 24, 25], but almost exclusively at the assembly code level. To our knowledge, no experiment targets CRT-RSA under such fault model in the literature. As there is no assembly instruction notion at the C code level, we propose a high-level extension of the *instruction-skip* fault model as follows:

Granularity	: C code line
Skip Width	: One C code line
(Spatial | temporal) control	: Complete | Limited
Persistence	: Transient
Multiplicity	: First order or higher
Type	: Skip of lines in C source code

FAULT MODEL 2: Line-skip

In practice, the fault simulator has been designed to permit arbitrary width line skips. However, a C line of code is often represented by several lines of assembly. Knowing that in the current state of the art, it remains difficult to skip multiple assembly lines, an attacker will unlikely be able to skip multiple C lines of code. Then, we will only consider faults with a width of one line.

Table 2 summarizes the differences of our fault models with state of the art, on several general criteria in order to show the diversity of existing analysis on this topic. HL denotes High-Level abstraction and LL denotes Low-Level abstraction.

Table 2. Comparison of our approach with state-of-the-art

Reference	Abstraction level	Type of fault model	Persistence	High order
[11,12]	HL (C)	Data-flow	Permanent	
[13,16]	HL (OCaml)	Data-flow	Transient	✓
[17]	HL (C) / LL	Control-flow	Transient	
[18,24]	LL	Control-flow	Transient	
[21]	LL	Control-flow	Transient	
[5]	Intermediate (LLVM)	Control-flow	Transient	✓
Our approach	HL (C)	Data-flow Control-flow	Permanent Transient	✓

The simulator mostly relies on a testing approach in the sense that the targeted implementation is not modified between simulations. However, a single mutation might be needed to decompose computations and let the intermediate values appear as one-time variables.

Faults are injected using the well known Gnu Project Debugger (GDB) [26] that makes it possible to pause the execution via breakpoints, change any variable's value and then resume the execution. Moreover, we enhanced the control and efficiency of our simulator by providing automation through Python scripts.

3.2   Test Protocol

Our testing protocol currently targets any single function in an implementation. Several parameters can be tuned to specify the fault model such as the fault multiplicity or which variable to attack or not. If not specified, every global variable of the file, local variable and parameter of the function will be faulted at each line of the function.

GDB commands are controlled by Python scripts, which, for each combination of faults (aka targeted variables, injection lines and new values set), will request GDB to:

1. Execute the target;
2. Set breakpoints where the fault shall be injected;
3. Inject the faults;
4. Get the system state post execution;
5. Repeat this sequence until the fault model is exhaustively explored.

This will spot possible attacks with respect to an oracle defined by the user. As we will see, there might be many of them.

We choose to allow the simulator to change the value of a variable even if this variable is not used at the targeted line. It means that every variable will be forced to every possible value (zero or one) at each line. This possibility could be realistic for example in a system where the values of the variables are stored in memory and loaded each time they are read. In a system where this assertion does not stand (basically all system with registers), only the realistic attacks will be included in the total set of attacks found.

Instinctively, such flexibility will create a relation between some attacks in a way that they can be regrouped as one generic attack and several ways to reproduce it. Thus, in Sect. 5, we will define precisely what we call redundant attacks. Then we will detail classification criteria in order to regroup such attacks.

4   Case Study

In this section we present a case study in order to show the validity of our tool. We concentrate on the process of signature using CRT-RSA. The objective is to ask a system to sign a random message m with its own key (p, q, d_p, d_q, i_q, N) and to obtain a prime factor p or q of N using a BellCoRe attack.

We will study the results of the simulator on an unprotected CRT-RSA implementation and on one using the Aumüller et al. counter-measure [15]. Both of them will be tested with the data fault model and the line-skip fault model explained in Sect. 3.1.

4.1   Study of an Unprotected Implementation of CRT-RSA

```
1  int  CRT_RsaSign(int  M ,  int  p,  int  q,  int  d_p,  int  d_q,  int  i_q)
2        S_p = M^{d_p}  mod p              /* Signature  modulo  p */
3        S_q = M^{d_q}  mod q              /* Signature  modulo  q */
4        S = S_q + q · (i_q · (S_p − S_q)  mod p)  /* Recombining  */
5        return  S
```

Listing 1.1. Unprotected implementation of CRT-RSA

Simulation 1 targets the unprotected CRT-RSA given in Listing 1.1 with first order attacks under the data fault model. For the rest of this paper, we will describe each simulation experiment with the following structure:

Target function	: Unprotected CRT_RsaSign
Success oracle	: Success of a BellCoRe attack on the signature
Fault model	: Data
Fault multiplicity	: 1 (first order)
Result	: **11 attacks found**

SIMULATION 1: Data model on unprotected CRT-RSA (first order faults)

By $\mathcal{O}(S, \widehat{S}, N)$ we denote the success oracle that returns true if a BellCoRe attack succeed with the given parameters, false otherwise.

Data Attack Example 1. The unprotected implementation of CRT-RSA is prone to numerous attacks. For instance, forcing the value of S_p to zero prior to the execution of line 4 reveals the prime factor q of N. Indeed,

$$S - \widehat{S} = q \cdot ((i_q \cdot (S_p - S_q) \bmod p) - (i_q \cdot (-S_q) \bmod p)) \text{ and } gcd(N, S - \widehat{S}) = q$$

Data Attack Example 2. An even clearer attack consists in zeroing the whole intermediate value $q \cdot (i_q \cdot (S_p - S_q) \mod p)$ prior to the execution of line 4 will result in $\widehat{S} = S_q$, thus we have a BellCoRe attack:

$$|\widehat{S}| \neq |S| \text{ and } |\widehat{S} \mod q| = |S \mod q|$$

Simulation 2 targets the same unprotected CRT-RSA with first order attacks according to the line-skip fault model. Results are shown below:

Target function	: Unprotected CRT_RsaSign
Success oracle	: Success of a BellCoRe attack on the signature
Fault model	: Line-skip
Fault multiplicity	: 1 (first order)
Result	: **4 attacks found**

SIMULATION 2: Line-skip model on unprotected CRT-RSA (first order faults)

Line Attack Example 1. Skipping the line computing $i_q \cdot (S_p - S_q) \mod p$ (on line 4 of Listing 1.1) led to $\widehat{S} = S_q + q \cdot (S_p - S_q)$ which allows a BellCoRe attack.

The line-skip fault model detected four vulnerable lines. Listing 1.1 shows a generic code of the naive RSA where several computations are gathered on few lines. There is a strong dependency between the implementation and the attack success rate with the line skip fault model. The latter can also recover several attacks found by the data fault model and count them as a single one, which explains the lower number of found attacks in Simulation 2.

For instance, if we consider a variable a that is used in an attacked exponentiation, with the data fault model, we can set it either to 0 or 1. However, with the line-skip fault model, the attack output will depend on the initialization value of a. Therefore, if a was initialized to 0, we would recover a *set-to-zero* data fault model. Moreover, if a was not initialized, we would recover a *random* data fault model and finally, if a was initialized to a constant value, we would recover a *set-to-value* data fault model. Even if the two latter data fault models are not directly considered by our simulation, the line-skip fault model can detect them.

4.2 Study of the Shamir Implementation of CRT-RSA

The counter-measure of Shamir [14] introduces a new factor r co-primed with p and q, random and small (less than 64 bits). Computations are thus performed modulo $p \cdot r$ (resp. modulo $q \cdot r$), which allows to retrieve the result by reducing modulo p (resp. modulo q). A verification is possible by reducing modulo r.

Our simulator shows that a first order fault is enough to break Shamir's implementation. For example, forcing the value of S_p to zero allows us to obtain the exact same attack than in Simulation 1, as the integrity test only relies on S_p' and S_q'.

4.3   Study of the Aumüller Implementation of CRT-RSA

The counter-measure of Aumüller [15] has been developed in order to enhance the version of Shamir against first order attacks. It stills introduce a new factor t co-primed with p and q. However, the computation of d_p and d_q is performed outside of the function which removes the use of d. Moreover, the ending verification introduced by Shamir is now *asymmetrical* and intermediate verification are also added. The Aumüller implementation of CRT-RSA is given in Listing 1.2.

On the Aumüller implementation of CRT-RSA, our results matches the one exposed in [13]. No first order attack is found by setting any variable or intermediate data to zero.

```
1  int CRT_RsaSign(int M, int p, int q, int dp, int dq, int iq)
2      t = rand()
3
4      p' = p · t
5      d'p = dp + random1 · (p − 1)
6      S'p = M^(d'p) mod p'              /* Signature modulo p' */
7
8      if ((p' mod p ≠ 0) or (d'p ≢ dp mod (p − 1))) {
           takeCounterMeasure() }
9
10     q' = q · t
11     d'q = dq + random2 · (q − 1)
12     S'q = M^(d'q) mod q'              /* Signature modulo q' */
13
14     if ((q' mod q ≠ 0) or (d'q ≢ dq mod (q − 1))) {
           takeCounterMeasure() }
15
16     Sp = S'p mod p
17     Sq = S'q mod q
18     S = Sq + q · (iq · (Sp − Sq) mod p) /* Recombining */
19
20     if ((S − S'p ≢ 0 mod p) or (S − S'q ≢ 0 mod q)) {
           takeCounterMeasure() }
21
22     Spt = S'p mod t
23     Sqt = S'q mod t
24     dpt = d'p mod (t − 1)
25     dpt = d'p mod (t − 1)
26
27     if (S_pt^(dqt) ≢ S_qt^(dpt) mod t) { takeCounterMeasure() }
28     else { return S }
```

Listing 1.2. Aumüller implementation of CRT-RSA

Simulation 3 targets the CRT-RSA implementation protected with the Aumüller countermeasure shown in Listing 1.2 above. Second order attacks are performed according to the data fault model, we obtain:

Target function : Aumüller CRT_RsaSign
Success oracle : Success of a BellCoRe attack on the signature
Fault model : Data
Fault multiplicity : 2 (second order)
Result : **802 attacks found**

SIMULATION 3: Data model on Aumüller CRT-RSA (second order faults)

The Aumüller implementation is not robust against second order attacks using this data fault model. The first fault is used to corrupt the computation while the second avoids the counter-measure to be triggered.

Data Attack Example 3. A *Set-to-one* fault on $(p-1)$ before the execution of line 5 sets up a BellCoRe attack. Secondly, performing the same fault on $(p-1)$ before the execution of line 8 avoids triggering the counter-measure.

Data Attack Example 4. The attack presented for unprotected and Shamir implementations consisting in setting the whole intermediate value $q \cdot (i_q \cdot (S_p - S_q) \bmod p)$ to zero before the execution of line 18 stills enables a BellCoRe attack. However, it will also trigger the counter-measure of line 20 (through the test $S - S'_p \not\equiv 0 \bmod p$). A second fault will disable it by setting the intermediate value $S - S_p$ to zero.

Such a huge number of attacks (802 in Simulation 3) makes results impossible to analyze by hand. Moreover it is obvious that most of these attacks found can be regrouped into some generic attacks with different ways to reproduce them. This example definitely shows the necessity of classification criteria and metrics.

Simulation 4 targets the same protected CRT-RSA with the Aumüller counter-measure but second order attacks are performed according to the line-skip fault model. Results are shown below:

Target function : Aumüller CRT_RsaSign
Success oracle : Success of a BellCoRe attack on the signature
Fault model : Line-skip
Fault multiplicity : 2 (second order)
Result : **13 attacks found**

SIMULATION 4: Line-skip model on Aumüller CRT-RSA (second order faults)

Line Attack Example 2. Skipping the line computing $i_q \cdot (S_p - S_q) \bmod p$ (on line 18 of Listing 1.2) led to $\widehat{S} = S_q + q \cdot (S_p - S_q)$ which allows a BellCoRe attack. It also triggers the counter-measure on line 20 which can be easily skipped by our fault model at the second order. This attack is very similar to the Data attack example 4.

Thirteen attacks are spotted by the line-skip fault model. Interestingly, the number of attacks found by the line-skip fault model in Simulation 4 is drastically lower to the one found by the data fault model in simulation 3. This can be explained knowing that it only depends on the lines while the data fault model also depends on variables and values. We will present deeper analyses of the link between these two models in Sect. 5.

To the best of our knowledge, some studies showed that the Aumüller implementation of CRT-RSA is weak against multiple fault injection such as [27] but none provides detailed experimental results.

5   Advanced Analysis

Criteria. We recall that a successful attack is the exploitation of a code vulnerability, which is induced by the fault injection. According to the transient value modification fault model, we provide a variable-centric criteria $\mathcal{C}_{val}$ by which we measure the code sensitivity. $\mathcal{C}_{val}$ only depends on the value taken by the targeted variable regardless the attacked line of code. It is defined as:

$$\mathcal{C}_{val}(targeted\_var, value) := \#\{line \mid \mathcal{O}(S, \widehat{S}, n) = true\}$$

For a given couple $(targeted\_variable, value)$, $\mathcal{C}_{val}$ describes the number of successful attacks obtained by setting $targeted\_variable$ to $value$ regardless of the lines. We define as non-redundant, the successful attack that has the greatest injection line number.

Table 3. Found Attacks with the Fault Simulation with Data Fault Model

	Unprotected (order 1)	Shamir (order 1)	Aumüller (order 1)	Aumüller (order 2)
Attacks found	11	15	0	802
Non-redundant attack	9	11	0	85

Table 3 summarizes the experimental results obtained by the fault simulator on CRT-RSA implementations with the data fault model on C variables. The first line shows how many attacks the simulator has found on each implementation. The second line displays how many non-redundant attacks are found. When the same targeted variable is modified to the same value at several different lines of the code, it describes the same attack. We call such groups of lines a vulnerability. This is why the second line of Table 3 report a lower number of found attack.

Line Skip Fault Model. We now provide a line-centric criteria $\mathcal{C}_{line}$ that for each line of the implementation under testing returns a boolean value depending on the presence of an attack with an injection on this line. In the end, for a given implementation, this criteria returns the set of lines where injecting a fault results in an attack. It is defined as follows:

$$\mathcal{C}_{line}(l, m) := \begin{cases} true & \text{if } \exists\, \mathcal{A}(l, m) \mid \mathcal{O}(S, \widehat{S}, N) = true \\ false & otherwise \end{cases}$$

For a given line l, C_{line} returns true if there exist a successful attack $\mathcal{A}$ on line l according to the fault model m denoted as $\mathcal{A}(l, m)$. For each implementation that we studied, we retrieve vulnerable lines filtered by C_{line} under the data fault model. Then, we check how many of these lines are also vulnerable under the line-skip fault model. For readability purpose, we define

$$Vulnerable\ lines_{model} := \{l \mid C_{line}(l, model) = true\}$$

Thereby, we compute the following ratio:

$$Gain := \frac{\#\{Vulnerable\ lines_{data} - Vulnerable\ lines_{lskip}\}}{\#\{Vulnerable\ lines_{lskip}\}}$$

It happened that for each of our implementations, this gain ratio was 100 % even considering redundant attacks. This means that each vulnerable line found with the data fault model is also vulnerable with the line-skip fault model.

Moreover, as we can see in Table 4, the first (resp. second) line displays the time taken by our tool for each implementation using the data (resp. line-skip) fault model. The third line is the ratio of the first and second lines. We can here conclude that simulations using the line-skip fault model are much quicker than using the data fault model. This is especially true when dealing with higher order faults.

Table 4. Line-skip Fault Model And Fault Simulation Timing Performances

	Unprotected (order 1)	Shamir (order 1)	Aumüller (order 1)	Aumüller (order 2)
Data	3,53 s	38,75 s	143,93 s	1361,45 mn
Line Skip	2,18 s	2,39 s	14,31 s	7,41 mn
Gain ratio	162 %	1621 %	1006 %	18373 %

In our experiments, every attack found by the data fault model seems to be reproducible using the line-skip fault model. As mentioned in Sect. 4.1, the general link between the two fault models is not straightforward. On one hand, the general effects of a line skip on a variable is a *Set-to-last-value*. It differs from *Set-to-0/1*. If we consider that an attacker has no control on intermediate values, the line-skip fault model can be seen as a *uncontrolled* value fault model. On the other hand, considering a single line of code, the data fault model targets only one variable while the line-skip fault model targets every modified variables of the line. Despite these differences, it still becomes really useful to run line-skip based simulations prior to data based simulation at high-level as it produces similar effects. Moreover, the large simulation performance improvement justifies this choice.

Finally, high-level line-skip allows discover attacks completely invulnerable to data fault models such as removing a `break` statement in a `switch` or adding/removing loop iterations. As a matter of fact, the last has been put into practice in [28] where the authors are able to increase the leakage of an AES key for side channels analysis. Generally, these high-level faults models can be considered as the consequence of low-level faults encompassing several of them.

Representativeness Discussion. Attacking the source code structure can break the data or the control flow as the targeted source code could represent one or several instructions, which can manipulate data or not. Post compilation, a human readable C variable or loop counter will consist in a memory address for the machine. An `if-then-else` expression, a `switch` or `break` statement or an arithmetic operation will consist in a hardware encoded instruction for the machine. A possible way to improve our approach could be the use of Abstract Syntax Trees (AST) instead of C lines. This Intermediate Representation (IR) would abstract the code structure but keep its semantic and therefore improve our approach accuracy and representativeness.

6   Conclusion

We propose an approach to evaluate the robustness of secured implementations against multiple fault injections. This approach works on high-level source codes (such as C). We propose a first fault model relying on data modification with the granularity of a C variable. This fault model has been automated in a Python tool that is able to try it exhaustively on a given implementation and log out the functions outputs. Helped by oracles, it can tell whether a combination of faults results in a attack or not.

We demonstrate the validity of our tool on three examples of CRT-RSA implementations and obtained results according to the current state-of-the-art. Moreover, we proposed a second fault model relying on line skipping that is faster. In our experiments, we found that it covers entirely the attacks found by the data fault model with a huge speed gain.

Finally, we proposed a set of criteria and metrics in order to regroup attacks found and quantify in term of security the robustness of an implementation. Further work is to refine the link we found between our data and control-flow fault models.

References

1. Boneh, D., DeMillo, R.A., Lipton, R.J.: On the importance of checking cryptographic protocols for faults. In: Fumy, W. (ed.) EUROCRYPT 1997. LNCS, vol. 1233, pp. 37–51. Springer, Heidelberg (1997)
2. Biham, E., Shamir, A.: Differential fault analysis of secret key cryptosystems. In: Kaliski Jr., B.S. (ed.) CRYPTO 1997. LNCS, vol. 1294, pp. 513–525. Springer, Heidelberg (1997)
3. CSE, Scssi, BSI, Nlncsa, CESG, Nist, and NSA. Common Criteria 2. https://www.commoncriteriaportal.org

4. Quisquater, J.-J., Couvreur, C.: Fast decipherment algorithm for rsa public-key cryptosystem. Electron. Lett. **18**(21), 905–907 (1982)
5. Potet, M.-L., Mounier, L., Puys, M., Dureuil, L.: Lazart: a symbolic approach for evaluation the robustness of secured codes against control flow fault injection. In: ICST (2014)
6. Joye, M., Lenstra, A.K., Quisquater, J.-J.: Chinese remaindering based cryptosystems in the presence of faults. J. Cryptol. **12**(4), 241–245 (1999)
7. Miani, R.-S., Cukier, M., Zarpelão, B.B., de Souza Mendes, L.: Relationships between information security metrics: an empirical study. In: Proceedings of the Eighth Annual Cyber Security and Information Intelligence Research Workshop, CSIIRW 2013, pp. 22:1–22:4. ACM, New York (2013)
8. Vaughn, R.B., Henning, R.R., Siraj, A.: Information assurance measures and metrics - state of practice and proposed taxonomy. In: HICSS, p. 331 (2003)
9. Savola, R.: Towards a taxonomy for information security metrics. In: Karjoth, G., Stølen, K. (eds.) QoP, pp. 28–30. ACM (2007)
10. Jansen, W.: Directions in security metrics research. DIANE Publishing, NISTIR 7564 (2010)
11. Christofi, M.: Preuves de sécurité outillées d'implémentation cryptographiques. Ph.D. thesis, Laboratoire PRiSM, Université de Versailles Saint Quentin-en-Yvelines, France (2013)
12. Christofi, M., Chetali, B., Goubin, L., Vigilant, D.: Formal verification of a CRT-RSA implementation against fault attacks. J. Crypt. Eng. **3**(3), 157–167 (2013)
13. Rauzy, P., Guilley, S.: A formal proof of countermeasures against fault injection attacks on CRT-RSA, vol. 2013, pp. 506 (2013)
14. A. Shamir. Method and apparatus for protecting public key schemes from timing and fault attacks. Patent Number 5,991,415, November 1999 (Also presented at the rump session of EUROCRYPT 1997)
15. Aumüller, C., Bier, P., Fischer, W., Hofreiter, P., Seifert, J.-P.: Fault attacks on RSA with CRT: concrete results and practical countermeasures. In: Kaliski Jr., B.S., Koç, Ç.K., Paar, C. (eds.) CHES 2002. LNCS, pp. 260–275. Springer, Heidelberg (2002)
16. Rauzy, P., Guilley. S.: Formal analysis of CRT-RSA vigilant's countermeasure against the bellcore attack: a pledge for formal methods in the field of implementation security. In: Jagannathan, S., Sewell, P. (eds.) PPREW@POPL, p. 2. ACM (2014)
17. Kauffmann-Tourkestansky, X.: Analyses securitaires de code de carte a puce sous attaques physiques simulees. Ph.D. thesis, Université d'Orléans (2012)
18. Heydemann, K., Moro, N., Encrenaz, E., Robisson, B., Formal verification of a software countermeasure against instruction skip attacks. In: PROOFS 2013, Aot, Santa-Barbara, États-Unis (2013)
19. ARM Architecture Reference Manual - Thumb-2 Supplement (2005)
20. Brayton, R.K., et al.: VIS: A system for verification and synthesis. In: Alur, R., Henzinger, T.A. (eds.) CAV 1996. LNCS, pp. 428–432. Springer, Heidelberg (1996)
21. Berthier, M., Bringer, J., Chabanne, H., Le, T.-H., Rivière, L., Servant, V.: Idea: embedded fault injection simulator on smartcard. In: Jürjens, J., Piessens, F., Bielova, N. (eds.) ESSoS. LNCS, vol. 8364, pp. 222–229. Springer, Heidelberg (2014)
22. The KLEE symbolic virtual machine. http://klee.llvm.org/
23. Vigilant, D.: RSA with CRT: a new cost-effective solution to thwart fault attacks. In: Oswald, E., Rohatgi, P. (eds.) CHES 2008. LNCS, vol. 5154, pp. 130–145. Springer, Heidelberg (2008)

24. Moro, N., Dehbaoui, A., Heydemann, K., Robisson, B., Encrenaz, E.: Electromagnetic fault injection: towards a fault model on a 32-bit microcontroller. In: FDTC, pp. 77–88. IEEE (2013)
25. Kosuri, V.K., Fazal, N.: FPGA modeling of fault-injection attacks on cryptographic devices. IJERA **3**, 937–943 (2013)
26. http://www.sourceware.org/gdb/
27. Kim, S.-K., Kim, T.H., Han, D.-G., Hong, S.: An efficient CRT-RSA algorithm secure against power and fault attacks. J. Syst. Softw. **84**(10), 1660–1669 (2011)
28. Dehbaoui, A., Mirbaha, A.-P., Moro, N., Dutertre, J.-M., Tria, A.: Electromagnetic glitch on the AES round counter. In: Prouff, E. (ed.) COSADE 2013. LNCS, vol. 7864, pp. 17–31. Springer, Heidelberg (2013)

Short Papers

Towards an Image Encryption Scheme
with Content-Based Image Retrieval Properties

Bernardo Ferreira$^{(\boxtimes)}$, João Rodrigues, João Leitão, and Henrique Domingos

Nova University of Lisbon / NOVA-LINCS, Faculdade de Ciências e Tecnologia,
2829-516 Caparica, Portugal
bernardof@acm.org, jm.rodrigues@campus.fct.unl.pt,
{jc.leitao,hj}@fct.unl.pt

Abstract. In this paper we introduce a new secure cryptographic scheme, named IES-CBIR, specifically designed for images and their outsourced storage and retrieval in large private image repositories. Our solution enables both encrypted storage and querying using Content Based Image Retrieval (CBIR), while preserving privacy. We have implemented a prototype system around the proposed scheme, and experimentally analyzed its performance when compared to similar proposals for privacy-preserving image retrieval. Our results show that IES-CBIR allows more efficient operations than existing proposals, both in terms of time and space overheads, while enabling less restrictive application scenarios.

Keywords: Data and computation outsourcing · Encrypted data processing · Privacy-preserving content-based image retrieval (CBIR)

1 Introduction

The amount of visual data being generated and shared by Internet users is growing everyday. The requirements for storing and sharing such large amounts of image data has been a key factor for the growth of data outsourcing solutions such as Cloud Computing and Storage services (e.g. Instagram, Flickr, etc.) [1]. Furthermore, in these services the ability to efficiently retrieve relevant fractions of the outsourced data comes of utter importance for usability.

Although data outsourcing seems like the perfect solution for supporting large scale image storage and retrieval systems, it actually raises new issues for users' privacy. On one hand, recent news have proven that privacy isn't preserved by outsourced storage providers [2,3]. On the other hand, honest yet curious or malicious system administrators working for the providers have access to all data on disk and memory in the hosting machines [4,5]. Finally, external hackers can exploit software vulnerabilities to gain unauthorized access to servers and their stored data.

The traditional solution to solve these issues and enforce users' privacy has been to outsource encrypted data and run computations on the users' devices,

© Springer International Publishing Switzerland 2015
J. Garcia-Alfaro et al. (Eds.): DPM/SETOP/QASA 2014, LNCS 8872, pp. 311–318, 2015.
DOI: 10.1007/978-3-319-17016-9_20

after it's transfer and decryption [6]. However, such approach limits it's own applicability, specially regarding online applications managing very large repositories. A promising approach is to perform operations on encrypted data, directly on the server side. Nonetheless, existing solutions are still of theoretical interest only (e.g. Fully Homomorphic Encryption [7]), or have complexity and scalability issues that limit their wide adoption [8, 9], particularly for supporting private image retrieval over large-scale repositories.

To address these challenges we introduce IES-CBIR (Image Encryption Scheme with Content-Based Image Retrieval properties), a cryptographic scheme proposal that supports outsourcing of private storage and search / retrieval of images in the encrypted domain. Key to the design of this scheme is the observation that in images, color information can be separated from texture information, enabling the use of different encryption techniques with different properties for protecting each of these features. Following this observation, and considering that texture is usually more relevant than color for object recognition, in IES-CBIR we make the following tradeoff: we choose to protect image contents first, by encrypting texture information with probabilistic encryption; then we somewhat relax the security of the remaining features, by using deterministic encryption on image color information.

2 Related Work

The related work on privacy-preserving image retrieval can be divided in two classes: Searchable Symmetric Encryption (SSE) based approaches [9] and partially-homomorphic approaches [8].

SSE approaches force clients, before outsourcing a repository, to generate an index referencing it's images, and then separately encrypting both images and index and uploading them to the outsourced servers. Image encryption is typically performed using conventional symmetric cryptography. To allow privacy-preserving search over it, the index is encrypted with a symmetric-key scheme displaying some form of homomorphic property, such as determinism [10] or order-preservation [11]. An example of such work is [9], where different approaches are proposed to extract and encrypt indexing structures from image repositories, while preserving the ability to perform CBIR based on color features. Unfortunately, these SSE-based approaches present significative limitations: clients have additional computational overhead, as they have to process images locally and extract their indexing structures; additional bandwidth consumption is required to move both the repositories and their indexes to the outsourced servers; and when a user adds images to his repository, he may be required to download image feature vectors and recompute their index, which exacerbates the previous drawbacks.

The alternatives to SSE that can be found in the literature are based on public-key partially-homomorphic encryption (PKHE) schemes such as Paillier [12] or ElGamal [13]. In these approaches clients encrypt images in a way that outsourcing servers can perform all image indexing and querying operations directly over the encrypted data, avoiding many of the practical issues of

SSE-based solutions. Unfortunately, PKHE presents much higher time and space complexities when compared with SSE schemes. For instance, in [8] the authors design a powerful CBIR algorithm for the encrypted domain (based on SIFT [8]) by resorting to the Paillier cryptosystem [12], a PKHE which enables additions on the encrypted domain. However, their approach results in big ciphertext expansion and slow encryption and decryption times (as we will experimentally prove in our evaluation Sect. 6).

With our proposal of IES-CBIR, we try to address the limitations of previous works, by aiming at a balance between cryptographic complexity and client's processing overhead in the presence of large, dynamically changing repositories.

3   System and Adversary Models

System Model. The envisioned system model where IES-CBIR would be applied (Fig. 1) considers 3 main entities: *Owners*, the entities that own images and outsource them to an externally managed repository, by encrypting and sending them to a third-party's infrastructure (the Store); *Store*, the entity responsible for storing images for the Owners and performing computations over them on their behalf, including feature vector extraction and indexing [14]; and the *Users*, which are entities authorized by one or more Owners to perform search operations over their repositories. Although being able to perform search operations, Users must still explicitly request an Owner for individual access to images that might interest them (i.e. returned by the Store in reply to their queries).

Owners have a trapdoor/search key per repository, which are shared with trusted Users to grant them search privileges over it; and multiple decryption/access keys (one per stored image) which are kept secret by the Owner, and only shared with a User if he wants to grant full access to a particular image. Key distribution between Owners and Users can be done by different mechanisms orthogonal to this paper.

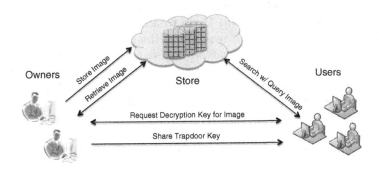

Fig. 1. System model

Adversary Model. In this work we aim at protecting the privacy of the Owner's images and User's query images. Attacks on privacy may come from curious or malicious administrators managing the Store's infrastructure, malicious Users that deviate from their expected behavior, or external Internet hackers. Malicious Store administrators may have access to all data stored on disk (at the Store), in RAM, and passing through the network. External malicious entities are assumed to only be able to access data passing through the network, or in the particular case of malicious Users, being able to issue search request over an Owner's repository (with or without access to the correct trapdoor key). Leveraging their capacities towards the system, the described adversaries will try to break any secure protocols or cryptographic schemes to gain access to the image contents. In this model, the Trusted Computing-Base is reduced to the Owners and Users personal infrastructures, and the Store's infrastructure and communication channels are considered as *not trusted.*

4   IES-CBIR Proposal

In this section we present our proposal of an Image Encryption Scheme with CBIR capabilities (IES-CBIR). We remind the reader that our scheme leverages the key observation that in images, color information can be separated from texture information and hence different levels of security can be applied when protecting each. Following this observation, and considering that texture is usually more relevant than color for object recognition, in IES-CBIR we protect image texture with probabilistic encryption and color information with deterministic encryption. Hence, privacy-preserving CBIR based on color can be performed on outsourced servers (the Store), without intervention of clients (Owners and Users), while fully protecting image texture. IES-CBIR is composed of four main algorithms, which we present in the next paragraphs.

Key Generation. IES-CBIR works with two different types of cryptographic keys, which are generated by two different algorithms: search/ trapdoor keys (tk) and access/decryption keys (dk). Trapdoor keys tk are used to give search privileges to a group of Users, and one is generated for each Owner. Decryption keys dk are unique to each encrypted image stored in an Owner's repository, and are only shared with (trusted) Users to accept explicit access requests to individual images. Both keys are required in the encryption and decryption of images. However, to generate trapdoors for searching an Owner's repository, only tk is required. The key tk is generated by making a random permutation (through a Pseudo-Random Number Generator function (PRNG) parameterized with a random seed) of all values in the range [0..100] (represents all values in HSV color space). In contrast, key dk is generated by requesting a 128-bit key from a Symmetric-Key Generator function, that will be used as a cryptographic seed for the probabilistic encryption counterpart of IES-CBIR.

Encryption. Image encryption in IES-CBIR is achieved through two steps: (i) pixel color value encryption and (ii) pixel rows and columns position shifting.

The goal of the first is to protect image color contents, by deterministically replacing each pixel color value in each color channel. This is achieved by mapping each pixel color value to it's encrypted counterpart, according to key tk. To further protect image contents, we rely on a second probabilistic step: random pixel rows and columns shifting. This step consists in instantiating a PRNG function with a previously generated decryption key dk as cryptographic seed. Then, for each pixel column, we request from the PRNG a new random value v between 1 and the image height and do a shift on that pixel column of v positions. The procedure is then repeated for the rows (with random values ranging between 1 and the image width).

Decryption. The decryption algorithm applies the different steps of encryption through the opposing order: rows shifting to their original positions, columns shifting, and then pixel color decryption. Note however that the random values must be generated in the same order as they were in encryption.

Trapdoor Generation. This algorithm generates trapdoors that Users use to search over image repositories. Trapdoor generation requires a query image (Q) as input, as well as a trapdoor key tk. Given a trapdoor key tk, the algorithm operates in a similar fashion to the encryption algorithm, where the decryption key dk is substituted by a User's randomly generated key.

5   CBIR in the Encrypted Domain

IES-CBIR enables content-based image retrieval tasks (for color features) to be performed on the encrypted domain without modification from their plaintext counterparts. As such, upon receiving new images for storage, the Store can process them, extract their feature vectors [14] and index them. Feature extraction consists in processing an image and extracting a reduced set of feature vectors that describe it. In this proposal we focus on color features in the HSV color model and their representation as color histograms. As such, for each encrypted image and each HSV color channel, the Store can build a color histogram representing it (yielding a total of 3 histograms per image).

After processing an Owner's encrypted images, the Store can receive search requests (trapdoors) from authorized Users. Upon receiving a trapdoor, the Store also extracts its feature vectors (the same way it did for the Owner's images) and finds the k most similar images in the repository by comparing their features vectors through histogram intersection [14]. After receiving these ranked results, Users can explicitly request full access to an image by asking its Owner for the decryption key.

6   Experimental Evaluation

In this section we perform an initial experimental evaluation to access the performance of a system prototype leveraging IES-CBIR, as well as similar systems

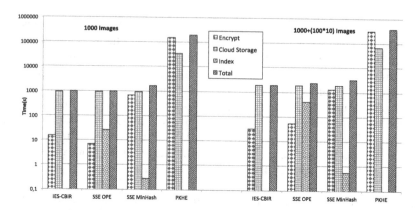

Fig. 2. Performance for the *Store Image* operation

leveraging competing alternatives found in the literature. In particular we compare the performance of our prototype with that of: (i) a system leveraging the Paillier cryptosystem described in [8] (labeled *PKHE*), and (ii) the two SSE-based solutions originally proposed in [9] (labelled *SSE OPE* and *SSE MinHash*). To conduct this experiment we measured the time taken by the *Store Image* operation with two distinct workloads: (*i*) One where 1000 JPEG images are simultaneously used to populate an outsourced repository, and another where after the initial upload of 1000 images, the Owner uploads another 10 different groups of 100 images per group. This last workload allow us to show hidden overheads of updating repositories in some alternatives described in the literature. These results present the performance from the perspective of users (i.e. we don't consider the computation in the outsourced infrastructure, as this can easily be scaled). In the experiments, client computations (i.e., Owners and Users) were performed on a Linux-Ubuntu Desktop with a Intel Core i3-2130 3.4 Ghz processor, running a OpenJDK 7 JVM with 2 GB of reserved memory, located in Lisbon, while the Store processing was carried on a Amazon EC2 Medium instance (Ireland datacenter) with a limited Internet connection of 30 Mb/s download and 3 Mb/s upload between clients and store.

Figure 2 summarizes the obtained results for each system, in terms of time required for sub-operations (*Encryption, Indexing* and *Cloud Storage*) and as a whole (*Total*). Results show that *IES-CBIR* offers overall better performance when compared with the remaining competing alternatives. More specifically, in terms of client processing *IES-CBIR* only requires encryption, while also presenting one of the highest cryptographic throughput. Alternatives either rely on indexing operations (*SSE OPE*) or slower cryptography (*SSE MinHash* and *PKHE*).

Furthermore, when adding additional images to the repository, our solution is the one that offers overall best performance, specially when compared with *SSE OPE*. This happens because with IES-CBIR, the Owner isn't required to fetch image feature vectors, re-indexing them, and re-uploading the newly generated indexes to the Store. Finally, we also observe that IES-CBIR offers similar cipher-text expansion as *SSE OPE* and *MinHash* (a ratio of $1,00005\%$ compared to $1,379\%$ and $1,003\%$, respectively), and much lower than *PKHE* (a ratio of 37%). This is further exacerbated by the data upload time to the Store in the different systems.

7   Conclusions

In this paper we have presented a proposal for a new cryptographic scheme, named IES-CBIR, which supports private outsourcing of storage and search/retrieval of images in the encrypted domain. Key to the design of IES-CBIR is the observation that in images, color information can be separated from texture information, enabling the use of different encryption techniques with different properties for each one. Leveraging IES-CBIR, we designed a secure system model focused on dynamic and distributed image outsourcing. We experimentally validated the performance of our proposal by comparing an early system prototype leveraging IES-CBIR with the relevant related works. The results obtained show that our proposal is as efficient as the related works, promises better scalability and demands lower computational overhead from clients.

References

1. Global Web Index: Instagram tops the list of social network growth (2013). http://blog.globalwebindex.net/instagram-tops-list-of-growth
2. Rushe, D.: Google: don't expect privacy when sending to Gmail. The Guardian (2013). http://tinyurl.com/kjga34x
3. Greenwald, G., MacAskill, E.: NSA Prism program taps in to user data of Apple, Google and others. The Guardian (2013). http://tinyurl.com/oea3g8t
4. Chen, A.: GCreep: Google Engineer Stalked Teens, Spied on Chats. Gawker (2010). http://gawker.com/5637234
5. Halderman, J., Schoen, S.: Lest we remember: cold-boot attacks on encryption keys. Commun. ACM **52**(5), 91–98 (2009)
6. Mahajan, P., et al.: Depot: cloud storage with minimal trust. ACM Trans. Comput. Syst. **29**(4), 1–38 (2011)
7. Gentry, C., Halevi, S., Smart, N.P.: Homomorphic evaluation of the AES circuit. In: Safavi-Naini, R., Canetti, R. (eds.) CRYPTO 2012. LNCS, vol. 7417, pp. 850–867. Springer, Heidelberg (2012)
8. Hsu, C.Y., et al.: Image feature extraction in encrypted domain with privacy-preserving SIFT. IEEE Trans. Image Process. **21**(11), 4593–4607 (2012)
9. Lu, W., et al.: Enabling search over encrypted multimedia databases. In: IS&T/SPIE Electron. Imaging, ISOP, February 2009. 725418–725418-11
10. Song, D.X., et al.: Practical techniques for searches on encrypted data. In: Proceedings of IEEE S&P, pp. 44–55. IEEE (2000)
11. Agrawal, R., et al.: Order preserving encryption for numeric data. In: Proceedings SIGMOD, pp. 563–574. ACM (2004)
12. Paillier, P.: Public-key cryptosystems based on composite degree residuosity classes. In: Stern, J. (ed.) EUROCRYPT 1999. LNCS, vol. 1592, pp. 223–238. Springer, Heidelberg (1999)

13. El Gamal, Taher: A public key cryptosystem and a signature scheme based on discrete logarithms. In: Blakely, G.R., Chaum, David (eds.) CRYPTO 1984. LNCS, vol. 196, pp. 10–18. Springer, Heidelberg (1985)
14. Swain, M.J., Ballard, D.H.: Color indexing. Int. J. Comput. Vis. **7**(1), 11–32 (1991)

A-PPL: An Accountability Policy Language

Monir Azraoui[1]([✉]), Kaoutar Elkhiyaoui[1], Melek Önen[1], Karin Bernsmed[2],
Anderson Santana De Oliveira[3], and Jakub Sendor[3]

[1] EURECOM, Biot Sophia Antipolis, Biot, France
{monir.azraoui,kaoutar.elkhiyaoui,melek.onen}@eurecom.fr
[2] SINTEF ICT, Trondheim, Norway
karin.bernsmed@sintef.no
[3] SAP Labs France, Mougins Sophia Antipolis, Antipolis, France
{anderson.santana.de.oliveira,jakub.sendor}@sap.com

Abstract. Cloud Computing raises various security and privacy challenges due to the customers' inherent lack of control over their outsourced data. One approach to encourage customers to take advantage of the cloud is the design of new accountability solutions which improve the degree of transparency with respect to data processing. In this paper, we focus on accountability policies and propose A-PPL, an accountability policy language that represents machine-readable accountability policies. A-PPL extends the PPL language by allowing customers to define additional rules on data retention, data location, logging and notification. The use of A-PPL is illustrated with a use case where medical sensors collect personal data which are then stored and processed in the cloud. We define accountability obligations related to this use case and translate them into A-PPL policies as a proof of concept of our proposal.

1 Introduction

Cloud computing marks a shift in the way organizations and individuals consume technology. Customers outsource large amount of data into the cloud and delegate the implementation of numerous security and privacy controls over these data to the cloud service provider. This new paradigm hence raises accountability concerns; in particular, business customers perceive data lock-in, loss of governance and non-compliance as major risks associated with the cloud [11].

As defined in [14], accountability concerns data stewardship regimes in which organizations that are entrusted with personal and business confidential data are responsible and liable for processing, sharing, storing and otherwise using the data according to contractual and legal requirements from the time the data is collected until when it is destroyed (including onward transfer to and from third-parties). In such a setting, clarifying the accountability relationships, i.e. who is responsible to whom and for what, with clear organizational policies will help overcome barriers to data governance in the cloud. Appropriate policies mitigate risks, provided that reliable tools to enforce them and to monitor their effectiveness are in place to allow audits.

© Springer International Publishing Switzerland 2015
J. Garcia-Alfaro et al. (Eds.): DPM/SETOP/QASA 2014, LNCS 8872, pp. 319–326, 2015.
DOI: 10.1007/978-3-319-17016-9_21

In this paper, we are interested in machine-readable representations of policies expressing accountability obligations. Such policies will help service providers deploy their automatic enforcement when personal data is processed. We propose a new policy language, A-PPL, that enables the expression of the accountability obligations. A-PPL (shorthand for Accountable PPL) extends the existing PPL language [15] by allowing the expression of accountability obligations such as rules on data retention, data location, logging and notification. We first present a number of design requirements for an accountability policy language. We then describe PPL and its limitations. A-PPL which aims at addressing these shortcomings is further introduced and finally illustrated with a healthcare use case.

2   Policy Language Requirements

Following an analysis of accountability relationships between cloud actors in [1,5], we derive a collection of eight requirements for the design of an accountability policy language. The new policy language should express data handling rules that correspond to (R1) Privacy Policies, (R2) Access Control Rules, (R3) Usage Control Rules and (R4) Data Retention Periods. The requirements related to accountability needs, often absent in existing policy languages, concern (R5) Reporting and Notification, (R6) Data Location Rules, (R7) Auditability and (R8) Logging. One may argue that these requirements can be expressed and enforced using multiple languages at different levels of the cloud technology stack. We advocate that centralizing these concerns in a single policy will improve the accountability of the actors processing personal data in the cloud, while decreasing the loss of governance, as policies will not be diluted across the service provisioning chain. Besides, rather than imposing a new language, we aim at choosing an existing language that fulfills the above requirements the best and which is extensible enough to add accountability extensions to it.

3   A-PPL: An Accountable Policy Language

In [1,5], we conduct an analysis of existing policy languages against the design requirements we identified in Sect. 2. As a result, we choose the PrimeLife Policy Language (PPL) as the best candidate language since it covers most of the requirements and PPL is an extensible language. Therefore, we create new extensions to PPL to build A-PPL.

3.1   PrimeLife Policy Language (PPL) and Its Limitations

PPL [15] was proposed by the European ICT PrimeLife[1] project to specify machine-readable privacy policies. PPL extends XACML [12] by defining a new obligation and authorization syntax. In PPL, an obligation is expressed using the pair Trigger-Action. Triggers are events related to an obligation and filtered

---

[1] http://www.primelife.eu/.

by conditions. Triggers fire Actions that are performed by the data controller. The complete list of available PPL Triggers and Actions can be found in [15]. Authorizations define the actions that the data controller is allowed or prohibited to perform: (i) authorization for purposes, allows the data controller to perform actions for a particular set of well-stated usage purposes; (ii) authorization for downstream usage, allows the forwarding of collected data to third-parties.

While PPL meets most of the requirements we identify in Sect. 2 (such as privacy policies (R1), access and usage control rules (R2)), it falls short in meeting other requirements such as data location (R6) or auditability (R7). Having identified the limitations of PPL, we propose in Sect. 3.2 our accountable policy language A-PPL that extends PPL based on each requirement.

3.2   The Syntax of A-PPL

In this section we present the extensions we add to PPL to create A-PPL. Note that we maintain the overall structure of PPL. More details can be found in [5].

Roles. A-PPL identifies different actors that can hold different roles: data subject, data controller, data processor and data protection authority. PPL already defines the first three roles. We create the auditor role. To make the identification of roles explicit in A-PPL, we introduce a role attribute identifier subject:role to be included as an attribute of the standard XACML element <Subject>.

Access Control Rules (R2). We introduce two new triggers which condition the execution of an obligation based on the result of an access decision. More specifically, we propose TriggerPersonalDataAccessPermitted and TriggerPersonalDataAccessDenied that occur when the evaluation of the access control on the targeted data results in "Permit" and "Deny", respectively.

Data Retention (R4). PPL provides an element Purpose that allows to specify for which purpose a piece of data can be collected or accessed. In A-PPL, we define the duration attribute for Purpose that allows to specify for how long the data can be processed for a particular purpose. This attribute implies that when all durations for each purpose have expired, the data has to be deleted, since the data cannot be used for any purpose anymore.

Reporting and Notification (R5). We modify the existing PPL ActionNotify DataSubject element and call the newly created action ActionNotify. We provide the attribute recipient that allows to indicate the recipient of the notification and the attribute type that specifies the type of notification to be sent to the recipient.

Controlling Data Location (R6). We propose in A-PPL a standard identifier region to specify the location in the AuthzUseForPurpose element. Thus we define the authorized locations of processing of data for particular purposes.

Auditability (R7). We propose two extensions that relate to audits and collection of evidence. This evidence collection is governed by a new A-PPL trigger `TriggerOnEvidenceRequestReceived`, and a new A-PPL action `ActionEvidence Collection`. The combination of these two elements initiates the evidence collection by the data controller.

Logging (R8). We extend the `ActionLog` element in A-PPL. We introduce several parameters to make explicit which information about an event needs to be logged: a timestamp, the action that is performed on the data, the identity of the subject who performed the action and the purpose of the action (e.g. `marketing`). Other details can also be written in the logs such as some security flags that may state whether the log entry is encrypted.

Note that possible conflicts between accountable obligations are not addressed by A-PPL. As studied in our report [5], we consider that these conflicts are solved before mapping the obligations to A-PPL policies.

3.3   A-PPLE (A-PPL Engine): The Extension of the PPL Engine

The policy engine supporting PPL was originally designed in PrimeLife project [15]. We briefly present the new architecture of A-PPLE whereby we extend and modify the PPL engine's architecture to implement the new features of the A-PPL policy language. The core elements of A-PPLE are the Policy Enforcement Point (PEP) and the Policy Decision Point (PDP). While the PEP acts as an orchestrator of the enforcement process and interfaces with the Web Services, the PDP is the component where the access control decision is taken. PDP relies on the access control engine implementation based on HERAS [9] for the evaluation of the XACML part of an A-PPL policy. Apart from the standard attribute-based access control, the other information evaluated by the PDP at the step of access control decision is usage authorization. The PEP coordinates two modules: the Event and Obligation Handlers. The functionality of the Event Handler is to fire the events related to the personal data lifecycle, e.g. when data is deleted from the Personal Data store or when it is shared with the third parties. The Obligation Handler keeps track of the triggers that are part of the obligation statements in the A-PPL policy. Once the events are observed, the action associated with the obligation is activated by the Obligation Engine. We also define an additional and central component for handling the audit requests which will facilitate the process of retrieving the necessary information from the systems (logs related to obligations, notifications, access control decisions and personal data lifecycle). Finally, each component in the engine architecture (Obligation Handler, Event Handler, PDP and PEP) are linked with the logging Handler to record all data sensitive actions in a non-repudiable manner. More details on the new A-PPL engine can be found in [1].

4   Example of Use of A-PPL

In this section we present a use case that illustrates how accountability obligations can be expressed using A-PPL. The use case that we describe is a healthcare system that will be used to support elderly people by analyzing medical data collected by sensors. We investigate a case where medical data from the sensors will be exchanged between the elderly, their families and friends, hospital caregivers and healthcare personnel. The proposed solution is the M Platform, which is a cloud-based service for medical sensor data collection, processing, storage and visualization. The sensor data will be transmitted to the cloud where they will be further processed and stored. The M Platform is offered to the hospital as a service from a European software and service provider M, which has outsourced both the initial storage of data collected through the sensors placed by hospital staff (Cloud x, which is provided by X) as well as the long-term data storage and back-up procedures (Cloud y, which is provided by Y). Further details about this healthcare system can be found in [1–3]. To comply with the European Data Protection Directive [7], as well as with the contractual relationships that must exist between the involved actors, a number of accountability obligations can be derived for the healthcare use case. Here we outline some of the most prominent ones with their mapping into A-PPL statements. Further details on the obligations can be found in [3].

Obligation 1: The right to access, correct and delete personal data. The hospital must ensure that the patients have read, write and delete access to their personal data that have been collected and stored in the cloud. The right to delete is expressed in Listing 1.1 as XACML rules that A-PPL is built upon. Similar rules can be specified for read and write access.

Listing 1.1. Access control

```
<Rule Effect="Permit"RuleId="DS_access">
 <Target>
  <Subject>
   <SubjectMatch MatchId="function:string-equal">
    <AttributeValue DataType="string">Data Subject</AttributeValue>
    <SubjectAttributeDesignator DataType="string"
      AttributeId="subject:role-id"/>
   </SubjectMatch>
  </Subject>
  <Action>
   <ActionMatch MatchId="string-equal">
    <AttributeValue DataType="string">delete</AttributeValue>
    <ActionAttributeDesignator DataType="string"
      AttributeId="action-id"/>
   </ActionMatch>
  </Action>
 </Target>
</Rule>
```

Obligation 2: Purpose of processing. The hospital must make sure that the patients' personal data is only processed for specific, explicit and legitimate purposes. Listing 1.2 shows an A-PPL statement that specifies the purposes and their respective durations of use of the collected data.

Listing 1.2. Authorization for the specified list of purposes

```
<a-ppl:AuthzUseForPurpose>
 <a-ppl:Purpose duration=2Y region=Europe>diagnosis</a-ppl:Purpose>
 <a-ppl:Purpose duration=5Y region=Europe>research</a-ppl:Purpose>
</a-ppl:AuthzUseForPurpose>
```

Obligation 3: Breach notification. In case of security or personal data breaches, cloud providers X and Y must notify M, which in turn must notify the hospital and the hospital must notify the patients. Listing 1.3 shows an example of the use of the `ActionNotify` element whereby the data controller is hold responsible for notification in case of a policy violation[2] or a loss of data.

Listing 1.3. Notify the data subject in case of a breach

```
<Obligation>
 <TriggersSet>
  <TriggerOnPolicyViolation/>
  <TriggerOnDataLost/>
 </TriggersSet>
 <ActionNotify>
  <Media>e-mail</Media>
  <Address>data-subject@example.com</Address>
  <Recipients>Patient:Data subject</Recipients>
  <Type>Policy Violation</Type>
 </ActionNotify>
</Obligation>
```

Obligation 4: Evidence of the correct and timely deletion of personal data. Cloud providers X and Y must be able to provide evidence to the platform provider M, and M must be able to provide evidence to the hospital on the correct and timely deletion of personal data. Listing 1.4 shows an example of logging of the delete action and Listing 1.5 collects these logs as evidence.

Listing 1.4. Log deletion

```
<Obligation>
 <TriggerPersonal-
DataDeleted>
 </TriggerPersonal-
DataDeleted>
 <ActionLog>
  <Timestamp/>
  <Action/>
  <Purpose/>
  <Subject/>
  <Resource/>>
 </ActionLog>
</Obligation>
```

Listing 1.5. Evidence of data deletion

```
<Obligation>
 <TriggerEvidenceRequestReceived>
 </TriggerEvidenceRequestReceived>
 <ActionEvidenceCollection>
  <Evidence>
   <Attribute AttributeId="evidence-type">
    <AttributeValue>Logs of deletion</AttributeValue>
   </Attribute>
  </Evidence>
  <Resource>
   <Attribute AttributeId="resource-id">
    <AttributeValue>Personal Data</AttributeValue>
   </Attribute>
  </Resource>
 </ActionEvidenceCollection>
</Obligation>
```

---

[2] Violations are detected by an external tool that takes A-PPL policies as inputs.

Obligation 5: Location of processing. Cloud providers X and Y, as well as the M Platform provider have contractual obligations towards their respective customers on the location of the data processing. Listing 1.2 presents an example of how to specify authorized location of processing.

5 Related Work

Various work design a language for specifying obligations such as [6, 10, 12, 13, 15]. But little focus has been put on a language for accountability. For instance, [10] proposes an extension of the XACML architecture to enable the enforcement of obligations related to access control decisions.

Contemporaneous work by Butin et al. [4] leverages PPL to design logs for accountability. They identify the lack of expressiveness of PPL `ActionLog` which does not provide sufficient information in the logs. Besides, they discuss the fact that the PPL element `ActionNotifyDataSubject` does not allow to specify the content of the notification. Our accountability language A-PPL proposes a solution for these two above problems.

Similarly, Henze et al. [8] identify location and duration of storage as the two main challenges in cloud data handling scenarios. They use PPL to specify *data annotations* that contain the data handling obligations (e.g. "delete after 30 days"). Without giving more details, they propose to extend PPL with elements that specify a maximum and a minimum duration of storage and with an element that restricts the location of data. A-PPL addresses these two challenges and we give in Sect. 3.2 the details of the extensions that solve these issues.

6 Conclusion

In this paper, we defined the design requirements for an accountability policy language. We presented A-PPL, an extension of PPL, that handles accountability specific requirements such as notification, logging and evidence collection. We also described an architecture of A-PPLE, the policy engine that enforces A-PPL policies. Finally, we extracted several obligations from a healthcare use case and defined the corresponding A-PPL rules.

Our future work will consist in the finalization of A-PPLE and its integration in a real setting that combines enforcement tools (such as an audit system).

Acknowledgments. This work was supported by the European Commission's Seventh framework A4Cloud (http://www.a4cloud.eu/) project. We thank Dimitra Stefanatou for her help on the analysis of accountability obligations.

References

1. Azraoui, M., Elkhiyaoui, K., Önen, M., Bernsmed, K., de Oliveira, A.S., Sendor, J.: A-PPL: An Accountability Policy Language. Technical report (2014)
2. Bernsmed, K., Felici, M., de Oliveira, A.S., Sendor, J., Moe, N.B., Rübsamen, T., Tountopoulos, V., Hasnain, B.: Use case descriptions. Deliverable, Cloud Accountability (A4Cloud) Project (2013)
3. Bernsmed, K., Kuan, H., Millard, C.: Deploying Medical Sensor Networks in the Cloud - Accountability Obligations from a European Perspective. Submitted for publication (2014)
4. Butin, D., Chicote, M., Le Métayer, D.: Log design for accountability. In: 2013 IEEE Security and Privacy Workshops (SPW), pp. 1–7. IEEE (2013)
5. Cherrueau, R.-A., Douence, R., Grall, H., Royer, J.-C., Sellami, M., Südholt, M., Azraoui, M., Elkhiyaoui, K., Molva, R., Önen, M., Garaga, A., de Oliveira, A.S., Sendor, J., Bernsmed, K.: Policy representation framework. Deliverable (to be published), Cloud Accountability (A4Cloud) Project (2013)
6. Cuppens, F., Cuppens-Boulahia, N.: Modeling contextual security policies. Int. J. Inf. Secur. **7**(4), 285–305 (2008)
7. European Parliament. Directive 95/46/EC of the European Parliament and of the Council of 24 October 1995 on the protection of individuals with regard to the processing of personal data and on the free movement of such data (1995)
8. Henze, M., Großfengels, M., Koprowski, M., Wehrle, K.: Towards data handling requirements-aware cloud computing. In: 2013 IEEE International Conference on Cloud Computing Technology and Science (CloudCom) (2013)
9. HERAS AF team. HERAS AF (Holistic Enterprise-Ready Application Security Architecture Framework). http://herasaf.org/
10. Li, N., Chen, H., Bertino, E.: On practical specification and enforcement of obligations. In: Proceedings of the Second ACM Conference on Data and Application Security and Privacy, pp. 71–82. ACM (2012)
11. Lin, A., Chen, N.-C.: Cloud computing as an innovation: percepetion, attitude, and adoption. Int. J. Inf. Manage. **32**(6), 533–540 (2012)
12. OASIS Standard. eXtensible Access Control Markup Language (XACML) Version 3.0. 22 January 2013. http://docs.oasis-open.org/xacml/3.0/xacml-3.0-core-spec-os-en.html
13. Papagiannakopoulou, E.I., et al.: Leveraging ontologies upon a holistic privacy-aware access control model. In: Danger, J.L., Debbabi, M., Marion, J.-Y., Garcia-Alfaro, J., Heywood, N.Z. (eds.) FPS 2013. LNCS, vol. 8352, pp. 209–226. Springer, Heidelberg (2014)
14. Pearson, S., Tountopoulos, V., Catteddu, D., Sudholt, M., Molva, R., Reich, C., Fischer-Hubner, S., Millard, C., Lotz, V., Jaatun, M., Leenes, R., Rong, C., Lopez, J.: Accountability for cloud and other future internet services. In: 2012 IEEE 4th International Conference on Cloud Computing Technology and Science (CloudCom), pp. 629–632 (2012)
15. Trabelsi, S., Neven, G., Raggett, D., Ardagna, C., Bournez, C., Bussard, L., Bezzi, M., Camenisch, J., de Capitani di Vimercati, S., Gey, F., Kuczerawy, A., Meissner, S., Neven, G., Njeh, A., Paraboschi, S., Pedrini, E., Foresti, S., Pinsdorf, U., Preiss, F.-S., Sendor, J., Tziviskou, C., Raggett, D., Roessler, T., Samarati, P., Schallaboeck, J., Short, S., Sommer, D., Verdicchio, M., Wenning, R.: D5.3.4 - report on design and implementation of the primelife policy language and engine. Deliverable, Primelife Project (2011)

Privacy-Preserving Electronic Toll System with Dynamic Pricing for Low Emission Zones

Roger Jardí-Cedó(✉), Jordi Castellà-Roca, and Alexandre Viejo

Dpt. d'Enginyeria Informàtica i Matemàtiques, UNESCO Chair in Data Privacy, Universitat Rovira i Virgili, Av. Països Catalans 26, 43007 Tarragona, Spain
{roger.jardi,jordi.castella,alexandre.viejo}@urv.cat

Abstract. Low emission zones (LEZs) aim to reduce pollution and traffic congestion in cities. Current proposals for managing LEZs introduce a significant error percentage in the detection of fraudulent drivers and represent a serious privacy threat for the honest ones. In this article, a new electronic toll system to improve both issues is proposed.

Keywords: Electronic road pricing · Low emission zone · Driver privacy · Security

1 Introduction

Traffic congestion has become a significant problem for almost all major cities and governments have introduced toll systems to solve it. These systems have received a lot of attention [1–8]. The main reason behind the success of this approach is that it enables an authority to restrict the access to drivers willing to pay a certain amount of money. In this way, a Low Emission Zone (LEZ) is a restricted area that vehicles can access in exchange for a payment according to the vehicles' carbon emissions. LEZs can adjust the variable prices to manage the flow of vehicles by increasing toll taxes in congested roads and suggesting drivers to take cheaper routes (i.e., they are dynamic).

In general, Electronic Road Pricing (ERP) systems calculate road usage pricing by considering the vehicles' itinerary. Vehicles are equipped with e on-board units (OBU) to record their paths. Each OBU is enabled with GPS and wireless communication capabilities; they periodically collect their geographical position; and send them to a service provider. To avoid fraud, current proposals adopt control mechanisms with the use of checkpoints ($Chps$), which are equipped with cameras and are randomly located in the LEZs. Chps take pictures of all vehicles and, hence, their number plates are stored together with the corresponding geo-positions and time. These three items allow the ERP to build a partial path of all the vehicles moving around the restricted area and verify that a certain driver has not altered the set of positions recorded by her car's OBU and provided to the SP during the billing period.

This fraud detection mechanism has a certain failure probability that directly depends on the number of Chps deployed in the restricted area. In addition,

© Springer International Publishing Switzerland 2015
J. Garcia-Alfaro et al. (Eds.): DPM/SETOP/QASA 2014, LNCS 8872, pp. 327–334, 2015.
DOI: 10.1007/978-3-319-17016-9_22

increasing the number of checkpoints directly affects drivers' privacy due to the fact that, the more checkpoints there are, the bigger the set of registered real drivers' locations will be; and therefore, the more accurate the drivers' paths will be.

In this article, a new prepayment *ERP* system for Low Emission Zones (*LEZ*s) is proposed. This system provides: (1) a non-probabilistic fraud control and (2) honest drivers' privacy through revocable anonymity. The system is presented in Sect. 2. The protocol is introduced in Sect. 3. Security is evaluated in Sect. 4, and conclusions are presented in Sect. 5.

2   System Model

Driver D is the person who drives. *Vehicle V* is the means of transport registered by a unique *D*. *V* has an identifier, the vehicle plate. Each *V* has a *Secure element SE* (tamper-proof module) and an *On-board unit OBU* (which has location capabilities and wireless connections).

A *LEZ* is divided into a set of street stretches. A *stretch* is a one-way section of street where *V*s have to pay every time they drive through it. Each stretch is divided into a *payment area* and a traffic *restricted area*. The prices of each stretch are dynamically set according to its traffic density. A *Beacon* is a device, placed at the *payment area*, which constantly warns the *V*s entering the stretch. A *Checkpoint Chp*, placed at the entrance of the *restricted area* of a *stretch*, aims to control the access of vehicles that enter the stretch. *Service Provider SP*, which manages both component types, offers an ERP service for urban areas. *Ticket Provider TP* issues tickets to *V*s.

A *Vehicle Certification Authority VCA* provides keys and certificates to *V*s. A *Payment Service PS* enables *D*s to pay. The electronic payment system is out of scope of this article. Finally, a *Punisher authority PA* knows the identity of the *V* owner and reveals it in case of fraud.

Anti-fraud Requirements. When a *V* enters a *stretch* of a *LEZ* through a *Chp*, it obtains a *ticket* ζ^*. This ζ^* contains information to prove that a specific *V* has the right to enter at a specific time. This *proof* is considered **valid** when it has the following properties: integrity, authenticity, non-repudiation, single-use and temporality. **Fraud** is commited when a *D* drives in a *stretch* without a ζ^*, with an invalid ζ^* or with a valid ζ^* associated with another *V/stretch*. A *SP* cannot **falsely accuse** an honest *D* of fraud.

Authenticity Requirements. At the entrance of a *stretch*, *V* and *Chp* must prove their identity to the other part.

Privacy Requirements. The system must (1) assure the privacy (the identity of *D* or *V* cannot be linked to any itinerary); (2) avoid the linkability between itineraries; and (3) provide revocable anonymity to *D*.

3   Protocol Description

3.1   Setup

Before starting the system, the next entities are initialized as follows:

1. PA obtains from authorities: (1) An asymmetric key pair (Pk_{PA}, Sk_{PA}), (2) its public key certificate $cert_{PA}$, and (3) a certificate repository of the authorities.
2. SP and VCA obtain from authorities: (1) An asymmetric key pair (Pk_{SP}, Sk_{SP}) and (Pk_{VCA}, Sk_{VCA}), (2) its public key certificate $cert_{SP}$ and $cert_{VCA}$, and (3) a certificate repository of the authorities.
3. VCA:
   i. Defines: (1) A set of vehicles $V = \{v_1, ..., v_{nv}\}$, where $n_V = |V|$; (2) a collection of sets $K = \{C_1, ..., C_{n_K}\}$ partition of V, where $n_K = |K|$, with $|C_i| = n_C, \forall i$
   ii. Generates and associates a certification entity VCA_{C_i} to each element of the subset K $(C_1, ..., C_{n_K})$: (1) An asymmetric key pair $(Pk_{VCA_{C_i}}, Sk_{VCA_{C_i}})$, $\forall i \in \{1, ..., n_K\}$ and, (2) a CA certificate $cert_{VCA_{C_i}}$, $\forall i \in \{1, ..., n_K\}$, which has an expiration time c_{exp}
4. TP and each Chp apply the following steps:
   i. Obtain a certificate repository of the authorities and entities
   ii. Generate an asymmetric key pair (Pk_{TP}, Sk_{TP}) and (Pk_{Chp}, Sk_{Chp})
   iii. Securely obtain a public key certificate $cert_{TP}$ and $cert_{Chp}$ from SP. $cert_{Chp}$ contains an extension $cert_{Chp}.loc$ with its location coordinates and a stretch identifier $cert_{Chp}.str$
5. Each $Beacon$ is initialized by SP with a warning advise $information\text{-}of\text{-}stretch$ $\beta_{str}{}^* = (\beta_{str}, \overline{\beta_{str}})$, where $\overline{\beta_{str}}$ is the signature of β_{str} $(Sign_{SP}(\beta_{str}))$, and where β_{str} contains information of: (1) the street stretch (str and GPS cord.); and (2) the TP connection (it defines how to access TP)
6. VCA certificates the Vs (it is assumed that the SE of each V has been previously initialized with a certificate repository of the certification authorities, identifying information of the vehicle V_{id} and its technical specifications): (1) Register V in an element of the subset K (in a C_i) and (2) download the certification entity VCA_{C_i} $(Pk_{VCA_{C_i}}, Sk_{VCA_{C_i}}$ and $cert_{VCA_{C_i}})$ associated to C_i by a secure channel in the SE.

3.2   Price Generation

Every fixed period of time τ, SP establishes the prices of each stretch str, depending on its traffic density, by performing the next operations:

1. Set the $prices$ per emission category (i.e. European Emission Standards), searching a balance between supply and demand.
2. Compose $information\text{-}of\text{-}prices$ $\alpha_{str} = (str, prices, p_{exp}, acc_d)$, where p_{exp} is the expiration time of the prices and acc_d identifies the SP destination account of the electronic payment system assumed.
3. Sign α_{str}: $Sign_{SP}(\alpha_{str}) = \overline{\alpha_{str}}$, send $\alpha_{str}{}^* = (\alpha_{str}, \overline{\alpha_{str}})$ to TP.

3.3 Certificate Generation

When V enters a LEZ, its SE generates new credentials. Its SE:

1. Computes an asymmetric key pair (Pk_{V_q}, Sk_{V_q})
2. Generates a public key certificate $cert_{V_q}$ with the next attributes: (1) An extension $cert_{V_q}.idS$ containing the probabilistic encryption of the vehicle identifier V_{id} with the public key of PA: $Enc_{Pk_{VCA}}(V_{id})$; and (2) an extension $cert_{V_q}.em$ containing its pollutant emission category.

3.4 Purchase

When a V enters a payment area, the purchase protocol is applied:

1. *Beacons* send *information-of-stretch* $\beta_{str}{}^*$
2. The SE of the V, with the help of the OBU, has to:
   i. Verify the signature $\overline{\beta_{str}}$: $Verif_{SP}(\beta_{str}, \overline{\beta_{str}})$ and its GPS location
   ii. Establish with TP a secure and secret communication channel
   iii. Extract str from β_{str} and send TP a request for the prices of str
3. TP sends $\alpha_{str}{}^*$ to V
4. The SE of the V, with the help of the OBU, has to:
   i. Verify the signature $\overline{\alpha_{str}}$: $Verif_{SP}(str, prices, p_{exp} \, acc_d, \overline{\alpha_{str}})$, and the freshness of $\alpha_{str}{}^*$:$|p_{exp}\text{-}current\ time| < \tau'$ (a fixed time)
   ii. Obtain the *amount* to pay, according to its pollutant emissions
   iii. Compose a *payment order* $\gamma = (acc_s, amount, acc_d)$, where acc_s is the source account of the user, and acc_d is the destination account
   iv. Sign γ: $Sign_{V_q}(\gamma) = \overline{\gamma}$ and send $\gamma^* = (\gamma, \overline{\gamma})$ and its certificate $cert_{V_q}$ to PS. γ includes additional information, which indicates the source account and authenticates its owner in front of PS.
5. PS has to: (1) Perform the actions belonging to the used payment system; and (2) compose $\delta = (trans_{id}, hash(\overline{\gamma}))$, sign δ: $Sign_{PS}(\delta) = \overline{\delta}$, and send $trans_{id}$ and $\overline{\delta}$ to V;
6. The SE of the V, with the help of the OBU, has to:
   i. Compute $hash(\overline{\gamma})$, recompose δ and verify $\overline{\delta}$: $Verif_{PS}(\delta, \overline{\delta})$
   ii. Compute $hash(\overline{\delta})$ and compose a *ticket request* $\epsilon = (str, ts, hash(\overline{\delta}))$, where ts is the current time
   iii. Sign ϵ: $Sign_{V_q}(\epsilon) = \overline{\epsilon}$, and send $\epsilon^* = (\epsilon, \overline{\epsilon})$ and its $cert_{V_q}$ to TP
7. TP has to:
   i. Verify the certificate $cert_{V_q}$ and the signature $\overline{\epsilon}$: $Verif_{V_q}(\epsilon, \overline{\epsilon})$
   ii. Verify the freshness of ts:$|ts\text{-}current\ time| < \tau'$, where τ' is a fixed time
   iii. Compute $hash(\overline{\epsilon})$ and the fingerprint $fing_{V_q}$ of $cert_{V_q}$
   iv. Compose a *ticket* $\zeta = (str, ts, fing_{V_q}, hash(\overline{\epsilon}))$, sign it: $Sign_{Chp}(\zeta) = \overline{\zeta}$, send $\zeta^* = (\zeta, \overline{\zeta})$ to V, and send ϵ^* and ζ^* to SP
8. The SE of the V, with the help of the OBU, computes $hash(\overline{\epsilon})$, and verifies the signature $\overline{\zeta}$: $Verif_{TP}(str, ts, fing_{V_q}, hash(\overline{\epsilon}), \overline{\zeta})$

3.5   Entrance

When a Chp detects the V, the protocol is applied:

1. Chp generates a nonce N_A, and sends N_A and the $cert_{Chp}$ to V
2. SE of the V, with the help of the OBU, has to:
    i. Verify the certificate $cert_{Chp}$, $cert_{Chp}.loc$ and $cert_{Chp}.str = str$
    ii. Generate a nonce N_B and compute the $fing_{Chp}$ of $cert_{Chp}$
    iii. Compose an *entrance request* $\eta = (N_A, fing_{Chp}, N_B, \zeta^*)$ and sign it: $Sign_{V_q}(\eta) = \overline{\eta}$
    iv. Generate a digital envelope of $\eta^* = (\eta, \overline{\eta})$ with the Chp's public key
    v. Send the digital envelope and its $cert_{V_q}$ to Chp
3. Chp has to:
    i. Open the digital envelope with its secret key obtaining η^*
    ii. Verify the certificate $cert_{V_q}$ and the signature $\overline{\eta}$: $Verif_{V_q}(N_A, fing_{Chp}, N_B, \zeta^*, \overline{\eta})$ and generate timestamp ts'
    iii. Verify the signature $\overline{\zeta}$: $Verif_{TP}(\zeta, \overline{\zeta})$
    iv. Verify $cert_{Chp}.str = str$ (extracted from ϵ, included in ζ) and verify the freshness of ζ^*:$|ts - ts'| < \tau''$, where τ'' is a time which is fixed according to the traffic volume of the stretch.
    v. Compute the $fing'_{V_q}$ of $cert_{V_q}$ and verify $fing'_{V_q} = fing_{V_q}$
    vi. If one of the verifications fails or ζ^* has not sent, Chp performs the following operations: (1) Generate an incidence number of entrance in_i; (2) Take a photo ph of V and extract the plate number plt; (3) Compose a *proof-of-entrance incidence* $\theta_i = (in_o, plt, ph, ts', \eta^*, cert_{V_q})$; (4) Sign θ_i: $Sign_{Chp}(\theta_i) = \overline{\theta_i}$ and send $\theta_i^* = (\theta_i, \overline{\theta_i})$ to SP.
    vii. If the verifications performed in 3ii–3v are correct, the Chp has to: (1) Compose *proof-of-entrance* $\iota = (ts', \eta^*, cert_{V_q})$; (2) Sign ι: $Sign_{Chp}(\iota) = \overline{\iota}$, and send ts' and $\overline{\iota}$ to the V
4. If the verifications performed in 3ii–3v are correct, SE of the V, with the help of the OBU, verifies the certificate $cert_{Chp}$ and the signature $\overline{\iota}$: $Verif_{Chp}(ts', N_A, fing_{Chp}, N_B, \zeta^*, \overline{\eta}, cert_{V_q}, \overline{\iota})$

3.6   Payment Verification

TP sends SP *ticket requests* ϵ^* and *tickets* ζ^* periodically. Each Chp sends *proof-of-entrances* ι^* and *proof-of-entrance incidences* θ_i^*. SP then forwards the incidences θ_i^* to PA. Moreover, SP verifies a posteriori the payment performed by each V according to the following operations:

1. Define a set of *proof-of-entrance* $I = \{\iota_1^*, ..., \iota_{n_\iota}^*\}$ and a set of *ticket request* $E = \{\epsilon_1^*, \epsilon_2^*, ..., \epsilon_{n_\epsilon}^*\}$, where n_ι is the number of *proof-of-entrance* and n_ϵ is the number of *ticket request* sent to TP
2. Select a subset E' from E (each ϵ_i^* has been used by some D)
3. Verify that there is a unique ϵ in the set E' with the same $hash(\overline{\delta})$
4. For each *proof-of-entrance* ι^*:

i. Extract str, ts and $hash(\bar{\epsilon})$ from $ticket$ ζ
ii. Recover the prevailing $information\text{-}of\text{-}prices$ $\alpha_{str}{}^*$ of the stretch str at time ts, and extract $prices$ from α_{str} and $cert_{V_q}.em$ from ι
iii. Obtain from $prices$ the $amount'$ to pay according to $cert_{V_q}.em$
iv. Verify whether the transfer, referenced by $hash(\bar{\epsilon})$, was successful, and recover the $amount$ of money paid
v. Verify that $amount = amount'$
vi. Verify that ζ^* is unique in the set I

5. If one of the verifications fails, SP then needs to:
   i. Generate an incidence number of verification in_v
   ii. Compose $proof\text{-}of\text{-}verification$ $incidence$ θ_v, including ι^* concerned: $\theta_v = (in_v, \iota^*)$. In the case of a reused ζ^*, add $\iota^{*'}$ to $\theta_v = (in_v, \iota^*, \iota^{*'})$. Moreover, when a $hash(\bar{\delta})$ is reused, θ_v is supplemented with both $ticket$ $requests$ of the $proof\text{-}of\text{-}entrances$ proving it: $\theta_v = (in_v, \iota^*, \iota^{*'}, \epsilon^*, \epsilon^{*'})$
   iii. Sign θ_v: $Sign_{SP}(\theta_v) = \overline{\theta_v}$ and send $\theta_v{}^* = (\theta_v, \overline{\theta_v})$ to PA.

3.7 Sanction

For each received θ, PA performs the following operations:

1. In the case of θ_i, PA verifies the signatures and extracts the number plate plt from the photograph ph, included in θ_i
2. In the case of θ_v PA has to:
   i. Verify all the signatures included in θ_v and the signatory of ι
   ii. Verify the right payment by repeating steps 4i–4v of phase Sect. 3.6
   iii. In case of a reused ζ^*, verify that it is the same in ι and ι'
   iv. In case of a reused $hash(\bar{\delta})$, verify the $hash(\bar{\epsilon})$ of ζ^* (included in ι references ϵ^*) and the $hash(\bar{\epsilon})'$ of $\zeta^{*'}$ (included in ι' references $\epsilon^{*'}$), and verify that both ϵ^* and $\epsilon^{*'}$ have the same $hash(\bar{\delta})$
   v. If the incidence is confirmed, recover the identifier V_{id} of V_q by opening the extension $cert_{V_q}.idS$ of the certificate $cert_{V_q}$, included in ι: Dec_{PA} $(cert_{V_q}.idS) = V_{id}$. In the case of a reused $hash(\bar{\delta})$, the identifier V'_{id} of the second vehicle V_q' is also recovered in the same way from ι'
3. Notify the owner of V, using plt or V_{id}, about the sanctioning procedure and request her contrary evidences to refute her accusation.
4. Verify the contrary evidences presented by the owner of the V. In the case of a reused $hash(\bar{\delta})$, the evidences should include the hashes, which allow to evaluate the pre-images of the hash chain, and the first value of the hash chain $\bar{\gamma}$, which proves the signature authorship.
5. Fine the owner of the V if the presented evidences are not valid.

4 Security and Requirement Analysis

The system preserves authenticity, non-repudiation, integrity, single-use and temporality for the $tickets$ to be considered **valid** since:

- The creation of fraudulent *tickets* is computationally unfeasible nowadays without the knowledge of Sk_{TP} in the signature.
- *TP* cannot deny their emission, the issuer's identity is linked to the proofs, and for the properties of the electronic signature scheme, it cannot deny its authorship.
- The modification of the content of the *tickets* by Vs is computationally unfeasible nowadays since the hash summary function used in the signature scheme is collision-resistant, and without the knowledge of the *TP* secret key.
- A *ticket* cannot be reused to enter a stretch without being detected because it is considered unique. A ticket can only be created by *TP*, only one ticket at the same time.
- *Tickets* cannot be used to enter a stretch after their expiration because each ticket cannot be modified and contains the time *ts* of its emission, which is verified by the *TP*.

The toll system is resistant to **fraud** since users who enter a stretch without a ticket (in step 3vi of Sect. 3.5), with no valid ticket, or with a valid ticket associated with another user or stretch, are detected (in step 3v of Sect. 3.5). Otherwise, the system protects users against **false accusations** since the protocol execution generates records signed by the involved entities, which prove the user has entered the stretch without committing fraud. She will then be able to retrieve some of these records and provide them to *PA* in order to prove its own honesty.

The system preserves **anonymity** and **traceability** between user itineraries (an itinerary starts each time V enters a *LEZ*) to honest drivers since: (1) The information that can identify a user ($cert_{V_q}.idS$, which contains V_{id}) does not reveal the user's identity because this information is encrypted using the public key of *PA*. The certificate $cert_{V_q}$ can be neither identify them thanks to the fact that the CA, is shared with several users and because each user is registered in an element of the subset K together with other users; and (2) the *SE* generates a new $cert_{V_q}$ for the vehicle in each new *LEZ* entrance. Nobody can neither relate the identity of the V of this itinerary with any other nor know whether two certificates belong to the same user, as there are K different CAs.

The system provides **anonymity revocation** for dishonest drivers according to how fraud is detected:

- In case of a reused ticket, the amount paid does not correspond to the tax determined for τ, or emissions of V, or a reused transfer reference $hash(\bar{\delta})$ are detected, *SP* sends θ_v to *PA*. *PA* verifies the incidence and identifies the user by opening the field $certV_q.idS$ of the certificate with its private key. Obtaining V_{id} allows the identification and punishment of the dishonest user.
- In other cases of fraud, the user is identified when she is photographed by the *Chp* at the entrance of a stretch. The user then loses her anonymity as the vehicle number plate is captured.

5   Conclusions

This paper has presented an *ERP* system for urban areas with an enhanced dynamic pricing, which provides a robust fraud control system and a high level of privacy. The entrance process of a *LEZ* is controlled so that the legitimate tax is dynamically computed depending on the traffic volume while the anonymity of the user is preserved. However, if a user commits fraud, she will then be identified by the picture of the number plate taken by the checkpoint in conjunction with the anonymity revocation system of the protocol.

Acknowledgments and disclaimer. This work was partially supported by the Government of Catalonia under grant 2009 SGR 1135 and by the Spanish Government under CO-PRIVACY TIN2011-27076-C03-01, ARES-CONSOLIDER INGENIO 2010 CSD2007-00004, BallotNext IPT-2012-0603-430000 and MOBILE KEY RTC-2014-2552-7 projects and the FPI grant BES-2012-054780.

References

1. Balasch, J., Rial, A., Troncoso, C., Preneel, B., Verbauwhede, I., Geuens, C.: Pretp: Privacy-preserving electronic toll pricing. In: USENIX Security Symposium, pp. 63–78 (2010)
2. Chen, X., Lenzini, G., Mauw, S., Pang, J.: A group signature based electronic toll pricing system. In: ARES, pp. 85–93. IEEE Computer Society (2012)
3. Day, J., Huang, Y., Knapp, E., Goldberg, I.: Spectre: spot-checked private ecash tolling at roadside. In: WPES, pp. 61–68. ACM (2011)
4. Garcia, F.D., Verheul, E.R., Jacobs, B.: Cell-based privacy-friendly roadpricing. Comput. Math. Appl. **65**(5), 774–785 (2013)
5. Hoepman, J.-H., Huitema, G.: Privacy enhanced fraud resistant road pricing. In: Berleur, J., Hercheui, M.D., Hilty, L.M. (eds.) HCC9 2010. IFIP AICT, vol. 328, pp. 202–213. Springer, Heidelberg (2010)
6. de Jonge, W., Jacobs, B.: Privacy-friendly electronic traffic pricing via commits. In: Degano, P., Guttman, J., Martinelli, F. (eds.) FAST 2008. LNCS, vol. 5491, pp. 143–161. Springer, Heidelberg (2009)
7. Meiklejohn, S., Mowery, K., Checkoway, S., Shacham, H.: The phantom tollbooth: Privacy-preserving electronic toll collection in the presence of driver collusion. In: USENIX Security Symposium, pp. 32–32 (2011)
8. Popa, R.A., Balakrishnan, H., Blumberg, A.J.: Vpriv: Protecting privacy in location-based vehicular services. In: USENIX Security Symposium, pp. 335–350. USENIX Association (2009)

Association Rule Mining on Fragmented Database

Amel Hamzaoui[1][✉], Qutaibah Malluhi[1], Chris Clifton[2], and Ryan Riley[1]

[1] Department of Computer Science and Engineering, Qatar University, Doha, Qatar
{Amel.Hamzaoui,Qutaibah.Malluhi,Ryan.Riley}@qu.edu.qa
[2] Department of Computer Science, Purdue University,
West Lafayette, Indiana, USA
Chris.Clifton@cs.purdue.edu

Abstract. Anonymization methods are an important tool to protect privacy. The goal is to release data while preventing individuals from being identified. Most approaches generalize data, reducing the level of detail so that many individuals appear the same. An alternate class of methods, including anatomy, fragmentation, and slicing, preserves detail by generalizing only the link between identifying and sensitive data. We investigate learning association rules on such a database. Association rule mining on a generalized database is challenging, as specific values are replaced with generalizations, eliminating interesting fine-grained correlations. We instead learn association rules from a fragmented database, preserving fine-grained values. Only rules involving both identifying and sensitive information are affected; we demonstrate the efficacy of learning in such environment.

Keywords: Anonymity · Fragmentation · Database · Association rule mining · Data privacy

1 Introduction

Worldwide, the amount of data being collected and stored every day is growing at a rapid pace. Because of this data explosion, organizations are increasingly looking to data outsourcing for storage and its management. In some cases, the data being outsourced may contain personal information of individuals and outsourcing it to a third party could result in a privacy violation for those individuals. In response to this, a number of approaches for anonymizing data have been proposed [2–4, 6, 7].

Complex data analysis, such as data mining, would need to involve computations from both the data host, who has a copy of the anonymized data, and the data owner, who knows the secrets required to de-anonymize the data. For example, revealing a new trend or relationship in the health care field can allow researchers to develop new advances to save lives or to prevent sickness.

We propose a mining technique that expands the data set on the server by using the groups (used for the anonymization) to extract association rules on a

© Springer International Publishing Switzerland 2015
J. Garcia-Alfaro et al. (Eds.): DPM/SETOP/QASA 2014, LNCS 8872, pp. 335–342, 2015.
DOI: 10.1007/978-3-319-17016-9_23

ID	Age	Disease	Treatment
A	30	Heart disease	Surgery
B	42	Flu	Intravenous therapy
C	28	Stomach	Intravenous therapy
D	35	Heart disease	Medicine
...	...	...	...

Fig. 1. Original database

fragmented database. We study the impact of the fragmentation/anatomy group size on the quality of the produced association rules. The approach we propose relies on the difficulty of applying mining tools on an anatomized database. Our work is different from mining in anonymous data because we deal with the fragmentation of the tables rather than generalization of the data values.

We conduct a set of experiments to evaluate our mining technique. We investigate the relationship between the group size and the matching between the rule produced from the original data and from the expanded data. We also study the rank of the first matched rules and the position of unmatched rules. Section 2 gives a detailed description of our proposed method. We evaluate the effectiveness of this approach in Sect. 3.

2   Our Approach

The basic idea behind our approach is to assume that all mappings between identifying and sensitive values in a group are equally likely. This is perhaps a naïve assumption, but is appropriate given our assumption that entities are randomly assigned to groups. We assume also that the k-anonymity is enforced directly on the private data before mining. We assume that data is divided into identifying and multiple sensitive data fragments using an anatomy approach; only the client is able to reconstruct the original identifiable data. Clients who are the source of the data are assumed to have no storage ability. The association rules sent by the server to the client are not confidential.

To accomplish this, we use the simple approach of expanding the data with all possible mappings and finding rules with appropriately scaled support and confidence thresholds. We do not claim this is the most efficient approach; the goal of this paper is to evaluate the utility of learning association rules on anatomized outsourced data rather than the optimal means of doing so. It does have the advantage of exactly preserving data distributions, including multivariate distributions entirely within the quasi-identifiers.

Figure 2 shows a simple example of anatomized database of the original database in the Fig. 1 with two fragments (Fragment 1 = Age and Fragment 2 = disease and treatment). Given no background information about the original data and as we know only the group ID (GID), we use it to expand the anatomized data (see Fig. 3). We produce a combination of the attributes values belonging to the same GID.

ID	Age	GID
1	30	1
2	42	1
3	28	2
4	35	2
...	...	...

Encrypted ID	Disease	Treatment	GID
Encr(1)	Heart disease	Surgery	1
Encr(2)	Flu	Intravenous therapy	1
Encr(3)	Stomach	Intravenous therapy	2
Encr(4)	Heart disease	Medicine	2
...	...	...	...

Fig. 2. Example of fragmentation of the original data (group size =2) where the attribute Age is the quasi-identifier attribute (fragment 1) and disease and treatment are the sensitive attributes (fragment 2)

New ID	Age	Disease	Treatment
1	30	Heart disease	Surgery
2	30	Flu	Intravenous therapy
3	42	Heart disease	Surgery
4	42	Flu	Intravenous therapy
5	28	Stomach disease	Intravenous therapy
6	28	Heart disease	Medicine
7	35	Stomach disease	Intravenous therapy
8	35	Heart disease	Medicine
9	...	...	...

Fig. 3. GID Expansion of the fragmented data: combination of values belonging to the same group ID (GID) from the two fragments.

Since the random assignment of entities to groups means that every group is of size k, it would seem that support and confidence values expressed as frequency ratios would remain the same. After the expansion, any association rule mining technique can be used; for our experiments we use a straightforward implementation of the *a-priori* algorithm from the Weka package [8].

3 Experiments

We investigate the relationship between the group size and the matching between the rules produced from the original data and from the expanded anatomized data. We look not only at the presence in the top rules, but also the frequency rank ordering of the rules. We use as data the Adult database from the UC Irvine machine learning repository [5], which contains census data, and has become a commonly used benchmark for data anonymization. The data set has 6 continuous attributes and 8 categorical attributes. We use three attributes (Age, Education Number, Hours-per-week) to construct two fragments with different combinations of these attributes. After records with missing values have been removed, there are 30,162 records. The only transformation of the data was to discretize the attribute Age into 10 bins. The Education Number attribute ranges from 1 to 16 and the hours-per-week attribute from 1 to 100. For our work, we assume that anonymization is done randomly. We evaluate across multiple such random assignments to determine how significantly this impacts the outcomes. We aim to study the impact of group size which is not well studied in the literature. An exception is [1] that studies the impact of k on the discernability of the data.

3.1 Matching Rule Scores

In this experiment, we are interested in the matching between rules produced by the original data and those produced by the expanded data. We aim to compute how many rules are in common between the rules produced by the server with the expanded data and those that normally would be found by the client with the original data. The experiment is conducted with the three possible combinations of attributes that construct the two fragments. We used:

- The attribute Age versus the attributes Education Number and Hours-per-week as shown in the Fig. 4(a). We denote this combination of attributes in the following as "Combination 1".
- The attributes Age and Education Number versus the attribute Hours-per-week as shown in the Fig. 4(b). We denote this combination of attributes in the following as "Combination 2"
- The attributes Age and Hours-per-week versus the attribute Education Number as shown in the Fig. 4(c). We denote this combination of attributes in the following as "Combination 3"

We obtain the 10, 15 and 20 rules with highest support and confidence for the original data and for the expanded data. As the group assignment is done randomly, for each group size, we repeated the experiment 100 times; Fig. 4 shows the matching scores across the trials. For the most part, the results were identical across the different trials.

We can see in this Fig. 4 that the 10 rules produced by the expanded data with group size from 2 to 128 are almost always the same as the rules produced by the original data; the score of matching is 100 % for the 2 different fragment combinations. Another aspect to consider in these experimental results is that for most of the cases, the result is the same as the group size increases from 2 to 128. In fact, data mining does not necessarily require the individual records, but only distributions and as the distribution is the same whatever the group size, we still have the same scores.

3.2 Top Matching Rule

After having the percentage of matching between the rules produced by the server with the expanded data and those that normally would be found by the client with the original data, we investigate on the ranking of the first relevant rules produced by the server with the expanded data. While for 10 rules, all the rules are good, for 15 and 20 rules the matching score is less than 100 %.

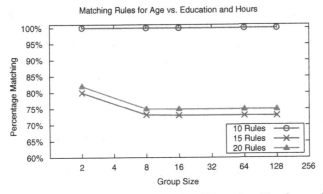

(a) Fragment 1 = Age, Fragment 2 = Education-Number and Hours

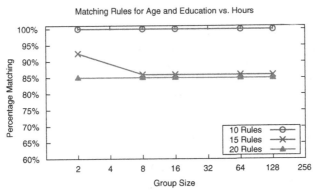

(b) Fragment 1 = Age and Education-Number, Fragment 2 = Hours

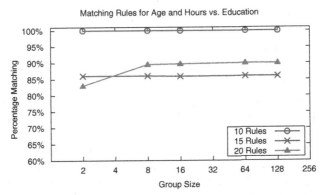

(c) Fragment 1 = Age and Hours, Fragment 2 = Education-Number

Fig. 4. Percentage of matching with the original rules of the rules produced by the expanded data for group size "GSize" (2, 8, 16, 64, 128)

We conducted this experiment to evaluate the ranking of the rules produced by the expanded data that matched with the original data, we call them "Top matching rules". The goal is that when the server receives the list of rules from the server produced from the expanded data, how many first rules the client can trust on knowing that the rules are not all good (percentage of matching is less than 100 % for more than 10 rules).

As before, the experiments are always repeated 100 times to avoid bias as the assignment of the groups is done randomly. Figure 5 shows the top matching for 20 rules produced in the expanded database with different size for the 3 attribute's combinations.

For 20 rules, in the main, the first 10 rules are relevant. This means that the first 50 % of the rules are relevant. As we repeated the experiments 100 times, in some cases the first unmatched rule can take different rank on the list, this is why the top matching rule is not the same for all trials of a group size. Let's consider this example of 20 rules from a data expanded with a group size = 8 by using "Combination 1":

1. Edu=9 $\Rightarrow$ Hours=40 conf:(0.53)
2. Age='(24.3-31.6]' $\Rightarrow$ Hours=40 conf:(0.48)
3. Age='(46.2-53.5]' $\Rightarrow$ Hours=40 conf:(0.48)
4. Age='(31.6-38.9]' $\Rightarrow$ Hours=40 conf:(0.47)
5. Age='(38.9-46.2]' $\Rightarrow$ Hours=40 conf:(0.47)
6. Age='(-inf-24.3]' $\Rightarrow$ Hours=40 conf:(0.46)
7. Edu=10 $\Rightarrow$ Hours=40 conf:(0.44)
8. Edu=13 $\Rightarrow$ Hours=40 conf:(0.43)
9. Hours=40 113184 $\Rightarrow$ Edu=9 conf:(0.36)
10. Age='(31.6-38.9]' $\Rightarrow$ Edu=9 onf:(0.33)
11. Age='(24.3-31.6]' $\Rightarrow$ Edu=9 conf:(0.32)
12. Age='(38.9-46.2]' $\Rightarrow$ Edu=9 conf:(0.32)
13. Age='(-inf-24.3]' $\Rightarrow$ Edu=9 conf:(0.32)
14. Hours=40 $\Rightarrow$ Edu=10 conf:(0.21)
15. Edu=9 $\Rightarrow$ Age='(31.6-38.9]' conf:(0.19)
16. Hours=40 $\Rightarrow$ Age='(38.9-46.2]' conf:(0.19)
17. Hours=40 $\Rightarrow$ Age='(31.6-38.9]' conf:(0.19)
18. Edu=9 $\Rightarrow$ Age='(38.9-46.2]' conf:(0.19)
19. Hours=40 $\Rightarrow$ Age='(24.3-31.6]' conf:(0.18)
20. Edu=9 $\Rightarrow$ Age='(24.3-31.6]' conf:(0.18)

The first unmatched rule of this list of 20 rules is the rule number 11 (Age='(24.3-31.6]' $\Rightarrow$ Edu=9). The Top matching is 10 as the first 10 rules are relevant (the first 10 rules match with rules produced on the original data by the client). There are 5 rules that did not match with those of original data in this trial (Rule numbers : 11, 12, 13, 18 and 20), therefore the score matching is 75 %. As shown in the Fig. 5(a), some trials have as top matching 9 instead of 10, this is due to the close confidence score between the two rules number 10 and number 11. As the assignment of group ID is done randomly, the expanded data is a little different, and the unmatched rule (Age='(24.3-31.6]' $\Rightarrow$ Edu=9) takes the rank 10 instead of 11 which produce a top matching score equal to 9.

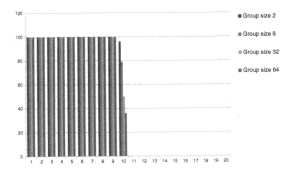

(a) Top matching score for the "Combination 1" in 20 rules

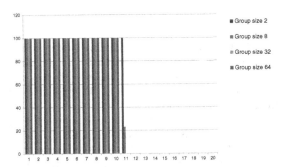

(b) Top matching score for the "Combination 2" in 20 rules

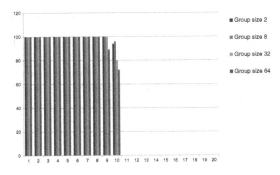

(c) Top matching score for the "Combination 3" in 20 rules

Fig. 5. Top matching scores of 20 rules produced on the expanded data for different group sizes with the different combinations of attributes

4   Conclusions

In this paper, we demonstrated the effectiveness of association rule mining performed on fragmented data. We proposed a mining technique that expands the data set on the server by using the groups to extract association rules on a fragmented database. Our experiments indicate that the 10 rules produced by the expanded data with different group size match completely with those produced by the original data. We have also investigated the relationship between the group size and the matching between the rule produced from the original data and from the expanded data and have shown that even when the matching score is not 100 %, the first ranked rules are relevant and can be used by the client.

Acknowledgments. This publication was made possible by NPRP grant #09-256-1-046 from the Qatar National Research Fund (a member of Qatar Foundation). The statements made herein are solely the responsibility of the authors.

References

1. Gal, T.S., Chen, Z., Gangopadhyay, A.: A privacy protection model for patient data with multiple sensitive attributes. IJISP **2**(3), 28–44 (2008)
2. Li, N., Li, T., Venkatasubramanian, S.: t-closeness: Privacy beyond k-anonymity and ℓ-diversity. In: ICDE 2007 Proceedings of IEEE International Conference on Data Engineering, pp.106–115, 2007
3. Li, T., Li, N., Zhang, J., Molloy, I.: Slicing: a new approach for privacy preserving data publishing. IEEE Trans. Knowl. Data Eng. **24**(3), 561–574 (2012)
4. Machanavajjhala, A., Gehrke, J., Kifer, D., Venkitasubramaniam, M.: l-diversity: Privacy beyond k-anonymity. ACM Transactions on Knowledge Discovery from Data (TKDD), (1), (Mar 2007)
5. Newman, D., Hettich, S., Blake, C., Merz, C.: Uci repository of machine learning databases, (1998)
6. Samarati, P.: Protecting respondents identities in microdata release. IEEE Trans. Knowl. Data Eng. **13**, 1010–1027 (2001)
7. Sweeney, L.: K-anonymity: A model for protecting privacy. Int. J. Uncertain. Fuzziness. Knowl.-Based Syst. **10**(5), 557–570 (2002)
8. Witten, I.H., Frank, E.: Data Mining: Practical Machine Learning Tools and Techniques (Morgan Kaufmann Series in Data Management Systems), 2nd edn. Morgan Kaufmann Publishers Inc., San Francisco (2005)

Author Index

Abughazalah, Sarah 147
Armando, Alessandro 266
Autrel, Fabien 183
Azraoui, Monir 319

Beckers, Kristian 216
Bernsmed, Karin 319
Bertino, Elisa 17
Bezzi, Michele 266
Blanco-Justicia, Alberto 47, 133
Bouyahia, Tarek 183
Bringer, Julien 293

Castellà-Roca, Jordi 327
Chothia, Tom 250
Clifton, Chris 335
Conti, Mauro 167
Cuppens, Frédéric 183
Cuppens-Boulahia, Nora 183

Davarynejad, Mohsen 201
De Oliveira, Anderson Santana 319
Dellas, Nikolaos 95
den Hartog, Jerry 233
Domingo-Ferrer, Josep 47, 133
Domingos, Henrique 311

Elkhiyaoui, Kaoutar 319

Ferreira, Bernardo 311

Gambs, Sébastien 58
Gaur, Manoj S. 167

Hamzaoui, Amel 335
Hartenstein, Hannes 114
Herrera-Joancomartí, Jordi 3

Idrees, Muhammad Sabir 183

Jardí-Cedó, Roger 327
Johansen, Christian 277
Jøsang, Audun 26, 277

Kaklamani, Dimitra I. 95
Köhler, Jens 114
Koukovini, Maria N. 95
Krautsevich, Leanid 216

Laxmi, Vijay 167
Le, Thanh-ha 293
Leitão, João 311
Lioudakis, Georgios V. 95

Malluhi, Qutaibah 335
Markantonakis, Konstantinos 147
Matteucci, Ilaria 233
Mayes, Keith 147
Metoui, Nadia 266

Naval, Smita 167
Novakovic, Chris 250

Önen, Melek 319

Papagiannakopoulou, Eugenia I. 95
Pieters, Wolter 201
Puys, Maxime 293

Raja, Sachin 167
Rajarajan, Muttukrishnan 167
Ranellucci, Samuel 58
Riley, Ryan 335
Rivière, Lionel 293
Rodrigues, João 311

Sabetta, Antonino 266
Sendor, Jakub 319
Singh, Rajiv Ranjan 250

Tapp, Alain 58
Tschersich, Markus 77

Venieris, Iakovos S. 95
Viejo, Alexandre 327
Yautsiukhin, Artsiom 216

Printed in the United States
By Bookmasters